There are __2__ items in this set.
Please return ALL items. Full
replacement cost of $35 will be
charged if any item(s) missing
upon return.

1 CD

D0689152

Audio Mashup Construction Kit

Audio Mashup Construction Kit

Jordan "DJ Earworm" Roseman

WITHDRAWN

BICENTENNIAL

1807

WILEY

2007

BICENTENNIAL

Wiley Publishing, Inc.

Audio Mashup Construction Kit

Published by
Wiley Publishing, Inc.
10475 Crosspoint Boulevard
Indianapolis, IN 46256
www.wiley.com

Copyright © 2007 by Wiley Publishing, Inc., Indianapolis, Indiana

Published simultaneously in Canada

ISBN-13: 978-0-471-77195-1
ISBN-10: 0-471-77195-3

Manufactured in the United States of America

10 9 8 7 6 5 4 3 2 1

No part of this publication may be reproduced, stored in a retrieval system or transmitted in any form or by any means, electronic, mechanical, photocopying, recording, scanning or otherwise, except as permitted under Sections 107 or 108 of the 1976 United States Copyright Act, without either the prior written permission of the Publisher, or authorization through payment of the appropriate per-copy fee to the Copyright Clearance Center, 222 Rosewood Drive, Danvers, MA 01923, (978) 750-8400, fax (978) 646-8600. Requests to the Publisher for permission should be addressed to the Legal Department, Wiley Publishing, Inc., 10475 Crosspoint Blvd., Indianapolis, IN 46256, (317) 572-3447, fax (317) 572-4355, or online at http://www.wiley.com/go/permissions.

Limit of Liability/Disclaimer of Warranty: The publisher and the author make no representations or warranties with respect to the accuracy or completeness of the contents of this work and specifically disclaim all warranties, including without limitation warranties of fitness for a particular purpose. No warranty may be created or extended by sales or promotional materials. The advice and strategies contained herein may not be suitable for every situation. This work is sold with the understanding that the publisher is not engaged in rendering legal, accounting, or other professional services. If professional assistance is required, the services of a competent professional person should be sought. Neither the publisher nor the author shall be liable for damages arising herefrom. The fact that an organization or Website is referred to in this work as a citation and/or a potential source of further information does not mean that the author or the publisher endorses the information the organization or Website may provide or recommendations it may make. Further, readers should be aware that Internet Websites listed in this work may have changed or disappeared between when this work was written and when it is read.

For general information on our other products and services or to obtain technical support, please contact our Customer Care Department within the U.S. at (800) 762-2974, outside the U.S. at (317) 572-3993 or fax (317) 572-4002.

Library of Congress Cataloging-in-Publication Data

Trademarks: Wiley, the Wiley logo, and related trade dress are trademarks or registered trademarks of John Wiley & Sons, Inc. and/or its affiilates, in the United States and other countries, and may not be used without written permission. ExtremeTech and the ExtremeTech logo are trademarks of Ziff Davis Publishing Holdings, Inc. Used under license. All rights reserved. All other trademarks are the property of their respective owners. Wiley Publishing, Inc., is not associated with any product or vendor mentioned in this book.

Wiley also publishes its books in a variety of electronic formats. Some content that appears in print may not be available in electronic books.

This book is dedicated to the memory of Charles F. Molle
I'll never forget you

About the Author

Jordan Roseman aka DJ Earworm, was born into a family of musicians and raised in Eastern Iowa. He earned degrees in music theory and computer science before gravitating toward the West coast. Having developed as a songwriter, music producer, and pianist, and inspired by mashups heard during a stay in London in the early 2000's, he switched gears toward mashup creation, finding the format able to satisfy his hunger for various genres of music. His productions include wide-ranging genres such as electro, rock, 80's, Top 40, and even country, blended together into a style that has earned him a global reputation. Most days, he can be heard blasting music out of an artist-filled Victorian mansion in the Pacific Heights neighborhood of San Francisco or deejaying at wild parties and underground events.

Credits

Executive Editor
Chris Webb

Development Editor
Brian Herrmann

Technical Editor
Matt Hite

Production Editor
Angela Smith

Copy Editor
Kathryn Duggan

Editorial Manager
Mary Beth Wakefield

Production Manager
Tim Tate

Vice President and Executive Group Publisher
Richard Swadlcy

Vice President and Executive Publisher
Joseph B. Wikert

Media Development Project Supervisor
Laura Carpenter VanWinkle

Media Development Specialist
Kate Jenkins

Media Development Quality Control
Angela Denny

Compositor
Chris Gillespie
Happenstance Type-O-Rama

Illustrator
Jeff Wilson
Happenstance Type-O-Rama

Proofreading
Jennifer Larsen, Word One

Indexing
Ted Laux

Cover Design
Anthony Bunyan

Contents at a Glance

Contents

Acknowledgments

There are so many people who have helped me become a musician, a mashup artist, and an author. I could never have gotten to this point without a tremendous amount of support.

To my family, who instilled a love of music in me; To my mother, who would endlessly entertain my sister and me playing the piano while we gathered around and sang; To my father, who would play the fiddle, banjo, or concertina, jamming Irish folk music with his friends on cold evenings in the middle of Iowa;

To Charles Molle, who taught me the importance of beauty, and whose unerring faith in me inspires me still to dedicate myself to music;

To Scott Brown, who recognized my potential to create mashups, and whose ideas, encouragement, and support helped make DJ Earworm a reality;

To Adrian and Deidre for their essential advice regarding all things mashup and their tireless support for the mashup scene both in San Francisco and globally; To Party Ben and the rest of the Bootie crew, and all the San Francisco bootleggers, who have inspired me to strive for excellence; To the wonderful people of GYBO, the amazing little global community, who have taught me most everything I know about mashups;

To the musicians whose music I sampled, without whom I would be still stuck making original music;

To my editors Brian Herrmann and Chris Webb, who have put up with my obsessive tweaking of this book as the months rolled on; To Matt Hite, mashup artist and technical reviewer, whose insight and suggestions tremendously enhanced the book's breadth and accuracy;

To Richard and Tatiana, who have always believed in me and given me encouragement when I need it the most, and whose presence adds so much to my daily life;

To all these people, I thank you with all my heart. I couldn't have done it without you.

Introduction

"A good composer does not imitate, he steals."
—Igor Stravinsky

This is a book on how to make mashups. But before addressing the question of how to make mashups, I'd like to talk a little about *why* make mashups.

Mashups are music compositions entirely assembled from pieces of previously recorded music. They are sometimes criticized that they rely on other people's originality and hard work.

But looking at the entire history of music, you'll find that it is full of borrowing and stealing. The taking of other people's ideas and transforming them is the basis for all music, in fact the basis of all culture and civilization. Ideas are meant to be shared and transformed, but within the past century or two, and increasingly in the past few decades, ideas are being treated more and more like things.

But ideas are not things. The problem is that if you take a thing from someone, the person no long has it. When you take an idea, not only do both people have it, but the person who takes it probably thinks about it, processes it, perhaps improves upon it, re-transmits it, and the process starts all over again.

This free flow of ideas is now often stifled by idea ownership, where every idea has a dollar value attached to it and the free flow of ideas is seen as a financial loss even when no ideas have actually been lost. You could argue that mashups are some of the purest-intentioned forms of music out there today, since very few artists have any illusions that they'll capitalize on their creations.

Every piece of music is composed of ideas from previous pieces of music. Mashups are just a bit more direct and honest about it. Originality is purely a matter of degree.

If you press play on your mp3 player, are you making art? How about when you make a really cool playlist? What if you make a playlist, but fade the songs in and out early at points of your choice? How about if you play your songs at the same time? What if you play only rearranged portions of them at the same time? How about taking extremely short samples of them and programming an entirely new song? What if you just sample a piano note and assign it to an electronic keyboard and perform it live?

Chances are, you won't think pressing play on an mp3 player is creating art, but performing an electronic keyboard is creating art. Mashups lie in that uncomfortably fuzzy area in between.

Whether or not a given mashup is art, the fact remains that people love to listen to them. Mashups give a type of stimulation not achievable by any other means, since they are using references to ideas that already exist in the listener's mind. An original song might be great, but the experience of a mashup cannot possibly be replicated without the sampled material.

A wise man once said "Anyone can make a mashup in 30 seconds."

It's true! Just drag a couple of mp3s into Sony ACID®, render it, and a never-before-heard musical concoction can be created before your morning coffee is done brewing. However, some mashups take many weeks or even months of work, crafting the arrangement, bending one song to fit with the other. It's all a matter of degree.

I got started making mashups after many years of making music, both electronically and acoustically. I had played around with ACID a lot, mostly with loops I had rendered in other programs. When ACID added the functionality to support entire songs, I started making mix CDs, just fading in one song as another song faded in. ACID allowed me to sync up the songs, so the blending was smooth. I started doing a bit of cutting up during one of these transitions, and my before I knew it I had made my first mashup.

Before long, I took some of my mashups to Adrian, a DJ and promoter of Bootie, a mashup club in San Francisco. He told me should put them on the web, get myself an alias (I chose DJ Earworm), and join GYBO, an online community of mashup artists. Soon, I was making mashups all the time, devoting much of my free time to it.

If you have half the fun making mashups as I've had, you're in for a good time!

Who This Book Is For

If you've never made a mashup, this book will take you step by step through the various aspects of mashup production and will provide you the necessary background in music and music soft-ware. No experience is assumed.

On the other hand, if you've made few mashups but want to know some tips and techniques, this book will also be helpful. This book covers everything from the very basics to advanced topics in song selection, unmixing, arrangement, and mastering.

How This Book Is Organized

This book hits the ground running, and you'll have created your first mashup within the first few pages. Once your appetite is whetted, you'll read a bit on the history of mashups and early predecessors in Chapter 2. A quick rundown of the software, hardware, and music files necessary for mashup construction is given in Chapter 3. If you're new to music, you should definitely read Chapter 4, which teaches you all the music theory you need to know for mashup construction. If you've never used ACID or Adobe Audition, Chapter 5 will show you the ropes.

Once the basics are covered, Chapter 6 goes in depth into the song selection, and Chapters 7 through 9 discuss how to get your songs in key and in sync. Chapter 10 reveals the black art of unmixing, where vocals and other parts are lifted and separated from the rest of the sound. Chapter 11 goes into depth on the topic of arrangement, and Chapter 12 covers mastering and effects. This is all followed up by a discussion on rendering, distribution and legal considerations in the final three chapters.

The appendices include information on the CD-ROM included with this book (Appendix A), a large list of links to software, mashup artists, and other useful web sites (Appendix B), and a handy glossary of music and music production terms used in the book.

Conventions Used in This Book

Throughout this book you'll encounter various icons. Here they are, along with their interpretations:

 Wake up! You'll regret not paying attention to these useful warnings.

 A helpful tip or a particular point about the subject being discussed.

 Points to other places in the book that elaborate on the subject touched upon.

 Directs you to download a particular audio file for use in the step-by-step examples.

 Directs you to listen to an audio file from the CD-ROM.

 Discusses features unique to the XPress version of ACID that don't pertain to the Pro 6 version.

 Discusses features available in ACID Pro 6 as well as earlier versions of ACID Pro.

 Discusses new features in ACID Pro 6 that weren't available in previous versions.

What You Need To Use This Book

This book assumes you have access to a Windows computer. ACID and other software on the CD-ROM require a computer with Windows with at least a 1GHz processor. The exact requirements are outlined in Chapter 3, but most personal computers still functioning will be able to handle the software.

Throughout this book you'll be directed to download various songs from the iTunes music store, to be used in step-by-step examples of mashup techniques. These songs cannot be used in ACID until they've been converted, and burning a CD is one of the easiest ways to do this (see Chapter 3 for more information on this rip-and-burn technique). You may wish to download several or all of the songs at once in order to burn multiple songs onto a single CD. Refer to Table B-1 at the end of Appendix B for a complete list of songs used in this book.

What's on the Companion CD-ROM

The CD-ROM contains both ACID XPress, which is a completely free version of Sony's ACID software, a preferred platform for mashup construction. Also included is a demo of ACID Pro 6, the top-of-the-line version of ACID.

To really understand mashup construction in depth, ACID Pro is recommended. Even if you eventually decide to use the XPress version, you will still have gained insight from using the more advanced version.

The CD-ROM also contains a demo of Adobe Audition, which contains amazing tools for unmixing (acapella extraction), as well as tONaRT which is software that can detect the key of a piece of music. Additionally, there is a spreadsheet that can help you manage your music collection in order to help make decisions in song selection. A thorough discussion of the CD-ROM is in Appendix A.

Booting Up

Welcome to the wonderful world of mashups, where you create your own collaborations with unwitting participants. Have you ever wondered what the Beastie Boys would've sounded like if they had rapped with the Beatles? What would a Green Day/ Oasis supergroup sound like? Would you enjoy Kelly Clarkson more if she were backed up by the Breeders? These are the sorts of questions mashup artists not only dare to ask, but attempt to answer, by lifting and dropping, cutting and pasting, unmixing and remixing, blatantly stealing and then kindly giving back, and raiding the annals of pop culture to create a disorienting recombinant nostalgia trip. Arguably one of the first new popular music genres of the twenty-first century, mashups are a global phenomenon enjoyed by people of all ages, cultures, and musical preferences.

At its most basic, a mashup is simply the vocals of one song singing or rapping over the instrumental of another song, assembled on a computer. Each component is edited to make sure the parts flow together seamlessly.

This chapter will give you a whirlwind tour of mashup production, just enough to get your feet wet. Afterward, throughout the rest of the book, the history of mashups will be explored, followed by some technical and musical background necessary for mashup production. After the fundamentals are covered, you'll read about mashup production in detail, including the issues of song selection, timing, pitch, unmixing, arrangement, and mastering. Distribution and legal issues will also be considered.

Quick Start

Rather than learning all the ins and outs before experiencing the satisfaction of mashup production, you can get a quick taste by following a few simple steps. All of this will be covered in much greater detail and at a much slower pace in later chapters.

in this chapter

☑ Quick start

☑ Moving on

Install the Software

On this book's CD-ROM are installations of two versions of Sony ACID, one of the more popular software packages for mashup production. See the Introduction for details on the different versions available. Choose the version that's right for you, run the installer, and follow the instructions. ACID and its installation are covered in depth in Chapter 5.

You will also need iTunes installed, available at www.apple.com/itunes, or some other means to acquire the component songs.

Download an Acappella

If you purchase your song from the iTunes store, you will need to convert it to either a wav or an mp3, two types of audio files that can be used in ACID. Wav files are higher-quality but large, while mp3s are much smaller, but not quite as high-quality. The simplest way to convert your purchased file is to burn a CD with your song and then reimport the song from the CD. This removes the copy protection, which would prevent the songs from being directly loaded up in ACID. This conversion technique (as well as several others) is covered in detail in Chapter 3 in the "Unprotecting Audio" sidebar.

 An acappella is simply the vocal for a song or rap without any of the background instrumentation. For simplicity's sake, it's good to start with a rap acappella (a selection is available for purchase at the iTunes Store). Try "Whoomp! (There It Is) [Acappella Mix]" by Tag Team.

Download an Instrumental

The great thing about rap acappellas (without any singing) is that they easily combine with a number of instrumental backgrounds as long as they have similar tempos. Eventually, you might decide to cut up a full song's instrumental sections and rearrange them into your own customized instrumental, but for now it's quicker to simply download an audio file that's already an instrumental.

 A good match for the Tag Team acappella is "Stand Up Tall (Instrumental Version)" by Dizzee Rascal, available at the iTunes Store.

The ACID Drop

After you get your audio files, drag them from iTunes and simply drop them into the upper-left half of the ACID window (see Figure 1-1): first the "Stand Up Tall" instrumental, and then the "Whoomp!" acappella. If a Beatmapper Wizard window (ACID Pro) or an upgrade window (ACID XPress) appears, click Cancel or Close to close that window.

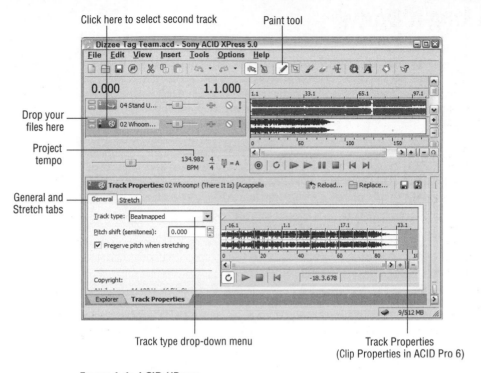

FIGURE 1-1: ACID XPress

Now select the second track by clicking 02 Whoomp! (There It Is) [Acappella Mix] in the upper-left portion of the ACID window (see Figure 1-1). The entire track names may not be visible, but they should start with 01 and 02.

In the General tab of Track Properties (ACID XPress) or Clip Properties (ACID Pro 6), switch from One-Shot to Beatmapped in the Track Type drop-down menu, as shown in Figure 1-1. Check the box that says "Preserve pitch when stretching," and then click the Stretch tab, which shows three parameters (not shown in Figure 1-1). Leave the Root Note as it is, and change the Original tempo to **129.000** and the Downbeat offset to **12,640**. You do not need to change the track/clip properties of Track 1. Also, make sure you are editing the downbeat offset in the Stretch tab of your Track or Clip properties, not in the Event Properties pop-up window.

Select the Paint tool by clicking its button in the toolbar (see Figure 1-1). At the beginning of Track 1, paint the entire track by clicking near the beginning of Track 1 while holding down the Ctrl key for track 2. Your ACID window should look something like Figure 1-1. Double-click the project tempo (see Figure 1-1) and enter a value of **134.982**.

Press Play. Congratulations. You just made your first mashup.

Breaking It Down

If this all seemed too easy, don't worry. It gets a lot more interesting. For example, what happens if your tracks aren't of similar tempo? If the vocals are sung, how do you find a good match? What happens when you can't find the instrumental or acappella of the songs you want (which is most of the time)? What do you do if the tempo is uneven? All these questions and more will be answered in the following chapters. Have fun!

What Is Mashup?

A *mashup* is a piece of recorded music composed entirely of other people's recorded music. Usually the lengths of the recordings are long, and typically their use is unauthorized. Although mashups have been popular in their current form only for a few years, their musical roots run much deeper. The idea of borrowing and changing the context of a piece of music has been around for centuries. As new technologies emerged, each new innovation spurred new musical developments, allowing new ways to reuse and rework preexisting musical pieces.

Predecessors

Many eras in history have brought about new technologies and practices that contribute to the art of the mashup as it exists today. An examination of the history reveals that rather than being a passing fad, mashups are not only here to stay, but are an inevitable consequence of musical tradition and technological progress.

Early History

Before the era of recorded music, composers would frequently borrow from folk music and other composers' music. In fact, the wholesale borrowing of preexisting music was the main form of early composed music. In the first millennium, Gregorian chants were spread by copying and varying existing melodies, and folk songs were picked up from wandering minstrels and then altered to take on a local flavor.

Soon, composers started to combine different pitches, as with the *organum* of the church of the eleventh and twelfth centuries, when composers would create new melodies that layered well with older, preexisting chants. Eventually, composers began to give the harmonies more voices and independent melodies. But composers would typically include other people's music in their own work.

The thirteenth century saw the birth of the *motet*, which dominated church music for many centuries. Motets were also always built on a preexisting chant, but they combined multiple melodies over the top, each with its own text, sometimes even in different languages.

In the fourteenth century, church masses were written in an increasingly multilayered style, and would not only place new music over old chants, but sometimes weave the melodies through different voices, and even go as far as borrowing entire multilayered arrangements from other motets or *chanson*, which were motets' rapidly developing secular counterpart. These masses would increasingly borrow from secular music, and even include the name of the song it borrowed from in the title of the mass. The practice of singing sacred music over secular melodies rubbed a lot of members of the church the wrong way, and might even be considered the first genre clash. In fact, the practice was banned, although it continued — only now with different titles that didn't reference the source.

The Baroque period saw the introduction of the *quodlibet*, a usually lighthearted composition that combined the words and music of songs, both layered and in series. The songs were typically deconstructed into fragments, and then the fragments were rearranged. This very much reflects the modern spirit of the mashup, where multiple parts are borrowed and layered together. One of the more well-known examples is the last of Bach's Goldberg variations, number 30, where the melodies and the words of the various components relate to each other and influence each others' meanings.

So for about half a millennium, during the birth of modern Western music, the main compositional method was to directly lift from preexisting sources and layer them with new and different material. During the seventeenth and eighteenth centuries, the practice of basing new pieces on preexisting music started to lose favor and dominance. People had learned so much about polyphonic composition, and it began to seem disrespectful to set sacred texts to a melody written for another text. *Through-composed* music gained popularity, in which each new section of text would have entirely new music written for it. During this period, rampant borrowing still happened all the time. Handel, Bach, Mozart, and Beethoven all regularly lifted passages from other composers. Another type of appropriation common during this era was a form of popular entertainment called the *ballad opera*, where plays would be presented that featured songs with new words written over popular melodies.

By the late nineteenth and early twentieth centuries, some classical composers were exploring the practice of *polytonality*, in which multiple keys play simultaneously. Usually different melodies, often borrowed, would play along with composed music and other preexisting melodies. Charles Ives, Igor Stravinsky, and Darius Milhaud created compositions in this style, where the individual components retained their individuality, yet blended together. Borrowed pieces were often included for their symbolic or emotive power.

Cross-Reference

Key relates to how different pitches are combined, and is discussed in Chapter 4, along with many other topics related to music theory. The ancient idea of combining different texts relates to the cut-up method of lyric manipulation in mashups, discussed in Chapter 11.

The Era of Recording Technology

With the industrial age came major shifts in the ways music was experienced. Suddenly music did not have to be listened to at the time or place of performance. Music could be stored and listened to later. Each new method of music storage brought about new artistic possibilities, and each new method of music distribution had a tremendous influence in shaping people's musical experience.

The Phonoautograph

The earliest attempts to record a sound wave did not have the reproduction of the sound in mind. Rather, the sound wave was studied by researchers in the field of *acoustics*, the science of sound.

As far back as 1806, Thomas Young was able to transcribe the *oscillations* (rapid back and forth vibrations) of a tuning fork onto a wax-covered drum in order to analyze the frequency. The *phonoautograph* was invented in 1857 by Edouard-Leon Scott, and used a hog's bristle to inscribe a sound's waveform onto a glass plate, and later, paper. Apparently it didn't occur to anyone for a while that this waveform could be converted back into actual sound. But even without actual sound reproduction, the idea that a waveform could be extracted from an actual sound and preserved for later analysis represented a big leap forward.

Possibly one of the more bizarre phonoautographs was invented by Alexander Graham Bell. Curious about how a sound wave might be able to be translated into an electrical representation, in 1874 he built a phonoautograph from the actual complete ear of a cadaver, along with a stalk of hay. He spoke into the dead man's ear, and the signal was inscribed on glass. This version of the invention was never mass-produced, but Bell went on to invent the telephone two years later.

Cross-Reference Visual waveforms, which have existed for 200 years, are discussed in Chapter 4, along with methods of reading them.

The Phonograph

In 1877, Thomas Edison and many others were fascinated with Bell's amazing new invention. He was working on improving the telegraph when he realized that if telephone messages were transcribed onto a piece of paper or tinfoil, they could be played back and reproduced, eliminating the need for Morse code. The original intention was for this invention to be used as a Dictaphone and telephone answering machine. Soon, the technology was applied to live audio rather than telephone messages, and the phonograph was born. The first recording is said to be Edison's voice saying, "Mary had a little lamb."

At first, the devices were marketed to business people, but soon the devices were retargeted toward the world of music. Early phonographs were expensive, but single-song jukeboxes soon appeared, and even though they only cost a nickel per play, the novelty was so great that they were huge financial successes. When the public was first exposed to phonographs (called *gramophones* outside the United States), they were shocked. It was quite disorienting to have a sound divorced from its source, and this idea of a sound being an independent object, played back at a different time and place than it was created, would fundamentally change the way people perceive music. Instead of listening to a piano in the parlor or a marching band, you could press a button and listen to a reproduction, at first with a jukebox at the local saloon, and by the turn of the century, with devices affordable enough to listen to in the comfort of your home.

The rapid availability of this new technology created a sudden demand for songwriters and musicians. Early records held about two or three minutes of recording time, and although there were already popular music forms with a similar duration, the use of phonograph technology helped to encourage people to write tunes that fit in this time frame. The sale of actual recordings began to overtake the sales from sheet music. Music had been transformed from a set of instructions on how to make sound to the actual sound itself. The phonograph spurred new forms of music and a new approach to sound.

Many serious musicians at the time were so put off by the horrible sound quality of these new devices that they refused to record them. Most of the early recordings were of vaudeville entertainers and other more "common" music.

The earliest phonographs could also create new records, and so home recording is almost as old as recording itself. Many of these early home records were off-color, and they had warning messages attached — a turn-of-the-century precursor to today's parental advisory warnings.

Although the earliest phonograph recordings were in the shape of a cylinder, the advent of disc-shaped records allowed even cheaper manufacturing and more compact storage. Also, the heavy new turntables maintained a more constant rotational speed, allowing for greater pitch (and tempo) fidelity. Both cylinder and disc formats were popular for the first several decades of the phonograph, but by 1929, Edison stopped manufacturing cylinders.

Early on, each new version of the phonograph was incompatible with previous versions, so recordings you bought for your old phonograph wouldn't work if you bought a new one. Eventually, a single format was agreed upon, and all records became fairly compatible. The initial format was a *78*, named for the number of revolutions per minute (or *rpm*) at which the discs were meant to spin. Later, *45s* gained in popularity, which reduced the record size to seven inches, and the larger *33 1/3* records were also introduced, which allowed 10 or more songs to be released on a single disc.

The idea of using the phonograph as a musical instrument had a gradual evolution. In Berlin of the 1920s, Stefan Wolpe is said to have played at least eight phonographs simultaneously as part of a live performance, each playing a different portion of Beethoven's Fifth Symphony at varying speeds. Ottorino Respighi wrote a piece called "Pini di Roma," where a record of a nightingale was to be played accompanying the orchestra. This is the first known example of a written piece explicitly calling for the inclusion of previously recorded material. From 1928 to 1930, Paul Hindemith and Ernst Toch created pieces called "Grammophonmusik," which were sound collages that used phonograph records with their speeds altered, creating tempo and pitch shifts. Ten years later, composer John Cage used variable speed phonographs, sometimes with simple electronic test tones as the recording. He also included live radio and various electronic gadgets, creating a collage of previously recorded material.

In 1948, Pierre Schaeffer was working in a radio station in France and started experimenting with sound effects played back at various speeds. He combined the phonograph sounds and then made new records from the combinations. He then manipulated the new records, pressing newer records of the manipulation. This practice, known as *music concrète*, soon became commonplace in the era of tape.

Optical Recording

Music wasn't the only art form revolutionized by sound recording. Filmmakers, themselves working in a medium that was a fairly recent invention, were keen to add sound to their then-silent movies. Although there were experiments with inscribing the sound directly on the film, most attempts involved putting the sound onto a record and then playing the record at the same time as the film was showing. The synchronization issues were a nightmare.

Starting around 1929, however, new technologies emerged that allowed filmmakers to store sound directly on the film optically. If you examine the film reels from this era, you can actually see a waveform right next to the frames. It looks very similar to the sort of waveforms you see in ACID. Light would shine through the waveform, and the amount of light that passed through was converted into an electrical signal, which then produced audio.

There are big differences between a reel of film and a record. With records, if you wanted to edit a performance, you would have to play back each portion of the performance on its own phonograph and then rerecord them onto a new record, all in real time. But for the most part, performances were recorded in their entirety and left untouched. With optical recording, the idea of editing sound gathered momentum. You could cut out certain sounds, rearrange them, replace them, copy them, and paste them.

Walter Ruttman, a German film director, is credited with creating the first recorded sound collage of recorded material. In 1930, he spliced together a variety of sounds on film to create a piece called "Weekend," which was meant to be a sound film for the radio. Although this technology wasn't used heavily in the production of music, the audio-manipulation concepts generated would be later applied to magnetic tape, samplers, and computer-based composition.

 Cross-Reference The section on single-song techniques in Chapter 11 goes into detail about rearranging audio material, using computers to do something similar to what the editing of optical sound allowed.

The Radio

Guglielmo Marconi is credited with the invention of the radio in 1894, although the technology took awhile to mature, and the first commercial radio station, KDKA (Pittsburgh), started transmission in 1920. The technology caught on very rapidly from that point onward. Although it wasn't an audio recording technology per se, radio revolutionized the transmission of recorded audio, allowing remote access to music without any physical object used to carry the audio.

Radio was initially primarily devoted to news and audio plays. However, after television was introduced, radio switched almost entirely to music because other information and entertainment needs were transferred over to the TV.

This, combined with the introduction of the vinyl 45 record, helped to spur an explosion in pop music, allowing the number of artists and composers to multiply. This wonderful diversity in pop music is one thing that makes creating mashups so rewarding.

Tape

Recording with magnetic tape had its origins back in 1898, when Valdemar Poulsen from Denmark invented a technology that would store audio waveforms by magnetizing steel wires. As with many of these technologies, it took a few decades to mature, but by the 1930s, Germany had made huge advances in magnetic recording, dropping the unwieldy steel wires in favor of the more reliable and technologically advanced acetate tape. After World War II, the United States captured some of these amazing machines and reverse-engineered them, improving them greatly.

Within a decade, the high fidelity and ease of use of magnetic tape made it quickly displace other recording technologies. In the studio, tape could be cut and spliced together much as the sound editors had been doing with optical film, but with the convenience of instant recording and manipulation. Tape was cut and spliced to itself to make loops, allowing the same events to occur repetitively. Errors in a performance could be also edited out and replaced with a portion from a better performance.

Les Paul is credited with the creation of multitrack tape recording. By adding an extra recording head to an existing tape recorder, he transformed the practice of recording music. Although multiple tape recorders had been used in the past, a single multitrack tape would ensure synchronization throughout the piece of music. Multiple performances could be played back at the same time, but recorded separately. The same performer could be on several tracks simultaneously.

Multitrack tape also popularized the practice of stereo recording, where two different channels of a tape could make the recorded audio seem like it had a specific location in space.

Note   A *track* is a discrete stream of sound, usually mixed in with other tracks. A *channel* is a discrete stream of sound that is played on an individual speaker in a sound system. So in music production, the first several tracks are recorded, each with different instruments. Then they are mixed together and output to several channels (two channels, left and right, in a typical stereo system).

The home tape recorder also premiered during this time, allowing music consumers to easily make copies of recorded material.

The era of tape recording saw the rise of the producer as artist. Because a majority of the sound manipulation could be performed after the recording, much of the arrangement actually took place in the studio on tape. Tape recording became so popular that the Beatles famously decided not to perform any more live shows, and directed their output to the form of recordings based on multitrack technology, many of which could never have existed in a live performance setting.

The tape era also gave birth to the first popular sound collage using other artists' prerecorded material, a precursor to the modern mashup. Dickie Goodman and Bill Buchanan produced novelty records by splicing up snippets of popular music and interspersing them with their own voices, usually for comedic effect. These pieces were called *break-in* records, and their first success was called "Flying Saucer," which was a huge hit in 1956. It spliced together parts from Orson Welles' "War of the Worlds" with The Platters, Little Richard, Fats Domino, and Elvis Presley, among others, in the form of an interview. Goodman would ask questions of various people (and Martians), and the response would come back as a segment of a song. Although they may be obvious or trite to today's ears, these recordings were quite inventive and stimulating to the audiences at the time. The Music Publishers Protective Association complained loudly that Goodman and Buchanan had not cleared the borrowed material and accused them of 19 cases of copyright infringement. But mysteriously, the record companies never sued. A funny thing happened. Sales of the infringed works went up, not down! "Flying Saucer" didn't replace the audience's need for the borrowed material, but actually whetted their appetite. Some of the songs sampled in the piece actually had to be reissued to meet the resurgence in demand. Eventually, the record companies struck a deal with Goodman and Buchanan, and they each went on to create break-in records for years to come.

In 1979, the Residents made an album called *The Residents Radio Special*. It contained a track called "Beyond the Valley of a Day in the Life," which consisted entirely of Beatles samples. This is an early example of taking the Goodman-Buchanan concept one step further by completely eliminating any original elements.

Cross-Reference The concept of layering and combining different sounds was brought to maturity with magnetic tape, and is fundamental to mashup construction. It is discussed at length in Chapter 11.

Beatmatching

The concept of taking multiple songs recorded separately and making them seem like a single song got its start in the late 1960s. In a nightclub called Salvation Too, DJ Terry Noel replaced the usual rubber mat on top of his turntable with a felt mat. This allowed the turntable to continue spinning when the record was held still. While a different song was playing on the other turntable, he would then place the needle in the record groove right where a strong beat was located. When he released the record, it would rapidly accelerate to full speed, because the turntable had been rotating at normal speed underneath. He would wait for just the right moment in the already-playing song to start the new song. This practice is now called *slip-cueing*, and the crowd loved it.

Noel progressed in his deejaying, and eventually allowed the first song to continue to play while the second song started in. There weren't finely adjustable variable-speed turntables back then, so he had to select records that had very similar tempos. This practice of playing two or more tracks simultaneously is known as *beatmatching*.

Francis Grasso was a go-go dancer at the nightclub, and although he loved the slip-cueing and beatmatching, he was bothered by the unevenness that sometimes occurred. One night, when Noel failed to show up due to an acid trip (a different kind of ACID), Grasso was asked to deejay. He did a great job, got promoted to DJ, and eventually perfected the art of slip-cueing. He got some variable-speed turntables, so that the beatmatching could be much more flexible and maintain synchronization for longer periods. He also added headphones to the multi-turntable setup, so if he was slip-cueing or beatmatching, he could monitor the new record and make sure it sounded right before his audience could hear it. Grasso is widely regarded as creating the modern practice of deejaying.

Cross-Reference Mashups are in many ways an extension of the practice Noel and Grasso began 40 years ago. Beatmatching is one of the most fundamental concepts in mashup construction and is covered in depth in Chapters 7 and 9.

The Remix

A *mix* refers to a set of levels and settings that transforms a multitrack tape recording into a stereo recording, whereas a *remix* refers not only to a different set of levels and settings, but new arrangements, and usually the addition of new material. The remix, along with hip-hop, had its roots in Jamaica in the late 1960s and early 1970s. At first, producer-DJs would create what they called *dub* versions of current songs by simply recording the multitrack tape without the vocal track. Soon they began to rearrange these dub tracks, by repeating certain sections, adding delay and echo effects. They would create these dub mixes both with material they were producing and with other artists' prerecorded material. These dub plates were the some of the first *white-labels*, which are records produced in very limited quantity, with no artwork, and sometimes not even any identifying text. The relative anonymity of white labels allowed producers the freedom to manipulate music without obtaining a license, and to this day, uncleared remix records, also called *bootlegs*, continue to proliferate.

In New York City in the 1970s, DJs would loop and edit their disco songs, altering the sound and extending the length. Soon, the vinyl 12-inch single format became popular, containing several remixes of the same song, each using previously recorded material, often combined with other rhythmic patterns and sounds from the remix producer.

In the early 1980s, Dutch producer Jaap Eggermont, under the pseudonym Stars On 45, produced a series of remixes that contained hits from a single artist over a disco rhythm. Generally, a series of musical pieces is called a *medley*, and is distinct from a mashup in that the musical pieces are not played simultaneously. The Eggermont remix medleys were huge successes. They may be considered an early example of the *megamix*, which continues to be produced. Megamixes are essentially long remixes of several songs, usually by a single artist. However, they are not typically layered on top of each other as mashups are.

Hip-Hop

Jamaican DJs of the 1970s would often talk rhythmically over the dub recordings as they played them. Sometimes they would even make nonsense rhythmic sounds along with the records. These practices eventually evolved into rap and beatboxing, once brought to the United States.

Meanwhile, in 1970's New York City, Bronx DJs went beyond simple slip-cueing and beat-matching, and were performing something called *scratching*, which was similar to slip-cueing, but with the audio turned on so that the audience could hear the back-and-forth motion of the record.

Grand Wizard Theodore, who along with Grandmaster Flash pioneered scratching, evolved the practice of the *needle drop* around the same time. Because slip-cueing required a few precious moments of preparation in a live setting, DJs began to make little marks directly on the record ahead of time, so they could then drop the needle right in the groove at just the right time without any previews. This allowed the DJ to essentially loop a bit of material he liked by performing a needle drop, letting the record play, going to the other record, and performing a needle drop at the same point at just the right time. DJs would often use drum fills, breaks, and the more percussive parts of previously recorded material. Because of this, early hip-hop was known as *breaks*. Entire live collages were performed that contained pieces of various artists' material — stringing together and sometimes layering different breaks from different artists.

These beats, combined with the rapping that was evolving at the same time, were eventually recorded into pieces of their own, starting in the late 1970s. Since then, the reuse of recorded material has spread into the collective musical consciousness.

The Sampler

A *sampler* is a hardware or software musical instrument that records and plays back short pieces of digital audio. Each piece is triggered from a keyboard played by a musician or an electronic signal.

In the United States in 1946, very early on in the magnetic tape era, Harry Chamberlin had an idea. He wanted to record himself playing the organ, and it struck him that if he could record an entire organ performance, why couldn't each key play back a tape recording of an instrument? He built an instrument called the *Chamberlin*, which did exactly that. A very small tape playback device was triggered for each key in the keyboard. The tape strips were short, lasting about eight seconds each, but the device was perfectly playable. When the performer's finger left the keyboard, the tape would rewind back to the beginning. The device was notoriously unstable, but for the first time, prerecorded music could be assembled into musically meaningful forms in real time. About 15 years later, the *Mellotron* was invented (some say stolen). The Mellotron had similar features, but worked much more stably, and found its way into recording studios all over the world. As with many inventions, the story behind the inventions of the Chamberlin and the Mellotron is in question, but the impact of the devices is clear. This was the first sampler. Listen to the Beatles' "Strawberry Fields Forever" for an iconic example of the Mellotron.

An early exploration of digital sampling, as well as an early example of a musical composition made *entirely* from unauthorized previously recorded material can be found in James Tenney's "Blue Suede," from 1961, where he manipulated Elvis Presley's "Blue Suede Shoes" by digitally sampling it on an IBM punch card machine, storing the audio on a huge stack of cards, and then shuffling up the cards and reconstituting the scrambled audio.

The first dedicated digital sampler was produced in 1976. Although it only played one note at a time, the fact that its sound playback involved no moving parts made it much more stable than the Mellotron. Stevie Wonder used the instrument on his album *Journey Through the Secret Life of Plants* in 1976. The album has the honor of being the first digitally recorded album of popular music.

In 1979, the Fairlight became the first polyphonic sampler, meaning that multiple digital recordings could be played back simultaneously. The Fairlight had a built-in sequencer and an extensive set of tools to look at and alter the digital waveform. Unfortunately, the instrument had an exorbitant price tag, and only the more successful recording studios could afford one. However, throughout the 1980s, samplers began to drop in price, until eventually, serious home musicians could afford them. Akai, E-mu, and Ensoniq all produced popular samplers.

The sampler greatly influenced hip-hop, which had already been looping bits of other people's music using vinyl in live settings and tape in the studio. Hip-hop artists sampled their own loops from all genres of music, and traded, bought, and sold premade loops. Typically, samplers didn't have minute upon minute of sampling time, so the idea of making a modern-style mashup wouldn't have been possible. But shorter snippets of previously recorded material spread throughout hip-hop and R&B, and soon migrated to many other genres of music as well.

Digital sampling and recording concepts are discussed in more detail in Chapter 4.

The Computer

The computer advanced digital sampling immeasurably. Starting in the late 1980s, computers became fast enough to handle digital audio recording and playback. Fast hard drives allowed for the playback of very long samples. As computers got faster and better, more tracks could be layered in real time. By 2000, even casual home users were able to record digital multitrack projects in the comfort of their bedrooms. The wide distribution of this powerful music-making technology democratized music production. During the era of tape recording, an aspiring producer would need to rent a very expensive music studio, but by the time computer recording became available, very little expenditure was required to have much more power than most music studios had a couple of decades before. New software platforms and signal processors proliferated. Much like the guitar in the rock and roll era, the computer today is the everyman's music tool — anybody can get started with it to easily make music, but there is so much depth to it that it can take a lifetime to master.

Software has gotten increasingly sophisticated, while the price has been dropping steadily. ACID XPress by Sony is a free version of their revolutionary ACID software. Even though it is free, it has capabilities well beyond what the most advanced software offered 10 years ago, especially when combined with ever-increasing processor speeds. Sony's ACID Pro adds more tracks, effects, automation, and other features that make it the tool of choice for serious mashup producers. The ability to take multiple tracks and control their pitch and tempo independently and precisely has generated a vast array of new musical possibilities. Because it's so easy, musicians can play around with ideas and listen to them in real time, rather than painstakingly calculating and planning the music beforehand, waiting for the sound to render, and then repeating the process.

Cross-Reference Chapter 5 discusses computer recording software, specifically Sony's ACID and Adobe's Audition.

The Internet

Like radio 70 years earlier, the Internet created vast new audiences for all kinds of music. Today, the typical music fan owns a much larger array of music styles than in previous eras, mostly owing to the availability of a large quantity of music on the Internet. Whether they purchase their music or download it from peer-to-peer (P2P) networks, many people have music collections on their hard drives that contain as much music as an avid record collector may have spent his whole life putting together. Many of the mp3 playback devices and software have shuffle functions and quick-search capabilities, which let people jump about in their music collection rapidly. Today, instead of putting on a CD and listening to it, many people will listen to a song, and then jump to another song from a different artist, era, or genre. This scattered musical attention landscape is the perfect breeding ground for the mashup.

The Era of the Mashup

In 1983, Club House created a track called "Do It Again/Billie Jean," which had the Steely Dan track "Do It Again" over the groove of Michael Jackson's "Billie Jean." The piece was a cover, and no actual recordings from the originals were used, but the concept was very similar to the modern mashup, although it was titled a medley. Other mashups appeared as remixes, often called *medleys* for lack of a better term. One such mashup was released in 1986 called "Propaganda for Frankie" and featured Frankie Goes To Hollywood's "Relax" played at the same time as Propaganda's "P-Machinery."

In 1988, John Oswald released an extended play (EP) called "Plunderphonics," which was composed entirely of unauthorized samples. This was very much a precursor to the modern mashup (as were his subsequent works), in that he blatantly took previously recorded material with no effort to mask their source. In fact, the knowledge of the source is what makes the music interesting.

The Evolution Control Committee's "Whipped Cream Mixes" from 1996 had vocals from Public Enemy over an instrumental by Herb Alpert. This is one of the first examples of the modern mashup, in which very long and relatively unaltered recordings of vocals are placed over long and relatively unaltered instrumentals.

In 2001, Erol Alkin produced a mashup of Kylie Minogue's "Can't Get You Out of My Head" along with New Order's "Blue Monday." The same year, Freelance Hellraiser's "Stroke of Genie-us" combined the vocal talents of Christina Aguilera with the indie guitar stylings of The Strokes. The next year, 2 Many DJs released their landmark album, *As Heard on Radio Soulwax, Part 2*, which was an essentially an extended mashup set. The modern mashup era had begun.

Mashup clubs started popping up in Europe, notably Bastard in London, which continues to this day. In San Francisco in 2003, Bootie became the first mashup club in North America, which continues to be very popular, and now has a branch operating in Los Angeles as well. Websites such as Boomselection, which is no longer active, appeared to chronicle events, and a website called Get Your Bootleg On (www.gybo.org), started by noted mashup artist McSleazy, became a global meeting place for mashup producers. Radio DJs around the world began playing mashups, such as James Hyman and Eddy Temple Morris at XFM London, DJ Zebra at Oui FM in Paris, and Party Ben at San Francisco's Live 105 in the now-defunct weekly "Sixx Mixx." All-mashup podcasts have been popping up as well, including Radio Clash (www.mutantpop .net/radioclash) and DJ Paul V.'s "Smash Mix," which is a rebroadcast of his popular radio show on Indie 103.1 in L.A. There are also some great dedicated blogs devoted to updates on the latest in the mashup world, like www.beatmixed.com and www.bootie.fm.

Cross-Reference For an extensive list of mashup-related links, including artists, forums, blogs, and podcasts, see Appendix B.

In 2002, a CD called *The Best Bootlegs in the World Ever* gave many people their first taste of mashups, including "Stroke of Genie-us" and "Smells Like Teen Booty," a mashup by 2 Many DJs (a.k.a., Soulwax), although it was mistitled and miscredited. This CD inspired *The Best Mashups in the World Ever (are from San Francisco)*, which is currently enjoying success in its second compilation. In early 2004, DJ Danger Mouse brought this emergent art form to the attention of many in the American public with the unofficial release of *The Grey Album*, a mashup of the Beatles' "*White Album*" and Jay-Z's *The Black Album*.

Early in 2004, MTV Europe aired a show called "MTV Mash," which featured music videos of mashups made by some great European artists, such as Loo & Placido, Lionel Vinyl, Go Home Productions, and McSleazy. Later in 2004, in America, MTV started a series of live mashups that combined rock bands with rappers. Although not mashups in their true form, this prompted another wave of interest throughout America. Z-Trip's *Uneasy Listening* was a vinyl-based mashup album (although he prefers to call them *blends*) that also sparked many people's interest. A spate of commercial mashups have been released recently, including Go Home Productions' "Rapture Riders," which features Blondie's "Rapture" with the Doors' "Riders on the Storm." "Doctor Pressure," mixed by Phil & Dog, features Mylo paired with Miami Sound Machine, and was a huge dance hit. Loo & Placido's "Horny As a Dandy," featuring the Dandy Warhols with Mousse T., is climbing the charts as of the writing of this book. Thus far, these releases haven't enjoyed as much commercial success in the United States as they have overseas.

Although most mashups continue to be the *A vs. B* variety, featuring the vocals of one track with the instrumentals of another track, the mashup genre is splintering in many different directions. For example, *glitch* usually attempts to mess with a single track at a time, and chop it up into very small fragments and rearrange them. Glitch features sounds one usually associates with digital recording errors, such as loud incongruous buzzing, and CD-skipping type sounds. *Sound collage* continues to evolve as well, using multiple sources and turning them into a single song.

While the word *mashup* is popular in the United States, many Europeans simply call them *bootlegs*, (*boots* or *booties* for short) and the genre as a whole is sometimes labeled *bastard pop*.

Breaking It Down

The precursors to mashups have been around for a while, but it's only recently that the technology and breadth of music have been widely available enough for this genre to take off. All in all, the mashup era seems to be still in its infancy, so it's a great time to start experimenting and see what you can do to contribute to this phenomenon! First, you'll read about what hardware and software you'll need, and then you'll learn a bit about music theory and music production software tools. Then it's on to making your own mashups.

Mashup Checklist

T he tools to make mashups are quite easy to obtain. Most people nowadays have a computer powerful enough to make mashups, and this book contains a CD-ROM and URL links to all the software necessary to create great-sounding mashups.

Assuming your computer can handle the software, you'll need to get some music files. There is only a handful of hardware and software platforms preferred for mashup construction, but the raw sonic material you can use is virtually limitless. After learning the basics, you will be able to try your hand at making mashups using any songs you can think of.

Hardware

Although it is quite possible to make mashups on Macs and even on Linux machines, the discussion here is limited to Windows-based machines. The reason for this is twofold:

- Windows machines are the most common type of computer today, and are accessible by most people.
- Sony's ACID works only on Windows machines.

To make the best use of this book, you need to have a computer powerful enough to run both Sony ACID and Adobe Audition. Your computer will need the following:

- Windows 2000 Service Pack 4 (SP4) or XP (SP2for Audition)
- Intel Pentium III or 4 or Intel Centrino, or other Simple Sharing Extensions-enabled (SSE-enabled) processor with at least 1 GHz processing speed
- 850MB available hard drive space (150MB for ACID, and 700 MB for Audition)
- 256MB RAM for ACID (512 MB recommended), and 512MB RAM for Audition (1GB recommended)
- Windows-compatible sound card

- 1024×768 display for Audition; 1280×1024 recommended
- CD-ROM drive; CD-R or CD-RW drive recommended to burn CDs
- Speakers and/or headphones, (both are recommended)

Software

Several software packages that are useful for making mashups are included on this book's CD-ROM.

 There is a fully functional demo of Sony's ACID Pro 6.0 on this book's CD-ROM, which allows you to try all the features for 30 days, with the exception of exporting to formats such as mp3 and AC3, which require additional licensing from third parties.

 This book's CD-ROM also includes Sony's ACID XPress, which is Sony's free version of ACID. It doesn't have all the features that ACID Pro has — most notably, it allows just 10 tracks, and doesn't have the beatmapper wizard, which can be helpful. Fortunately, most mashups have far fewer than 10 tracks, and the methods of mapping beats without the wizard are discussed in Chapter 7.

Also included on the book's CD-ROM is a 30-day fully functional demo of Adobe Audition, a sound-editing environment that is particularly useful for extracting sounds from audio files. Chapter 10 relies heavily on this software. However, this level of sound editing is not necessary for basic mashup construction. If you already have a clean acappella that you want to use, chances are you won't need Audition at all. More ambitious mashup projects may require advanced sound-editing capabilities.

Microsoft Excel is required to use the song selection spreadsheet in Chapter 6. If you don't have Excel or don't want to use it, alternative methods are presented as well.

tONaRT is a small piece of software that helps detect the key of an audio file. It is available at www.zplane.de/Downloads/tONaRT.zip, and will be discussed in greater detail in Chapter 6.

Many other downloadable pieces of software will be discussed throughout this book. For a complete list of software mentioned in this book, please refer to Appendix B.

Acappellas

The word *acappella* may remind you of a vocal group singing together in rich five-part harmonies. But as far as remixers and mashup artists are concerned, an acappella is any vocal track that has been separated from the background track that normally accompanies it.

Sometimes artists will release acappella versions of their songs, especially on vinyl 12-inch or CD singles marketed to dance DJs. A skilled DJ, after years of practice, is able to play the acappella vocals of one song over another song on the other turntable or CD deck, keeping perfect timing. Fortunately (and much to the dismay of some experienced turntablists), you will be able to do this as soon as you finish Chapter 7.

Often acappellas will be available in mp3 form, as any Internet search for *acappella* will show you. Be aware that some of the mp3s you will find this way may not be legal. It is your responsibility to be aware of the copyright status of the material you download.

An *mp3* is an audio file with some parts removed in order to make the file smaller. Although it is easier to transmit on the Internet or store on a hard drive, the sound quality suffers as the file size decreases. A *wav* file is an uncompressed audio file, identical in quality to CD audio.

Unfortunately, most songs don't have acappella versions available anywhere. There are many ways to partially isolate vocals from the background music. This will be discussed in much greater detail in Chapter 10.

Searching for Accappellazz

One of the most challenging aspects of finding an acappella is figuring out just how to spell it. Searching on iTunes, you'll find it under "acapella," "acappella," "a cappella," "a capella," and even "accappella," "accapella," "acapela," "accappela," "acca pella," "aka pella," or just plain "pella." What's going on? Are people who make vocal-only versions just reely bad spellerz?

Well, yes and no. The term has a history that goes back before the Beastie Boys released their unadorned rap vocals on their website. Way before . . .

A cappella literally means *in the manner of a chapel* in Italian. Around the time of the Renaissance, large Catholic churches had organs, but smaller chapels did not so singers would sing without accompaniment. For many centuries, the term referred only to religious music sung in this context. Because Latin was the primary language used in the church, the phrase could be spelled *A capella* from the Latin spelling. However, as musical terminology spread across Europe, Italian became the preferred universal language, and the double-*p* predominated.

By the twentieth century, the term was applied to music sung without instruments, whether sacred or secular, and started showing up in the context of pop music, especially in the doo-wop era. The term was typically compressed into *acappella* or *acapella*. By the end of the century, the remix era had dawned, and the term was applied to the pure vocal version of songs that originally had instruments. People in the remix and mashup communities sometimes shorten it to the slang term *pella*, and many variations on this term can be found, like *string-a-pella* or *perc-a-pella*. Today the proper spelling is either one or two words, has one *c*, either one or two *p*'s, and two *l*'s, but due to general confusion, there are even more variants. When searching for acappellas, it's useful to try many spellings.

Instrumentals

The complement to an acappella is an instrumental. This can sometimes be a version of a popular song with the vocals removed, released on vinyl 12-inch or CD single.

You can also often extract the instrumental portion of the music from the vocals using similar techniques to the acappella extraction. This will be covered more in Chapter 10.

Perhaps most commonly, people obtain full songs and then find the portions of those songs that don't have any vocals. Often there is an instrumental introduction and usually at least one instrumental break in most songs. It is often possible to cut those portions out of a song, loop them, and lay an acappella over them. For more information about creating your own instrumental sections, check out Chapter 11.

Obtaining Digital Music Files

There are many sources for music available online. You can do any of the following:

- Purchase mp3s online from any of the popular download services
- Rip mp3s or wav files from purchased CDs or other media
- Download mp3s from websites, P2P networks, or newsgroups

As always, it is your responsibility to be aware of the copyright status of any audio files you download and the implications of removing any copy protection.

Music Download Services

For the purposes of this book, iTunes will be used exclusively. It is very easy to use and install, and is available at www.apple.com/itunes. With the iTunes site open, simply click the Music Store icon in the left panel, and then type the name of the song you are looking for in the search box in the upper-right corner. You can preview any song by double-clicking its name, which gives you a 30-second snippet. Clicking the Add Song icon starts the process of buying the song, and you will be guided through the process of entering your personal information and credit card number. After you have purchased and downloaded the song, it will be in your library, ready to be played. Songs purchased through iTunes cannot be directly loaded into ACID, because their usage is restricted.

Ripping Your Own

The main advantage to creating your own audio file from a CD is the quality. If you want pristine audio in your mashup, you need to start with the best quality sound you can find, and the downloadable compressed formats are generally inferior. Ripping is covered in the "Unprotecting Audio" sidebar.

Unprotecting Audio

Media corporations have devised various *copy protection* technologies that are aimed at preventing consumers from making unauthorized duplication of their content. The only problem is that sometimes you'll want to use your purchased music in ACID and other software, and the copy protection prevents you from loading the files. For this reason, you may find yourself in the position of needing to eliminate the copyright protection from your legally purchased audio files. Depending on the method you use, this process can be entirely legal, or somewhat questionable.

Burning refers to creating your own CDs from audio files. *Ripping* is converting CD audio to an audio file on your computer. The burning-and-ripping method is the easiest way to convert a purchased audio file into usable form. First, in iTunes, press Ctrl+N to create a new playlist, and title it "CD" or whatever you feel like. Drag the songs you want to use into the new playlist, click on the playlist, and then click the Burn Disc icon in the upper-right corner. iTunes will prompt you to insert a blank disc if you have not done so, and then it will burn the playlist onto a regular audio CD. As soon as you are done, your new CD should be selected, and the Burn Disc icon will turn into an Import CD icon. Click this icon, and your songs will be reimported without copy protection.

Keep in mind that the songs will be imported into the format specified in iTunes' preferences, which defaults to Apple's *AAC* format. AAC in some ways has better compression than mp3, but it has not yet achieved the popularity and interoperability of the mp3 format. AAC format files have an .m4p extension for copy-protected songs and .m4a for unprotected songs. The default import format for iTunes should be changed to either wav or mp3. If you have not yet changed this, go into the preferences (Ctrl+,), click the Advanced tab and then click the Importing tab. Change the Import Using drop-down menu from AAC Encoder to either WAV encoder (highest quality) or MP3 encoder (smallest file).

The advantage to this technique is that it's easy and legal, as long as you don't share your unencrypted file. The disadvantage is that it uses up a CD. You can always use a CD-RW disc if this is a concern.

Another method is to use a handy little piece of sound editing and recording software called Audacity, located at `http://audacity.sourceforge.net`. With Audacity, you can directly record the output of another program operating on the same computer. This is great for accomplishing any of the following:

- You can record the output of your audio player and record copy-protected audio.
- You can record the output of demo software that won't allow you to save or render.
- You can capture streaming audio from the web.

There are other techniques involving virtual CDs, audio loopbacks, and outright hacking the protected files. You can find a great guide to all of this at `http://wiki.ehow.com/Convert-Protected-Audio-Into-a-Plain-MP3`.

Websites

There are a number of websites that offer free mp3s. Some offer content that has been cleared by the copyright owner, and others do not verify the status of the content they index. Google "free mp3s" and you'll find many websites to download from. If you are concerned about making sure your downloads are legal, Google "free legal mp3s" instead.

P2P

Using P2P networks is one of the easiest ways to find audio files, including a wide variety of acappellas. P2P networks consist of a network of users who are both downloading and sharing their files. Keep in mind that some of the shared files may be subject to copyright, and it is your responsibility to know the status of the files you download and share. The most popular and easy-to-use P2P client is LimeWire, located at www.limewire.com. LimeWire uses the pervasive Gnutella network, and there are tens of millions of files available for free download.

There are a number of fake files and viruses on the Gnutella network, and it is easy to unwittingly compromise the security of your computer using LimeWire or other Gnutella clients.

Another good P2P platform is BitTorrent. BitTorrent is usually better for larger files, sometimes up to several gigabytes in size. There are many BitTorrent clients available, but Azureus has a great selection of features and is easy to use. The latest version is available at http://azureus.sourceforge.net/download.php. Unlike LimeWire and other Gnutella-based P2P platforms, BitTorrent does not have a search capacity, so to search, you must use the web. Just google your search terms and then add the word *torrent* at the end. A variety of torrent search engines can be unearthed by Googling "torrent search." If you are looking for a single song, BitTorrent may not be the best route to go.

Chapter 15 has more information regarding BitTorrent and other P2P networks.

Newsgroups

One of the most overlooked sources for material is the Usenet newsgroup. Usenet has been around for more than 25 years, and is similar to the BBS systems that predated the Internet. It is organized into topics, and is hosted by thousands of news servers operated by various ISPs. It is quite likely that the ISP that you currently use to access the Internet also hosts a news server. Check with your ISP to find out the URL. Although Usenet was originally designed for text-based discussions, it is now dominated by file sharing. Getting up and running on the newsgroups takes a bit of time and getting used to, but the rewards are manifold. An entire book could conceivably be devoted to the subject, but here is a quick rundown:

1. **Find a news server.** Your ISP probably runs one, but if you are serious about Usenet, you will probably need a dedicated news server eventually. Because of the vast quantities of data posted, news servers only hold the most recent posts. Just how much data is retained depends on the hosting company. Your ISP will probably offer you free access to Usenet, but might only hold a day or two of posts from the groups you are interested in. This means that you have to be quick to get the files you want, and that there will be a number of incomplete files, because the pieces of the file may trickle in over time. To gain access to a longer retention period and more data and complete files, you may want to look into a paid Usenet subscription service, such as Giganews or Astraweb.

2. **Find a newsreader.** This is specialized software used to access the newsgroups. Many e-mail clients also have the ability to access Usenet, but the handling of binaries can be awkward to impossible. Agent (`http://forteinc.com`) is one of the better platforms, although there are many. Xnews (`http://xnews.newsguy.com`) is a good alternative as well.

3. **Find a newsgroup.** When you have a news server and reader, you can retrieve a list of all groups. The bulk of the mp3s are in groups, starting with alt.binaries.sounds.mp3. You can subscribe to any number of groups, download the headers, and then search through the headers for music of interest. Alternatively, you can go to `http://audiofind.com`, which catalogs the mp3s available on Usenet. This website enables you to search through all mp3-oriented newsgroups at once and is highly recommended.

Breaking It Down

Got your software installed? Grabbed a few choice music files? It won't be long now! Fasten your seatbelt . . .

How Music Works

Before diving in to the actual process of making a mashup, it is essential to develop an understanding of the basics of music theory. This can improve your mashups in some noticeable ways:

- Understanding rhythm will help you get your component tracks to lock together and sound tight.

- Understanding pitch and key will help you make your mashup sound like one seamless track rather than two different songs thrown on top of one another.

- Knowledge of both rhythm and key can help you select songs that have high potential to blend well.

- Awareness of music structure can help you get your finished track to flow and maintain the listener's interest.

This chapter covers the basics of rhythm, pitch, key, tone, and form.

Basics of Sound

Whenever an object vibrates, it pushes the air molecules immediately surrounding it, creating a disturbance of pressurized air that travels through space in all directions from the source. Each vibration of the object creates another wave of pressure. While the sound waves travel through the air very rapidly, the molecules themselves only move back and forth a very short distance. This is similar to the ripples in a pond after you throw a pebble into it. The ripples expand outward, yet the water itself doesn't travel far. Figure 4-1 illustrates this concept.

You typically will see a sound wave represented graphically as a *waveform*, which displays a sound wave's intensity over time, like the graph in Figure 4-2. The upper half of the graph represents the areas of *compression* (increased pressure), and the lower half of the graph represents the areas of *decompression* (decreased pressure). This graph could also be thought of as representing the back-and-forth movement over time of the vibrating object that produced the sound wave, such as the *oscillation* (back-and-forth movement) of a string or vocal chord. Figure 4-2 represents the purest sound wave possible, a *sine wave*. In practice, most waveforms look more complex.

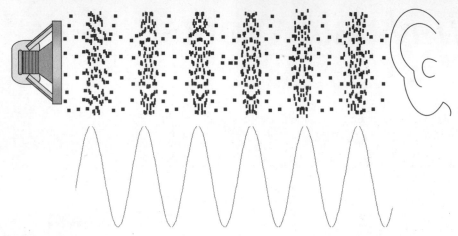

FIGURE 4-1: A sound wave traveling through air molecules, creating zones of high and low pressure

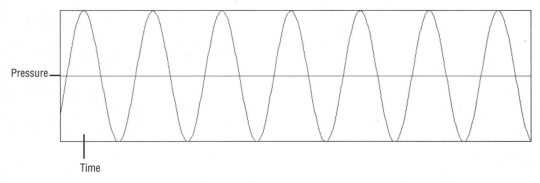

FIGURE 4-2: A waveform representing a pure sine wave

The height of the wave corresponds to the intensity of compression, or the *amplitude* of the wave. Listeners experience this musically as *volume* or loudness. Amplitude is typically measured in *decibels*, abbreviated as *dB*. A difference of a single decibel is close to the smallest change in amplitude a person can detect.

The rate at which the waves occur is called the *frequency*. Musically, this is simply called *pitch*. *Wavelength* is the physical distance between peaks in the sound wave. As the wavelength decreases, the frequency increases. Frequency is measured in *hertz*, typically abbreviated as *Hz*, which measures the number of waves per second. A *kilohertz* is 1,000 Hz and is abbreviated as *kHz*.

When a wave travels through the air and into your ear, it vibrates a membrane called an *eardrum*, which then passes the vibrations through a few small bones to a snail-shaped part of the inner ear called the *cochlea*. Inside of the cochlea are many *hair cells*, each of which is tuned to a different frequency. When a hair cell is vibrated, a signal is sent to the brain that signifies the presence of sound energy at that frequency. The brain then recompiles all the frequency information it receives into a single unified sense of sound. The ear can hear as low as 16 Hz and as high as 20,000 Hz. The highest perceivable pitch gets lower as you age, and as you destroy your ears by listening to loud music in your headphones.

Reading Waveforms

Throughout computer music production, you will often encounter waveforms. Most modern recordings are in two channels (stereo), with the left channel's waveform displayed on top and the right channel displayed on the bottom, as in Figure 4-3.

You won't be able to hear what a waveform would sound like by simply looking at it, but there are many sonic features that become visually recognizable at various levels of time magnification.

Figure 4-3 shows the song "Wake Up," by Missy Elliott, loaded into ACID XPress and zoomed all the way out, so that the entire song is visible. There are two rulers visible. At the top is the beat ruler, counting the number of measures and beats, which will be discussed in detail later this chapter. At the bottom is the time ruler, here displaying hours, minutes, and seconds. At this level of magnification, you can tell the following:

- The song is in stereo.
- The song is about 4 minutes long (time marker 00:04:00).
- There is a fade-out for about the last 15 seconds of the song.
- The volume is fairly constant throughout the song, except for periodic sudden drops in volume. In this song, sometimes the drum sounds drop out momentarily, and then start up again, the first time being at around 16 seconds into the wave.

Continues

Reading Waveforms *Continued*

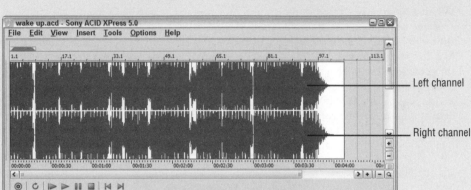

FIGURE 4-3: Missy Elliott's "Wake Up," zoomed out all the way

Figure 4-4 shows the same song at a slightly higher level of magnification. Notice that the waveform is still the same height, but the horizontal scale has changed. You are now looking at just over 8 seconds of music. At this scale, the following features become apparent:

- The individual drum sounds become visible, appearing as a series of wedge-shaped forms.
- The drum sounds have regular horizontal spacing. Different drum sounds have different waveforms, accounting for the variability of each wedge shape.
- Repeating patterns are visible.
- The two channels have very similar contours. If sounds are located in the center of the stereo field, rather than the left or right, the waveforms will be identical in both channels.

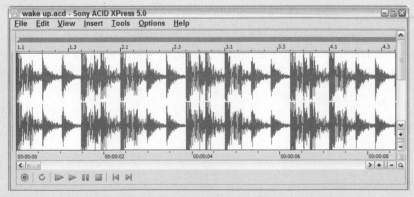

FIGURE 4-4: Missy Elliott's "Wake Up," zoomed in from Figure 4-3

Continues

Reading Waveforms *Continued*

If the time is magnified even further, as in Figure 4-5, a new level of detail shows itself. A half-second of music is now displayed and the following changes are apparent:

- You are looking at two distinct rhythmic sounds, the first one starting at 0 seconds, labeled A, and the second one starting around .3 seconds, labeled B.

- You can actually see the individual oscillations of the waveform. These would correspond with the individual vibrations of a drum or other sound-generating object.

- The second sound has more visual density, because it has higher frequencies. Even this level of magnification is not enough to see all the details of the second wave. (Frequency will be discussed in greater detail later in this chapter.)

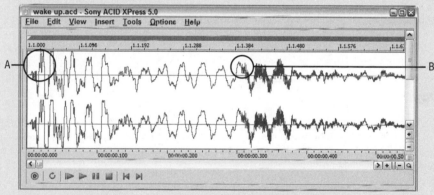

FIGURE 4-5: Missy Elliott's "Wake Up," zoomed in again

As you get more familiar with working with waveforms, you will be able to navigate more quickly without having to rely solely on your ears. If you want to cut up a song into a perfect loop or layer two tracks in perfect sync so that they sound like one track, recognizing the features in a waveform will be invaluable. You can zoom in to adjust the sound almost imperceptibly, and you can zoom out to get a big picture without having to listen to the whole wave.

Basics of Rhythm

Rhythm refers to a pattern of sound events over time. Underlying all Western music is a regular repetition of sounds, which creates patterns of varying levels of emphasis.

Because these patterns are delineated by the exact time the sound events occur, it is helpful for the sounds that define the rhythm to be sudden, rather than gradual. For instance, when an object is struck, it begins to vibrate suddenly, and a quick increase of sound intensity is generated. This is easily perceived as a rhythmic event because of its quick onset. Slower, more evolving sounds, such as a string section, are not as useful in defining rhythm. A typical rhythmic event will have a wedge shape similar to those in the waveform pictured previously in Figure 4-4. Its onset (or *attack*) is well-defined, but the dissipation of the sound (or *decay*) is more gradual.

Beat

Nature is full of repetitive motion, whether it is the vibration of a fly's wings or the slow dripping of water. A series of regularly repeating events is experienced as a *pulse*, and a single event in the series is called a *beat*. When you nod your head or tap your foot to a song, you instinctively feel the pulse, which is the rhythmic building block for most of the world's music. You hear a sound, another sound a moment later, and then yet another sound a moment after that, and your brain automatically creates a grid-like mental map of the events over time and builds up an expectation of another sound a second later.

Note   Beats do not need to have drums in order to define a pulse. There is an additional distinct usage of the word *beat*, which refers to drum patterns or the overall groove of a song.

Tempo

The most readily recognizable pulses are those that happen at the pace of natural human motion. A typical heart rate at rest is between 70 and 75 beats per minute (bpm), and a typical walking pace is a bit faster. Beats occur in similar human-scale time intervals. This pace is known as the *tempo*, and is also measured in bpm.

Meter

Beats are typically arranged in groups of two, three, and four, with the majority of current popular music being in the four-beat group. The grouping of beats into patterns is called *meter*, and a single group of beats is called a *measure*, or sometimes a *bar*. Often there is a pattern of stressed beats, called *accents*, or changes of pitch, harmony, and tone that can also help to give different beats different prominence. You can count along with most songs, and if the measures have four beats, you will be able to count "one two three four, one two three four" fairly easily. The "one" is called the *downbeat*. In much of popular music, there is a snare drum or hand clap on beats two and four, while a kick will often occur on beat one. When mashing up songs, it will be important to correctly identify the downbeat, or your music will likely have a disturbing offset.

A note that lasts for a single beat is usually called a *quarter note*, because there are four beats per measure in the most common meter. A note that lasts for two beats is called a *half note*, and a note that lasts for four beats is a *whole note*. There are also durations of less than a beat: A half of a beat is called an eighth note, and a quarter beat is called a sixteenth note. Thirty-second and sixty-fourth notes are not unheard of, but are rare in popular music. If a note is *dotted*, it takes on a value of one and a half times its normal value. So a dotted quarter note would last for one and a half beats, while a dotted half note would last for three beats.

The most common meter of four beats per measure is commonly referred to as *4/4* (pronounced "four four"), referring to the fact that there are four quarter notes per measure. A meter of three quarter notes per measure would be written as *3/4* ("three four").

When a meter is defined, the brain actually performs an internal rhythm following the beats as they are grouped together. Actual sounds do not have to occur on beats for the pattern to become discernable. Some beats in a rhythm are silent and implied, but they are still felt by the listener. The human mind has a predilection to perceive these grids even with incomplete information, filling in the blanks mentally. In fact, if you hear a series of unaccented uniform beats, you will likely start to organize them into a meter inside your own head without even trying.

A musical rhythm is built on top of this metrical grid. When you look at a waveform, you can often see the drums draw out the grid visually. Notice the regular spikes in the waveform in Figure 4-6.

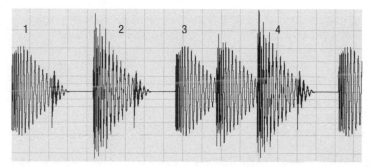

FIGURE 4-6: A waveform representing a simple drum pattern without a lot of other sounds

The beats are labeled for you. In this case, there is a kick on every beat, as well as an extra kick between beats three and four. Because beats are spaced at regular intervals, you know that this extra spike in the wave is not a beat, but rather a sound made halfway through the beat. You can also see the little hi-hat spike halfway through beats one, two, and four, neatly dividing each beat in half. Notice the denser lines at the beginning of beats two and four. This is the snare, performing its most typical rhythmic pattern.

Audio Example 4-1: Simple drum pattern pictured in Figure 4-6.

In most real-world examples, the waveforms may look more complicated, but with a little practice, you will be able to both hear and see the beats.

In mashup construction, the tempos and meters of the component tracks will be manipulated until they are identical, and the underlying grids of the tracks will line up, with the emphases of both tracks occurring simultaneously in parallel. The end result is that the two rhythmic grids merge into a single rhythm.

Basics of Pitch

While sound events are mapping out a rhythmic grid in time, a different grid is being built from the various frequencies that occur. There are just over 100 audible pitches available in Western music, and the distance between them is standardized into a regular grid of pitches, each consecutive pitch having a constant ratio to the previous one. In a given piece of music, a subset of this larger collection of pitches will be played, each with varying emphasis. This map of differently emphasized pitches defines the music just as much as the collection of rhythmic events.

Octaves

When there are two different pitches either played simultaneously or in sequence, the relationship between them is called an *interval*. This is a musical word for the distance between the two pitches.

Rhythm is perceived linearly, meaning that if there are two durations, each ten seconds long, they will be experienced as equivalent. Pitch, however, is perceived logarithmically, and the difference is measured in ratios rather than absolute distance. This means that a frequency of 1,000 Hz seems to be just as distant from 500 Hz as it is from 2,000 Hz. Likewise, the perceived interval between 10,000 Hz to 20,000 Hz is equivalent to the perceived interval between 20 Hz to 40 Hz.

The human brain seems to be hard-wired to recognize certain intervals instinctively, especially ones that are commonly found in nature. Frequency ratios of 2-to-1 and 3-to-2 are often created by naturally occurring phenomena, and our ears instantly recognize the pitches as being related without any musical training. A 2-to-1 ratio is called an *octave*. If one pitch is an octave higher than a second pitch, it has twice the frequency of the second pitch. Pitches an octave apart are so similar that even the most untrained singer can sing a melody an octave higher or lower than a melody they've heard, often without even knowing they are doing it. This phenomenon is called *octave equivalence*.

Audio Example 4-2: Two notes in sequence an octave apart.

Audio Example 4-3: Two simultaneous notes, an octave apart. The pitches are so similar that they become almost impossible to distinguish.

Pitches

Because pitches that have the interval of an octave are so similar, they are given identical names in music. For instance, musicians have given the name of A to the pitch that has the agreed-upon frequency of 440 Hz (also known as *concert A*). But 880 Hz is also called A, as is 220 Hz. Each octave is split into 12 equally sized intervals called *semitones*, and from these pitches all of Western music is created. Octave equivalence allows you to perceive the 100-plus semitones within the range of human hearing as just 12 simple pitches. This makes the map of varying pitch weights much simpler. The pitches, in order, are as follows:

1. A

2. A-Sharp (A♯) or B-flat (B♭)

3. B

4. C

5. C-Sharp (C♯) or D-flat (D♭)

6. D

7. D-Sharp (D♯) or E-flat (E♭)

8. E

9. F

10. F-Sharp (F♯) or G-flat (G♭)

11. G

12. G-Sharp (G♯) or A-flat (A♭)

1. …And then back to A again as the pattern repeats itself.

The pitches played in this order are known as a *chromatic scale*. Figure 4-7 shows the pitches as they appear on a piano keyboard. The white keys have letter names, and the black keys referred to as *sharp* (♯) versions of the note below or *flat* (♭) versions of the note above. It is important to realize that the distance between each consecutive pitch is the same, whether they are sharp, flat, or *natural* (neither sharp nor flat). The distance between B and C is the same as the distance between F and F♯, but half the distance between D and E. So even though some notes look different on the piano or have more complicated names, they are musically all equivalent.

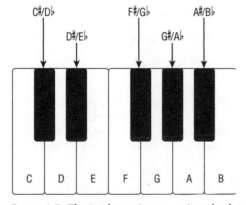

FIGURE 4-7: The twelve notes on a piano keyboard

Other Intervals

Just as there are 12 standard pitches available, there are also 12 common intervals, ranging from a single semitone to 12 semitones (an octave). Intervals greater than 12 semitones behave similarly to the octave-equivalent smaller interval, meaning that a 15-semitone interval can be treated as a three-semitone interval, subtracting 12 from 15.

Half Steps and Whole Steps

The smallest interval in Western music, a semitone, is also known as a *half step*, and is the distance between two consecutive pitches, such as C and C♯, or E and F. It is also known as a *minor second*.

A whole tone is two semitones, such as the interval between F and G, or B♭ and C. It is also known as a *whole step* or a *major second*.

Generically, a *step* is the interval between adjacent notes in a scale, usually consisting of one or two semitones. Scales are discussed in the next section.

The Fifth

Besides the octave, the most important and easily recognizable interval is the *fifth*, sometimes called a *perfect fifth*. While there are 12 semitones between two pitches in an octave interval, there are seven semitones in between two pitches in a fifth. So a fifth above the B would be an F♯, and a fifth above a G would be a D. Like an octave, pitches in a fifth relationship blend together well. These relationships will be important later in deciding which songs to mash up together.

Audio Example 4-4: Two notes in sequence a fifth apart.

Audio Example 4-5: Two simultaneous notes a fifth apart. The pitches blend together quite well.

If you take the lower note of a fifth and raise it an octave, you create an interval of five semitones, which is known as a *perfect fourth*, or simply a *fourth*. Due to octave equivalence, a fourth is very similar to the fifth.

Fourths and fifths are so named because they count steps in a scale rather than semitones. Scales are discussed in the next section.

The Cent

The *cent* is equal to a hundredth of a semitone. Pitches a cent apart are virtually indistinguishable from each other. Some people may be able to hear a 5-cent difference, and most people will detect a 10-cent difference. Sometimes recordings will not have perfect pitch where A is at exactly 440 Hz, and you will need to shift the pitch in small fractions of semitones. These pitch shifts will usually be measured in cents.

Tempo and Pitch

Tempo measures the rate of pulses in a piece of music, and pitch measures the rate of the oscillations in a sound wave. In fact, if you play a sound at a fast enough rate, it will stop being perceived as a rhythm and will be perceived as an audible pitch instead. A pulse at 1200 beats per minute (bpm) corresponds with a pitch of 20 Hz, the low end of the human threshold for pitch detection. If you were to play sixteenth notes, you'd only need a tempo of 300 bpm to become pitch instead of rhythm.

Because of this, tempo and pitch are inextricably linked in sound recordings. When you speed up a recording, you raise the tempo, but you also raise the pitch at the same time. Doubling the speed will double the tempo and raise the pitch of every sound by an octave. Likewise, slowing a recording down to half-speed will cut the tempo in half while lowering the pitch an octave.

Independent manipulation of tempo and pitch is one of the features of ACID that makes it a great platform for mashup construction. Pitch shifting is covered in Chapter 8.

Basics of Key

You've learned about pitches and intervals, which relate to the placement and distance between pitches. Just as meter helps the listener set up expectations of rhythmic events occurring at a certain times, key sets up expectations of certain pitches occurring more than others. Key is as critical to successful mashup construction as rhythm.

Scales

A *note* is an instance of a musical event with a specific pitch and rhythmic duration. A *scale* is a collection of notes with seven of the 12 possible pitches. These are arranged in a specific order of half steps and whole steps. Scales can begin on any note, but after the first note is chosen, the pattern of half-step and whole-step intervals is always the same for each *mode*, or type of scale. The initial pitch of a scale is known as the *tonic*. There are two significant modes of scales in modern popular music: *major* and *minor*. When a piece of music uses melodies and chords made up of pitches from a certain scale, it is said to be written in the *key* of the scale.

Major Scale

The major scale consists of two whole steps, followed by a half step, followed by three more whole steps, followed by another half step. For example, the E♭ major scale is as follows:

1. E♭

2. F (whole step above E♭)

3. G (whole step above F)

4. A♭ (half step above G)

5. B♭ (whole step above A♭)

6. C (whole step above B♭)

7. D (whole step above C)

8. E♭ (half step above D)

The major scale is often considered the happier and more cheery of the two scales. Figure 4-8 shows the E♭ major scale on a piano keyboard.

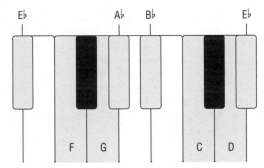

FIGURE 4-8: The notes in an E♭ major scale

Audio Example 4-6: The E♭ major scale.

Minor Scale

The most commonly used form of the minor scale consists of a whole step, followed by a half step, followed by two more whole steps, followed by another half step, followed by two more whole steps. For example, the F minor scale is as follows:

1. F

2. G (whole step above F)

3. A♭ (half step above G)

4. B♭ (whole step above A♭)

5. C (whole step above B♭)

6. D♭ (half step above C)

7. E♭ (whole step above D)

8. F (whole step above E♭)

The minor scale is often considered the sadder and more brooding of the two scales. Figure 4-9 shows the F minor scale on a piano keyboard.

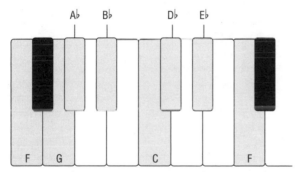

FIGURE **4-9: The notes in an F minor scale**

Audio Example 4-7: The F minor scale.

Keys

Typically, a song will mostly use pitches from just one of the major or minor scales. Although the scale itself will not be performed, the pitches in the song will be mostly from notes in that scale, often emphasizing the first pitch of the scale. Because there are 12 pitches, and you can have a major or minor key built on each of these, there are 24 possible keys. It's not important to memorize or even figure out what the pitches are in each key, but it's important to realize that a given key will share more pitches with some keys than others. For example, C major and G major have six of their seven pitches in common, but F major and E major don't have a single pitch in common. This will be very important later when you're choosing the component songs for your mashups. If the keys of the songs are dissimilar, it will sound jarring.

Chords

When you play three or more pitches from a scale at the same time, it makes a *chord*. The simplest and most common chords are three-pitch chords called *triads*. They consist of a pitch from the scale, called the *root* of the chord, and the pitches two and four steps above the root. The steps are either half steps or whole steps, depending on the intervals in the scale. For example, suppose you are in the key of E♭ major (refer back to Figure 4-8), and you are building a triad starting on E♭, the first note of the key's scale. The other pitches would be G and B♭, the third and fifth notes of the key's scale, two and four steps above E♭. When you play these three notes simultaneously, you hear a harmonious blending of all of the notes. Figure 4-10 shows the notes in an E♭ major chord.

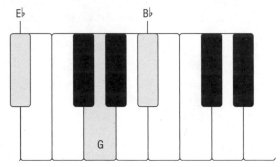

FIGURE 4-10: An E♭ major chord

Audio Example 4-8: The E♭ major chord: E♭, G, and B♭ separately, and then together.

Major chords consist of the chord's root, the pitch four semitones above the root, and the pitch seven semitones (a perfect fifth) above the root. Minor chords consist of the root, the pitch three semitones above the root, and the pitch seven semitones (a perfect fifth) above the root.

Audio Example 4-9: The E♭ major chord, followed by the E♭ minor chord.

There are many other kinds of chords as well. The important thing to know is that most music is built on a series of chords within a key, known as a *chord progression*, or more generally as *harmony*. So not only do you have to make sure that the keys of your mashup components are compatible, but the chord progressions within each component song need to be compatible as well. Some brief or small discrepancies can be tolerated. But even if two songs are in the exact same key, but they have lots of simultaneous chords that don't share any pitches, they will be perceived as clashing.

Melody

A *melody* is a series of notes, one after the other. This is in contrast to harmony, which relates to a series of groups of notes. Any time you sing, it is a melody. A melody will also convey rhythm with the timing and duration of its notes. Because melodies voice some pitches more than others, they can also help to transmit a sense of harmony. The pitches within a melody typically fall exclusively within the set of pitches in the current key, and tend to favor pitches within the underlying chord progression, especially when the note falls on a rhythmic accent.

Melodies consist of short segments called *phrases*, which have about as many notes as you could sing before taking a breath. Consecutive notes within a melody are close in pitch more often than not, with larger leaps being more uncommon. Because of this, melodies give a sense of a rising and falling pitch contour. Often, melodies end with a descending pitch pattern, resting on the tonic of the scale. If melodies come to rest on other pitches, it may sound unresolved, especially if the pitch isn't within the current underlying chord. Likewise, if the melody frequently hits pitches outside of the current key, it will have a jarring effect. This will be very important to remember later, when you're laying down a vocal from one song over the instrumental of another.

Basics of Tone

Figure 4-2 introduced the sine wave, the purest form of oscillation. You will notice that most real-world waveforms have much more complex shapes. But any sound wave, no matter how complicated, can be reproduced by combining various sine waves of different frequencies. You may need thousands of sine waves to produce some of the more complex sounds, but it can be done. Each component sine wave has its own amplitude that varies over time.

Because these sine wave components have clear relationships of frequency, amplitude, and phrase to each other, the ear groups them all together and experiences them as a single sound with a characteristic *tone* or *color*, which is also called *timbre* when referring to the characteristic tone of an instrument. Two sounds with different tones may have identical pitch and volume, but because the sine wave components vary, you can tell the difference between different instruments and sound sources.

Overtones

Suppose you tune a guitar string to a concert A of 440 Hz and then pluck it. You would hear a sound that included a sine wave at 440 Hz. But the guitar has a sound that is perceived to be brighter than a simple single sine wave. This brightness is actually an indication of the presence of sine waves at frequencies other than 440 Hz. In fact, there are additional vibrations occurring at 880 Hz, 1320 Hz, 1760 Hz, and many other frequencies. These higher frequencies are called *overtones*, and the lowest and usually loudest frequency is called the *fundamental*. Almost all naturally occurring sounds contain overtones.

Pitched musical sounds tend to have overtones in integer multiples of the fundamental, which are called *harmonics*. Harmonics usually tend to decrease in amplitude with each higher frequency.

A flute, with a relatively pure tone, will have few harmonics, while a brass instrument, with a bright tone, will have many audible harmonics. The collection of harmonics at the various amplitudes is referred to as the *harmonic spectrum*. Instruments with harmonic overtones are perceived as stable, and transmit a clear psychological sense of a single pitch, even though they are in fact made up of multiple related component frequencies.

Note Interestingly, the intervals that music is based on seem to correspond with the series of harmonic overtones. The interval between the fundamental and the first harmonic overtone is an octave. The interval between the first and second overtone is very close to a fifth, and the first six overtones together closely approximate a major chord.

If there are strong levels of fractional overtones or *inharmonics*, the ear will perceive the sound to be dissonant or jarring. A crash cymbal is a great example of a sound with many fractional overtones. You can't really say what pitch a cymbal is. Tones without clear mathematical relationships are simply experienced as noise.

Resonance and Formants

When an acoustic guitar string is plucked, and its characteristic series of related frequencies is created, the sound is transmitted from the string through the body of the guitar, where it is amplified. Because of the particular shape of the guitar, certain frequencies of the strings get amplified more than others. This selective frequency amplification is called *resonance*.

Resonance alters the harmonic spectrum of a sound. The frequency of a sound may change, along with its overtones, but the resonance will often stay the same. As a simplified example, suppose an object had a resonant peak at 440 Hz. If a string were plucked with a fundamental frequency of 440 Hz, the fundamental would be amplified, and all the harmonics would be less prominent in comparison. However, if a string were plucked with a fundamental frequency of 220 Hz, the first harmonic (440 Hz) would be amplified. So even though the tone of the vibrating string may be constant at various pitches, the constant frequency of the resonance would shape the tone differently at different pitches.

A similar phenomenon happens with vocals. The vocal chords generate a vibration with plenty of harmonic overtones. Different vowel sounds are made simply by changing the shape of the mouth and throat. Every singer has a characteristic range of vowel resonant patterns, each with a series of characteristic frequency peaks that *amplify* (increase the amplitude of) the vocal chord's vibrations. These peaks, also known as *formants*, do not change when the pitch of the sound changes, because the size and shape of the mouth and throat do not change.

Cross-Reference Formants will become important in Chapter 8, which discusses realistic pitch shifting without shifting the formants, giving processed vocals a more natural sound.

Transients

Transients are very brief sound components, often overtones, usually heard during the attack portion of a sound. Transients can be inharmonic even when the tone itself is mostly harmonic. A flute, for example, has mostly harmonic overtones, but the attack portion can contain a lot of noise. Because of their sudden onset, transients can be useful for defining rhythm, even when the remainder of the sound is fairly smooth. In vocals, explosive consonants tend to have lots of transients, but the vowels do not.

 Software exists that can emphasize or de-emphasize transients in a sound recording, which is one of several useful tools for *unmixing*, discussed in depth in Chapter 10.

Basics of Form

As discussed earlier, pitch and rhythm are essentially about the same thing: the pattern of events over time. In the case of rhythm, the pattern is readily apparent because it happens on the human time scale of heartbeats and footsteps. In the case of pitch, the recurring events (oscillations) happen so fast that we don't sense them individually, but only the general pace at which they occur. In music, structure is also occurring at a slower pace than either pitch or rhythm. A piece of music is typically broken down into sections, and the larger structure is generally referred to as musical *form*, and specifically, in the case of modern popular music, as *song structure*. Instead of the structural units being a single beat, in song structure they are in measures. They might be 8, 16, or 32 measures, although this is not set in stone. These sections are most readily recognizable from the melodies and lyrics (if any), and also harmonic progressions and instrumentation.

Because mashups typically deal with popular music with vocals, the sections of a typical song will be discussed next. Modern popular song structure almost always has sections known as choruses and verses, and usually other sections as well. Although there are no hard and fast rules, usually the sections alternate, so the listener doesn't get too bored. An appropriate balance of repetition and variety is what makes a structure pleasing. Too much repetition will make a song get grating. Too much variety will swamp the listener with too much information. A perfect structure will strike a balance between a little novelty and familiarity.

Chorus

The *chorus* is the part of the song that is most recognizable and important. The lyrics are typically the same for each repetition of the chorus, and the melodies are memorable. If you don't know a song well, usually the chorus is the part where you can start singing along. Sometimes the lyrics will mention the song's title in the chorus, often as the first or last words. Most pop songs ever written have a chorus.

Here are some examples:

- **Michael Jackson, "Billie Jean":** The section starting with the lyrics "Billie Jean is not my lover."

- **Beyoncé, "Crazy in Love":** The section starting with the lyrics "Got me looking so crazy right now, your love's got me looking so crazy right now."

- **Madonna, "Like a Virgin":** The section starting with the lyrics "Like a virgin touched for the very first time."

- **Kelly Clarkson, "Since U Been Gone":** The section starting with the lyrics "Since you been gone, I can breathe for the first time."

- **Prince, "When Doves Cry":** The section starting with the lyrics "How can you just leave me standing alone in a world so cold."

Verse

Along with the chorus, the *verse* is a defining characteristic of a modern pop song. Verses within a song will have the same melody, but different lyrics, as opposed to the chorus, where both the lyrics and melody are the same. Verses tend to have lower energy than the choruses and can be less catchy. Lyrically, the verses are where the background story is being told, and the chorus sums up the main point of the song. Usually, there are several repetitions of the verse followed by the chorus within a song. The verse will often be the first words sung in the song.

Bridge

Often the verses and chorus don't provide quite enough variety to carry an entire pop song. After two or three verse-and-chorus repetitions, the listener can be taken to a third place called the *bridge*. In the bridge, the lyrics tend to provide a new perspective on the material covered in the verses and the chorus. The harmonic progression shifts, and can even wander into other related keys from the main song. The bridge will typically occur around two-thirds of the way through a pop song.

Intro

An *intro* simply refers to the first part of a song, usually without any vocals. Often, an instrumental *hook* (a recognizable and catchy riff or melody) will be introduced. Intros are typically short, but effectively set the mood for the song. In dance music, the intro can be quite long to give a DJ time to mix into the song.

Outro

While technically not an actual word, the *outro* is the most common terminology for the ending part of a song. This is simply the part of the song after the verses and choruses are all done, and the song is winding down. In some songs, the outro simply consists of a gradual fade to silence, although this is falling out of fashion. In rock and roll, the outro can be where the guitarists and the drummers all go crazy and then all end together in a big power chord. As with intros, in dance music, the outros will typically be extended to allow the DJ to mix into a different song.

Breakdown

A *breakdown* will usually happen before, after, or in place of the bridge. Many pop songs do not have this section. A breakdown is usually completely instrumental and will feature much sparser instrumentation than the rest of the song. In dance music, breakdowns are *de rigueur*. They will often gradually build up into a peak moment of the song, sometimes an instrumental hook or perhaps the chorus.

Pre-Chorus

Often there is a short section after the verse and before the chorus, where the energy and tension build, waiting for the release brought on by the chorus. If there is a pre-chorus, there is less likelihood that there will be a bridge.

Instrumental Break

There are other instrumental sections besides the breakdown, intro, and outro. Often there will be a short instrumental after a chorus and before the next verse. Sometimes the hook introduced in the intro will be repeated. Maybe there will be a blazing guitar solo. Sometimes an entire verse will be played by instruments, although this is not as common as it once was.

Refrain

A refrain is somewhat similar to a chorus, in that it contains the same melody and the same words each time. However, a refrain usually consists of a single phrase repeated over and over, and may not have the energy peak that a chorus has.

Song Structure

Even though most songs won't have all of these sections, there is a typical pattern in a pop song. It starts with the intro, has a couple verse-and-chorus repetitions, goes to the bridge, and then possibly another verse (although it's often left out), followed by a few chorus repetitions, and then the outro. Even if there are not obvious verses and choruses in a song, there will be a repeating structure of sections. Understanding typical song structure is essential to creating a good mashup, because your mashup should have a similar structure. To make a mashup interesting, the instrumental backing of the verses and the choruses should be different. Sometimes the bridge of the mashup is an opportunity to throw in some material from an entirely different song or otherwise violate the listener's expectations.

It is a useful exercise to dissect songs to determine their structure. After choosing the component songs for your mashup, but before constructing it, if you examine each song's structure it may provide guidance on how your mashup should be structured. Here are some examples of structures from a few pop songs (notice the similarity of the structures):

- Michael Jackson, "Billie Jean"
    - Intro: 14 bars
    - Verse: 20 bars
    - Pre-chorus: 8 bars
    - Chorus: 12 bars
    - Verse: 20 bars
    - Pre-chorus: 8 bars
    - Chorus: 20 bars
    - Instrumental break: 8 bars
    - Chorus repeats and fades out
- Kelly Clarkson, "Since U Been Gone"
    - Intro: 2 bars
    - Verse: 16 bars
    - Pre-chorus: 6 bars
    - Chorus: 10 bars
    - Instrumental break: 2 bars
    - Verse: 16 bars
    - Pre-chorus: 6 bars
    - Chorus: 10 bars
    - Bridge: 8 bars
    - Breakdown: 8 bars
    - Double chorus: 21 bars
    - Outro: 4 bars
- Nirvana, "Smells Like Teen Spirit"
    - Intro: 12 bars
    - Verse: 8 bars
    - Pre-chorus: 8 bars

- Chorus: 12 bars

- Instrumental break: 8 bars

- Verse: 8 bars

- Pre-chorus: 8 bars

- Chorus: 12 bars

- Instrumental break: 16 bars

- Verse: 8 bars

- Pre-chorus: 8 bars

- Chorus: 21 bars

Cross-Reference

When constructing your own mashup, it's important to periodically take a step back and look at the entire structure as a whole. You may want to create a structure similar to that of a standard pop song. The structure may mimic the structure of one of the mashup components, or you may create your own structure. Arranging your mashup will be discussed in Chapter 11.

Breaking It Down

The fundamentals of music theory outlined in the chapter are the building blocks for mashup and all music creation. Adjusting tempo and rhythm are discussed in Chapters 7 and 9, and adjusting the pitch is covered in Chapter 8. Both key and tempo figure heavily in song selection, which is discussed in Chapter 6. Mashup form and structure are discussed in Chapter 11. But first, you'll need to learn a bit about how to use ACID software, which is in the next chapter.

Using the Software

Before you dive into making mashups, you'll need to gain some familiarity with the tools you'll use. This chapter is not intended to be a thorough discussion of each piece of software, rather just the subset of functions you will most likely use in constructing your mashup. The actual mashup construction will take place within Sony ACID, but some advanced audio editing functions will use Adobe Audition.

Sony ACID

ACID, formerly from the company Sonic Foundry, started out as a loop-based music construction tool. In early versions of the software, you could only drop in wav files that were pre-cut into repeatable loops. Soon ACID introduced *beatmapping*, the use of tempo and beat placement information, to handle longer sound files while independently manipulating tempo and pitch. In many ways, ACID has helped to spur the mashup revolution, and has long been the mashup artist's tool of choice.

ACID Pro versus ACID XPress

Sony provides several versions of ACID at varying prices. ACID Pro is the most frequently used version of the software, but carries a large price tag. However, it contains features not available in other versions that are useful in learning mashup construction. Even if you eventually opt to use the XPress version, which Sony gives away for the low, low price of free, it's a good idea to start with ACID Pro. There is a 30-day demo of ACID Pro 6.0 on this book's CD-ROM, which should give you enough time to familiarize yourself with its features and decide for yourself which version is best for you.

 Throughout this chapter and the rest of this book, features available in ACID Pro 6, and not the XPress version, will be marked with the ACID Pro icon. These include the Beatmapper Wizard, effects, and envelopes. For a full list of ACID Pro features, go back to Chapter 3 and take a look at Table 3-1.

Installation

The ACID Pro 6.0 demo provides a good way to learn the basics of mashup construction. If after 30 days, you decide not to purchase ACID Pro, you'll need to uninstall the demo and install ACID XPress instead.

Installing either version is straightforward. Insert this book's CD-ROM, and double-click the setup executable for either ACID XPress or ACID Pro 6. Simply follow the on-screen instructions, and ACID XPress or Pro will be added to your list of installed programs.

To uninstall the ACID Pro demo, go to Add or Remove Programs in the Control Panel, located in the Start menu. Select Sony ACID Pro, click Remove, and follow the on-screen instructions.

Projects

A *project* is a set of instructions to create a single piece of music. Each mashup you create will most likely have its own associated project. An ACID project will have the extension .acd on your computer. Each time ACID starts, it loads the most recent project you were working on. ACID also attempts to periodically auto-save your project, so if your program or computer crashes, ACID may have a recently stored version of your most recent project, which it will attempt to automatically load the next time you run ACID. Even so, it is important to save your work often to avoid unnecessary frustration. Not only is it maddening to have to retrace your steps, often the "fun factor" is missing in reconstruction, which can be discouraging. Pressing Ctrl+S to save your work every once in a while is a good habit to get into, even with ACID's auto-save feature.

Also, if you find yourself making significant changes to your project, but you are a bit unsure of whether you actually want to permanently go in your new direction, you might want to save a copy of your project with a different name. That way, if you change your mind, you can always revert to a previously saved state. To do this, select Save As from the File menu and choose a new name. It is not uncommon to have 5 or 10 versions of a project saved on your hard drive by the time you are finished.

Another issue to keep in mind in maintaining the future integrity of your project files is that ACID does not store the project's sound files in the .acd file. It simply stores the path to the mp3s (or wavs), which means that if you later move the audio files, ACID will have to search for and relocate them. If you delete or move the sound files from your computer, ACID will not be able to load your project correctly. This also means that if you transfer your .acd file to another computer, your project may not load correctly. Luckily, ACID has a feature that lets you save the .acd file along with all sound files in it. If you select Save As and then choose ACID project with embedded media (*.acd-zip) from the Save As Type drop-down menu, ACID will create a file that contains all the information you will need to safely archive or transfer the project.

For this chapter, the examples will use the Dizzee Rascal/Tag Team mashup from Chapter 1.

Overview of the ACID Window

There are four main sections of the ACID window, as shown in Figure 5-1:

- **The menu and toolbar at the top.** The menu holds a wide variety of commands along with many associated keyboard shortcuts. The toolbar contains shortcuts to many of the same functions, as well as several tools that perform various functions.

- **The track list.** On the left side of the window directly below the toolbar, the track list is where each track's volume and pan are set, as well as the overall tempo of the project.

- **The timeline.** This is where the actual audio data for the tracks is displayed. Most of your editing will be performed in the timeline. Each track can contain many audio events. While ACID XPress demands that each event in a given track have the same audio file as its source, ACID Pro 6 adds the ability to put multiple audio files on a single track. The upper part of the timeline is the beat ruler, which marks the number of measures and beats. The lower part of the timeline is the transport bar.

- **Dockable windows.** At the bottom of the ACID window are various windows that can be shown or hidden at will. These windows allow for detailed control of many features.

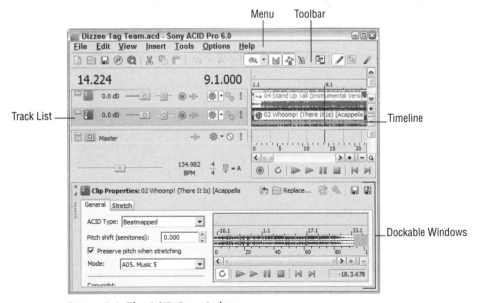

FIGURE 5-1: The ACID Pro window

ACID XPress looks similar to this, but a few controls are missing.

Toolbar

There are many buttons that provide functionality in the toolbar, but perhaps the most important of these are the draw tool, selection tool, paint tool, and envelope tool (see Figure 5-2). These tools are mostly used to edit events, and will be discussed throughout this chapter. To switch tools, click the appropriate icon.

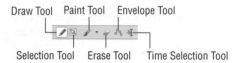

FIGURE 5-2: ACID's toolbar

Transport Bar

The transport bar is located just under the timeline and just over the dockable window area, as shown in Figure 5-3. It contains the following buttons, some of which may be familiar to you from the controls of a CD, DVD, or mp3 player:

- **Record:** You will probably not need this in mashup construction. In fact, a pure mashup will not use any original material whatsoever.

- **Loop Playback:** This toggles the loop functionality. With the loop on, ACID plays through the current time selection, and loops back to the beginning of it when it hits the end. To make a time selection, position your cursor over the beat ruler, and then drag the cursor from the point where you want the loop to start to the point where you want the loop to end. You may not end up using the Loop Playback button in mashup construction, but it's handy if you want to repeatedly listen to a portion of your track while making adjustments.

- **Play from Start:** Perhaps not needing explanation, this plays a selection from its start.

- **Play:** Plays a selection from the cursor's current position.

- **Pause:** Pauses playback, and leaves the cursor where it was when you paused it.

- **Stop:** Stops playback, and returns the cursor to where it was before you started playback.

- **Go to Start:** Sets the cursor at the start of the selection.

- **Go to End:** Sets cursor at end of the selection.

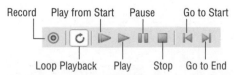

FIGURE 5-3: **The transport bar**

To get a quick feel for these buttons, first click the selection tool from the toolbar, and then click the timeline somewhere in the middle of the project. Click the Play button, and the project will start playback from where you positioned your cursor. Now click the Stop button, and you will notice that the cursor has returned to where it was when you first clicked the timeline. Now click the Play button again, and the project will start playback from the same place. If you click Pause, you will notice that the cursor has moved. If you click Play again, the playback will resume from the new cursor position. Click the Play from Start button, and you will hear the project start from the beginning. However if you click Stop, the cursor will again revert to its most recent position in the middle of the song. Click the Go to Start button, and the cursor repositions itself at the beginning of the project. Now if you click Play and then Stop, the cursor will return to the beginning.

Track List

Now it's time to play around a little bit with the track list features. The components of the track list are detailed in Figure 5-4.

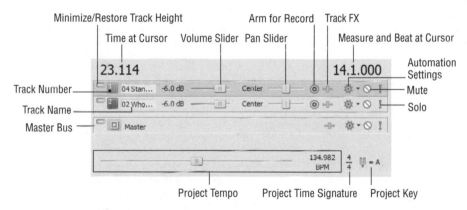

FIGURE 5-4: ACID Pro's track list

 ACID XPress has a single multipurpose slider instead of separate pan and volume sliders.

Click the Play from Start button, and while the project is playing, drag the volume slider for one of the tracks to the left and then to the right. Notice how the volume is reduced when you drag to the left and increased when you drag to the right. Press Ctrl+Z to undo the changes you just made.

 If you have ACID XPress, click Vol, right next to the slider. A drop-down menu will pop up. Select Pan instead of Vol, changing the multipurpose slider mode.

Now drag the pan slider from right to left. Assuming you are listening in stereo, you should hear the track moving from right to left as well. Press Ctrl+Z to undo this action. If you want to adjust the volume or pan only slightly, try pressing the Ctrl key while you are dragging the sliders. You can move the sliders in smaller increments this way.

Now click the Mute button on one of the tracks, play the project, and notice how the track is silenced. Click the Mute button again to un-mute it. Now click the Solo button on the same track and click Play. Notice everything is muted except the soloed track. Click the Solo button again to un-solo it.

Now it's time to mess around with the tempo a little bit. It's probably best to do this with "Whoomp!" soloed, because the "Stand Up Tall" track is a one-shot and is therefore unresponsive to project tempo (more on that later). After soloing track 2 ("Whoomp!"), drag the tempo slider all the way to the right and let go. You'll hear the vocals speed way up, although their pitch will remain unaltered. Now drag the tempo slider all the way to the left and let go. You'll hear the vocals playing back veerrryyy ssslllooowwllyy. Notice as you drag the tempo slider that a bar appears next to each track, informing you of how much the track is slowed down or sped up. A percentage value signifying the amount of tempo shift appears at the right of each track while you move the tempo slider. Now press Ctrl+Z to reset the tempo to the original bpm. Click the Solo button for track 2 to undo the soloing.

The project key, which is located to the right of the tempo slider, tells ACID what key to transpose the tracks to. This affects only tracks for which the root note has been set, and will be discussed later in this chapter in the section on track/clip properties.

It is easy to rearrange the order in which the tracks appear. Click track 1, either on the track name or the icon with the track number and type. Now drag the track downward until the cursor is below the second track and let go. Notice how the track order was rearranged. The playback will still sound identical, however. The reason you might want to rearrange tracks is primarily so that related tracks are visually close to each other.

You can also cut, copy, paste, and delete entire tracks. Select a track by clicking on the track name or the icon with the track number and type. Now press the Delete key. You will see the entire track disappear. Press Ctrl+Z to undo this action. Now press Ctrl+X to cut the selection (the scissors icon in the ACID toolbar has the same effect). You will again see the entire track disappear, but this time the track is sitting in the computer's clipboard, waiting to be pasted. Press Ctrl+V to paste the selection, and you will see that the track has returned. Press Ctrl+V one more time just to prove that you are indeed pasting a track from the clipboard. You will notice that there are now two identical tracks. Press Ctrl+Z to revert your project to just two tracks. Now select the other track and press Ctrl+C to copy it. You won't see anything disappear, but ACID has made a copy of the track and put it into its clipboard. Press Ctrl+V (paste) to prove this, and then press Ctrl+Z again to return the project to its original two-track state.

If you want to change the playback pitch of the entire track, select the track (in the track list, not the timeline) and click the +/= button (or press the + key on the number pad) to raise the pitch, or click the – key to lower the pitch. These keys will change the event's pitch one semitone at a time.

If you press Shift while holding down either of these keys, the pitch will change four semitones at a time. The behavior of the pitch-shifting depends on the track type, as discussed in the section on track properties windows later in this chapter.

Note

With the introduction of clips in ACID Pro 6, you can shift the pitch in both the track and the individual clips. In ACID XPress, these are the same parameter.

Cross-Reference

Chapter 8 covers pitch-shifting in depth.

To add a new track from an mp3 or a wav file you have on your hard drive, you can choose File ➪ Open, and then navigate to your sound file. But a method that is usually easier and quicker is to simply drag your sound file from either Windows Explorer or iTunes and drop it into ACID.

Scroll and Zoom

You can perform two kinds of scrolling and zooming in ACID. Horizontal scrolling moves you forward and backward in time, allowing you to see different time periods of the project, and horizontal zooming allows you to see more or less time in the ACID window. Vertical scrolling allows you to view various tracks if all of your tracks do not fit in the ACID window at once, and vertical zooming allows you to either show more tracks at once, or examine each track in greater detail.

The vertical scroll bar is located on the left edge of the timeline, and the horizontal scroll bar is on the bottom edge of the timeline, as previously shown in Figure 5-1.

Horizontal Scroll and Zoom

Figure 5-5 shows the time scroll bar as well as the time zoom buttons. Click the Zoom In Time button a few times or simply click and hold it for a short duration, and you will notice that you will see less time displayed but in greater detail. The zooming will be centered in time where the cursor is placed. Now click the Zoom Out Time button a few times or click and hold it. You will see the opposite effect, until the entire time of the project is displayed. Now click the small bar in between the Zoom In Time and the Zoom Out Time buttons, and drag from left to right and back again. Notice how the time zooms in and out with a single button.

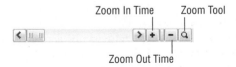

FIGURE 5-5: Horizontal scroll and zoom

Now make sure you are zoomed in a little bit, and click the center of the horizontal scroll bar and drag it from left to right and back again. Notice how the time shifts along with the scroll bar. Now click to the left and right of the horizontal scroll bar, in the white space. The scroll bar will move and the time will shift. If you click the left and right arrows at the end of the horizontal scroll bar, the time will also shift, although not as quickly. You can also click and hold either the white space or the arrows for a continuous movement.

Now click the left or right edge of the scroll bar and drag it from left to right and back again. Notice how the time zooms in and out. The length of the horizontal scroll bar directly corresponds to the portion of time displayed compared to the length of the entire project.

Vertical Scroll and Zoom

Figure 5-6 pictures the vertical zoom bar, which functions similarly to the horizontal zoom, except that instead of more and less time being shown, more or fewer tracks are shown. You can press the Zoom In Track Height button, the Zoom Out Track Height button, and the little button between them, just like with the horizontal zooming. You can also drag the vertical scroll bar up and down as well as clicking the up and down arrows and the white space in the scroll bar, similarly to the horizontal scroll bar. You can't zoom with the vertical scroll bar, however. You may find yourself using the vertical scroll and zoom capabilities less frequently than the horizontal ones.

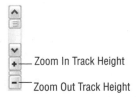

— Zoom In Track Height

— Zoom Out Track Height

FIGURE 5-6: The vertical scroll and zoom

Additionally, you can zoom in vertically on individual tracks. To change the height of a single track, click the lower edge of the track in the track list and drag it up or down. Alternatively, you can click the Minimize/Restore buttons (shown previously in Figure 5-4) or the Maximize/Restore buttons, which become visible if the track height is sufficient.

There is one last zoom function to discuss: the zoom tool. This is unlike other tools in that ACID will revert to the previously selected tool after using it once. Click the zoom tool and then click and drag diagonally across the events you want to zoom in on, outlining a rectangle around your desired zoom area. ACID's window will zoom in both horizontally and vertically at the same time, and your tool will revert to whatever it was previously. Now click the zoom tool again and click in the event area without dragging (or just double-click the zoom tool). ACID's window will zoom out all the way, both horizontally and vertically.

The Beat Ruler and Time Ruler

You may have noticed that during all of this scrolling and zooming, the numbers and tick marks move and shift in the area above the events. These numbers count off the number of measures, beats, and beat subdivisions elapsed since the beginning of the project. The beat subdivisions show up only if you are zoomed in enough, and there are 768 of them per beat (384 per eighth note and 192 per sixteenth note). Because you will typically be lining up your tracks to measures and beats, the beat ruler is usually enough of a time reference, but if you want to see time in another format — minutes and seconds, for example — you can view an additional time ruler by choosing View ⇨ Time Ruler and checking the Show Time Ruler item. The time ruler will appear below the events and above the transport bar, as shown previously in Figure 5-1. You can also change the format to various other time formats in the View menu's Time Ruler submenu.

Events

The bulk of the work you'll do in ACID will involve *events*. Events are basically instructions that tell ACID what part of the audio file to play, when to play it, and for how long. A mashup gets built by piecing together and layering various events.

 In ACID XPress (and earlier versions of ACID Pro), tracks are associated with a single audio file. Every event within the track is a portion of that audio file.

 ACID Pro 6 introduces tracks that can contain multiple sources for audio. These sources are called clips. Each track contains a collection of clips called a clip pool. The audio for events in a track comes from one of the clips in the track's clip pool.

Tools for Event Manipulation

When a new mp3 or wav file is added to your project, ACID XPress automatically creates an associated blank track. ACID Pro 6 creates it with a single-clip clip pool. To get the track to make any sound, you have to create events on the track in the timeline. You can use the paint tool, as you did in Chapter 1, or you can use the draw tool. After you create your events, you can select some of them and move them about. Again, the draw tool comes in handy for this, as does the selection tool.

The Paint Tool

Although the draw tool is typically more useful, the paint tool has a few capabilities that the draw tool lacks. For example, the paint tool can do the following:

- Create events on more than one track in a single drag, so if you drag across multiple tracks, it will create events on each of those tracks

- Join adjacent beatmapped events together on the same track if you paint across both of them (one-shots as well in XPress)

- Behave just like the erase tool if you right-click

The paint tool behaves slightly differently in ACID Pro 6 than in earlier versions. If you paint a one-shot clip (discussed shortly), a new event will be painted at each grid line. You can paint one-shots in intervals other than the currently displayed grid by clicking on the little downward arrow next to the paint tool (previously shown in Figure 5-2) and selecting a spacing of your choice.

The Erase Tool

The erase tool simply gets rid of sound for any part of the event you drag over. If you drag over the entire event, the event will be erased, and if you drag from the beginning or end of the event, you will shorten it accordingly. If you erase the middle of an event, the event will split into two events with a gap in between them.

The Selection Tool

Not surprisingly, this tool is for selecting events. When you click on an event, you select it, and when you click on a second event, your previous event is deselected as the new event is selected. However, like many other Windows applications, the Shift and Ctrl keys affect the selection process. If you select an event, and then Shift+click another event, both events will be selected along with every event in between them. This works both vertically across tracks and horizontally across time. However, if you select an event and then Ctrl+click another event, only the two clicked events will be selected. To add more events to your selection, Ctrl+click again. If you need to remove an event from a multiple-event selection, you can Ctrl+click on a selected event, and it will unselect that event, leaving the rest of your selection intact.

With the introduction of clips in ACID Pro 6, you can also make selections according to clip source. Either right-click an empty area in the track and choose a clip from the Select Events Using Clip submenu, or right-click an event and choose Select Events Using This Event's Clip.

You can also use the selection tool to move events across time. Simply make a selection and then click and drag it to the left or right, watching your events move backward and forward in time.

You can also delete, cut, copy, or paste your selection, as follows:

- If you make a selection and press the Delete key, the selection disappears, never to be seen again (unless you press the magic Ctrl+Z to undo).

  - Pressing Ctrl+X cuts your selection, and the selection also disappears. However, the selection is in the computer's clipboard memory, waiting for you to paste a copy of it somewhere else.

  - Pressing Ctrl+C places a copy of your selection in the computer's clipboard memory without removing the original copy.

- There are a few different kinds of pasting. For each of these to work, you need to have a selection in the clipboard from a previous cut or copy.

- Ctrl+V pastes the clipboard's selection beginning at wherever you've placed your cursor. Typically, you will cut or copy a selection, move the cursor, and then paste the selection at another location.

- Ctrl+Shift+V also pastes the selection where you've placed your cursor. However, this has the effect of inserting time equal to the length of your selection. This time will be inserted across all tracks.

- If you want to insert time at the cursor on all tracks without pasting, select Time from the Insert menu, and then enter the number of bars and beats you want to insert.

- If you press Ctrl+B, a Paste Repeat dialog box pops up, allowing you to paste multiple copies of your selection, either end-to-end or at some other regular interval.

- One other factor that affects the behavior of both Ctrl+B and Ctrl+V (but not Ctrl+Shift+V) is the *ripple edit*. You can toggle ripple edit on and off either by selecting it from the Options menu or by pressing Ctrl+L. When ripple edit is activated, you can paste (Ctrl+V) and paste multiple (Ctrl+B), but the material is inserted into your track, pushing everything after it back a duration equal to the length of your selection. Without ripple edit on, you would simply overwrite the existing events. Note that ripple edit only pushes back the events on the tracks on which you are pasting, and paste insert (Ctrl+Shift+V) pushes back events on all tracks.

 Ripple editing is available in ACID Pro, but not ACID XPress.

To select all the events on a track, right-click anywhere on the track and choose Select All on Track. To select an event and all events on the track that occur after that event, right-click the event and choose Select Events to End. To select all events on all tracks, simply press Ctrl+A.

If you drag the cursor across several events using the selection tool, you will select all events within the rectangle you just outlined. Just be sure that you don't begin your drag over an event that is already selected, or you will find yourself moving the existing selection instead of creating a new one.

 ACID Pro allows you to paste events from one track into another track. The event's clip will be added to the clip pool if it isn't in it already.

The Draw Tool

As opposed to the paint tool, which can only draw and erase events, and the selection tool, which can only manipulate events, the draw tool can both draw and manipulate events. For this reason, it will probably be the most frequently used tool in your toolbox.

Like the selection tool, you can click, Shift+click, and Ctrl+click to make your selection. Also like the selection tool, you can click on your selected events and drag them forward and backward through time. The draw tool is also similar to the paint tool in that you can click on an empty space in the track and drag to create an event. One very useful feature of the draw tool is the capability to resize your event. If you grab your event at the back or front edge, and then drag it, you will change the length of your event. This is similar to how a paint tool operates if you paint over the same edge of a beatmapped event. However, if you grab the edge of the event near the very top and then drag towards the middle, you will produce a fade-in or fade-out for the event rather than shortening it.

Hover over the middle of either edge of any event in your project. You'll notice that the standard Windows cursor changes to a double-arrow and a rectangle, letting you know you are in the proper zone for resizing your event. Now hover the cursor over the uppermost portion of the event's edge. The cursor still has the double-arrow, but the rectangle is a quarter-circle now, letting you know that you are in the zone to create a fade.

In ACID XPress, if you have two events on different tracks, and you want to create a quick cross-fade between them that lasts the duration of their overlap, select the overlapping events and press the F key. Just be sure that there are only two events overlapping in your selection at any one time, or ACID will not perform the fade at all.

With version 6 of ACID, single-track cross-fading is introduced. Simply overlap the events on a single track and the cross-fading is automatically performed, creating a simultaneous fade-in and fade-out for each of the two events.

The Time Selection Tool

Although the time selection tool is not as frequently used as some other tools, it has unique properties that may be useful. Similar to the draw tool and selection tools, you can click, Shift+click, and Ctrl+click to make a selection. If you then drag the cursor across the beat ruler above the timeline, you will select a time region apart from the event selection. If you cut or delete with a time region selected, you will operate only on the section of your selected events within the selected time range. If you have no events selected, the time selection will operate on all tracks within the range.

Also, if you make a time selection and press Ctrl+T, you will delete all material *outside* of your time selection for the tracks with selected events.

If loop playback is activated, the time selection controls the amount of material played.

Choosing a Clip Source in ACID Pro 6

Each track in ACID Pro 6 has an active clip, which is in the track's clip pool. To switch active clips, right-click anywhere in an empty area of the track in the timeline or in the track list, and select Paint Clip (followed by the name of the clip) from the pop-up menu. In the Paint Clip Selector submenu that pops up, select the clip from the clip pool that you want to make active. Now, any events that you draw or paint will use the new clip.

ACID XPress has one audio file assigned to each track, so whenever you paint or draw on a track, events are created with the track's audio file. ACID Pro can have multiple clips in each track's clip pool, allowing you to use the paint and draw tools to create a new event from several other events.

To change the clip source for an existing event, right-click the event, select Event Clip (followed by the name of the clip) and select your desired clip from the Paint Clip Selector menu that appears.

The Paint Clip Selector menu also appears in your track list if your track's height on the screen is large enough. It will show up in the lower-right corner of the track in the track list.

Snap

By now you may have noticed that when you draw or move events, they aren't placed exactly where you put your mouse, but they are rounded to the nearest currently visible grid markers. This automatic rounding of event placement is called *snap*. Snapping to the grid is particularly useful if your events are properly beatmapped. With snap turned on, your rhythmic elements will stay in sync with ACID's internal grid, no matter where you draw or move your events. As you zoom in, and more grid lines become visible, your resolution becomes greater as well. If the smallest currently visible grid markers on the beat ruler are a bar apart, you will move events a full bar at a time. Similarly, if you've zoomed in so that your grid markers are only a beat apart, you will move your events exactly a beat at a time. You can toggle snap off and on at any time by pressing F8, but it's generally good to leave it on.

Although it is usually convenient to have the grid line set up with the currently visible ruler marks, you can override this setting and set the grid to a fixed time value, independent of the current level of zoom. To do this, choose Options ➪ Grid Spacing and select a new grid duration. Set this value to Ruler Marks to return the grid to the variable zoom-dependent value.

Splitting and Joining

There are many occasions when you might want to split an event into multiple events without actually moving or erasing any portion of the sound. For example, you might want to copy a short segment of an event or otherwise manipulate it. *Splitting* an event creates two events, one on each side of the cursor. Simply make your selection, position the cursor where you want the split to occur, and press the S key. The audio is unchanged, but you can manipulate each part of it separately.

The opposite of splitting is *joining*, which is done by selecting two or more adjacent events and pressing the J key. This converts all the events into one event. The first event will still sound the same, but if adjacent events were previously shifted in time, they may now be playing different material. This is similar to using the paint tool and dragging from left to right across beatmapped events. Joining is used less frequently than splitting in the creation of mashups, because you are usually trying to bend the existing music into new shapes instead of returning altered material to its original form.

Pitch and Volume for Events

Each event can have its own pitch and volume value. To re-pitch an event, simply select it and press either the +/= or − key, which is just like re-pitching the entire track except that only one event has been selected. Just as with track re-pitching, if you press Shift while pressing either of these keys, the pitch will change four semitones at a time.

 Event pitch is only available in ACID Pro.

To lower the volume of a single event, position the draw tool cursor near the top of the event. The cursor will change to a hand with a pointed index finger with an up/down arrow next to it. Click and drag down. Your gain will appear next to the cursor as you drag. If you are zoomed out vertically, the event volume cursor may not appear. If this happens, zoom in vertically and try again.

In addition, you can right-click an event with either the draw or select tool, and choose Properties from the pop-up menu. This will bring up an Event Properties window, where you can enter the pitch shift manually, allowing you to enter values in increments as small as a thousandth of a semitone.

Reversing Events

ACID Pro has a fun feature that lets you quickly reverse each event in your selection. Simply make a selection and press the U key. A backward arrow will appear, and the events will play in reverse. Select the reversed event and hit U again to play it normally.

Window Docking Area

A number of windows can be displayed either as a free-floating window, placed wherever you want them on your screen, or as a docked window attached to the lower half of the ACID window. These windows include the Track and Clip Properties windows and the Mixer window, all used extensively in mashup production. To open one of these windows, select it from the View menu. To close a window that's either undocked or docked, click the little x in the upper-left corner. To move a docked window, drag it from its left side, and to move an undocked window, drag its upper edge. To dock a floating window, drag it to the docking area, and to undock it, drag it away from the docking area. If you place windows on top of one another in the docking area, they will become tabbed, and you can switch between them by clicking their respective tabs. If you want to see several windows simultaneously within the docking area, drag the windows so they are not overlapping.

Track/Clip Properties Window

The Track/Clip Properties window displays detailed information about the currently selected track/clip, mostly relating to ACID's built-in pitch-shifting and time-warping capabilities. When sketching out your mashup and playing with ideas, you'll most likely use this warping functionality. ACID allows your tracks/clips to play back at whatever tempo and pitch you want them to, regardless of the audio material's original tempo and pitch. This capability, more than any other, has made ACID the mashup producer's tool of choice. A shortcut to showing the Track Properties window (in XPress and Pro 6) is to double-click the track's name or number in your track list. A shortcut to bringing up the Clip Properties window in ACID Pro 6 is to right-click an event and select Clip Properties from the pop-up menu. The Track/Clip Properties window has two tabs: General and Stretch.

With the introduction of clips in ACID Pro 6, most of the features formerly included in Track Properties have been moved over to Clip Properties. Throughout this book, when you encounter "Track/Clip," this simply means "Track" if you are using XPress, and "Clip" if you are using ACID Pro 6. ACID Pro 6 still has a Track Properties window, but it contains the clip pool, because tracks can contain multiple clips.

General

You can choose three types of audio tracks/clips in ACID from the General tab's ACID Type drop-down menu:

- **Beatmapped**: Used for long audio files that need to slow down and speed up along with the master tempo. Chances are most audio files you'll use in your mashup will have this setting. If you choose to beatmap a track/clip, a checkbox will appear called Preserve Pitch When Stretching. If this option is checked, the track/clip will not change pitch no matter what the project tempo is. If this option is unchecked, the pitch will rise and fall with the tempo, much like slowing down or speeding up a record or tape. If your track/clip has little pitch information, you may not need to preserve the pitch. However, if you have pitched tracks/clips and you are trying to blend the pitches harmonically, you'll probably want to preserve the pitch. One other factor to consider is that pitch preservation requires some audio processing, which may slightly reduce the fidelity of your audio. Time warping and pitch shifting issues are discussed in depth in Chapter 8.

- **One-shot:** Plays the audio file without any time-warping or pitch-preservation. If you shift the pitch, the sound will slow down or speed up just like a standard recording. The speed of playback in a one-shot is independent of the master tempo.

- **Loop:** Used for shorter audio segments that have already been trimmed to the length of a regular repeating loop. The duration will often be 1, 2, 4, 8, 16, or 32 bars. The loop is usually trimmed in an external sound editor, such as Adobe Audition, to ensure the proper start and end points. Most mashups will not need tracks/clips in the loop setting.

The General tab also features a Pitch Shift parameter, which can be typed in manually. This allows you to fine-tune the pitch of the track/clip to a thousandth of a semitone.

Stretch

The Stretch panel contains parameters that instruct ACID on how to warp your audio. This panel is only visible in Loop and Beatmapped mode, because the One-shot mode does not involve stretching.

In Beatmapped mode, the Stretch panel shows parameters for Root Note, Original Tempo, and Downbeat Offset, which work like this:

- If the Root Note is set to a value other than Don't Transpose, you are letting ACID know that the track/clip is in the key with your selected root. ACID will then transpose the track/clip up or down to match the project key, in whichever direction requires the least amount of transposition. This is done before the manual pitch shift is performed, if you have set the pitch shift to a value other than zero. If you are using the root notes and the overall project key, it's probably not necessary to use the manual pitch shift. However, it's usually best to leave the Root Note parameter set to Don't Transpose, and only use the manual pitch shift. This method allows you the maximum amount of control, because you are deciding the direction of the pitch shift instead of letting ACID decide.

- The Original Tempo parameter needs to be set at the tempo of the track/clip's audio. ACID will then speed up or slow down the track/clip to the project tempo. The easiest way to set the track/clip tempo is to use the Beatmapper Wizard, discussed in detail in Chapter 6.

- The Downbeat Offset setting is the number of samples of the track/clip that ACID should skip before starting playback of the audio file. Because this setting is measured in individual samples, if your sampling rate is at 44.1 kHz, then a one-second offset would have a downbeat offset of 44,100. Again, the easiest way to set the downbeat offset is to use the Beatmapper Wizard.

 The Beatmapper Wizard is only available in ACID Pro.

In Looped mode, the Stretch panel displays many settings unique to that mode. Looped mode is suitable for very short audio files, especially drum loops, and won't be used much in this book.

Track Properties Window of ACID Pro 6

The Track Properties window in ACID Pro 6 consists of a toolbar and a clip pool, as shown in Figure 5-7. The clip pool lists all the clips available in your currently selected track.

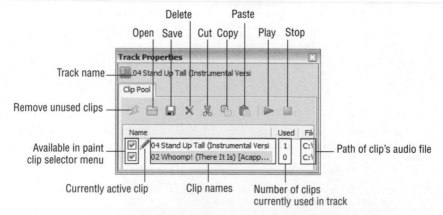

FIGURE 5-7: ACID Pro 6's Track Properties window, showing the clip pool

If you need to remove a clip temporarily from the Paint Clip Selector menu, uncheck its box in the clip pool. Although it remains in the pool, it will not show up in the menu. The currently active clip is indicated by a pencil icon next to the clip. A count of events on the track using each event is displayed next to each clip name.

If you delete every event in the track from a clip, the clip remains in the clip pool, but it will show up with a count of zero, as is shown for "Whoomp!" in Figure 5-7. To remove all clips without events, click the Remove Unused Clips lightning bolt. To add new clips to the pool, click Open in the toolbar and navigate to your file. Alternatively, you can drag your file into the clip pool from Windows Explorer or iTunes. Clicking the Save button will re-save your audio file with any beatmapping properties embedded. Delete, Cut, Copy, and Paste all behave as you would expect. Sometimes you need to copy and paste duplicates of the same clip so that you can modify the properties in each. Play and Stop allow you to hear the currently selected clip.

Envelopes

ACID's envelopes control a track's volume, pan, and other parameters, allowing you to vary these settings during your project's playback. If your overall volume or pan setting for a track is inappropriate for a section of the track, you can adjust it for only that time period, or you can to create gradual and smooth change in these values. The envelope's control of parameters over time is called *automation*.

 Envelopes are available in ACID Pro, but not in ACID XPress.

To insert either a volume or pan envelope, right-click a track in either the track list or the timeline, and add a check mark to either volume or pan from the Insert/Remove Envelope menu item. You can have multiple envelopes of several types on a single track. A shortcut to adding or removing the volume envelope is to press Shift+V, and the shortcut for adding or removing the pan envelope is to press Shift+P. Simply pressing V or P will hide and redisplay these envelopes without deleting them.

Envelopes are made up of a series of points, representing a series of values at different times. ACID draws lines through the series of points you have specified, so there is a continuous stream of changing parameter values for each envelope that you draw.

To understand this, click the first track of your project, "Stand Up Tall," and follow these steps:

1. Press Shift+V to create a volume envelope. Notice that it consists of an initial point, represented by a small square, followed by a line projected indefinitely toward the end of the project.

2. Hover your mouse over the first square without clicking it. The pop-up tooltip says "Volume at 1.1.000 is 0.0 dB." This tooltip tells you what envelope you are editing (Volume); the time represented by bars, beats, and ticks (1.1.000); and the value of the envelope at that time (0.0 dB).

3. Add another point to the envelope by double-clicking the line at any point to the right of the initial point. A second point appears on the envelope. If you hover over the second point, the tooltip tells you that the Volume at that point in time is 0.0 dB.

4. Click the second point and drag it all the way up to 6.0 dB. Notice how the envelope between the first two points changes continuously from the initial value of 0.0 dB to the second value of 6.0 dB. Also notice how the remainder of the envelope to the right of this point has risen to 6.0 dB.

5. Create a third envelope point, to the right of the second one, again by double-clicking the envelope. Now drag this third point all the way down to the bottom of the track, to a value of −Inf dB, representing silence.

6. Play back your project, and listen to the track as it gets louder and then fades to silence.

To adjust the envelope, click any point and drag it up or down, left, or right. Alternatively, you can click a line segment between two points and drag it.

Select the event you have just drawn the envelope on top of, and drag it to the right. Notice that the envelope stays in place while your audio material shifts. Press Ctrl+Z to undo this action. Now select Lock Envelopes to Events from the Options menu. Again, select the event you have drawn the envelope over, and drag it to the right. Notice that this time, the envelope has moved along with your event, preserving the relationship between the sound material and the event.

Although envelopes are most frequently used for adjusting volume, they can just as easily change the pan during the project playback. They can also adjust parameters of effects, which are discussed in the next section.

ACID Pro 6 adds real-time recording of envelopes. To record an envelope in real time, click Automation Settings (previously shown in Figure 5-4). Press the Play button and move the slider for the control you want to create an envelope for. Pan and volume envelopes will be created automatically, but effects envelopes (discussed shortly) need to be created first. After recording, click Automation Settings again to disable this feature.

ACID Pro 6 includes a feature for free-hand envelope drawing. To draw an envelope, select the envelope or draw tool and Shift-click on an existing envelope, drawing the envelope shape you desire.

Effects

Many types of effects are available in ACID, including reverb, EQ, delays, distortion, chorus, and others. Each effect is discussed in detail in Chapter 12, but there are some general methods for adding and controlling all effects that are briefly described here. In addition to the effects that are shipped with ACID, you can use VST plug-in effects, again discussed in Chapter 12, hugely increasing the sonic potential of ACID.

Effects are available in ACID Pro, but not ACID XPress.

Click the Track FX button (previously shown in Figure 5-4) of track 1 in the track list. An Audio Plug-In window pops up that looks like the one shown in Figure 5-8. When a new track is created, an effect called Track EQ is automatically added. This effect can potentially alter the color of your audio track, but because each frequency band defaults to 0.0 dB, it will not initially alter the sound.

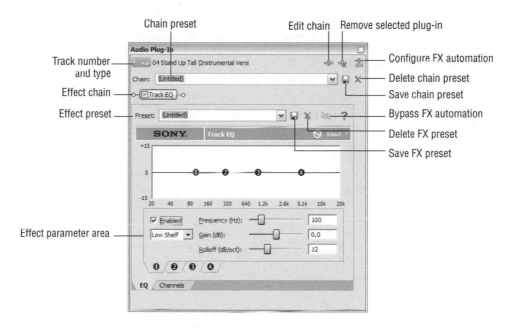

FIGURE 5-8: The Audio Plug-In window, also called the Audio Track FX window

Each track can have a series of effects that process the track's audio, one after another. This series of effects is called an *effects chain*. The majority of the Audio Plug-In window is taken up by the effects parameters for that particular effect. This window changes depending on what effect you are currently editing.

Note When the Audio Plug-In window is docked, it is called Audio Track FX instead of Audio Plug-In. There is no significance to this; it's just an idiosyncrasy in the ACID software.

Presets

Effects presets appear in a drop-down window near the top of the effect parameters frame. The effects preset drop-down is not to be confused with the Chain drop-down window, which appears at the top of the Audio Plug-In window previously shown in Figure 5-8, and outside of the effects parameter frame. The preset drop-down window includes a number of effects presets, each of which changes every parameter within the effect. Click the down-arrow next to the effects preset drop-down window and select any preset. Do this a few times with a few different presets, and notice how all the parameters change. Presets are useful in a few ways. First, you can quickly try out different sets of parameters that are preinstalled with ACID, and second, you can store your own presets for later use.

To store your own preset, change any of the parameters in the effects parameter frame. In the case of Track EQ, these settings include Frequency, Gain, and Bandwidth. EQ is discussed in greater detail in Chapter 12. After you have altered the effects parameters, type the name of your new preset in the Preset drop-down box, and click the Save FX Preset button. Your preset is now saved, and any time you load up the current effect (in this case, Track EQ), you will have your preset available. To delete the effects preset, select the preset and then click the Delete FX Preset button.

Chains

The effects chain area appears in the Audio Plug-In window above the effects parameters frame (previously shown at the top of Figure 5-7). In the top row are buttons that add, remove, and configure automation for effects. In the second row are controls related to chain presets, and in the third row is a representation of the current chain.

Plug-In Chooser

To add new effects to the chain, click the Edit Chain button. The Plug-In Chooser window appears, showing you all the possible effects you could add to your chain (see Figure 5-9). Double-click the Flange/Wah-wah effect to add it to the end of your chain. An alternate way to do this would be to click Flange/Wah-wah and then click the Add button.

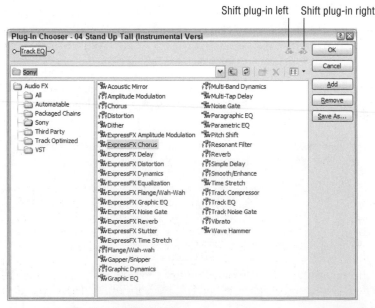

FIGURE 5-9: The Plug-In Chooser

After you add the Flange/Wah-wah effect, it is displayed to the right of the Track EQ. This means that the track is first processed by the Track EQ, and then by the Flange/Wah-wah. If you want to change the order so that the Flange/Wah-wah is processed first, drag the Flange/Wah-wah button to a position to the left of the Track EQ button, or drag the Track EQ button to a position to the right of the Flange/Wah-wah button. Another way to do this is to select the button of the effect you want to move, and then click the Shift Plug-In Left or Shift Plug-In Right button.

To get rid of an effect in your chain entirely, select the button with the effect, and click the Remove button.

To save your entire chain for later recall, click the Save As button. You will be prompted to enter the name of your chain.

To accept the effects you have added, click OK, or to revert back to the chain you had before opening the Plug-In Chooser, click Cancel.

Chains In the Audio FX Window

Some of the functionality of the Plug-In Chooser is duplicated in the upper portion of the Audio Plug-In Window. You can remove a plug-in from the chain by selecting it and clicking the Remove Selected Plug-In button. You can save the current chain by clicking the Save Chain Preset button. You can rearrange the order of the effects by dragging their buttons to the left and right.

Additional functionality includes the ability to temporarily bypass an effect without actually removing it from the chain. Each effect's button has a check mark by default. If you uncheck the button for an effect, it will not alter the sound. To turn the effect back on, just recheck the button.

To load up an entire previously saved chain, replacing all effects in your current chain, select the new chain from the Chain Preset drop-down menu. There are no preset chains that ship with ACID, so if you have not saved any chains yet, this drop-down will initially be blank. To permanently remove the chain preset, click the Delete Chain Preset button.

 Remember that both chain and effects presets are saved globally and can potentially be accessed not only by other tracks in your project, but by tracks in entirely different ACID projects. Keep this in mind before deleting any presets!

FX Automation

Many of the effects available in ACID have parameters that can be automated, similar to volume and pan automation. There are two ways of adding or removing effects automation. One way is to right-click the track either in the track list or the timeline, and select FX Automation from the FX Automation Envelopes menu. (This menu item only becomes available when there is an effect that can be automated somewhere in the track's effects chain.) This will bring up the FX Automation Chooser window shown in Figure 5-10. Another way to bring up this window is to click the Configure FX Automation button in the upper-right corner of the Audio Plug-In window (previously shown in Figure 5-8). Yet another method for viewing the

FX Automation Chooser is to click the small down arrow to the right of the Track FX button in the track list and click the FX Automation menu item in the drop-down menu.

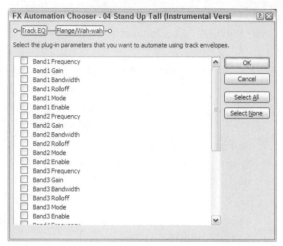

FIGURE 5-10: The FX Automation Chooser window

The FX Automation Chooser displays every parameter in the currently selected effect that can be automated. To switch to another effect within the chain, click that effect's button. To automate a parameter, click the check box to the left of that parameter. To select all parameters, click the Select All button, and to deselect all parameters, click the Select None button. When you're satisfied with the parameters you've selected, click OK. If you change your mind and decide you do not want to add or remove any automation envelopes, click Cancel.

Try it out. Check the Band3 Gain parameter of the Track EQ effect and then click OK. An envelope shows up in your track, appearing as a horizontal line at a value of 0.0 dB, which is the current value of the Band3 Gain parameter. At this point, ACID is instructed to put the Band3 Gain at 0.0 dB and just leave it there, which is basically the same thing that would have happened without any automation at all. Now double-click the envelope at some point toward the middle of the track. A new envelope point appears. Drag this point all the way to the top of the track, representing a Band3 Gain of 15 dB. Now create a third envelope point after the second one, and drag it all the way to the bottom of the track. It will have a value of -15 dB. Now if you play the project from the start, you will hear the tone of the track radically change throughout the track, with Band3 first amplifying and then attenuating.

Now bring up the FX Automation Chooser window again, and uncheck the Band3 Gain check box. If you get a pop-up warning, click Yes. The envelope will be removed, and the radical automated EQ will be gone.

Busses

You may often encounter situations where you want to process several tracks with the same effect or automation. For instance, you might wish to apply reverb to all the tracks, but using different amounts of reverb for different tracks. Or perhaps you want to perform a gradual fade on a group of tracks, but leave the others untouched. The way to implement these and other tricks is to use *busses*.

 Busses are only available in the Pro version of ACID.

You've already been using busses this whole time, perhaps without realizing it. The audio for all tracks is routed by default to the master bus, which is located at the bottom of the track list. On the master track, you can click the Master FX button and add effects onto the entire mix, just as you did for the individual tracks. You can also automate the pan, volume, or effect parameters for the entire mix just as you can with individual tracks. Your envelopes will not be drawn over events, as they were in the individual tracks, because busses do not hold events, but rather process the output of other tracks or busses.

But what if you want to affect the volume of only a subset of your tracks with a volume envelope? Rather than copying the envelope in each track, which would create all sorts of headaches if you wanted to change the envelope later, you can route the tracks to a new bus. Although in practice, this would be useful only for projects of more than two tracks, you can learn the techniques on this two-track project by following these steps:

1. Choose Insert ➪ Bus. If you cannot see a new bus appear at the bottom of your track list, click the divider between the track list and the master bus, and raise it until you see Bus A underneath the master bus.

2. On each of your tracks, a square icon appears to the left of the Track FX button. If you click one of these square icons, a drop-down menu appears, letting you choose where to route your signal. Change the routing for each of your tracks to Bus A.

   You will see the square icon replaced with the letter A. What this means is that your tracks' audio is routed to Bus A instead of directly into the master bus. Bus A is then routed to the master bus. Your tracks will first be sent through whatever effects and automation are on the individual tracks. The audio is mixed together onto Bus A, and then processed by any effects or automation you want to put on Track A, mixed together with the output of any other busses, and processed by any effects or automation you have on the master bus.

 If you were to play your project at this point, it would sound the same as it did previously, because Bus A contains no automation or effects yet.

3. Click the Bus FX button of Bus A, and select the Reverb effect.

4. In the Audio Plug-In window (it may be called Bus FX if it's docked) drag the Dry Out parameter slider all the way down to its lowest value of –Inf. Press the Play button. The entire mix sounds drowned in reverb.

5. Click the A button to the left of the Track FX button in Track 1, and change the routing from Bus A back to the master bus. Press the Play button again. Now the vocals are drowned in reverb, but the instrumental is unaffected.

What if you want just a little bit of the reverb effect on the instrumental, and a little bit more reverb on the vocals? Luckily, you can route the track signal to the master bus, and at the same time route some of it to Bus A. Here's how:

1. Click the A to button the left of the Track FX button of Track 2, and change the routing from Bus A back to the master bus. The mix will now have no reverb, because no sound is routed to Bus A.

2. Zoom in vertically using the vertical zoom controls. If you zoom enough, all the controls will be displayed in the track list, including a multipurpose slider on each track labeled Bus A. These sliders control how much of the signal is sent to Bus A in addition to the main routing, determined by the letter (or square) appearing to the left of the Track FX button.

3. Turn up Track 1's Bus A value to around -10 dB, and turn up Track 2's Bus A value all the way up to 6 dB.

4. Press the Play button. Notice how you can hear both tracks clearly, and the instrumental has a touch of reverb, while the vocal has a lot.

5. Play around with the Bus A sliders to hear the effect that different values have on the overall sound.

If there are multiple busses (or assignable effects, discussed shortly), you can change the multi-purpose slider by clicking the label to the left of the slider and selecting the bus you want to control.

Using busses in this manner can play an important part in mastering, which is discussed in detail in Chapter 12.

Mixer

The *mixer* is another essential dockable window in ACID. It controls the levels of all the busses. You can view the mixer by choosing View ➪ Mixer. The mixer panel will have one fader for each bus currently in your project, plus an additional fader called Preview. The faders for the busses are located in the track list and the mixer, and the master bus fader is located exclusively in the mixer. The Preview fader controls how loud the sound is from the Beatmapper Wizard, metronome, and other playback functionalities not in the actual mix. The mute, solo, automation, routing, and Bus FX functionalities are duplicated in the mixer for convenience.

If you unlock the fader channels by clicking the lock icon below the master fader, the left and right channels of the master bus become independent from each other, and the fader becomes a dual left-right fader, with each channel having its own volume.

Assignable Effects

Assignable effects are very similar to busses, with an important distinction. Although you can control the output of any bus, you can control only the input levels on the tracks and other busses that are routed to that bus. Assignable effects have an input control in addition to an output control. This is useful because there are some effects — distortion and compression, for example — that sound quite different depending on the input level, apart from the impact on the net output level.

In traditional mixing parlance, assignable FX are similar to sends, and Track FX are similar to inserts.

You can add an assignable effect in much the same manner as you would a bus, by choosing Assignable FX from the Insert menu. The familiar Plug-In Chooser will be displayed, and you will need to choose an effect to create an effects chain. If your mixer is open, you will see two faders associated with this specialized bus: one for the input and the other for the output. Assignable FX are not full busses in that you cannot route an entire signal to the assignable FX instead of the master bus. You can send only a portion of the signal, either by creating an automation envelope or by adjusting the levels with the multipurpose slider, in the same manner as you would a regular bus.

Rendering

To convert your project to a wav or mp3, choose File ⇨ Render As. A Render As window pops up that allows you to choose your destination name and type, and also lets you either render out the entire project or just the current time selection. Rendering is discussed in detail in Chapter 12.

 ACID Pro allows you unlimited mp3 renders, but ACID XPress is limited to 20 free encodes. Using Audacity to record ACID XPress's output to a wav may be in violation of your agreement.

Adobe Audition

Most of your mashup work will be done in Sony ACID, but some more advanced techniques involve the use of Adobe's Audition. The current version is 2.0, but version 1.5 or higher will suffice. The main purpose of using Audition for mashup construction is for *unmixing*, a process that attempts to isolate instruments or vocals from a mix to the highest degree possible. This is covered extensively in Chapter 10.

Installation and Startup

Adobe Audition is a very powerful program that can not only lay down and mix multiple tracks, similar to ACID, but can also edit the actual waveforms, something that ACID cannot directly do. Although Adobe has a great amount of potential, for the purposes of this book and mashup construction, there will be a very narrow focus on a subset of this program's capabilities.

Installation

This book's CD-ROM includes a 30-day trial of Adobe Audition. To install it, navigate to the CD-ROM's installation folder, and double-click Audition 2.0 Setup.exe. Follow the on-screen instructions, and Adobe Audition will be added to your list of installed programs. You may have to reboot at the end of installation.

Startup

When Adobe Audition initially starts up, it shows what is known as the *multitrack view*. This may be reminiscent of ACID with its many tracks. However, for this book you will only use the Edit View. Select View ➪ Edit View (or press 8). Unless you change views again, the next time you start up Audition, you will see this view, so you don't have to worry about this any more.

Audition's Edit View

Audition has several controls similar to ACID's controls. The transport and zoom controls behave similarly, and the actual waveform may look somewhat familiar. To open up a wav or mp3, drag it into the Audition window, either from iTunes or Windows Explorer. Alternatively, you can open up the file by choosing File ➪ Open. The following sections detail the essential components of Adobe Audition's Edit View.

Main

The Main window is where the waveform is displayed, as shown in Figure 5-11. Like ACID, both channels are displayed, but unlike ACID, you can select a portion of either channel or both.

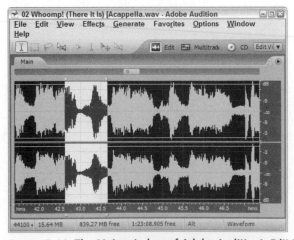

FIGURE 5-11: The Main window of Adobe Audition's Edit View

Selecting

To select a portion of the waveform, just drag your mouse from one end of your desired selection to the other. The vertical position of your mouse should not be very close to the top or bottom of the waveform, however. The selection will have a white background (as shown previously in Figure 5-11). If you want to select just a single channel for the same portion of the wave, drag your mouse across your desired time selection, but position your mouse vertically near the very top of the waveform to select the left channel, and near the bottom for the right channel. A small *L* (for *left*) or *R* (for *right*) will appear next to your cursor to let you know you are in the single-channel zone.

If you want to expand or contract your current selection, Shift+click at the position of the new start or end of your selection. Audition will determine whether you are clicking closer to the start or end of your previous selection, and assumes that you are editing either the start or end point accordingly. If you press Ctrl+A (for *all*), you will select the entire wave.

Additionally, a few keyboard tricks limit your editing to one or both channels of the wave:

- **Ctrl+R**: Allows you to edit only the right channel.
- **Ctrl+L**: Allows you to edit only the left channel.
- **Ctrl+B** (for *both*): Returns you to editing both left and right channels.

Although these do not affect your selection directly, they will affect any processing done.

Dragging

There are two ways to drag the window backward and forward in time. If you hover over the numbered timeline below the waveform, you will notice that the cursor changes to the drag icon of an open hand. If you click and drag to the right or left, the waveform will move accordingly.

Additionally, hovering over the pale-green scroll bar directly above the waveform will change your cursor to the open hand, allowing you to drag the scroll bar left or right. Clicking to the left or right of the scroll bar will move the scroll bar in larger increments. If you have selected a portion of the wave, you may notice a light-grey stripe in the otherwise darker-grey scrollbar background. This represents the position of the selection in the entire wave. If the light-grey stripe is inside the scroll bar, then the selection will be visible on the screen. Otherwise, your selection will be off-screen.

Cutting and Pasting

Selections can be cut, copied, pasted, and deleted similarly to the selections in ACID. Pressing the Delete key while you have material selected eliminates the selected material. If your selection spans both channels, the time is deleted, and the material after the selection will become attached to the material before the selection. If you have only one channel selected, the material is simply replaced with silence in that channel. Cutting (Ctrl+X) has the same effect as deleting, except that the material will be retained in the clipboard for later pasting. Copying (Ctrl+C) puts the material in your clipboard without affecting the original wave. Pasting material from the clipboard will insert the audio material at the cursor's position. If you have a portion selected, it will be replaced by the new material.

If you want to create a new wave quickly from your current selection, you can choose Edit ⇨ Copy to New. If you want to create a new wave quickly from material that has already been copied or cut, choose Edit ⇨ Paste to New. Otherwise, you can create a new blank waveform by pressing Ctrl+N (for *new*) and then pasting in the material.

Transport

The Transport window, shown in Figure 5-12, has many of the same buttons that ACID has. Stop, Play, Pause, Play Looped, Go to Beginning, Go to End, and Record all have similar functionality. Additionally, there are Rewind and Fast Forward buttons that speed backward and forward through the audio file, and a Play from Cursor to End of View button that stops playback when the cursor reaches the edge of the screen. You can toggle the Transport's visibility by selecting Transport Controls from the Window menu.

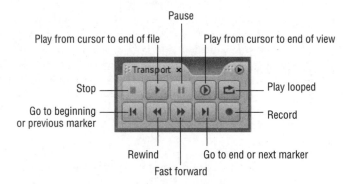

Figure 5-12: Audition's Transport window

Zoom

The Zoom window, shown in Figure 5-13, contains a group of buttons that are similar in look and function to the zoom buttons in ACI. Zooming in and out horizontally displays less and more time of the waveform, like the horizontal zoom in ACID. Similarly, zooming in or out vertically exaggerates or reduces the visualization of the waveform's amplitude. The Zoom Out Full Both Axes button acts like double-clicking the zoom tool in ACID, and displays the entire wave in both the horizontal and vertical directions. If you've selected a portion of the waveform, there are a few zoom buttons that come in handy. The Zoom To Selection button fills up the entire viewable waveform area with your selection. The Zoom In To Right Edge of Selection and Zoom In To Left Edge of Selection buttons function like more like the Zoom In Horizontally button, except that while the Zoom In Horizontally button zooms in to the center of the currently displayed waveform portion, the Zoom In To Right Edge of Selection and Zoom In To Left Edge of Selection buttons are centered on the edge of the selection.

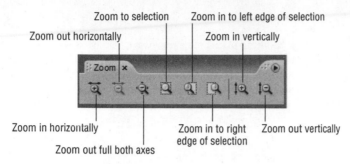

FIGURE 5-13: Audition's Zoom window

Selection/View

The Selection/View window is a numerical way of looking at the portion of your waveform that is selected and currently in view. You will notice these numbers changing as you scroll and zoom your view and alter your selection. You can manually type in new values to affect both your selection and your view. To alter the start point of your selection, type the new beginning point in the Begin box. To alter the end point, either type the new end point in the End box or the new length in the Length box. The View parameters behave similarly, defining the amount of material displayed on your screen.

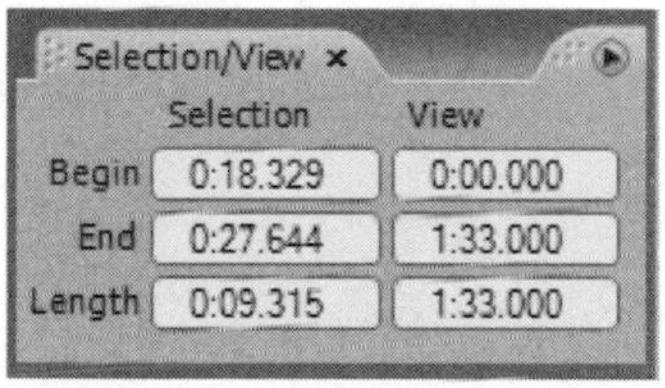

FIGURE 5-14: Audition's Selection/View window

Processing

An entire book could be devoted to Adobe Audition, but mashup producers will be interested primarily in its audio processing capabilities, most notably the Center Channel Extractor. To apply an effect, first you need to select a portion of your wave. If you do not select any portion, Audition will automatically select the entire wave before processing. There are a variety of effects available, mostly in submenus of the Effect menu. The Amplitude, Delay Effects, Filters, Restoration, Special, and Time/Pitch submenus each have a bunch of cool effects. Feel free to play around with these effects and see what they do. A few of these effects are discussed in detail in Chapter 10.

Saving

After you've altered your wave to your liking or created a new wave, you need to save it before you can use it in ACID. Exercise caution in this area, or you may end up accidentally overwriting your original wave. There is no undo button for this! To be on the safe side, use File ⇨ Save Copy As (Ctrl+Alt+S). If you load an mp3, perform an acapella extraction on it (see Chapter 10), and then simply press Ctrl+S to save, or choose File ⇨ Save, you will *overwrite* your original file. Eliminate potential headaches by steering away from Save or at least use *extreme caution*.

Breaking It Down

Now that you have the fundamentals of both music software and music theory, it's time to get this thing started! The next chapter will help you choose your songs, and then you'll learn how to sync them up, get them in key, and put them together. Enjoy!

Choosing Your Songs

Much of the craft of the mashup takes place even before the beatmapping, cutting, and pasting begins. If you choose the right songs, making the mashup can be a breeze, almost as if the mashup were making itself. On the other hand, the vast majority of songs simply won't sound good together, no matter how much you try to coax them.

Many factors contribute to the matching of your component songs, but the two most important factors are key and tempo. All songs in your mashup must be in the same or closely related keys and tempos, or your mashup is guaranteed to be a mess.

Other factors in song selection are as follows:

- Genre
- Era
- Mood
- Lyrics
- Title
- Taste
- Intuition
- Availability

These other factors are discussed before diving into key and tempo in depth.

Genre

One of the most stimulating and entertaining aspects of mashups is that they often cross genre lines, blurring the categories. In the United States, mashups first became popularized using rap versus rock, but any genre clash can be satisfying, whether it's country versus new wave, metal versus R&B, or indie rock versus teen pop. Although it's entirely possible to have a successful mashup all within a single genre, a lot of the fun factor comes from the brain simultaneously digesting songs from different corners of pop culture. Quite often, mashups rely on ironic juxtaposition, using genres and artists far removed from each other. The classics "Smells Like Teen Booty," featuring Nirvana vs. Destiny's Child, or "Stroke of Genie-us," featuring Christina Aguilera vs. The Strokes are both excellent examples, as is Danger Mouse's rock-versus-rap *Grey Album*.

A typical DJ will try to create smooth transitions between similar genres, but the mashup producer slams different genres together, creating new unexplored hybrid genres and hopefully introducing listeners to styles of music outside of their usual musical experience.

Era

In addition to combining different genres, mashup producers often mix together songs recorded in different eras, adding to the experience of cultural overload. If you're trying to find a song to pair with the current hot song in heavy rotation on the radio, try searching through some songs from the 1980s or some classics from the 1960s. Mashups are supposed to mess with your mind, and an era clash can give a disorienting sensation, with different memories and associations being triggered simultaneously in the listener's mind.

Recycling vintage material also expands the potential audience for your mashup. Older listeners who don't typically appreciate modern music can be seduced by a guitar riff lifted from a song from their adolescence. Younger listeners can be painlessly introduced to classics from before they were born.

Mood

Mood is a highly subjective aspect of music. You may want to incorporate various moods within a given piece, taking people on an emotional journey. Sometimes, overlaying songs of differing moods will add up to material with an entirely different mood altogether. Other times, the moods of the various components will be quite similar, each complimenting the other.

Lyrics

The words of the songs can inspire the particular combination. If you are using vocal elements from more than one song, and if the words relate to each other, it can be wonderful. Songs may share key words or simply relate to each other thematically. One song may twist the meaning of the other, altering the context. Another song may ask a question that the other song answers. A worthwhile goal is to somehow tell one continuous story from the lyrics of several songs.

Chapter 11 discusses combining lyrics from different songs.

Title

There is a long-standing tradition to title mashups using words from each component song or sometimes the artist's name. Examples include the classic "Smells Like Teen Booty," which is "Smells Like Teen Spirit" combined with "Bootylicious." An inspired example is "Stroke of Genie-us," which combines "Genie in a Bottle" with a song by The Strokes. I once combined "Personal Jesus" and "Train" to make a mashup called "Jesus is my Personal Trainer." Often the best titles are ones that have a sense of humor, using puns and twists of meanings.

Titles can actually be the inspiration for the song pairing. You may conceive of a title so striking or funny that a mashup is generated as an afterthought.

Intuition

Although you can be quite methodical in your song-selection process, often the biggest factors in successful song selection and matching are the intangible elements of intuition and inspiration. The greatest ideas often come in a flash. You might be walking down the street, singing a song to yourself, and all of a sudden, another song pops into your head, generating an idea for a mashup. The first time you hear a new song on the radio, it might remind you of an old song you know. Listening to music in challenging environments can actually help by blocking out large portions of the sound. You might be in a crowded and noisy bar, mistakenly identify a song being playing over the sound system, and then realize the song's true identity, giving you an idea for a mashup. Or you might be listening to a low-quality radio in the shower or overhear a neighbor's stereo. Inspiration could come from anywhere. Just be ready for it and remember to write it down before you forget.

Taste

You probably won't be happy with your mashup if you don't start off with songs you like on some level. If you don't personally enjoy a song, you'd better have a really good reason for mashing it up. Some mashup producers will select whatever songs are popular at the moment, hoping the popularity of the components will spill over into the popularity of the mashup. This approach may work for some, but it's more likely that your mashup will come off as uninspired.

Acapella Availability

There is a tendency to simply use acapellas that are easily obtained. Clean acapellas can be difficult to find, so many mashup producers end up using the same acapellas. Although there is no problem mashing up the same song that everyone else is mashing up, your creations may not stand out as much. Also, your possibilities are limited if you just stick to the songs with officially released acapellas.

You may wish to create your own custom acapellas. Chapter 10 covers the issue of acapella extraction at length.

And don't forget, many great mashups have been made using two full songs without any acapellas. Don't let a limited supply of acapellas in your collection stop you from exploring the music you want to hear.

Tempo

Although clashing may be entertaining in era or genre, it is not so pleasant where tempo is concerned. It is essential that the component songs synchronize. If two songs have different tempos, the slower song will need to be sped up or the faster song slowed down until the songs have the same tempo.

Be aware that the more you alter a song's tempo, the stranger it may sound. Altering a song significantly (by more than 10 percent or so) can have results that sound obviously altered. Although successful mashups have been made with extreme warping of time, as a general rule of thumb, the less tempo alteration you perform, the better the mashup will sound.

Speeding up a song while preserving the pitch generally has better fidelity than slowing a song down while preserving the pitch. This phenomenon is discussed in detail in Chapter 8.

Some interesting results can be achieved when you combine two songs where one tempo is twice that of the other. A ballad at 70 bpm layered with a techno song of 140 bpm might be quite compatible with no time-warping whatsoever.

No matter what your tempo strategy, an accurate measurement of tempo is essential. You will eventually be using ACID to mix these songs, so you may as well use it for your measurement of the tempo. If you use ACID Pro's Beatmapper Wizard, this has the added benefit of enabling you to simply drag the beatmapped audio files into ACID at any point in the future.

Modern versus Vintage Recording Techniques

Believe it or not, music wasn't always performed by machines and recorded on computers. At one point in time, people were forced to make music with clunky physical devices called *instruments.* Not only that, but these primitive sounds were captured by imperfect recording devices such as analog tape and vinyl.

The problem with all this organic sound production is that the tempos are variable. No drummer can keep absolutely perfect rhythm, and even the mechanics of tape decks and vinyl have potential for some imperfections and variability.

You may want to know what tempo a song is, but sadly for most live music, the exact tempo is quite variable. Even early electronic music can have surprisingly unstable tempos. This can create massive headaches for the aspiring mashup producer.

However, the digital recording era has introduced songs that are recorded digitally, mastered digitally, and distributed digitally. Nowadays, particularly in electronic-based music, the tempo that was programmed into the original musician's computer-based sequencer is identical to the tempo of the final song. Even rock songs, traditionally driven by the rhythmic sensibilities of the drummer, are now often synchronized to a click track piped in through the drummer's headphones. The result is that some recently recorded rock songs have almost the same precision as modern electronic songs.

In ACID, there are two distinct methods to aligning constant or variable tempos. With constant tempos, you can use the techniques touched on in the next section and elaborated upon in Chapter 7. For variable tempos, a bit more effort will be required, involving methods described in Chapter 9.

ACID's Beatmapper Wizard

Although the Beatmapper Wizard is primarily a tool used to ensure components stay in sync, it is introduced here because it can assist in tempo detection as well, which will help you pick out your component songs.

 The Beatmapper Wizard is a feature of ACID Pro. Even if you are planning to use ACID XPress to construct your mashups, it is helpful to learn how this feature works. After you learn how to beatmap with the wizard, you can approximate those results manually in the XPress version of ACID, which is discussed in Chapter 7. The next section describes how you can use methods other than the Beatmapper Wizard for tempo detection.

A beatmapped clip (Pro 6) or track (XPress) contains two vital pieces of information:

- A precise tempo

- A precise offset, signifying the number of samples between the beginning of the audio file and the first detectable downbeat. For example, if your audio file's sampling rate is the standard rate of 44.1 kHz, and the first detectable downbeat occurs two seconds after the audio file starts, the offset would be $44,100 \times 2$, or 88,200.

The Beatmapper Wizard helps you to determine these two values. Songs recorded using modern recording techniques will beatmap quite well, while vintage recordings and most rock and roll will not. However, even with songs that are impossible to beatmap, the wizard will usually give you a reasonable approximation of tempo that will at least allow you to determine compatibility with other songs.

By default, ACID Pro is set up so the Beatmapper starts automatically when long sound files are loaded. You can load up new songs in several ways:

- Choose File ➪ Open, and then navigate to the wav file or mp3 you want to load, and double-click it.

- Click the Explorer tab in the bottom window in ACID Pro, navigate to the wav file or mp3 you want to load, and double-click it.

- Locate the song you want in Windows Explorer or iTunes, and then drag the song into the ACID Pro window.

After you load up a song, the Beatmapper Wizard opens and guides you through the process of finding the tempo and offset for your new clip or track. The steps are as follows:

1. Determine the location of the first downbeat. The wizard attempts to locate this for you, often guessing correctly.

2. Determine the length of the first measure. The wizard again tries to guess the appropriate value, and can be accurate sometimes, but you will verify this yourself.

3. Step through the entire song, making sure that each downbeat in the music aligns with the downbeats of the beatmapper.

Stand Tall

In Chapter 1 you downloaded the instrumental version of Dizzee Rascal's "Stand Tall." Locate the wav file (or mp3) in Windows Explorer or iTunes and drag it into the tracklist area of the ACID Pro window. As long as your have your preferences set to "Automatically Start the Beatmapper Wizard for Long Files," the wizard should start up after you drop it into ACID Pro. Figure 6-1 shows the Beatmapper Wizard's initial guess of the first downbeat. What you are looking for is a drum sound (often a kick drum) where a strong beat occurs. On the downbeat, you should be able to start counting off the beats 1 through 4 and then starting off again at beat 1. Beat 1 should be a strong beat, and can often be the first drum sound, but not always.

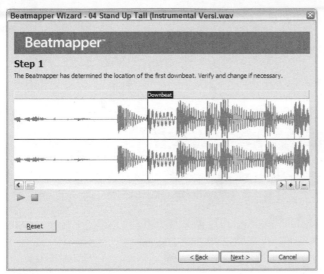

FIGURE 6-1: The Beatmapper Wizard of ACID Pro guessing the first downbeat of "Stand Tall"

Click the triangular Play button to listen. You may notice that it doesn't seem to start at the beginning, although it did choose a percussive event. If there are drum sounds in your song, and for some reason the Beatmapper Wizard chooses a non-percussive sound for the downbeat, it is usually preferable to locate a drum sound instead. You can use the scroll bar to move through the waveform until you see a candidate for the downbeat, you can zoom out to see more of the waveform at once, or you can click and drag the downbeat.

Since it seems that the initial guess was a bit late, click the downbeat (either on the blue Downbeat label on the vertical cursor) and drag it all the way to the left edge of the Beatmapper Wizard window. The visible waveform will start scrolling backwards in time. Drag until the downbeat is at the very beginning of the waveform. It should be visually obvious that the downbeat is placed on a significant percussive sound now, but perhaps you've moved it back far enough to hear the actual downbeat.

Press Play again, and watch the cursor move as the sound plays. Once the drums start, count off 1, 2, 3, 4. If you start counting on the very first drum sound, you will notice that the 1 indeed falls on the strongest rhythmic accent. This verifies that the first drum sound is indeed the downbeat. Click near the beginning of the first drum sound. You may need to press Play again and watch the cursor as you listen, to visually locate it. You do not need to be exact for now, as long as you are close. Your Beatmapper Wizard will look similar to Figure 6-2.

Now that you are close to the downbeat, zoom in a few times by clicking the plus button. Notice that the new cursor position becomes centered. The idea is to zoom in as much as possible to refine the placement of the downbeat marker. Keep an eye on the beginning of the downbeat, because you don't want to zoom in so far that this feature leaves the screen. You can simply click the minus button if this happens. In some cases, your initial estimate of the downbeat is so rough that you will need to refine your estimate after zooming in and then repeat the process. Eventually, you will see a drum sound with a clear attack at a high level of magnification. The downbeat should be placed at the very beginning of the sound, right before the attack, as shown in Figure 6-3.

FIGURE 6-2: Step 1 of the Beatmapper Wizard with a rough guess of the first downbeat

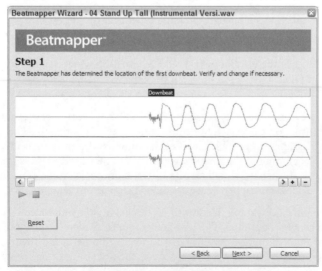

FIGURE 6-3: Step 1 of the Beatmapper Wizard, zoomed in with a more precise guess of the first downbeat

If the attack does not appear to be sharp, it is possible that you've zoomed in too far. At a high level of magnification, even the sharpest attack appears to be gradual. Slight differences of downbeat placement at this amount of zoom may have negligible effects on the beatmapping results. It's also possible that you've chosen a sound without a sharp attack. Zoom out, and then find another point in the song where there is a downbeat with a strong attack. Keep in mind that you do not have to choose the very first downbeat. If a song has an intro without a downbeat with a strong attack, you can choose any downbeat in a later measure in the song.

If your song has no sharp percussive sounds at all, or it is an acapella, beatmapping is a bit trickier. Chapter 7 covers this situation in detail.

Click Next. ACID will guess the tempo and display it, along with guesses for the first four beats, as pictured in Figure 6-4. Click the Play button, or hit the space bar. A perfect four-bar loop should play, along with a metronome clicking at every beat. You can toggle the metronome off and on by clicking on the Metronome checkbox. You'll also notice that the Wizard's initial tempo guess is shown underneath the waveform: Tempo (BPM): 135.226.

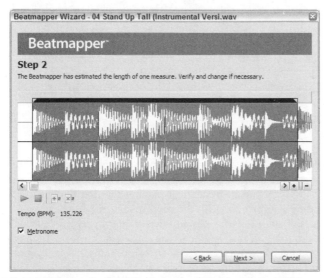

FIGURE 6-4: Step 2 of the Beatmapper Wizard with its initial tempo guess

In this case, the Beatmapper Wizard guessed fairly well, but often the initial guess isn't close. Sometimes the Wizard gets confused and guesses a value close to half or double the actual tempo, and the metronome plays twice per beat or once every other beat. If this happens, click the "÷2" or "×2" buttons. If the Wizard is off by some other amount, click and drag the little yellow triangle in the upper right corner of the shaded area. You could also re-adjust the down-beat by dragging the yellow triangle in the upper-left corner. The goal at this step is not to precisely determine the overall tempo, but to get a rough idea of the tempo of the first measure, which will act as an initial guess of the overall tempo. Because the Wizard guessed well in "Stand Tall," you can simply click Next without any adjustment.

After a quick analysis, the Beatmapper Wizard moves on to step 3, pictured in Figure 6-5, where the tempo is determined throughout the entire song.

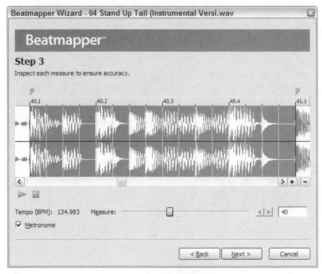

FIGURE 6-5: Step 3 of the Beatmapper Wizard

Press Play with the metronome on. Now step through the measures of the song either by using the measure slider, the back and forward arrows to the right of the slider, or by typing in the measure number to the right of the arrows. Check each of the first few measures, making sure that the metronome stays in sync with the rhythm and that the beat markers line up with significant percussive sounds. If the tempo is accurate for the first few consecutive measures, you can start skipping measures, going two measures at a time, then four, eight, and so on. The exact number of measures you skip isn't important, but if you have a song with an unwavering tempo, the amount of likely additional error decreases as the measure number increases. So as you progress through the song, checking every single measure becomes more and more unnecessary.

If the metronome and gridlines become misaligned at any point, grab either golden wedge shape above the waveform and drag it slightly to the left or right. These wedges signify the beginning and ending of the current measure, and moving one will move the other. You can click the plus and minus buttons to zoom in and out if necessary. When you are close to the end of the song, find a downbeat that's visually clear, and zoom in on it. Now, using the golden wedge, move the beat marker until it's precisely placed on the beginning of the sound, as shown in Figure 6-6. This will obtain a beatmap and tempo with the highest possible degree of accuracy.

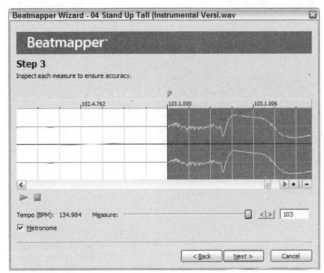

FIGURE 6-6: Step 3 of the Beatmapper Wizard, with the final beat precisely located

The final tempo, 134.984, is significantly more accurate than the Wizard's first guess of 135.226 back in step 2, and slightly more accurate than the Wizard's guess of 134.983 at the beginning of step 3. Next time you drop this audio file into ACID, the tempo and offset information will be remembered, and you will not have to go through this beatmapping process again.

Note The Beatmapper Wizard has only one tempo approximation for the entire song. Adjusting the placement of the gridlines in any measure will move the gridlines for every measure.

Other Tempo Detection Methods

If you have ACID XPress, you'll want a simple method of determining tempo, although you'll still have to eventually create an accurate beatmap without the wizard as described in the next chapter. Even if you have ACID Pro, the process of beatmapping each track just to determine tempo may become unwieldy. Luckily, there are a variety of other methods for determining tempo.

aufTAKT

aufTAKT is a piece of software from a company in Germany called ZPlane, which also created the amazing tONaRT key recognition software discussed later in this chapter. You can download aufTAKT from www.zplane.de/Downloads/aufTAKT.zip and unzip it into a directory of your choice. Double-click aufTAKT.exe, and a small program opens up that looks like Figure 6-7.

FIGURE 6-7: aufTAKT tempo detection software

Operation is simple, but you'll need a wav file. Click the Load button and navigate to your wav. Your tempo estimate will appear in the aufTAKT window. It's that easy!

 If you want to have a bit of fun, click the Play button, and then click the Loop It! button. aufTAKT will automatically loop a measure of the song with amazing accuracy.

TapTempo

TapTempo from AnalogX, shown in Figure 6-8, is a very simple program that counts the tempo at which you tap the spacebar. You can download it from www.analogx.com/CONTENTS/download/audio/taptempo.htm.

FIGURE 6-8: AnalogX's TapTempo

To use TapTempo, play your audio file in iTunes or any other player. If you play it in ACID, make sure your clip (Pro 6) or track (XPress) is playing back in One-Shot mode, rather than Beatmapped or Loop. As the audio file plays, bring TapTempo to the foreground and tap the spacebar along with the beat. Within 10 to 20 keystrokes, your tempo should stabilize and give you a good estimate. Remember, when determining tempo for song-selection purposes, it's not important to be extremely accurate. If your estimate is a couple of bpm off, it won't make a big difference.

TapTempo shows three figures. The Tempo is the average tempo of recent spacebar keystrokes, the Last Tempo is calculated from the most recent two keystrokes, and the Average MS is the number of seconds between average keystrokes. (Yes, the number of *seconds*, even though it displays the term *ms* twice, suggesting that it's counting the number of milliseconds. This is obviously an error and may be corrected by the time you download this. The program still works well for tempo.)

Manual

If all else fails, you can always count the tempo manually. Look at a clock with a second hand or get a stopwatch, and count the number of beats in one minute. If a minute is too long, count the number of beats in 30 seconds and double it, or count the number of beats in 20 seconds and triple it. This method is the least accurate, but it may be sufficient for song selection.

Converting mp3s to wavs

There are many occasions when you need to convert an mp3 to a wav in order to process it with a piece of software. There are several ways to go about this. Two methods are outlined here: one using ACID and another using iTunes.

Rendering to wav with ACID

Drop your mp3 into ACID, and skip the Beatmapper Wizard if you're using Pro. Look at the ACID Type drop-down menu in the General tab of the Track/Clip Properties. If it says Beatmapped or Loop, change it to One-Shot. Using the Paint tool, Ctrl+click toward the left of the empty track, and then solo the track. Choose File ➪ Render As. In the window that pops up, make sure that *.wav is selected in the Save As Type drop-down menu. Type the name of your wav and click Save.

Rendering to wav with iTunes

If your mp3 is already in iTunes, this is the easiest way to go. Right-click the mp3 you want to convert. If Convert Selection to WAV shows up, click it, and you're done. If the pop-up menu shows a conversion to some other format, you'll need to change some iTunes preferences. Choose Edit ➪ Preferences, click the Advanced tab and then click the Importing tab. Use the drop-down list to change the Import Using selection to WAV Encoder and click OK. Then right-click the mp3 or AAC file you want to convert, and select Convert Selection to WAV. The new wav file will be created in the same location as the original audio file. If you can't find it, go to iTunes, right-click the file you're looking for, and select Show Song File. Windows Explorer will open up and show you the location of your file.

Key

Matching the tempo of the component songs is crucial, but equally important is matching the songs' keys. Even if your mashup is perfectly in sync, if the component songs are out of key with each other, it will sound quite jarring. Ideally, all the songs would be in the exact same key, although there are different levels of compatibility between keys that make it possible to combine different keys.

Rap versus Singing

The easiest way around trying to find a compatible key for your vocals is to simply find a vocal with no key at all. Because most rap has no key, it will combine readily with backgrounds of any key. Many beginning mashup producers find initial success working with rap acapellas, and I recommend them for learning mashup basics without worrying about key issues. In fact, due to the ease of layering rap 'pellas, there is an amazing proliferation of Missy Elliot, Eminem, and Beastie Boys mashups. Of course, if there is a singing break in the rap, or the rapper is using the popular style of rap that is half-sung, you will need to treat the song the same as a non-rap song, determining the key and matching it appropriately.

Key Detection Techniques

Before you can start matching the keys of your songs, you need to figure out what keys they are in. This is not as simple as determining the tempo, and there are a variety of techniques available. You can try to determine the key by ear, or by using ACID's built-in piano or the wav files provided on this book's CD-ROM. If you are having difficulty using either the piano or the chord files, you can also use the provided tONaRT software to attempt to automatically detect the key.

Using the Chord MIDI Files

Provided on the CD-ROM is an ACID file containing 2 MIDI files representing all possible major and minor keys. MIDI files are different from audio files in that they provide instructions for an instrument on what notes to play, when, and for how long. It's kind of like using a player piano scroll to record a piano piece instead of a tape recorder. The great thing about a MIDI file is that you can transpose it as much as you like without the weird artifacts that can happen when transposing audio.

The technique to determine the key of your song is fairly simple. First, drag the A Major.mid file from the CD-ROM directly into your ACID timeline, and then open your song with the unknown key. With the Paint tool, Ctrl+click on the track containing your song to insert the entire song. Then paint the MIDI track for the duration of your song, or at least for a good portion of it. If there are other tracks besides the two mentioned, mute them. Click the Play button in ACID, and listen to the chord play along with the song. Select the A Major track from ACID's track list (the left side of the screen), and transpose the MIDI track by hitting the plus key. Listen again. Repeat this process until the transposition reads +11 in the track list. Take note of which transpositions sound best with your track. Now drag the A Minor.mid file from the CD-ROM into the ACID timeline and mute the previous MIDI track. Repeat the process, transposing the new MIDI file to each of the 12 possible keys. Most chords will sound unpleasant and discordant, but a few will sound good. The transposed chord that sounds best with your track most likely represents the key of the song. For example, if the A minor chord sounds best with a +2 transposition, the key is probably in B minor. If the A major chord sounds best with the +9 transposition, the key is probably in F♯ major.

Using ACID's Built-in Piano

Alternatively, you can use the piano keyboard that comes bundled with ACID. To view the piano, choose Insert ➪ Soft Synth, and then double-click Sony DLS Soft Synth. You will see a piano like the one shown in Figure 6-9. If you are unfamiliar with the piano keyboard, the notes are labeled for you. Remember that even though the white keys and black keys are different sizes and shapes, they are all equal in terms of pitch.

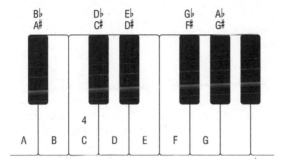

FIGURE 6-9: ACID's built-in piano

The process of determining the keys using the piano is similar to using the chord MIDI files. You play each pitch of the piano, listening for which pitch sounds most "at home" with the song. Usually one pitch will sound stronger than the rest. This will be the tonic of the song's key. Now you need to determine whether the song is in major or minor. The simplest way to do this is to play the pitch three semitones above the root and the pitch four semitones above the root, and decide which blends better with the song. For example, if you decide the song is in C, play both E♭ and E and listen for which sounds better with the music. If the pitch three semitones above the root sounds best, the key is probably in minor, whereas if the pitch four semitones above the root sounds best, the key is probably in major.

Using tONaRT Key Detection Software

tONaRT is a piece of software written by the good people over at ZPlane, who brought you the aufTAKT tempo-recognition software discussed earlier in this chapter. It is one of the few algorithms that can determine the key of a sound file. Although it is not always correct, it is fairly accurate, and often the incorrectly identified keys are at least related to and compatible with the true key. Always keep in mind, however, that the detected key and pitch may not be 100-percent accurate. However, this is the case with a human as well!

tONaRT needs a wav file as input. If you only have an mp3 file, you will need to convert it into a wav first. See the "Converting mp3s to wavs" sidebar earlier in this chapter for a couple ways to do this.

When you have a wav file available, open the tONaRT software, provided on the CD-ROM. Click the Load File button, navigate to your wav file, and double-click it. tONaRT will start analyzing your wav immediately. When it's done, tONaRT will show you the key information, as shown in Figure 6-10.

FIGURE 6-10: tONaRT key detection software

tONaRT's estimation of key in this case is G♯ minor. Check the Classic Mode check box. The detected key may or may not change. Classic Mode uses a slightly different algorithm. Unchecking the box may provide more accurate key detection, but not always. Either way, it's nice to have both estimates, kind of like a second opinion. If both modes provide the same key estimate, there is an even greater chance that the key is correct.

Click the Analyze and Play button. The song should start playing. Now click the Play Root Note button. You will hear a sine wave tone that tONaRT believes is the tonic of the key of the song. This pitch should feel very much "at home" with the song. If Classic Mode detects a different key than the non-Classic Mode, check and uncheck the Classic Mode check box, and listen for which pitch sounds most harmonious with the song. The key displayed while the more harmonious note is playing represents the most likely key. In the majority of songs, tONaRT will guess correctly in at least one of the modes.

Note If your song has lots of key changes or sections with noise or breakdowns, you may want to create a wav file with only a portion of the song for tONaRT to analyze. You can do this in ACID by painting or drawing only the portion of the audio that seems melodic and simple and then rendering it to wav, or you can use an audio editing platform such as Adobe Audition or Audacity to delete most of the audio and then save the simple melodic portion as a wav file.

In addition to key, tONaRT also estimates the standard pitch, which is the frequency (in hertz) of the pitch A. Ideally, pitch A is exactly 440 Hz (concert A). If the actual pitch is significantly different from 440 Hz, you may end up with a tonal clash in your mashup no matter what key either song is in. If the detected pitch is off only by one or two hertz, your ears may not be able to detect it. In fact, tONaRT's standard pitch detection isn't perfect, and ZPlane only claims an accuracy within one or two hertz. So the question remains: How much do you need to adjust the pitch to compensate for a standard pitch that significantly deviates from 440 Hz? The formula for the necessary compensation in semitones is as follows: $-12 * Ln(H/440)/Ln(2)$, where H represents the standard pitch in hertz.

For those of you whose eyes have just glazed over as you slipped into a mathematical coma, the simplest thing to do is refer to Table 6-1, which converts standard pitch to fractional pitch. Only values between a half-semitone up or down are listed, because if the standard pitch is off by more than a half-step, the key detection will detect a different key. Therefore, it is impossible to be off by more than .5 semitones. Keep in mind that most songs have a standard pitch close to 440 Hz, and fractional pitch compensation will be totally unnecessary. However, there are many songs that are tuned to other than a concert A. This can happen if all the instruments in a rock band tune to each other without an outside reference, and the singer then sings in the same detuned key. This can also occur if the analog tape playback is sped up or slowed down slightly for various reasons. If you have a digital recording of a tape or vinyl, the playback speed may not have been perfect, and the pitch will be slightly shifted.

Table 6-1   Standard Pitch-to-Pitch Shift Conversion

Standard Pitch, in Hz	Necessary Pitch Shift Compensation, in Semitones
427	0.519
428	0.479
429	0.438
430	0.398
431	0.358
432	0.318
433	0.278
434	0.238
435	0.198
436	0.158
437	0.118
438	0.079
439	0.039
440	0
441	-0.039

Table 6-1   *Continued*

Standard Pitch, in Hz	Necessary Pitch Shift Compensation, in Semitones
442	-0.079
443	-0.118
444	-0.157
445	-0.196
446	-0.234
447	-0.273
448	-0.312
449	-0.351
450	-0.389
451	-0.427
452	-0.466
453	-0.504

Cross-Reference   Pitch-shifting is covered in greater depth in Chapter 8. When you're finished with that chapter, you'll be able to finely adjust your pitch-shifting to compensate for standard pitch irregularities.

Other Key Detection Ideas

There are other software packages that detect key. Rapid Evolution (www.mixshare.com/software.html) is a music database program that some claim is superior to tONaRT for key detection. It also duplicates some of the features of the spreadsheet discussed later in this chapter. It's fairly full-featured and its key detection works quite well, although its interface is awkward and takes some getting used to.

DJ Prince (http://djprince.no) operates a database of tempo and keys for popular music. Go to his website and type the name of your song in the Quick Key and BPM Search box. If your song is in the database, you're good to go!

And the folks at Camelot Sound Services (www.harmonic-mixing.com/services.mv) will sell you a list of songs by key and bpm.

Trial and Error

Sometimes you may not be able to figure out what key a song is in. It may have complex jazz harmonies, or it may have strange atonal sounds. tONaRT may give you two different keys, neither of which sounds right to you. As a last resort, you can always simply plop any two songs into ACID and see if they sound good together. In fact, I imagine that's what most mashup producers do initially. This can be a laborious and time-consuming process, because most songs are quite incompatible. After you have loaded two songs into ACID, you can transpose either of them up or down a semitone. If you really want to, you can transpose them up or down two semitones, but the pitch-shifting will start to become obvious, especially in the vocal. Instrumentals allow a bit more flexibility. If you do not transpose, there is only a 1-in-24 chance the keys will be identical, assuming an equal chance that a song will be in any key. If you allow yourself two semitones up or down, there is a 5-in-24 chance. If you consider compatible keys, as discussed in the following section, you will have a higher chance of having a compatible key with or without transposition.

It is important to know your ear, however. If you have a hard time figuring out what key is best using the piano or the chord files, you may also encounter difficulty arriving at compatible pairings. tONaRT is strongly recommended in this case.

Resolving Key Ambiguity

Sometimes you just can't figure out which of two keys a song is in. Often, the confusion will be between two similar or compatible keys. If a key is incorrectly identified as a compatible key, it is possible that the resulting song combinations will still sound good. The resolution of key ambiguity is covered in detail in the next section.

Additionally, it is quite possible that a single song is actually written in two keys. Sometimes a songwriter will write the verse in one key and the chorus in a related key. Sometimes the bridge will be in a key far-removed from the rest of the song. These songs can be difficult to mash up. You may need to use only one section of the song, or find a different song pairing for each of the key areas. In practice, most mashup producers simply avoid songs with complicated key changes.

Key Compatibility Relationships

Typically, when you're combining different songs, you want the songs to be in the exact same key. However, there are situations where songs in different keys will blend well. Because each key is a collection of seven pitches chosen from the available 12 pitches, any given key will share more pitches with some keys than with others. Generally speaking, the more pitches two keys have in common, the more compatible the two keys will be. Not coincidentally, many of the times that there is ambiguity when trying to determine which key a song is, the confusion will be between two or more closely related and compatible keys.

Relative Minor/Major Relationships

Both the major and minor scales consist of seven intervals, two of which are a semitone, and the other five of which are two semitones. The only difference between major and minor scales is the order in which these intervals appear. If the semitone intervals are the third and seventh intervals, the scale is major, and if the semitone intervals are second and fifth intervals, then the scale is minor. Table 6-2 details the pattern of semitones in the major and minor scales.

Table 6-2   Number of Semitones in Minor and Major Scales

Interval	Semitones in Major Scale	Semitones in Minor Scale
Tonic–2nd	2	2
2nd–3rd	2	1
3rd– 4th	1	2
4th–5th	2	2
5th–6th	2	1
6th–7th	2	2
7th–Octave	1	2

The funny thing about this is that if you rearrange the order of the notes, any minor scale will have the exact same notes as any other major scale. The major scale has a root that is exactly three semitones above the root of the minor. The relationship between the two keys is known as *relative major* and *relative minor*. As an example, F major is the relative major of D minor, and B♭ minor is the relative minor to C♯ major. You may wonder if they have the same notes, doesn't this mean they are the same scale? Well, not exactly. Although the two scales may have the exact same seven notes, melodies and chords written in each key tend to gravitate towards some of the notes more than others. The first pitch of the scale, or the root, receives the most attention, but the fifth pitch is also quite often prominent, with the fourth pitch playing a supporting role.

For example, the keys of C major and A minor have the same collection of pitches. In C major, melodies tend to gravitate toward the pitch of C (the root), and to a lesser extent G (the fifth). These are the third and seventh notes in the scale of A minor, the relative minor. In the key of A minor, the melodies will gravitate toward the pitch of A (the root), and to a lesser extent E (the fifth). These are the sixth and third notes in the scale of C major, the relative major.

Even though they have subtle differences, these two keys can be quite compatible, so much so that it is quite possible for material recorded in A minor to sound quite harmonious when mixed with music in C major. If a melody is written in C major and accompanied by an instrumental in A minor, when the melody comes to rest on C, it corresponds to the third pitch of the A minor scale. This sounds relatively stable and at rest, especially when accompanied by an A minor chord, which is common in the key of A minor. However, when a melody in A minor is accompanied by an instrumental written in C major, the melody comes to rest on A, which is the sixth pitch of the C major scale. This pitch does not sound as resolved. The results are a mashup that sounds fairly in key, but doesn't seem to come to a stable resting point that the listener normally expects. It doesn't sound totally wrong, but it doesn't sound quite right either.

Sometimes a single song will slip between relative minor and major as it goes from verse to chorus, making determining the key that much more difficult. Fortunately, in this case if you are incorrect in identifying the key, you will mistake it for a very compatible key, and the mashups could still sound good.

Fourth/Fifth Relationships

Another important relationship is between the fourth and fifth keys. These are the keys that are built on the fourth and fifth pitches of any minor or major scale, corresponding with five and seven semitones above the root. Major and minor scales built on the same root share identical fourths and fifths. For example, the fourth pitch of E minor is A, and the fourth pitch of E major is also A. The great thing about keys that are a fourth or fifth apart is that they share all but one pitch, as long as they are both major or both minor. E major has the same pitches as A major, except that E major contains a D♯, and A major contains a D natural. As previously discussed, melodies tend to gravitate primarily toward the root, and to a lesser extent the fifth. So melodies in A major can have lots of E's in them, because E is the fifth pitch in A major. And melodies in E major may have some A in them, because A is the fourth pitch in E major, but it will not seem as stable a resting point. Because of this, it is more likely that a melody written a fifth above the instrumental will sound better than a melody that is a fourth above.

If the tonic of one key is on the fifth pitch of a second key, then the tonic of the second key is on the fourth pitch of the first key. So whenever you have two keys with a fifth relationship, you will have two keys with a fourth relationship as well.

As in the relative minor/major relationship, a single song may often slip between its primary key into a different key, based on the fifth of the primary key, and sometimes the fourth. In fact, this is probably the most frequent source of key ambiguity there is. More often than not, when you are confused about which key a song is in, chances are that the two potential keys are in a fourth/fifth relationship. Because melodies and chords gravitate towards the fifth of a given scale more than the fourth of the scale, chances are that the actual key will be the lower pitch of the two keys in a fifth relationship (the upper pitch of the two keys in the fourth relationship).

For example, you may be trying to determine a key using ACID's built-in piano. Both the F and B♭ notes may sound equally "at home" with the song. By referring to the list of notes back in Chapter 4, you can see that B♭ is the second note in the A chromatic scale, and that F is the ninth note. There are seven semitones between them, which is a perfect fifth. In this scenario, B♭ is the more likely key — the lower note of the perfect fifth.

As another example, you may be trying to determine a key using the chord MIDI file, and can't decide whether B minor (A minor transposed +2) or E minor (A minor transposed + 7) sounds best. Subtracting two from seven, you know there are five semitones between B and E, which is a fourth relationship. The most likely key in this scenario is the upper of the two notes in the fourth, or E minor.

Sometimes even tONaRT will have fourth/fifth relationships between its guesses for the key in Classic Mode and Regular Mode. You may try to use this technique to identify the more likely key of the two, but as always with tONaRT, it's best to let your ears confirm the choice.

Parallel Minor/Major Relationships

One more key relationship worth mentioning is that of parallel keys. A *parallel* key is simply a key with the same root but different mode. So the parallel minor to C major is C minor. Now on first glance, it might seem obvious that C major would be compatible with C minor. But a closer look reveals that out of the seven pitches, only four are identical: the root, the second, the fourth, and the fifth. In fact, there are nine other keys that share more pitches with C minor than C major. With this information, you might wonder why any compatibility exists at all.

As previously mentioned, melodies and chords gravitate toward the root as well as the fifth. Parallel keys have identical roots and fifths. So for music that gravitates more heavily toward these two pitches, parallel keys can be quite compatible. For music that has strong melodies and lots of notes, parallel keys are not quite so compatible. Simple rock songs, some hip-hop, and less melodic dance music can often have such simple harmonic structure that you can't really tell if it's in minor or major. And sometimes the cues are so subtle that there can be compatibility with the parallel key.

Other Relationships

You may combine relative minor/major and fourth/fifth relationships, although the compatibility will not be as strong as the relative or fourth/fifth relationships by themselves.

For example, the relative minor of F major is D minor. The fifth above D minor is A minor. Therefore, F major is related to A minor. In fact, they share six of seven pitches.

Table 6-3 simplifies all of these relationships.

Table 6-3   Key Relationships

Major Key	Minor Key
C major	A minor
G major	E minor
D major	B minor
A major	F#/G♭ minor
E major	C#/D♭ minor
B major	G#/A♭ minor
F#/G♭ major	D#/E♭ minor
C#/D♭ major	A#/B♭ minor
G#/A♭ major	F minor
D#/E♭ major	C minor
A#/B♭ major	G minor
F major	D minor
C major	A minor

In this table, relative minors and majors are right next to each other in the same row, and fourth/fifth relationships are above and below each other in the same column. Combinations of relative and fourth/fifth relationships are in cells that touch each other diagonally. Parallel relationships are not included in the table, but are quite simple to figure out because they share the same root. In case of key ambiguity between two keys that are above or below each other, the more likely candidate would be the lower of the two. The number of rows that separate the two keys is identical to the number of pitches that are different between the keys. For example, you can see that C minor is three rows away from C major, and the two keys have three pitches out of seven that are different.

Transposition

So far it's been determined that for any key, there are three other keys that may be strongly compatible (fourth, fifth, and relative), and three more keys that may be somewhat compatible (parallel, fourth above relative, and fifth above relative). This is all assuming that you don't shift the pitch of the songs. In practice, you can usually pitch-shift any song by moving vocals up or down a semitone, with sonically acceptable results. With instrumentals, you may be able to transpose two or three semitones. If you use formant-corrected pitch shifting (discussed in Chapter 8), you may be able to stretch these results even further.

As you saw previously in Table 6-3, E minor and F minor are as incompatible as any two keys can be. They are seven rows away from each other, and they have no pitches in common. When played against each other, you will have heavy amounts of guaranteed key clash. However, because they are only one semitone apart, a simple one-semitone pitch shift will get them into the same key, and they will be most compatible.

As you can see, with all of these key relationships and transposition possibilities, almost any key can be made compatible with any other. Although there is no universally accepted measure of key compatibility, I usually rank key compatibility using relative relationships, fourth/fifth relationships, and transposition. The most compatible keys with C major are listed below. This ranking is my own and is rather subjective, because it forces a comparison between key relationships and transposition.

The keys most closely related to C major are as follows:

1. C major (obviously!)

2. A minor (relative minor)

3. B major and C♯/D♭ major (C major, transposed one semitone)

4. F major and G major (fourth and fifth above C major)

5. G♯/A♭ minor and A♯/B♭ minor (transposed one semitone from the relative minor)

6. D minor and E minor (fourth and fifth above the relative minor)

7. C minor (parallel minor)

8. D major and A♯/B♭ major (transposed two semitones)

9. E major, F♯/G♭ major, and G♯/A♭ major (fourth and fifth above, transposed one semitone from F major and G major)

10. B minor and G minor (relative minor, transposed two semitones)

11. C♯/D♭ minor, D♯/E♭ minor and F minor (fourth and fifth above relative minor, transposed one semitone)

12. D♯/E♭ major and A major (fourth and fifth above C major, transposed two semitones)

13. F♯/G♭ minor (relative minor, transposed three semitones)

So with key relationships and transposition, the number of compatible songs expands considerably. Having an accurately identified key is essential to choosing the right songs.

Keeping Track of Your Tracks

You've gotten a lot of information so far in this chapter on choosing your component songs. You've learned about genre, era, and mood, as well as lyrics and titles, and you've read about tempo and key at length. It may have occurred to you that finding the key and tempo of a song takes a good deal of time and effort, and if you were to try to find a good match for a given song, you might need to try out many songs until you find one. If you were to analyze the tempo and key of every potential match each time you make a new mashup, it would be a lot of work! That is why it's important to keep a record of the tempo and key of songs you've analyzed, especially the ones you *don't* use. If you've gone through all the trouble of analyzing the song, you must like the song or at least think it's worth considering. If you write down the key and tempo of every failed match for every mashup, you will eventually have a massive list of tempos and keys, and save yourself a lot of time and effort in the future.

This section discusses two methods for keeping track of this information. One uses a simple text file, and the other uses Microsoft Excel.

Using a Text File

Creating a text file is a humble yet effective way of organizing all your mashup info. The method is quite simple. First, you open a blank document with Notepad, WordPad, Microsoft Word, or any other word processor you like. You then type a list of all 24 keys. You can enter them in any order you like, but the simplest thing to do would be to just put them in order: A major, A♯ major, B major, all the way through G♯ major, followed by A minor, A♯ minor, and on to G♯ minor (see Chapter 4 for a discussion of keys).

When you analyze a new song, enter the following information underneath the key that the song is in: tempo, song, and artist. Feel free to include any other information or notes you feel are important. If there are already songs in your list in the same key, make sure to put your new song before any songs with higher tempos and after any songs with lower tempos. As you build your song list, you will have up to 24 lists of songs, each with tempos from slowest to fastest. An example follows:

A Major

Tempo	Song	Artist
115.1	"Together Forever"	Rick Astley
120.5	"Shake Your Love"	Debbie Gibson
122.9	"We Don't Have to Take Our Clothes Off"	Jermaine Stewart
123.2	"Heaven Is a Place on Earth"	Belinda Carlisle
133.0	"Wait"	White Lion
134.1	"Baby Don't Forget My Number"	Milli Vanilli

A♯ Major

Tempo	Song	Artist
100.3	"Sara"	Starship
144.1	"We Built This City"	Starship

G Major

Tempo	Song	Artist
56.8	"Lost in Love"	Air Supply
137.5	"When You Close Your Eyes"	Night Ranger

G♯ Major

Tempo	Song	Artist
97.8	"Say You, Say Me"	Lionel Richie
128.4	"Nothin' But a Good Time""	Poison

A minor

Tempo	Song	Artist
102.7	"Who's Crying Now"	Bobby Brown
111.5	"You Got It (The Right Stuff)"	New Kids on the Block

G♯ minor

Tempo	Song	Artist
114.6	"Strut"	Sheena Easton

Your music collection may differ from this example (there's no accounting for taste), but the important thing is how it is organized. Even though none of these songs may have made it into a mashup so far, next time you are wondering what goes well with a song, you can analyze its key and tempo, and then look up the key in your document and find the tempo that most closely matches. Of course, you can look up closely related keys as well. It's that simple. If you're planning to make more than one or two mashups, you won't regret the effort a little record keeping requires.

Using Microsoft Excel

If you have access to and are comfortable with using Microsoft Excel, I recommend this method for song management. Included on the CD-ROM is a spreadsheet (called Mashup Song Database) into which you can enter the tempo and key information for songs in your collection. You can then enter a target key and tempo, and the spreadsheet will calculate a relevance score for each song in your collection, and then display a report ranking each song and detailing the key and tempo relationships. Half- and double-tempo relationships are considered as well as relative, fourth/fifth, and parallel key relationships.

Note   If you don't have Microsoft Excel, there is a full-featured spreadsheet program available as part of Open Office, an open-source alternative to Microsoft Office. You can download it for free at http://download.openoffice.org.

For example, Table 6-4 shows the results if you enter into the spreadsheet the collection you compiled in a text file, a target tempo of 90 bpm, and a target key of G minor.

Table 6-4   Sample Spreadsheet Output

Rank	Score	Title	Artist	Relationship
1	97.37%	"Who's Crying Now"	Bobby Brown	"Who's Crying Now" is 102.7 bpm and is in the target key of A minor. Slow it down 2.7% to the target tempo of 100 bpm.
2	89.69%	"You Got It (The Right Stuff)"	New Kids on the Block	"You Got It (The Right Stuff)" is 111.5 bpm of and is in the target key of A minor. Slow it down 11.5% to the target tempo of 100 bpm.
3	79.99%	"Strut"	Sheena Easton	"Strut" is 114.6 bpm and is in A♭ minor. Transpose it up one semitone to the target key of A minor. Slow it down 14.6% to the target tempo of 100 bpm.
4	78.93%	"Sara"	Starship	"Sara" is 100.3 bpm and is in B♭ major. Transpose it up two semitones to the target key of C major, the relative major of A minor. Slow it down 0.3% to the target tempo of 100 bpm.
5	76.65%	"Say You, Say Me"	Lionel Richie	"Say You, Say Me" is 97.8 bpm and is in A♭ major. Transpose it down one semitone to the target key of G major, the relative major of E minor, a fifth above A minor. Speed it up 2.2% to the target tempo of 100 bpm.
6	75.26%	"Lost in Love"	Air Supply	"Lost in Love" is 56.8 bpm and is in F major, the relative major of D minor, a fourth above A minor. Slow it down 13.6% to the target tempo of 50 bpm (half the target tempo of 100).
7	69.50%	"Together Forever"	Rick Astley	"Together Forever" is 115.1 bpm and is in A major, the parallel major of A minor. Slow it down 15.1% to the target tempo of 100 bpm.

Table 6-4   Continued

Rank	Score	Title	Artist	Relationship
8	66.39%	"Shake Your Love"	Debbie Gibson	"Shake Your Love" is 120.5 bpm and is in A major, the parallel major of A minor. Slow it down 20.5% to the target tempo of 100 bpm.
9	65.09%	"We Don't Have to Take Our Clothes Off"	Jermaine Stewart	"We Don't Have to Take Our Clothes Off" is 122.9 bpm and is in A major, the parallel major of A minor. Slow it down 22.9% to the target tempo of 100 bpm.
10	64.94%	"Heaven is a Place on Earth"	Belinda Carlisle	"Heaven is a Place on Earth" is 123.2 bpm and is in A major, the parallel major of A minor. Slow it down 23.2% to the target tempo of 100 bpm.
11	62.18%	"When You Close Your Eyes"	Night Ranger	"When You Close Your Eyes" is 137.5 bpm and is in F major, the relative major of D minor, a fourth above A minor. Slow it down 37.5% to the target tempo of 100 bpm.
12	61.04%	"Nothin' But a Good Time"	Poison	"Nothin' But a Good Time" is 128.4 bpm and is in A♭ major. Transpose it down one semitone to the target key of G major, the relative major of E minor, a fifth above A minor. Slow it down 28.4% to the target tempo of 100 bpm.
13	60.15%	"Wait"	White Lion	"Wait" is 133 bpm and is in A major, the parallel major of A minor. Slow it down 33% to the target tempo of 100 bpm.
14	59.66%	"Baby Don't Forget My Number"	Milli Vanilli	"Baby Don't Forget My Number" is 134.1 bpm and is in A major, the parallel major of A minor. Slow it down 34.1% to the target tempo of 100 bpm.
15	57.04%	"We Built this City"	Starship	"We Built this City" is 144.1 bpm and is in B♭ major. Transpose it up two semitones to the target key of C major, the relative major of A minor. Speed it up 28% to the target tempo of 200 bpm (double the target tempo of 100).

Each time you encounter a new song, enter the tempo and key information into the Excel spreadsheet in the Song Collection worksheet. Pretty soon you'll have a useful catalog of songs you like, and the more compatible songs will make themselves apparent next time you need them.

In the Excel system, scores are automatically calculated and will range from 0 to 100 percent. If a song is exactly the same tempo and key as the target tempo, it will have a score of 100 percent. These calculations are a bit complicated and are detailed in Appendix A.

Other Methods of Keeping Track

There are a variety of other ways of keeping track of your audio files.

Some people use iTunes to sort their files, with ID3 tags to store key and tempo information. For example, you might sort your tunes into 24 play lists, one for each key, sorted by tempo.

Some people use Windows Explorer to sort their files, storing them in 24 folders, one for each key. The tempo is added to the beginning of the filename, so it will be sorted in order of tempo.

You can use Rapid Evolution, discussed earlier in this chapter, to store your bpm and key data. It will analyze this data for you and store it, although it's a bit awkward to use.

MixedInKey (www.mixedinkey.com) is software similar to Rapid Evolution that uses tONaRT as its key detection engine. It is not free, however.

Breaking It Down

So you've chosen some songs, taking mood, genre, personal taste, lyrics, and titles into account. You've gotten a good estimate of tempo, and your songs have tempos that are close to each other. Your songs are in the same or compatible keys.

It's finally time to put your mashup together! You'll sync up the tracks, get them in key, arrange them, and polish them up, before presenting your creation to the world.

Aligning the Tracks

Probably the most readily apparent feature of a proper mashup is the synchronization of the tempos. If you are using two or more rhythmic tracks, a well-synced mashup will have the rhythms practically melt into each other. Individual sounds will be so synchronous that they seem to be one sound. If you are using an acapella, the vocal will be in the pocket of the rhythm, as if the singer were actually singing to your borrowed background tracks.

Your tracks need to start in sync, and they need to stay in sync. All too often, a decent mashup starts off sounding acceptably tight, only to drift over time as ACID's beat grid and the track's rhythmic grid drift and diverge.

This chapter will guide you through lining up two tracks with steady tempos, lining up the sounds both with ACID's grid and to each other.

Snapping to ACID's Grid

The best way to make sure that your tracks don't drift is to line them up with ACID's internal beat grid. For maximum simplicity, use a recording with a constant bpm, probably recorded in recent years — either an electronic-based song, such as a dance, pop, or hip-hop song, or a live recording where the drummer was playing along with a click track during the recording.

Choose recordings with absolutely unwavering tempos that will allow you to "set and forget" the tempo in ACID. If music you want to mash up has a variable tempo, there are a variety of techniques to handle this situation, as outlined in Chapter 9. But for learning mashup basics, it's probably better to start off with a static tempo. It's also a good idea to manipulate rhythmic songs at first as opposed to raw acapellas. Drum sounds are relatively easy to line up visually with ACID's grid. In fact, mixing two complete songs is a great way to start mashing stuff up, because the rhythmic cues are solid. Acapellas are a bit trickier, and will be addressed later in the chapter.

Most rhythms do not have a note resolution finer than sixteenth notes. In many situations, most attacks of the drum sounds will line up with ACID's grid when it is magnified to sixteenth notes. If they are magnified beyond this, sixteenth notes will occur every 192 ticks, so the attacks will occur at 0, 192, 384, and 576 ticks. However, if your rhythm track has any swing to it, as is the case with much hip-hop and house music, every other sixteenth note will be slightly delayed. If this is the case, you can only count on visually lining up the eighth notes, which correspond with 0 and 384 ticks. The rhythmic elements that would ordinarily be at 192 and 576 ticks will be off by different amounts, because swing levels vary with each song.

Working Without the Beatmapper Wizard

 If you're using ACID XPress, you won't have access to the Beatmapper Wizard feature and will need to line up your track to ACID's beat grid manually.

Here are a few steps for beatmapping without the Wizard:

1. Drop your audio file into ACID XPress, and if there are other tracks in your project, solo your new track.

2. Find the "first" beat by clicking the Play button and listening for the beats. If you nod your head or tap your foot, it will probably fall naturally on the beat.

Note Because beats are usually grouped in measures of four, ideally you can find the first beat of a measure, which often feels a little bit stronger than the other three. Furthermore, because measures are grouped into longer sections, it would be great if the beat you selected were in the first measure of a new section. It is less important to capture the absolute first beat that is audible in the track than to select a first beat of a first measure of a section. For example, if there is a vocal and/or string intro with no discernable rhythm, you can skip over that to the beginning of the next section. This doesn't mean you are throwing out the intro, but rather that you are using a clearly defined rhythmic sound to anchor your frame of reference.

3. When you have found your perfect beat, place the cursor shortly before it, zoom in a bit, and play the track again. Repeat this process several times until you can see the sound's attack clearly and you have your cursor placed immediately before the first beat.

4. Press S to split the sound right at the cursor. Select the portion of the sound to the left of the cursor and press the Delete key to get rid of it. If you have Quick Fade selected in your audio preferences, it is quite possible that the sharp attack at the beginning of the remaining waveform has been softened by the automatic fade. Either deselect quick fade in your audio preferences, or zoom in until you can see the fade-in and remove it, dragging the upper-right corner to the left.

5. Zoom out and slide the remaining waveform all the way to the left until it hits the beginning of the track.

   If your mashup is already underway, and there are other tracks besides your new one, make a note of the current tempo, because you'll want to return to it shortly. But temporarily at least, you'll be bringing the project tempo in line with your new track.

   The first beat of the first measure of a section is already lined up to the first beat of the first section of ACID XPress, and it's time to line up the remainder.

6. Click the Play button while you listen and look for the second beat. The second beat needs to line up with beat grid 1.2.000. If you can see beat markers for 1.1 and 2.1, you should be zoomed in sufficiently. Chances are, the second beat of your track isn't lined up with beat 1.2.000, so move the tempo slider in the same direction you need to move the snare.

Often, but not always, the second beat will have a snare drum on it. For this reason, the second beat is often more visually defined than the first beat. If you can't see it well, you may need to zoom in a bit, but not so much that the screen scrolls too fast for you to see what is happening.

Note Don't forget, you can press the Ctrl key while moving the slider to move it in very small increments, but don't worry about a fine level of precision quite yet. Try to get it close though.

If both your first and second beats were *exactly* lined up, then every beat afterwards would also line up. However, even a very small error will eventually have a large impact. The difference between your estimated tempo and the actual tempo will accumulate, each beat growing more out of sync until it becomes unpleasantly obvious. That is why you need to sync up beats beyond the first and second beats. But because you are close, the other beats shouldn't be far off.

7. Repeating the process you used for the second beat, line up the third beat to beat marker 1.3.000, and then line up the fifth beat to beat marker 2.1.000. Each of these adjustments should be slight compared to the initial adjustment.

8. Continue this process, doubling the number of beats each time. The entire process is similar to the following:

  - **1 beat after the first beat:** Second beat, or 1.2.000 (already done in step 6)

  - **2 beats after the first beat:** Third beat, or 1.3.000 (already done in step 7)

  - **4 beats after the first beat:** First beat of measure 2, lined up with 2.1.000 (already done in step 7)

  - **8 beats after the first beat:** First beat of measure 3, lined up with 3.1.000

  - **16 beats after the first beat:** First beat of measure 5, lined up with 5.1.000

  - **32 beats after the first beat:** First beat of measure 9, lined up with 9.1.000

  - **64 beats after the first beat:** First beat of measure 17, lined up with 17.1.000

  - **128 beats after the first beat:** First beat of measure 33, lined up with 33.1.000

  . . . and so on.

You do not need to precisely double the number of beats each time. The reason why you expand to larger and larger time scales each time is that the timing error doubles when you double the length of the material you are trying to sync. Stepping through the whole track one or four beats at a time might be very useful at first, when the errors tend to be large, but this gets tedious and inefficient by the end of the track, because each new measure has an increasingly smaller offset error. By the end of this process, you should have a track where most every major percussive event lines up perfectly with one of the sixteenth note gridlines in ACID XPress. If there is swing, at least the eighth note drum sounds will line up.

Cross-Reference If for some reason your beats seem to be more and more misaligned as you get further along in your song, make sure that your downbeat is properly positioned. If the problem persists, it is quite possible that you are dealing with a variable tempo, which is discussed in Chapter 9.

9. Switch the track type to Beatmapped, and check the Preserve Pitch When Stretching check box. The track's tempo will be automatically set to the current value of the project tempo, and you can revert the tempo back to its original state, and unsolo the track. Your track is now synchronized no matter what tempo you choose.

   Although all events on your track will be at the correct tempo, you have only defined the correct starting point, or *offset*, for the one event you have drawn. If you were to use the draw tool to create a new event, it would start at the very first sample of the audio file, and probably wouldn't sync up. For this, you need to define the track's downbeat offset. Luckily the event's start offset gives you the value you need.

10. Double-click the event you've just drawn, or right-click it and select Properties from the context menu. The start offset is measured in numbers of samples, just like the track's downbeat. Copy the value of your event's start offset to the downbeat offset for the track located on the Stretch panel of track 1's properties, so that when a new event is created with either the paint or draw tool, the event's start offset will be correct. (This is located in the Stretch panel of the clip if you are manually beatmapping in ACID Pro 6.) The event's start offset will adjust itself to compensate for the new track downbeat offset, so you may have to re-paste the value into the event start offset after pasting it into the track downbeat offset.

What you've just done is duplicate the functionality of the Beatmapper Wizard of ACID Pro. Because it's a lot easier and less time-consuming, you should use the wizard if you have ACID Pro. If you have the Beatmapper Wizard, but bypassed it when you dropped the track in, you can always pull it up again by clicking the Beatmapper Wizard button on the Stretch panel of the Track/Clip Properties.

Manual Beatmapping Example: "Policy of Truth"

Download "Policy of Truth" from the iTunes Store and convert it with a CD burn, and reimport it within iTunes.

Now give this example a try by following these steps:

1. Drop the track into ACID XPress and turn it into a one-shot, as shown in Figure 7-1. Use the horizontal zoom to see the individual rhythmic sounds, and place the cursor near the initial beat, verifying it with both your eyes and ears.

2. Zoom ACID XPress in horizontally, refine the cursor's position, and repeat the process until the cursor is just before the first beat's attack. Split the waveform and manually remove the automatic fade-in, as shown in Figure 7-2.

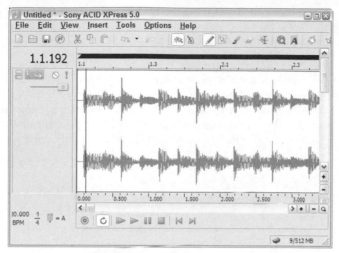

FIGURE 7-1: Initial beat estimate

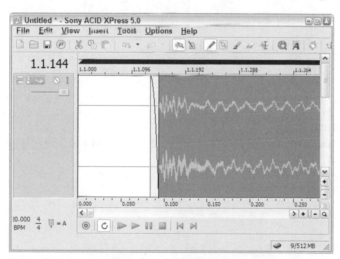

FIGURE 7-2: Cursor right before the initial beat

3. Delete the silence before the initial beat, zoom out the project until you can see the second beat, and adjust the tempo until beat two of the beat grid approximately lines up with beat two of the track. Notice how defined and visible the snare of beat two is in Figure 7-3.

4. Repeat this process for beats 1.3, 2.1, 3.1 5.1, 9.1, 17.1, 33.1, and 65.1, eventually pressing the Ctrl key while adjusting the tempo to fine-tune it.

At 129.1, the track gets a bit complex and full, and the beat, although visible, is not as visually well-defined as the beats surrounding it. In this case, it is a bit easier to sync up 129.2, as shown in Figure 7-4. (Those snares on beats 2 and 4 can really come in handy!)

5. Go back through the waveform and ensure that earlier beats are still synchronized. If they are not, you may have made an error at some point, or perhaps the tempo is actually variable. Set your track type to Beatmapped and check the Preserve Pitch When Stretching check box. In this case, in the Stretch tab of the track's Properties window (the clip's Properties window in Pro 6), the tempo will be around 114.23, and the downbeat offset will be around 4,143. If your values differ from these values slightly, don't worry. There is a little bit of wiggle room.

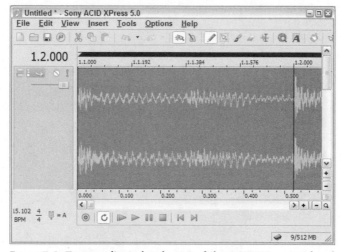

FIGURE 7-3: Tempo adjusted so beat 2 of the ACID XPress grid and the song nearly line up

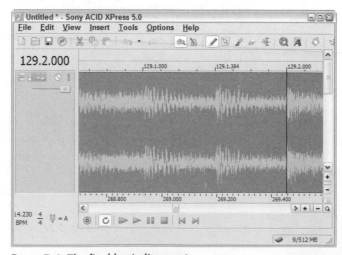

FIGURE 7-4: The final beat alignment

Complex Tracks

You can't count on the vocals of a track visually lining up with ACID's grid. Additionally, sometimes the vocal or other sounds will be so loud that you cannot clearly see the drums or other sounds through it. In this case, you may need to rely on percussive sounds that you can clearly see. As previously mentioned, the snare is often more visible than the kick.

Suppose you are going through your track, doubling the length of material you are synchronizing with each iteration, and then you find yourself with an area where the track doesn't have visually defined rhythmic points. This is not a problem. Simply find a nearby point that *is* rhythmically well-defined, and use that as a reference point. This may be the beat directly after the beat you were attempting to sync up, or it may be many measures off, if you are in a long section with no clearly defined rhythmic markers. The idea of doubling the length each time is not a strict rule in any sense. As long as you increase the magnitude of the beat number you are synchronizing each time, you should be okay.

There may be a case where you cannot even see the initial downbeat well, but the snare is clearly visible on that second beat. You can do a little variation of the beatmapping method, like this:

1. Set the track (or clip) to one-shot. Then find the snare from the second beat and put your cursor immediately before it, zooming in for refinement.

2. Split the event just before the snare and zoom out until you can see the grid line for beat 1.2.000, as in Figure 7-5.

3. Slide the snare so that it lines up to the 1.2.000 gridline, instead of the beginning of the track, as in Figure 7-6.

4. Assuming that there is a snare on both beats two and four, slide the tempo slider until the second snare is pretty near beat 1.4.000, as shown in Figure 7-7.

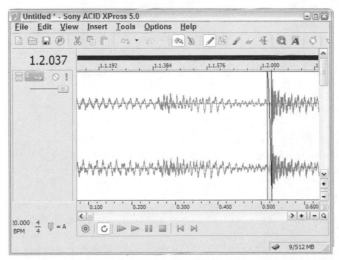

FIGURE 7-5: The event split just before the snare, with beat 1.2.000 visible

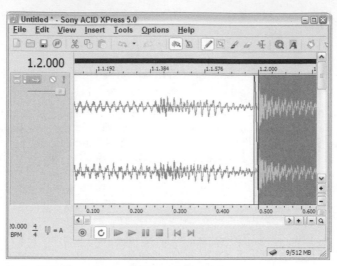

FIGURE 7-6: The snare exactly on gridline 1.2

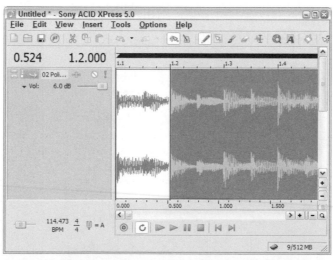

FIGURE 7-7: The second snare lined up approximately with beat 1.4

5. Continue with the third snare, lining it up approximately with beat 2.2 (one measure beyond your starting point of 1.2). Then line up the fifth snare with beat 4.2, followed by snares 9, 17, 33, 65, and so on, just like you did in the previous method, except that you're lining up the upbeats to the second beats of the measure instead of the downbeats to the first.

6. When you're done, and all the visible rhythmic elements are aligned, delete the first event. Use the draw tool to grab the left edge of the event and drag it back to the downbeat of 1.1.000, as shown in Figure 7-8.

7. Switch the track setting to beatmapped, unsolo it, and copy the offset of the event to the track, just like in the previous method.

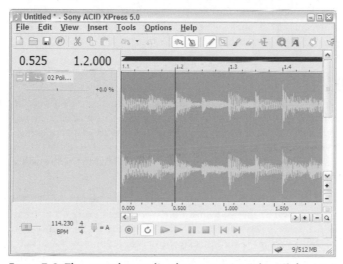

FIGURE 7-8: The second snare lined up approximately with beat 1.4

Adjusting While in Beatmapped Mode

It's convenient to adjust the project tempo to the tempo of the track you are trying to beatmap simply because the tempo slider moves smoothly and you have immediate visual feedback as the tempo varies. However, there are situations where you want to map the beats while staying at your original project tempo, varying the track's tempo instead. This is equally possible.

Set the track's type to beatmapped instead of one-shot. Find the downbeat, trim off the beginning, and move the remainder over to beat one. Now instead of varying the project tempo, vary the original tempo of the track in the Stretch panel of the track's Properties window (this would be the clip's Properties window in Pro 6). You can type in a new value, click the up and down arrows, or hold down the up and down arrows for continuous movement. This is great for fine-tuning, but the quickest way to adjust this value for the initial approximation is to grab the little area on the screen between the up and down arrows next to the original tempo, and drag it up and down. If it moves too fast, hold down the Ctrl key while you drag. You will be performing the exact same technique as before, syncing up beats 2, 3, 5, 9, 17, and so on, but this time you're adjusting the track's tempo to match your project tempo instead of the other way around.

Don't forget to copy the event's start offset over to track's downbeat offset, so that future events will be synced up to the grid.

Syncing at Various Time Scales

When synchronizing two tracks, you'll need to line them up at several time scales simultaneously. As the timescale increases, the synchronization becomes more subtle and complex, but no less important. Most obviously, the rhythmic sounds need to be synchronized, as do the beats and measures, and then the longer sections. Misalignments at a small scale are usually obvious, but larger-scale synchronization is easier to overlook. In fact, one of the most common mistakes beginning mashup artists make is neglecting to address the tracks' interactions at this larger time scale.

Syncing Rhythmic Elements

If you want your mashup to sound tight, the individual rhythmic sounds should line up to the highest degree possible. If your tracks line up to ACID's grid, this will happen automatically. When you zoom in time with your project, you should see two attacks happening simultaneously, so much so that the ear may be unable to distinguish the two sounds. If your tracks start to drift apart from each other, you will hear the drum sounds start to double, sounding a bit like a messy DJ. This is rarely desirable.

One factor to consider when you're thinking about synchronization at a sub-beat level is swing. When a rhythm is swung, every other sixteenth note (sometimes every other eighth note) is delayed. Sometimes the delay is very subtle, and other times the first sixteenth note can be up to two or three times longer than the second sixteenth note. If you zoom way in on your track, you'll be able to tell whether the drums on every other sixteenth note line up with ACID's grid. Sometimes, a quarter or eighth note is divided into three equal rhythmic durations instead of two. Blues rhythms and many ballads from the late 1950s and early 1960s come to mind. This is similar to a swing where the ratio is 1 to 2.

Whether your track has a swing or is in triple meter, it may present challenges in syncing up all the rhythmic elements. If you try to mix a track with swing with a track without swing, every other sixteenth note (or eighth note) will be slightly misaligned. While some people may like the looseness, it ought to be a conscious decision rather than done out of laziness, ignorance or neglect. If a track has a triple rhythm or strong swing, it is probably best paired up with another track with similar rhythmic characteristics.

Syncing Beats and Measures

Even if your rhythmic elements are perfectly aligned, your beats and measures need to be lined up as well. Chances are that you will be able to feel the beat pretty easily. If you've beatmapped your audio file, hopefully this level of synchronization will be taken care of. If you click Play while listening to a single track, and look at the time counter above the track list, you will see it counting off the measures, beats, and tick marks. The tick marks go by too fast for the eye to discern individual marks, but the measures and beats should change at a more reasonable rate. If you watch the beat counting from one to four and then repeating, it should happen at the same time as the beats of the music. You may even want to count along with the beat number,

"ONE, two, three, four, ONE, two…" emphasizing the first beat. If the "ONE" sounds inappropriately placed, perhaps your downbeat is misplaced in your beatmapping. You may also want to use the metronome in the Options menu. This will play a click track with the downbeat louder and higher in pitch than the other beats.

Sometimes, although it is not terribly common, a song will have a partial measure and skip a beat or two. If this happens, you'll have to give special treatment to that area, and cut up one of your tracks to realign them after the irregularity. Or, you could get rid of the irregularity altogether, deleting the partial measure.

Another kind of irregularity can occur in some electronic music from before the mid-1990s when digital audio recording took over. Older recordings used magnetic tape, which was often physically cut with a razor and spliced to reorder and remix a song. If the razor didn't cut at a precise location, a song with an otherwise constant tempo may have a blip.

It is easy to have your beats lined up, but not the measures. If you are off by half a measure, and both tracks have snare sounds on beats two and four, the snares will still line up, giving an overall impression of synchronicity, but the phrases will be off. Misalignments of a single beat are also common, especially if there's no snare on the upbeats. The easiest way to avoid this situation is to solo each track and make sure that the downbeat of ACID's grid (the "ONE" when you are counting) lines up and feels right with the track. It's important to solo the track, because hearing the correct timing of one track may trick you into missing the incorrect timing of the other.

Missynchronization of the beats and measures occurs quite frequently when you're handling pure acapellas. The vocals sound tight and seem to lock in with the background rhythm. And the fact is that if someone had never heard the original song that the acapella came from, it would sound in sync and wouldn't present a problem. In fact, offsetting the vocal by a number of beats or measures is a perfectly valid artistic choice. But it's important to be aware of the listener's expectations. If an original version of a rap recording has the vocal starting on the second beat of a measure, and your mashup has the vocal starting on the first, the difference will be apparent and jarring to the listener familiar with the vocals. It may sound good this way to you, or it may just be your own spin on things, but all too often, these subtle misalignments are a result of ignorance or laziness, instead of a sense of purpose. I've heard a perfectly good mashup have the acapella of the first couple of verses line up with the backing track on the identical rhythmic placement as the original. The third verse was a couple of beats late, and because of this inconsistency, it didn't seem purposeful. So go ahead and misplace your beats or measures, but just be aware when you are doing so, and have a reason. It's a good idea to initially try to position your events in their original placement before moving them about.

Syncing Sections

Now you've got your tracks lined up all the way from the sixteenth notes to the whole measures. When you count off the beats in one track, it's the same as when you count off the beats in the other track. Beats and measures either line up or they don't. It's pretty black and white. In the larger scale, synchronization is where the artistry and subtlety comes in. Section definition can be ambiguous compared to measures. You may not be sure if a pre-chorus is actually a different section or just a part of the verse. A subtle change in the instrumentation may or may not signify a new section. When you're dealing with lining up the tracks at this level, your ear and imagination are your guides. For this reason, this is where the fun really starts!

Back in Chapter 4, you read about intros, outros, verses, choruses, breakdowns, bridges, and other elements of song structure. It's perfectly fine to just mess around with your tracks, cutting them up and lining up different sections of them to see what sounds good, but at some point you need to step back and look at the overall structure of your component songs. It's easy to make a mashup where each passing moment sounds great, but after listening to it for the few minutes it plays, the larger structure seems to be missing. Or perhaps the backing track doesn't ebb and flow with the singer. Ideally, the exciting parts of the song, often the chorus, should coincide with the exciting parts of the backing track, often using increased instrumentation, volume, or rhythmic density. But there are no absolute rules.

Even so, it's important for you to be aware of what you think the structure of the song is. You may even want to write it down, counting out the number of measures for each section, as you did in Chapter 4. You may want to draw the entire song as an event, and then to split it into sections in ACID. You may just want to listen and commit it to memory. The important thing to remember is this: Sections of your foreground track generally need to line up with sections of your background track. The sections need not happen in the same order as in the original at all. But if your vocal is going from the verse to the chorus, perhaps the backing track can simultaneously change to a different section with fuller instrumentation. When your vocal is going to the bridge, perhaps your backing track could switch to the instrumental breakdown. These specific types of changes are only suggestions, but in general, it's not a good idea to lazily maintain an unchanging background while the foreground switches between sections. Likewise, don't let the background section change halfway through a foreground section just because that's when the background happened to change in the original recording. It can be tempting to simply allow the two tracks to continue each at their own pace. After all, the beats are staying in sync, and as long as nobody's singing at the same time as anyone else, it might not sound blatantly horrible. However, if the goal is to create one cohesive piece of music, you'd never intentionally have the backing track change up at a different time than the foreground.

The length of the sections of the two tracks will almost never be the same throughout. As you saw in Chapter 4, some sections are two measures long and others are 16. And although these section lengths made perfect sense in the context of the original recordings, *they will need to be adjusted in the context of your mashup*. Don't be a slave to your source tracks' section length and pacing. You are the boss here. You can shorten a section if need be, or loop a section of it to lengthen it. Remember, if you are trying to create an illusion of a single song out of many, your mashup has to have sections every bit as well-defined as an original song. If your component tracks each communicate different section lengths and placement, your mashup will sound slightly disorganized to the listener. This point cannot be emphasized enough. Laziness and inattention to section flow is all too often what makes a mediocre mashup mediocre.

Cross-Reference   Altering sections so they line up is covered extensively in Chapter 11.

Syncing Rhythmic Tracks

The most traditional form of mashup pits an acapella of one song over the instrumental of another, but it's probably easier to start off mixing two songs with rhythmic accompaniments. The rhythmic cues are much easier to hear and see, and the ability to visually line up your tracks can be very helpful.

To follow along with this example, go to the iTunes Store and download the Eurythmics' "Sweet Dreams (Are Made of This)" from the album of the same name, and then convert it to an mp3 or wav.

If you've been following along with the examples in this chapter, you've already beatmapped Depeche Mode's "Policy of Truth." If you do not already have this song loaded up, drag it into a blank ACID project. You'll also need to drag "Sweet Dreams" from iTunes or your Windows Explorer and drop it into ACID. Beatmapping "Sweet Dreams" is pretty easy, because the song starts on an easy-to-see downbeat. You can perform your own beatmapping, either with ACID Pro's Wizard or manually in XPress, or you can enter the following information into the Stretch tab of the Track/Clip Properties:

- Original tempo: 125.462
- Downbeat offset: 18,488

You may also need to check the Preserve Pitch When Stretching check box, if your preferences do not do this automatically.

Although "Sweet Dreams" and "Policy of Truth" have very little of the genre or era clash so enjoyable in many mashups, their keys are compatible, and the chord progressions blend quite well. Additionally, they each have a quirky six-measure section, and have similar chord progressions. The lyrical content shares a similar cynicism, and the songs' moods are compatible. Most importantly, they simply sound good when played together. Draw an event that lasts the duration of the song on each of your two tracks, and click Play. You can tell right away that the songs blend well and have synergy. Even though the sections don't line up, and there are competing vocalists starting at bar 17, the tracks sound great together and exhibit potential. This is the quickest way of determining song compatibility: beatmap the tracks, draw the entire song in each track, and click Play. The results are rarely as listenable as the simple mashup in Chapter 1, but the less it hurts your ears or assaults your sensibilities, the greater the chances that you have the beginnings of a successful mashup.

At this point, the two tracks are in pretty good sync, even though the sections do not line up perfectly. The ability to recognize and correct these misalignments is very helpful. Try out the following example to purposely misalign the tracks at varying degrees so you can hear what the misalignments sound like:

1. Place your cursor at beat one, measure one, and zoom in horizontally until you can see beat marker 1.1.048, one sixty-fourth note into the ACID project. This is such a small interval that it will probably not register as a rhythmic duration.

2. Slide the "Sweet Dreams" track over so that it starts right at 1.1.048. Click the Play button.

The music will sound not horrible, but a bit sloppy. This is kind of what it sounds like when an unskilled DJ is trying to do beatmatching. Although it's possible that this sort of looseness is desirable, it is usually the result of accidental misalignment rather than purposeful loosening of the rhythm.

Your ears are usually the first clue to this sort of misalignment, and then you can zoom in and visually confirm the source of the looseness. The solution is either to drag the event over until it lines up, or if you've incorrectly beatmapped the track, you may have to redo the process. If you're dealing with a track with variable rhythm, these slight misalignments will happen all the time, and require extra work to fix. This is covered in detail in Chapter 9.

3. Place your cursor at beat one, measure one, and zoom in horizontally until you can see beat marker 1.1.192, one sixteenth note into the ACID project.

4. Slide the "Sweet Dreams" event over so that it starts a sixteenth note late, and the event starts playing right at 1.1.192.

5. Click the Play button. The music will just sound wrong. Both of these songs have rhythms that emphasize eighth notes, and in fact there are no sixteenth notes in either song. Many songs do have sixteenth notes, however, but usually a misalignment this small will be as obvious and jarring as it is with these two songs.

6. Move the "Sweet Dreams" event a little further forward, so that it starts on beat 1.1.384, an eighth note too late, and click Play. The track now sounds tight again, but somehow off. The vocals of the Eurythmics come in too late, and the kick drums of the "Sweet Dreams" track fall in between the kick drums of the "Policy of Truth" track, creating a very busy kick drum pattern.

■ It can be quite difficult to figure out exactly what's wrong with a couple of misaligned tracks, and usually the best thing to do is to solo each one, figure out where the downbeat is, and make sure the downbeat of the track falls on beat number one in the beat grid.

■ Another useful technique is to pan one track all the way to the right and pan the other track all the way to the left, and play them, preferably through headphones. This has the effect of unmixing the two tracks and letting your brain more easily discern where the problem is.

7. Try playing the two tracks with "Sweet Dreams" starting on beats 1.2 and beats 1.3, representing quarter and half note misalignments. The trouble with these offsets is that the rhythm sounds so tight. The kick drums of "Sweet Dreams" line up perfectly with "Policy of Truth." But at the same time, certain sounds just don't seem to land in the ideal spots. Again, the easiest way to correct this is to solo each track and look for the downbeat in each one, making sure that they line up.

8. If you start the "Sweet Dreams" event on beats 2.1 or 3.1, the two tracks will sound really good together. However, the sections still don't exactly line up, and the changes seem to occur in one track right in the middle of the other track's section. In fact, this section-level misalignment will occur even when both tracks start right at 1.1.

9. Drag "Sweet Dreams" back to 1.1 again and click Play.

It sounds pretty good. There is a four-measure instrumental introduction, and then Annie Lennox starts singing. Her first vocal section is eight bars long. However, halfway through it, at 9.1.1, the Depeche Mode track's main instrumental hook starts in. A new section begins in the Depeche Mode track, right in the midst of a "Sweet Dreams" section. Although you may want the instrumental hook to begin there, it shouldn't be out of laziness, but rather because you want it to start right in the middle of the "Sweet Dreams" section.

Quickly looking at the lengths of the sections from the beginning of each song, you can see where the problem lies. The "Sweet Dreams" track starts with a four-measure intro, followed by an eight-measure vocal section, followed by yet another eight-measure vocal section. The "Policy of Truth" track starts off with an eight-measure instrumental section, followed by another eight-measure instrumental section (with the main hook), followed by an eight-bar vocal track. These sections are visualized in Figure 7-9.

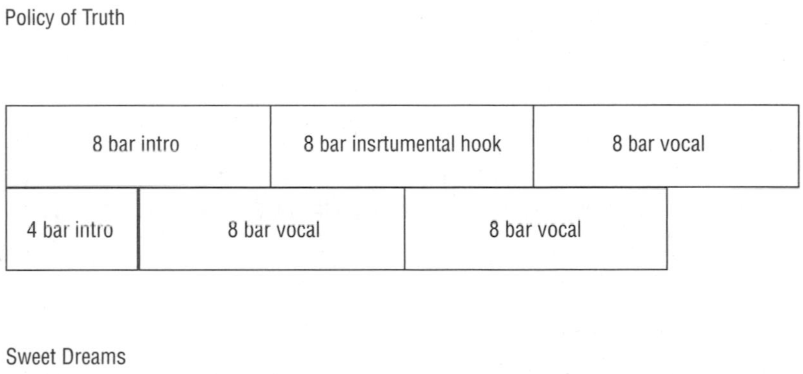

Policy of Truth

8 bar intro	8 bar insrtumental hook	8 bar vocal
4 bar intro	8 bar vocal	8 bar vocal

Sweet Dreams

FIGURE 7-9: An example of section misalignment

10. Line up the sections in one of the following ways:

- Double the "Sweet Dreams" intro so that the instrumental hook of "Policy of Truth" comes in right when the vocals come in. In this case, the Depeche Mode vocals starts right when the second vocal section of the Eurythmics started. Usually you do not want to have two vocals playing at the same time, so you probably would want to replace one of the two competing vocal sections with an instrumental section, cut and pasted from elsewhere in the track. This potential solution is shown in Figure 7-10.

- Shift the Depeche Mode event four bars later, lining up its intro with the first vocal section of "Sweet Dreams" while the eight-bar instrumental hook is lined up with the second vocal section from "Sweet Dreams." Then cut the Depeche Mode eight-bar intro in half, and copy and paste it to the beginning, layering it with the four-bar Eurythmics intro, as shown in Figure 7-11.

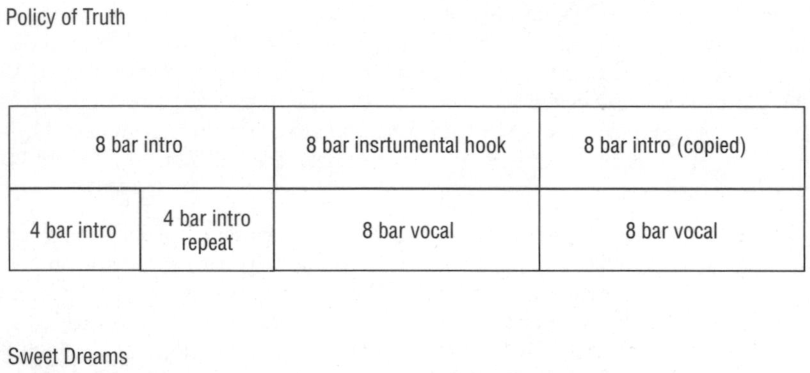

Policy of Truth

8 bar intro		8 bar insrtumental hook	8 bar intro (copied)
4 bar intro	4 bar intro repeat	8 bar vocal	8 bar vocal

Sweet Dreams

FIGURE 7-10: One solution to the section misalignment in Figure 7-9

Policy of Truth

half of 8 bar intro	8 bar intro	8 bar instrumental hook
4 bar intro	8 bar vocal	8 bar vocal

Sweet Dreams

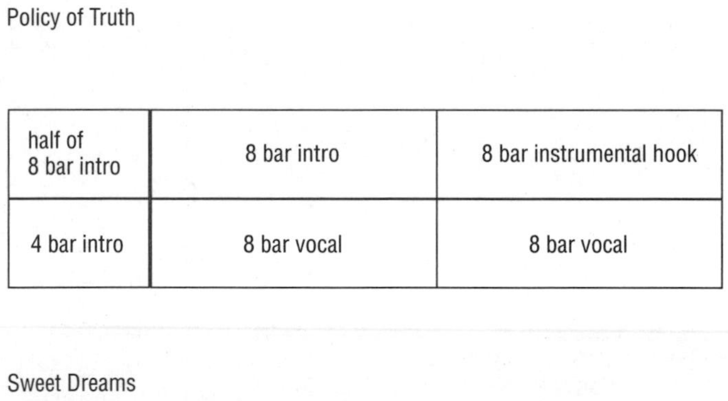

FIGURE 7-11: Another solution to the section misalignment in Figure 7-9

You need to line up the right foreground and background sections to make your mashup flow smoothly. The order in which the sections play is also very important. Chapter 11 discusses arrangement in much greater detail.

Syncing Acapellas

Lining up rhythmic events to ACID's grid is pretty straightforward. The fact that there are visually detectable rhythmic elements helps you line up the percussive sounds with precision beyond even what you can easily hear. Lining up acapellas to ACID's grid can be a bit more difficult. Even the most rhythmic of rappers will not be robotic like a drum machine or click track. Because of this, you need to take extra steps when handling acapellas.

Using the Full Song

The easiest way to line up an acapella to ACID's grid is to first get your hands on the full song with vocals and instruments. Line it up to ACID's grid using the method already outlined in this chapter, assuming it has a constant bpm. Then, drop the acapella into the project, and line it up to the full version so the two vocal tracks sound exactly like one. Afterward, you can remove the full version, and your acapella will retain the same timing as the full song without you having to make a bunch of judgment calls or errors, or do a lot of hard work. Sometimes the acapella will have a slightly different arrangement from the full mix, in which case, you can only line up the portions that are identical. Other times, the vocals from the full mix and the acapella will be identical throughout. Because the full song is only being used for reference, it doesn't matter so much if it has low-quality audio.

If you want to work along with the example, download "Whoomp! (There It Is) [Radio Edit]" from the iTunes Store, and convert the audio file to an mp3 or wav. This is the full version, not the acapella from Chapter 1, although you'll need the acapella as well for this exercise.

Drop the file into ACID and beatmap it using either the Beatmapper Wizard if you have ACID Pro, or using the manual beatmapping method outlined in this chapter. "Whoomp!" has a pretty well-defined first beat. There is a short vocal, and then the first kick drum signifies beat 1.1 as is so often the case. The tempo should be around 129.421, and the downbeat offset should be around 105,359. Don't worry if your values differ from these slightly. As long as your percussive sounds line up with ACID's grid, you should be okay.

Listening to the acapella of this song, it starts with the line "Party people." This is the same vocal that starts off the full song, right before beat one kicks in. The problem is that because it comes before beat one in the beatmap, the intro vocal is cut off when you draw or paint the event. Ideally, you'd like to line up the two vocals starting from the very first utterance, which in this case is not yet audible or visible in the ACID project because it comes before beat number 1. There is just over one bar of pure vocals in the full song before the drums kick in, so drag the full song event over to beat marker 3.1. Any beat marker will do, as long as there is enough room for the intro. Now, using the draw tool, extend the left side of the full song all the way to the left until you reach the beginning of the track. Make sure you drag the left edge of the event, or you will just move the event instead of extending it. Your event should now start somewhere right before beat 1.4.

Snap Warning

It's important to realize something about ACID's snapping function at this point. When you drag an event in ACID, the beginning of the event snaps to ACID's grid. This is great when your event starts right on a downbeat, but it has undesirable effects when your event starts at some other point. Now that you've extended your event to start at some point before the initial downbeat, your event no longer starts at a point that should be lined up to the grid. This event will remain perfectly in sync as it is, but if you were to drag it now, the new beginning would line up to ACID's grid instead of the downbeat lining up to the grid. For this reason, you need to take extra effort when dragging events that do not start on a downbeat. The usual method is to shorten the event so the beginning does start on a downbeat, and then drag the event to its new location, allowing the snap to maintain synchronicity between the event's internal beat and ACID's beat grid. Then, lengthen the event again so the event starts where you want it to. Another approach is to lengthen your event so it starts at an earlier downbeat, drag it, and then shorten it again. This extra step is inconvenient, but it is a lot easier than manually realigning your event each time you move it.

Now you can drop in the "Whoomp!" acapella into ACID, canceling the Beatmapper Wizard if you are using ACID Pro, and follow these steps:

1. In the General tab of the acapella's Properties window, set the type to Beatmapped if it is not already, and make sure the Preserve Pitch When Stretching check box is checked. This will be in the clip's Properties window in ACID Pro 6.

2. In the Stretch tab of the acapella's Properties window, set the Original Tempo to the same value as the Original Tempo of the full song. Also, make sure the downbeat offset of your acapella is set to 0 (zero), because you will not necessarily be snapping the beginning of your acapella to a significant beat in ACID's grid.

 Note There is no guarantee that the acapella's bpm will be identical to the full version, but it's usually a good starting point, unless your full song is a remix where the original tempo has been significantly altered. If you are manipulating an officially released acapella, chances are the more recently your acapella was released, the more likely that the tempos will be identical between the full version and the acapella.

3. Line up the first vocal phrase of the two tracks, moving the acapella so it speaks at the exact same time as the full song. Remember to concentrate only on lining the first phrase at first, dragging the acapella so that it sounds close, zooming in and refining, and repeating the process until the two vocal tracks sound like one. It should sound like one single vocal with no echoes or doubling.

In the case of "Whoomp!," it turns out that the beginnings of the two tracks will pretty much line up with each other and they will sound like a single voice. Both will start around beat 1.3.657, although your numbers may differ. As long as the two vocals sound like one *at the beginning*, you're in good shape.

Note Sometimes you can line up the vocals visually, but most of the time the nonvocal elements in the full mix obscure the vocals, making visual synchronization difficult. Your ears are the best judge, because you can tell pretty easily whether it sounds like two vocals or one. If there is an echo, it can be hard to tell which track is speaking or singing first. If this happens, you can try panning one track all the way to the left and the other track all the way to the right. In this case, a perfectly synced acapella will sound like it's panned dead center, while all the instruments are panned all the way to one side.

4. Click the Play button and listen to the tracks to make sure that they stay aligned throughout.

   If the acapella's bpm differs from the full song's bpm, the two vocals will start to sound slightly doubled, eventually becoming an obvious echo. You will notice this happen with the two "Whoomp!" tracks. Even though they start perfectly aligned, pretty soon the echo becomes obvious and sloppy. What this means is that you will need to adjust the acapella's bpm. It's easiest if you adjust it while listening to a later portion of the track where the misalignment has become more obvious.

5. In the Stretch tab of the acapella's Properties window, adjust the Original Tempo. If you don't initially know whether to speed up or slow down the acapella, simply try to adjust it one way, and if the echo gets worse, try adjusting it the other way. Pressing the Ctrl key while dragging the bar in between the up and down arrows next to the Original Tempo text box is a quick way to adjust this tempo while listening to the results. In this example, the acapella in "Whoomp!" is a bit slower than the full song, and you will need to bring the Original Tempo down to a value of about 129.369. At this tempo, the tracks not only start out in sync, but finish in sync as well.

Sometimes there may be a bit of silence before the acapella's initial vocal, although it's very short in this example. But you may possibly encounter a silence long enough that when you find the new tempo that syncs up the vocals toward the end of the track, that the initial phrase is now offset. If this happens, simply realign the initial phrases, and then fine-tune the tempo again so the ending lines up. To minimize this potential effect, trim off any silence at the beginning of your acapella before starting the syncing process.

Syncing Acapellas Without Having the Full Song

If you don't have access to the full song containing the acapella you want to use, you can still sync the vocals up to ACID's grid. The method is similar to matching up rhythmic material, but because the rhythmic cues aren't as distinct, sometimes it takes a few adjustments and readjustments. Try this:

1. Sync up your background track to ACID's grid, using the techniques described earlier in the chapter.

2. If your background track has vocals in it, find a one, two, four, eight, or sixteen bar instrumental section that sounds good looped. One easy way to find this section is to click the Loop Playback button in ACID's transport (or simply type **Q**), and then adjust the loop bar above the timeline. You can change the length of the loop bar by dragging either end of it to the left or right.

3. Trim this loop, either by using the Time selection tool and the trim function (Ctrl+T) or by splitting the event on either side of the loop. Select and copy the loop by clicking on it and pressing Ctrl+C. Now position your cursor at beat 1.1 and press Ctrl+B to paste repeat. Paste it in 100 times (or some large number) end-to-end. You now have an instrumental backing track, although it's a bit dull.

4. Listen to the acapella and select a fairly rhythmic portion of it near the beginning of the song. If the beginning isn't rhythmic — like the "party people" shouted at the beginning of "Whoomp!" — you may need to look further.

5. Draw the entire acapella track in ACID, and trim it so it starts just before the rhythmic portion you've identified. Place this vocal portion on the beat at which it occurs in the regular song. This is where familiarity with the full mix helps, even if you don't have it on hand.

6. In the Stretch panel of the Track/Clip Properties window, roughly adjust the bpm so the first few seconds of your vocal sound in sync. (It doesn't matter if there isn't a high level of precision at first.)

7. This step is similar to manually beatmapping a rhythmic audio file. Go through the song, roughly doubling the number of your beat markers each time, and adjust the tempo at each point, fine-tuning the synchronization, until you are to the end of your track. If you find at some point that the initial vocal has lost its sync, move the initial vocal and repeat the process. If your acapella has a constant underlying bpm, you should be able to line up the vocals pretty tightly with this method.

If after considerable struggle, the vocals just don't seem to line up throughout, perhaps your acapella doesn't have a constant bpm. Chapter 9 covers variable bpm songs.

Breaking It Down

As long as your tracks have a constant tempo, you should be able to sync them up pretty well. Well-matched rhythms are the foundation of good mashups. Now it's time to get your component songs in key, which is equally important and is covered in the next chapter.

Shifting the Pitch

One of the features of ACID that has made it the mashup producer's tool of choice for years is its ability to alter pitch and tempo independently of each other. In fact, it is this capability that helps to distinguish computer-based mashups from traditional turntablism, where tempo and pitch are inextricably linked together.

When matching two records, a vinyl-based DJ will usually have to speed up or slow down one of the records. Beatmatching is the most fundamental aspect of blending two records, and if they drift out of sync, it will be obvious to all listeners, regardless of their musical background. Songs that are out of key with each other are sometimes tolerated in a vinyl environment. Often the transitions are short enough that the key clash isn't too painful, and often in dance remixes there are long stretches where there are no pitched elements, so that the blended portions don't contain any key clash. Often the key clash is simply tolerated. Sometimes a DJ can actually find two records that are in the same key and near enough to the same tempo that the pitch shift introduced when slowing down or speeding up one of the records doesn't shift the pitch so far that it sounds out of key.

With ACID, any two tempos and keys can potentially be pitch-shifted and time-stretched until they match. This allows for consistent layering of beat-matched tonal music without key clash.

Time-Warping Basics

In all likelihood, the songs you select will not be precisely the same tempo, although they may be close. If you're using ACID's built-in time warping, there is an important distinction between speeding a song up and slowing it down.

If you don't preserve the pitch when stretching, the pitch will go up and down with the tempo, much like vinyl or tape. No new information is created or destroyed: A slower speed lowers all frequencies within the sound wave, literally stretching the waveform itself. Conversely, speeding it up will raise all the frequencies in the sound wave, simply compressing the waveform.

Fast Fourier Transform

In the early 19th century, a French mathematician named Jean Baptiste Fourier discovered that any waveform could be precisely recreated by adding up pure sine waves of various frequencies. Each of these pure tones would have its own varying amplitude and phase. *Fast Fourier Transform* (*FFT*) is a signal processing mathematical technique that breaks apart a waveform into these component sine wave bands. Each of these signals added up should approximate the original waveform. Breaking the signal apart in this way allows various forms of manipulation of the audio data that would otherwise not be possible. Most time-warping and pitch-shifting algorithms employ FFT, as do center channel extraction algorithms, discussed in Chapter 10.

Although any waveform can be represented by a number of sine waves, the number of discrete frequencies necessary to create a *perfectly* identical copy may be very large, even infinite. FFT approximates this perfect solution by reducing the number of sine wave components to a manageable amount.

Because almost all waveforms have varying frequency components over time, FFT takes a series of snapshots, called *frames*, each one containing a complete set of frequencies with phase and amplitude information. The smaller these frames get, the more precise the timing information is. Unfortunately, the frequency information becomes less precise because there is less data to analyze per frame. Conversely, as the frame size increases, the frequency information gets more accurate because there is more data per frame to analyze. Alas, because each frame represents a larger amount of time, the timing becomes less accurate. There is no way around this unpleasant tradeoff of frequency precision versus timing precision. Nevertheless, FFT's powerful form of analysis makes it a frequent element of signal-processing algorithms.

When you preserve the pitch while speeding up a waveform, FFT is usually employed. Although ACID's exact method of time-warping is a trade secret, it most likely involves some flavor of FFT. If you speed up a song while preserving the pitch, you actually destroy information. The number of frames from the FFT analysis will need to be reduced in order to play them back faster, and some frames will be discarded. A new waveform will then be generated by summing up the frequency components in each remaining frame. Contrast this with non-pitch-preserving speeding up, where the frequencies increase, the wavelengths shorten, and no information is lost. The same waveform is playing, just at a higher speed. This has higher fidelity, but doesn't allow you to manipulate pitch and speed independently.

If you preserve the pitch while slowing down the same waveform, there will not be enough frames to fill up the new, longer duration. An FFT-based time-stretching algorithm will need to add extra frames to fill in the gaps. These new frames are derived from existing frames, calculating reasonable values from the surrounding frames. In this case, you are actually creating new information rather than destroying it. If you were to slow down the sound wave without pitch preservation, the waveform would simply be stretched, and no information would be gained or lost.

For this reason, time stretching with pitch preservation can create some nasty *artifacts*, undesirable components of sound waves created as a result of processing. When the algorithm adds the new frames, sometimes the rapid attack of percussive sounds can be doubled, making an unpleasant out-of-sync sound, similar to when two instrumental components aren't lining up properly, even though you only have one audio file playing. Other times, the sharp attacks are simply diffused, so that the attack is more gradual and less defined. This is known as *transient smearing*. These artifacts are often worse in pitch-preserving time-stretching than in pitch-preserving time-compression.

Note Smearing is practically eliminated for integer ratios of stretching. So if you exactly double the length of a wave, you will probably get very crisp results. However, this is a pretty radical tempo shift!

Figures 8-1 and 8-2 show this effect clearly. A *pulse wave* is a waveform with a series of evenly spaced spikes that will graphically show the unpleasant artifacts possible with ACID's pitch-preserving time stretching. In Figure 8-1, they are evenly spaced, and there is a series of single spikes, representing an extremely sharp attack. As you can see in Figure 8-2, each spike is irregularly doubled after being processed with ACID's time-stretching algorithm.

There is a simple lesson to be learned from all this. If you are preserving the pitch, usually speeding up audio is preferable to slowing it down.

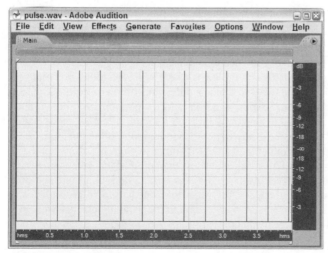

FIGURE 8-1: A pulse wave

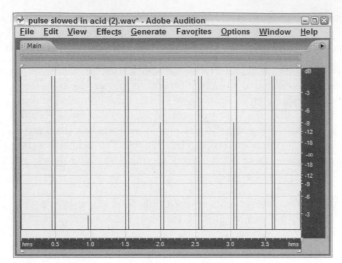

FIGURE 8-2: The same waveform as Figure 8-1, slowed down with ACID's pitch preservation

Using ACID's Built-In Pitch-Shifting

Unless you are using unpitched source material, you will often need to use ACID's built-in pitch-shifting and time-warping. Although ACID does this in real time, as you've just seen, the results can be less than perfect.

 In ACID Pro, when you check the Preserve Pitch When Stretching check box in the Stretch panel of a track's properties, the drop-down box becomes enabled, allowing you to choose from various types of time-stretching and pitch-shifting. Here is where ACID Pro allows you more control over the software's compromise between sustained notes and transient notes. Some modes focus more on percussive (transient) sounds, and others focus more on long, drawn-out (sustained) sounds. The crisper the percussive (transient) notes sound, often the more warbly the sustained notes will sound. When your sustained notes sound smooth, often the drums will actually echo, sounding like two drums rather than one. With other settings, the attacks of the drums will smear. For this reason, even ACID Pro can sound less than professional when you're pitching up or slowing down a track. However, ACID does a reasonably good job at pitching down or speeding up a track, because data is actually lost rather than needing to be generated, and the smearing or doubling of transients is not an issue. Although the default mode will work in many situations, it may be worthwhile to experiment with these various modes to discover the ideal mode for your audio.

Shifting the pitch couldn't be easier in ACID. Simply select a track and press the plus or minus key on your computer keyboard. A number will appear next to your track name, signifying the number of semitones the track has been shifted. If you want to shift only part of a track, select just the event or events you want to transpose, and press the plus or minus key. A number will show up in the lower-left corner of each shifted event, signifying the amount of transposition. If you want to shift a clip in ACID Pro 6, you'll need to enter it manually into the Pitch Shift setting in the General tab of the Track/Clip Properties. You can alter a track's tempo pretty significantly and still have it sound realistic, but altering the pitch has a much more noticeable effect. Transposing a track by a semitone may not be noticeable by some, but those more famil-iar with the source material may notice the difference. Transposing a track by two semitones will probably be noticeable by most people, even if they are not familiar with the source mate-rial. Transposing by three or more semitones will have obvious effects. Transposition is most noticeable on tracks with vocals. If your source material has no vocals, or you are using only the instrumental portions, you may be able to get away with a larger amount of transposition.

Because of the lower quality of time-stretching and pitch-shifting when audio data is being created rather than being destroyed, you may want to use external time-stretching/pitch-shifting software in these cases. Indeed, you may choose to use external software in all cases. Another way to ensure higher quality is to make sure that you are never shifting the pitch upward or slowing the tempo while preserving the pitch. If your two tracks are a semitone apart, you may want to transpose the higher one down a semitone. If your two tracks are in the same key but different tempos, you may want to speed up the slower one rather than slow down the faster one.

The Relationship Between Pitch-Shifting and Time-Warping

Stretching or compressing the time while preserving the pitch is very similar to shifting the pitch while preserving the tempo. As previously discussed, FFT is required for pitch-preserving time-warping. However, simply speeding up or slowing down the audio playback will not require any fidelity-reducing FFT operations.

If you stretch audio while preserving the pitch, you'll generate new audio data. If you then simply speed up the stretched audio by increasing playback speed, you'll have an audio signal with the original tempo but a higher pitch.

If you compress the audio while preserving the pitch, you'll lose audio data. If you then slow down the compressed audio by lowering the playback speed, you'll have an audio signal with the original tempo but a lower pitch.

Therefore, the algorithm for time-stretching is similar to that of pitch-shifting upwards, both creating new audio data, and the algorithm for time compression is similar to that of pitch-shifting downwards, both losing audio data.

But what happens if you are simultaneously pitch-shifting and time-stretching? How do you know if you are creating or destroying data? If you are both slowing down and pitching up, you are performing two similar operations that both create data, neither of which sounds great with ACID's built-in capabilities. If you are speeding a track up while pitching it down, you are destroying data in both cases, and ACID's built-in capabilities may sound okay. If you are speeding up a track and pitching it up, or slowing it down while pitching it down, you might want to figure out whether your tempo adjustment is greater or less than the amount of pitch adjustment. As a rough guide, transposing a track down one semitone produces a data loss of between 5 and 6 percent, so if the amount of tempo increase (in percent) is less than 5 or 6 times the number of semitones transposed up, you're probably in a situation where ACID is creating rather than destroying data, and the stretching may double the drums or sound warbly or smeared. Likewise, if your percentage of tempo decrease is greater than 5 or 6 times the number of semitones transposed down, you may also be in a data-creation mode, which might not sound great in ACID. Although this effect can be subtle to some ears, it is nearly impossible to get truly professional-sounding results within ACID in pitched up/slowed down situations.

If you are altering both the tempo and pitch of a track, it is easy to be confused as to which mode you are in. This book's CD-ROM contains a spreadsheet that will tell you with precision whether or not you are in a data creation or destruction mode. If you open the Up Time Stretching Pitch Shifting.xls file in Excel (or Open Office), you can type in the original tempo of the track and the new tempo. You can also type in the number of semitones that you are transposing the track. The spreadsheet will then tell you the amount of data loss or gain, the equivalent tempo shift without pitch shift, and the equivalent pitch shift without tempo shift. If there is a net data gain, you may want to consider external time-stretching and pitch-shifting algorithms, described later in this chapter.

Chipmunk Alert

You may have heard of Alvin and the Chipmunks, a popular musical act from the late 1950s and early 1960s. They had a series of hits featuring high-pitched, squeaky voices that are humanly impossible to produce. In the studio, the background tracks were recorded normally and then played back at half-speed. The vocalists then recorded the singing at a normal pitch but a very slow tempo. After recording, the playback was set back to normal speed, and the vocalists' voices were sped up, raising their pitch by an octave. Although a vocalist could have simply sung it in the final pitch and tempo, the technique of speeding up the tape had quite a different effect on the *tone* of the voice. The voices sounded like they were coming from a smaller creature with a smaller mouth and throat than a regular human. This effect was no accident, and in fact won the Chipmunks' creator a Grammy award for engineering.

This effect is interesting and fun, but it is not a substitute for the vocalist actually singing in the higher pitch. So what is it that makes a sped-up recording sound like it's coming from a small woodland creature rather than a singer just singing in a higher pitch? Formants.

Formants

As briefly discussed in Chapter 4, *formants* are natural peaks in the frequency spectrum that occur in the resonance of a tone. In the human voice, the vocal chords produce a tone with a large number of overtones. This sound is then amplified in the mouth, throat, and nose, which act as resonating chambers. As with all resonance, certain frequencies are amplified more than others, depending on the chamber's size and shape. If you've ever wondered why many musical instruments have such strange shapes, it is mostly so that the resonating chambers will have an appropriate tone. The larger a resonating chamber, the lower the frequencies that are amplified. It's important to note that the fundamental frequency is not changed, but rather, different overtones are emphasized.

When a vocalist produces a tone, a broad array of frequencies is generated, including many overtones of the fundamental pitch. The vocalist then shapes his or her mouth and throat, which produces various sets of formants that we recognize as different vowels. No matter what the resonated pitch is, each vowel's formants stay constant. A smaller mouth and throat will produce a higher set of formants.

When you're performing a simple upward pitch shift on vocal material, the fundamental frequency, overtones, and formants are all shifted equally, whether or not the tempo is preserved. This has the effect of not only transposing the vocal, but making the vocal appear to be coming from a smaller mouth and throat as well. If you were to have a more natural-sounding pitch shift, you would shift the fundamental frequency and all its overtones, but keep the formants untransposed. ACID doesn't offer this type of pitch-shifting. Indeed, most available software packages do not allow for the independent manipulation of formants.

The easiest way to grasp the difference between formant-corrected pitch-shifting and ordinary pitch-shifting is to listen to some audio examples. Listen to the following audio examples on the CD-ROM. First is an unaltered recording of George W. Bush's 2001 inauguration speech.

Audio Example 8-1: George W. Bush.

Now, listen to the same speech transposed up an octave without any formant preservation. This is the classic chipmunk effect. Notice how it sounds like it's coming from a very small creature with a tiny mouth.

Audio Example 8-2: George W. Bush transposed up an octave without formant preservation.

The next example is also transposed up an octave, but the formants are preserved. It still sounds a bit strange, because an octave is a pretty extreme amount to transpose a track. In practice, an octave shift probably won't sound realistic no matter what, but for the purposes of these examples, it highlights the effect of preserving formants. Go back and forth listening to Audio Examples 8-2 and 8-3 to hear the difference.

Audio Example 8-3: George W. Bush transposed up an octave with formants preserved.

The next example has the same recording lowered an octave without formant preservation. Notice how the vowels become unintelligible. This is because vowels are each defined by a set of formants. If those formants are shifted too radically, they become unrecognizable.

Audio Example 8-4: George W. Bush transposed down an octave without formant preservation.

The final example, although still a bit scary-sounding, has the formants preserved, and is quite intelligible.

Audio Example 8-5: George W. Bush transposed down an octave with formants preserved.

These examples show the value of formant preservation in pitch-shifting, which can add intelligibility and realism to your processed vocals.

Using External Pitch-Shifting

If you really want professional quality pitch-shifting, you will need to outsource your transposition needs to external software, and then replace your original audio material with the doctored results. If you are not too fussy, you can simply let ACID do all the work for you. The improvements achieved through using other software can be subtle, and it is up to you to decide whether it's worth the effort.

It may be because ACID is capable of performing multiple real-time pitch shifts simultaneously, or perhaps it's just the algorithm ACID uses, but other dedicated pitch-shifting tools outperform ACID, especially for slow-downs and pitch-ups, with minimal flanging, warbling, or smearing artifacts. Not only is the sound quality improved, but some pitch-shifting software can preserve the formants of a transposed track, allowing you greater control of the tone quality, especially with a transposed vocal.

Software Platforms

If you are going through all of the trouble to use an external pitch-shifter, you might as well get your hands on one that can preserve the formants. There are two approaches.

If you are using the Pro version of ACID, you can use a real-time VST plug-in, like Waves' Ultrapitch, Arboretum's Hyperprism, or FMJ's AnyTime, all of which correct formants.

The advantage to this approach is that you can get real-time formant-preserved pitch-shifting without leaving ACID. A drawback, however, is that you may be using ACID's time-stretching in addition to an external pitch-shifter, performing two pitch/time altering operations instead of allowing ACID to perform it all in one step. Pitch and time scaling is never 100% clean, so the fewer operations you can do, usually the better. However, it is not possible to outsource your time-stretching to a plug-in, since plug-ins operate in real time.

Non-real-time standalone platforms offer the possibility of high-quality time-stretching and pitch-shifting all in one step. This will enhance the quality of your final sound, but requires a bit of effort, because you will need to replace your original audio material with the altered sound file. If you are performing external time-stretching, the timing of your new track will differ from the original, and your event offsets in ACID will be displaced and need to be corrected. Standalone platforms include Prosoniq's TimeFactory and Celemony's Melodyne, both of which offer formant correction.

Prosoniq's TimeFactory

Prosoniq's platform is the only tool of this bunch that claims to preserve pitch on a polyphonic audio file, whereas others operate only monophonically. *Monophonic* means that only one note is playing at a time, and *polyphonic* means multiple notes are playing simultaneously. Translated, that means that TimeFactory can perform formant-preserving pitch-shifting on both full songs and acapellas, and other platforms perform well only on acapellas with no background or overlapping vocals.

Celemony's Melodyne

Melodyne is a remarkable tool that can not only manipulate the pitch and timing of an acapella, but can retime and repitch individual notes, changing the melody or rhythm of the vocal, all with formant correction. Because the audio file's pitch is detected throughout the duration of the acapella, much more advanced control is offered than within ACID.

ZPlane's élastique

Included on this book's CD-ROM (or downloadable at www.zplane.de/Downloads/ elastiquePro.zip) is a free demo of some formant-preserving time-stretching/pitching-shifting software from ZPlane, (the same people who make tONaRT, the key detection software discussed in Chapter 6). Unfortunately, this software doesn't allow for the export of the resultant sound, so unless you use internal audio recording software such as Audacity (introduced in Chapter 3), you will be unable to actually export the sounds into ACID. However, it may be educational to play around with it and listen to various pitch-shifting with and without formant correction. If you want to listen to a sound pitch-shifted with formant preservation, select monophonic mode, and if you want to listen to the regular pitch-shifting, set it to default mode (see Figure 8-3). The newest version of élastiquePro includes pitch-shifting with polyphonic formant preservation, so it's worth a download.

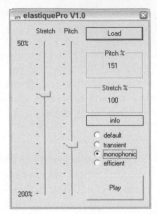

FIGURE 8-3: élastiquePro set to
monophonic (formant-preserving) mode

Replacing the Track

If you are performing no time-stretching in your external pitch-shifting software, replacing your audio file with the altered one is straightforward. Toward the upper-right corner of the Track/Clip Properties window in ACID is a button labeled Replace (shown in Chapter 5 in Figure 5-1). This will be the Track/Clip Properties window in ACID Pro 6. Simply click this button and navigate to the replacement file. If your new file is an mp3 and the tempo has been left unchanged, your track will retain the timing with the new file. However, if your replacement track is a wav file (which it most likely is), ACID will treat the replacement as a one-shot, discarding the timing information. You will then need to switch back to Beatmapped mode in the Track/Clip Properties window and reenter the original tempo and downbeat offset in the Stretch tab of the window. Because of this unwanted switch to one-shot mode, it's a good idea to jot down these two settings before replacing the wav. If you forget, don't worry — simply press Ctrl+Z to undo the replacement, write down the two numbers, and perform the replacement again.

If you're performing external time-stretching or compression, however, the situation is considerably more complicated. The problem is that ACID stores each event's duration in beats, but the start offsets are measured in samples. So while the duration of each event will be correct in a time-shifted replacement track, the start points will all be incorrect, and will need to be fixed individually! As you might imagine, this can be a time-consuming pain. For this reason, if you do opt for external pitch/time manipulation, it's best to do it early on in your project, before you cut and paste a lot and create many events. As soon as you have decided to take your project seriously, and you have determined the final desired key and tempo, you can perform your external time-stretching.

There are two parts to this process. First, you'll create the retimed and repitched wav file, and then you'll replace the original. For the purposes of this chapter, external time-stretching will be described using Prosoniq's TimeFactory, but other tools will work as well.

Follow these steps:

1. Convert your audio file into a wav file, if it is not already in that format. You can do this easily in iTunes or ACID. The method is described in the "Converting mp3s to wavs" sidebar in Chapter 6.

Many time/pitch software platforms will actually accept mp3s as input, but very few will accept Apple's proprietary format. TimeFactory accepts only wav and aif files.

2. Choose Open Audio File from the Edit menu and navigate to your wav file. Alternatively, you can just drop the wav file onto the TimeFactory window.

3. Under the Algorithm menu, choose Monophonic/Voice/Instr if you are processing an acapella, or choose Polyphonic (best) if you are processing a full track. Make sure the Preserve Formants check box is checked if you are altering the pitch.

4. Enter the amount of semitones and cents (hundredths of a semitone, as described in Chapter 4) you want to shift the pitch. Negative numbers are acceptable.

5. Enter the percentage you want to expand or compress the time. This is calculated by dividing the original tempo of the audio file by the tempo of your project. The original audio file can be found in the Stretch tab of the Track/Clip Properties of your beatmapped track.

If you are slowing the track down, your percentage will be greater than 100, and if you are speeding it up, your percentage will be lower than 100.

6. Save the wav file with a new name, using Save As from the File menu.

If you want to use other software to alter the time and pitch of your track, you can achieve good results. Just remember that tempo and duration have an inverse relationship, so if you are increasing the duration by 20 percent, or 1.2 times the original length, you are multiplying the tempo by a factor of 1/1.2, or .8333, decreasing the tempo by 16.7 percent. To put this another way, the new tempo divided by the old tempo is the amount the bpm is altered, and the old tempo divided by the new tempo is the amount the duration is altered.

After you've saved your new wav file, it's time to replace the old one in ACID. Follow these steps:

1. Duplicate your original track (right-click the track in the track list and select Duplicate Track). Retaining a copy of the original track lets you mess around with the replacement track without fear of irrevocably messing it up. Also, you'll need to refer to the events in your original track to calculate the offsets in your new track. Figure 8-4 shows a duplicated track with multiple events ("Stand Tall," from Chapter 1, stretched to 120 bpm).

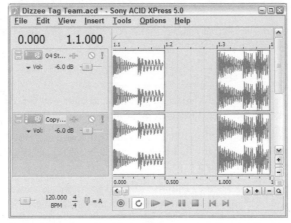

FIGURE 8-4: A track with multiple events after duplication

2. Replace the audio file using the same method outlined in the first paragraph of this section, clicking Replace and navigating to the new wav. This time you do not need to switch the one-shot back into Beatmapped mode, because the tempo of your new wav file is identical to your project. However, all your timing will be off, as shown in Figure 8-5.

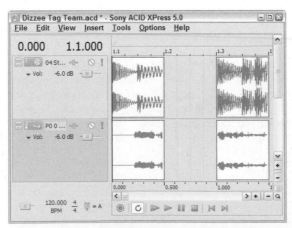

FIGURE 8-5: The second track replaced with an externally stretched copy

Note In general, if your project tempo matches the tempo for one of your audio files, leave the track or clip as a one-shot. Even beatmapping a track without any time warping or pitch shifting will have lower fidelity than a one-shot.

3. For every event in your duplicated track, do the following:

   ▪ Open the Event Properties window by right-clicking the event and selecting Properties. Find the Start Offset (samples) parameter, which is the start offset of the corresponding event in the *original* track. (Do not confuse this with the downbeat offset in the Stretch tab of Track/Clip Properties.)

   ▪ Multiply the offset by the amount the duration was altered (the old track tempo divided by the new track tempo, which is the same as the project tempo). If you slowed the track down, the number of samples will increase, and vice versa.

   ▪ Select the event in your new track and change the Start Offset to this calculated value. Figure 8-6 shows the second track with the new timing information entered for the first event.

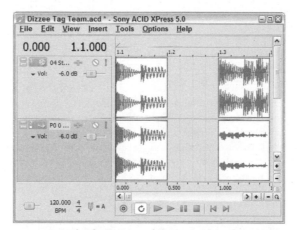

FIGURE 8-6: The first event of the second track with the calculated start offset

After performing this operation for each event in your track, the new, clean-sounding one-shot track should have the same timing and pitch as your beatmapped (and possibly pitch-shifted) track, but with superior sound quality.

4. Delete the old track, or at least mute it if you are not ready to let it go yet.

This may seem like a lot of work for only a small improvement in sound quality, but flanged/doubled drums sound pretty amateurish, and if you can get your hands on a good formant preserving pitch shifter, chances are your listeners won't even realize the sound has been manipulated, which is generally a good thing.

Microtuning

What happens when your songs seem to be in the same key, but still sound a little bit off? It's possible that your tracks are actually not perfectly in key. If you recall from Chapter 4, a perfectly in-tune track will have the pitch of A at 440 Hz. However, due to variations in tape or vinyl, or even out-of-tune guitars in the actual recording, some tracks veer significantly away from perfect intonation.

When the Beatles recorded "Strawberry Fields Forever," for example, they recorded some takes in A and other takes in B♭. They liked portions of both takes, so they decided to use parts of each. They sped up the recording of the takes in A, and slowed down the ones in B♭, until they were both in the same key. However, because A and B♭ are one semitone from each other, the resultant song was pitched somewhere between the two keys. If you played portions of this song with either A or B♭, it would clash.

The way to correct this is through *microtuning*, which is adjusting the pitch of the track in less than whole numbers. A pitch shift of 1.000 will raise your track a semitone, a pitch-shift of 0.100 will raise it 10 cents, and a pitch shift of .010 will raise it one cent. If you feel that your tracks are just a bit out of tune, you can try to shift the pitches in increments of less than a semitone.

This is dangerous, however, because you need a very keen ear to determine whether the keys are in absolutely perfect harmony. and there are many other potential sources of clash besides microtuning, so you might inadvertently make the problem worse!

If you suspect microkey clash as the source of your problem, it's probably best to use tONaRT (described in Chapter 6) to analyze your keys. Assuming your tracks are already generally in key, the only number you're interested in is the Standard Pitch (shown in Figure 6-10 in Chapter 6). If either of your tracks is more than 1 Hz or 2 Hz, you may want to perform a micropitch-shift, entering in fractional values for pitch-shift in the General tab of the Clip or Track/Clip Properties window. Look up the amount of necessary pitch compensation (as described in Table 6-1 in Chapter 6), and add that amount to your current integer pitch-shift value.

Avoiding Chord Clash

Okay, so now you've gotten your tracks perfectly aligned and in key. You've tightened them, de-munchkinized them, microtuned them, and lined them up to submillisecond accuracy. They're both playing at the same time and sound great together. Suddenly, it hits a rough patch. Did the guitarist play a sour note? Did the vocalist sing off key? Listening to the tracks alone, they each sound great, but there's this one part where it just sounds . . . clashy. You've probably encountered *chord clash*. If you remember the discussion about chord progressions in Chapter 4, you'll know that it isn't simply enough for the keys to be aligned, but the chord progressions from each of the component tracks need to be compatible — not identical, but definitely compatible. So what defines compatible chords? Generally, the more notes that two chords have in common, the better they will sound together. So if you are in the key of C major, and have a guitar hitting an F major chord (F, A, C) while a piano is hitting a D minor chord (D, F, A) in a different track, it will sound pretty good, because they share two notes in common. Likewise, if a vocalist is hitting a note within the accompanying chord, it will sound good. If the vocalist hits a note in the background scale that is not in the chord, depending on the melodic contour and emphasis, chances are it'll be okay. However, if the vocalist veers off into pitches not in the scale of the background, you are in trouble!

Note Keep in mind that music will sometimes switch keys, either temporarily or permanently. Sometimes the chorus will be in a different key than the verse. Sometimes a songwriter will insert a key change toward the end of a song, transposing it up a whole step to add extra drama. This is more common in ballads.

There are several approaches to avoiding chord clash.

First, make sure that your songs are in tune with each other. There should be long stretches that don't clash. If you have an acapella that seems to temporarily clash with the background, you can separate the notes that clash into separate events and try to transpose each one separately. For example, if you have one bum note, split the event right before and right after the note, select it, and then raise or lower it with the plus or minus key. This is risky, however, because you are actually altering the vocal melody, which is often the most recognizable component of the mashup. This may be jarring to the listener. Additionally, you need to be careful to split the vocal track at moments of silence, or at the very least, right before an attack. You can visually verify both of these types of potential split points. The elegant solution to altering a melody is to outsource the task to Celemony's Melodyne. This software is amazing, and it is absolutely the perfect tool for reshaping an unadorned vocal melody.

Another solution to all types of chord clash is simply to not use one of the clashing parts. Chances are that one of the clashing tracks is a little harder to find compatible material with than the other. Trash it! Don't forget, you're trying to make one song out of two, so some material will have to go anyway. This is your opportunity.

Supposing the problem-causing section is essential to the track? You can try to cut up the other track and rearrange it until it fits. Sometimes a combination of cutting up and rearranging the other track is necessary. The arrangement you choose can play a large role in the prevention and cure of chord clash. (Chapter 11 covers the concept of arrangement in detail.)

Breaking It Down

ACID's time-stretching/pitch-shifting software is great for rapid prototyping, but lacks the professional quality of other software. Using external software, especially applications that offer formant correction, can enhance a pitch-shifted track's sound quality. With your tracks in the right key and aligned, you are almost ready to assemble your mashup. But first, the next chapter goes a little more in depth about handling hard-to-sync rhythms.

Beyond the Beatmapper: Handling Uneven Tempos

chapter

9

Until now, you've been encouraged to use tracks with constant tempos. Unfortunately, because ACID's beatmapping cannot handle tempo changes within a song, unwavering tempos are much easier to work with. But most of the history of recorded music was performed with live musicians without computerized click tracks. The problem encountered when manipulating these sorts of tracks is that when ACID's rigid tempo is set, the beats will start to drift off of the grid.

You can use any of the following strategies to line up ACID's beat grid with the actual beats in the track:

- You can cut up the track into chunks, lining up each section with ACID's beat grid.

- You can vary ACID's master tempo, creating an uneven beat grid that lines up with the track's beat throughout.

- You can ignore ACID's beat grid entirely, using rhythmic cues from one track to position parts of the other.

- You can open the track in a separate program that can beatmap a variable-tempo song, render it, and then import it back into ACID.

You may also choose to use a combination of techniques if your project has multiple variable-tempo tracks.

This chapter describes the lining up of an entire audio file. In practice, you will line up pieces and chunks more often than an entire song. But if you can line up a whole song, lining up parts of it should be no problem.

Constant Tempo Techniques

Adjusting a component track's beat to ACID's master grid is the most common way of handling uneven tempos. This allows multiple tracks to line up to the same grid. Here are the two general approaches:

- If the tempo variability isn't too great, you can simply cut up the track where the beats start to become offset from the grid and nudge the chunks into place.

- If the variability is so great that cutting and nudging becomes impractical, and you're using ACID Xpress, you can copy the track, set a new tempo for the duplicated track, and possibly combine this technique with the cut-and-nudge method (described in the next section). In ACID Pro 6, you can duplicate the clip and set a different tempo for the new clip all within one track.

Cut and Nudge

When a track with a variable tempo starts to drift off of ACID's grid, often the simplest thing to do is to split the track and realign the remainder to the beat grid. Ideally, you want to do this before the beats get too far misaligned, but not so frequently that every measure is a new chunk. Each time you split the track and move the audio, there is the challenge of making it sound smooth so that there are no sudden changes in the audio signal. The track shouldn't sound like it was cut up.

So how often do you need to realign a variable tempo track? A general rule is that when you can hear the tracks obviously misaligned, it is too late in the timeline. It's important to fix the problem earlier in the timeline, before you can even hear that there is a problem. Fortunately, with ACID's zooming tools, you can often see that there is a problem before you can hear it.

First, create a rough beatmap to get a general tempo for the track. In Chapter 7, when you beatmapped a track with a constant tempo, you repeatedly doubled the amount of audio material you were syncing, refining the overall tempo each time until you had a high level of precision. This technique will not work on a variable tempo track. Each time you double the amount of audio material, the drift may double as well, and if you skip too many measures, you may actually line up measure 99 in ACID with measure 100 from the audio track. For this reason, if you are to obtain an overall average bpm, it's important to step through the entire audio file, adjusting ACID's beat grid every few measures to realign it with the song's beats. Alternatively, you can manually count the number of measures as you listen, and then adjust the tempo until the last discernable measure lines up with the corresponding beat grid in ACID. If finding the average bpm gets too confusing or laborious, you can simply use the initial tempo, although the likelihood of needing multiple beatmaps increases (as described later).

Note You can get a reasonable tempo approximation only if there are small variations in tempo. For more radical tempo shifts, you will need to use the duplicate and re-beatmap method outlined later.

After you've performed this beatmapping process, you'll have a track that starts out perfectly in sync and ends up perfectly in sync, but drifts considerably off the beat grid somewhere in the middle. The following steps show how to fix the drift (the next section contains a step-by-step example of the cut-and-nudge technique):

1. Draw an event as long as the entire track starting at beat one. You can do this with a Ctrl-click with the Paint tool.

2. Solo the track in question and turn on the metronome (in the Options menu). This will create an audible click on each beat of ACID's grid when played.

Note Use the preview slider in the mixer window to adjust the metronome's volume, if necessary.

3. Play the project, and listen to the click track gradually lose sync with the audio file.

4. When you notice that the clicks and beats are becoming misaligned, place the cursor about halfway between the audibly misaligned point and the last beat that was perfectly aligned (beat number 1 in this case). If you prefer extra precision, or if you have difficulty hearing the misalignment until it's very obvious, you may want to go back even more than halfway.

   The point at which you place your cursor is somewhat flexible, but it should be close to a clearly visible rhythmic element that is close to, but slightly offset from, an ACID beat grid line.

5. After you've identified an obvious rhythmic sound (often a kick drum or a snare), zoom in and place the cursor right before the sound's attack. You may need to zoom in a few times and reposition the cursor.

6. Press S on the keyboard, split the audio into two separate events, and reposition the second event so it now starts exactly on ACID's beat grid.

Speeding Up

If the song's tempo has drifted lower, the second event will be too late, and you will have to shift it earlier a bit in time, to the left on the timeline. When you do this, you will be moving the new event so it partially covers the old event — only the small bit of audio after ACID's beat grid has occurred, but before the audio file's rhythmic event has actually occurred. This small bit of audio will be lost in ACID XPress, and cross-faded in ACID Pro 6. For this reason, it's important to realign your track frequently enough that the adjustments are not jarring or audible. If the rhythm seems to lurch forward at your transitions, you may need more frequent adjustments.

Sometimes, the rhythm doesn't seem to lurch forward, but there is still an audible glitch between the two events. If your split point is in the middle of a sung phrase or big note, sometimes the brief drop-out can be quite annoying. Additionally, ACID's default mode is to create a quick fade when an event ends or starts. This is to prevent clicking, which can occur if a waveform jumps in value suddenly. The key to preventing this rough transition between events is to find a very quiet place in the audio, where not so much is going on. This doesn't mean you need to find a new realignment point. Your new event is properly aligned; it's just that the transition is audible. The usual solution is to extend the edge of the second event backwards in time (using the draw tool) until the transition occurs at a quieter and less obtrusive point.

 ACID Pro 6 handles these sorts of transitions more gracefully due to its automatic crossfading feature. However, when you're dragging a clip to the left, the beginning of the clip is automatically crossfaded from the previous clip, making the crisp attack you've identified fade in instead. When this happens, simply drag the beginning of the second clip to the left to a point slightly before the attack of the second event, and then drag the end of the first clip to the left as well, so the crossfade is totally completed before the attack occurs.

Slowing Down

A different set of circumstances happens when the song's tempo has drifted higher, and the second event is now too early. You will need to shift the second event later in time, to the right on the timeline. This can create a jarring gap in the audio that needs to be filled in. Again, this is best done by using the draw tool to drag the left side of the second event to the left until it meets the previous event, or overlaps in the case of ACID Pro 6. With ACID XPress, you may need to drag it a bit further if you can find a better transition point that doesn't have a lot of sound going on. It's important to extend the second event to the left, filling in the gap with the quiet portion of the waveform preceding the attack, rather than extending the first event to the right, creating a nasty double attack.

 Sometimes you may simply not be able to smooth out the transition between your clips even though the rhythm sounds accurate. No matter where you place the transition before the correctly timed attack, the switch between the events is audible. You've tried adjusting the fade-in and fade-out points to no avail. What you need is the smoothing cross-fading of ACID Pro 6, but you are working with ACID XPress. If this happens, duplicate your track, delete the second event (right after the split) from the original track, and then delete everything except this event from the duplicate track. Drag the beginning of the second event from the new duplicated track slightly to the left so that it overlaps the first event. Then select both events on the two tracks and press F on the keyboard to automatically crossfade between events.

Beatmapping Example

This example of beatmapping variable-tempo tracks uses "I Know There's Something Going On" by Frida, a hit from 1982. This track can be found on the *Something's Going On*

(Remastered) album at the iTunes Store. This song has a fairly variable tempo (even with Phil Collins on the drums!), and so you will need several different beatmaps to keep it in sync without cutting it up into a million pieces.

The song can be purchased from the iTunes Store, burned to a CD, and then reimported into iTunes as an mp3, as described in Chapter 3.

Drag the song into ACID, using the Beatmapper Wizard if you have ACID Pro, or following the instructions in Chapter 7's "Working Without the Beatmapper" section. Do not attempt to beatmap the entire song, but only the intro, or the first eight measures. You'll start off with an initial tempo of around 108.15 bpm and a start offset of around 31,000 samples. It's okay if your numbers are a little different — the exact placement of beats is somewhat of a judgment call. Because the first eight measures are beatmapped, the beats should maintain alignment with ACID's beat grid throughout. There is, however, a danger that the initial window of eight measures is too large, and that there is significant tempo variability even within that short time window. If the tempo varies a lot, the largest displacement would usually be toward the middle of the section. You may want to zoom in toward the center of the beatmapped area, in this case at beat 5.1. The kick at beat 5.1 seems to be slightly offset from the beat grid, but perhaps not enough to be unacceptable. To find out for sure, listen to the track with the metronome turned on. Indeed, the metronome sounds lined up with the track pretty well until around measure 11.

If the beat is perfectly aligned at the beginning of measure 9 and audibly misaligned by the beginning of measure 11, probably the best place for realignment is the beginning of measure 10, halfway in between. Positioning the cursor at beat 10.1 and zooming in, the offset becomes visible, although it still may not be audible at this point, as shown in Figure 9-1. The attack visibly starts at 10.1.024, when it should have ideally started right at 10.1.000.

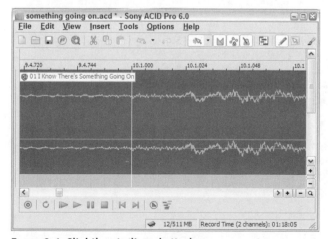

FIGURE 9-1: Slightly misaligned attack

If you are using Acid Pro 6, place the cursor right at 10.1.024, press S to split the event, and then drag the event to the left until it starts at 10.1.000, as shown in Figure 9-2. As you can see, ACID Pro 6 has created a smooth transition between the events that removes glitches, and at the same time removes the sharp attack. The effect is subtle, because the offset is small, but when the transition is longer and the attack sharper, the percussive sound may disappear altogether. Drag each side of the crossfade to the left, maintaining a similar length of crossfade but moving it so that it is complete before the attack, as shown Figure 9-3. This preserves the integrity of the attack and moves the crossfade to a less noticeable and quieter portion.

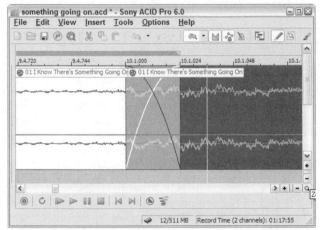

FIGURE 9-2: Properly aligned attack in ACID Pro 6, muted by the automatic crossfade

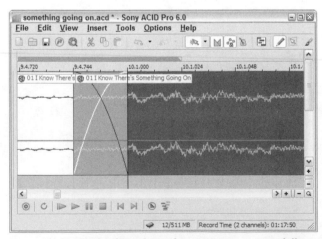

FIGURE 9-3: Properly aligned attack in ACID Pro 6, now fully audible

ACID XPress can produce equally good results, but it may take a little more work. Place the cursor right at 10.1.024, press S to split the event, and then drag the event to the left until it starts at 10.1.000, as shown in Figure 9-4. This is different from the method used in ACID Pro 6, because ACID XPress simply plays one track or the other. Additionally, with the automatic fade-in turned on, if your attack point was selected with precision, it may not be fully audible, as you can see in Figure 9-4 where the fade-in overlaps the attack.

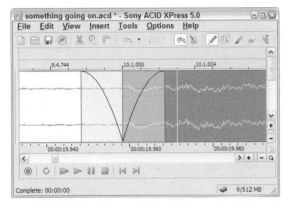

FIGURE 9-4: Properly aligned attack in ACID XPress, with automatic fade affecting the attack

There are two methods that you can use to solve this fade-in issue. One is to simply remove the fade-in by dragging the upper-right corner of the fade-in to the left, eliminating it, as shown in Figure 9-5.

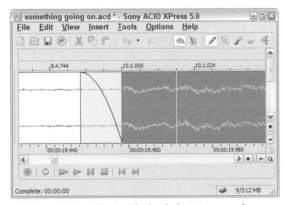

FIGURE 9-5: Transition with the fade-in removed

The other way you can solve the fade-in issue is to move the split point to an earlier, quieter portion, dragging the right edge of the first event to the left, and then the left edge of the second event. The results are shown in Figure 9-6.

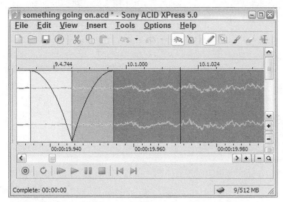

FIGURE 9-6: Transition with the split point displaced

Duplicate and Re-Beatmap

The simple cut-and-nudge technique works quite well for tracks with mild amounts of tempo variability, such as early electronic tracks or live tracks with very tight drummers. However, if you are performing this technique, and you have an accurate average bpm of the whole song, but you find that you need to make an edit after every measure (or more frequently), then this single-bpm approach may not be for you. Different portions of the song may need to have different beatmapped tempos so the edits happen less frequently.

This second technique (duplicate and re-beatmap) is a variation of the cut-and-nudge technique with a few important differences. When you're determining the tempo of your track, this time you only need to make sure it starts out accurately. You are not looking for the average tempo this time, but rather the initial tempo. After you've determined your starting tempo, perform the cut-and-nudge technique as you did previously. After a while, the tempo will have drifted enough so your edits become more and more frequent. This is a sign that your beatmapped tempo has drifted enough to warrant a new beatmap.

There are basically three steps that are repeated, as follows:

1. Beatmap as much audio as can be accurately beatmapped.

2. Cut and nudge until the cuts become frequent.

3. Duplicate the track/clip and go back to step 1.

Here are more detailed explanations of the process for each flavor of ACID.

With ACID XPress, duplicate the entire track. Delete everything to the right of the last split point in the first copy, and everything to the left of the same split point in the second copy. Now slowly adjust the beatmapped tempo of the event in the second copy so the rhythm lines up with the beat grid at four or eight measures from the split point. Perform the cut-and-nudge technique on the new track with the new beatmapped tempo until the cuts start to happen frequently enough to repeat the process all over again.

 With ACID Pro 6, you can have the same audio file with different beatmapped tempos on a single track by using multiple clips. When the tempo seems to have drifted significantly, open the Track Properties to view the Clip Pool. Select the clip you have just split, click the Copy button (which looks like two pieces of paper), and then click the Paste button (which looks like a clipboard with a piece of paper). Right-click the new clip and select Rename. Choose a slightly different name than the original clip so you can tell the difference. (The simple addition of a number at the end should suffice.) Now, right-click the event in your track after the split point, and choose the name of your newly created clip from the Event Clip submenu. You now have a single track with multiple clips, all from the same audio file. Each clip has its own beatmapped tempo, so you can adjust the second event's tempo in the Stretch tab of the Clip Properties window. Make the first four or eight measures line up to ACID Pro 6's beat grid, and then when the offsets become audible, perform the cut-and-nudge technique until the tempo has drifted enough so the cuts become quite frequent. At this point, repeat the process, creating another clip.

Variable Tempo Technique

An altogether different strategy from trying to force an organic tempo into ACID's strict grid is to instead adjust ACID's grid so it has a variable tempo that exactly matches the tempo of the track you are working with. This has the advantage of never creating overlaps or gaps that need to be smoothed, but instead, locking in the tempo of the entire project to the tempo of one sound file within the project. It also has the advantage of allowing the variable-tempo track to play as a one-shot, which allows for the highest level of sound quality in ACID. Although other tracks within your mashup can be slaved to this variable tempo, they need to either originally have a constant tempo or be adjusted with the cut-and-nudge method.

 If you are using ACID Pro, and you have any effects that are tempo-dependent (such as simple delay), tempo changes will alter the effect during playback but not during rendering. This seems to be a bug and will hopefully be resolved in future versions.

The variable technique is pretty straightforward. You determine the initial tempo for the first few bars, maybe 4, 8, or 16. If you have ACID Pro, you can use the Beatmapper Wizard; otherwise, you will again need to use the method outlined in "Working Without the Beatmapper" in Chapter 7. After finding this value, you must change the clip type (or track type in ACID XPress) from Beatmapped to One-Shot for this technique to work. You will not be adjusting the clip's tempo, but rather, *slaving* the entire project's tempo to the track. An added advantage to switching your audio to One-Shot is higher fidelity, because you won't be performing any time warping.

Set the project tempo to your initial tempo. Put the cursor at the number of bars for which you've determined the tempo. For example, if you determined the initial tempo for the first eight measures, put the cursor at beat grid 9.1.1. Type **T** to place a tempo marker at that point, and then press Enter to accept the value from the pop-up window, which should create a tempo marker with a value equal to the project tempo at this point. This tempo may not be equal to the tempo moving forward, but it will be adjusted shortly.

Now, to align the beat grid to the song's rhythm, repeat the following steps:

1. Starting at the last tempo marker, listen for the first beat that is audibly out of sync. Place your cursor right on the beat grid line where the sound's attack *should* be. This will be close to but not exactly where the sound's attack actually occurs.

2. Type **M** to place a time marker on the grid line where you want the attack to move to.

3. Zoom in on the actual attack and place the cursor right before it occurs.

4. Zoom back out if necessary, right-click your time marker, and select Adjust Tempo to Match Cursor to Marker. The tempo for the previous tempo marker is "automagically" adjusted.

5. Type **T** to place a new tempo marker in the same spot as your time marker. Press Enter to accept the current tempo value.

6. (Optional) Right-click the time marker (*not* the tempo marker) and select Delete.

Repeat this process as many times as necessary, and you will end up with a project that slaves its tempo to your variable-tempo track. Any songs added will now play back at the variable tempo of your first track.

Living off the Grid

There is yet a third approach to forcing the rhythm to the grid lines or forcing the grid lines to the rhythm. For some projects, you may choose to simply avoid using the grid lines at all. This usually works best if you are trying to sync up pure acapellas to a variable-tempo instrumental. Multiple tracks containing rhythmic material would present considerable difficulties without using the grid.

Basically, you lay down the instrumental as a one-shot, and then hack apart the acapella into phrases, adjusting the acapella's bpm by ear. You may need to use multiple tracks in ACID XPress or multiple clips in ACID Pro 6, similar to the duplicate and re-beatmap method described earlier in this chapter. There is a high potential for sloppy timing using this method, so you shouldn't try it until you have a bit of experience under your belt.

Third-Party Software Techniques

Perhaps the easiest way to deal with a variable-tempo track is to turn it into a straight-tempo track. It would be great if ACID had that capability, but as of version 6.0, it has not been implemented. There is, however, a software package that can perform variable tempo beatmaps: Ableton Live. Ableton Live can not only effectively straighten out loose rhythmic patterns, but it's a great mashup production platform in itself. Many mashup producers use Ableton Live exclusively. As of version 5, the sound quality of the time-stretching algorithm has improved greatly, and the addition of mp3 support makes it a very attractive tool to bootleggers. The downside is that there is no free version like there is with ACID XPress. So if you want to use it, you'll have to shell out some cash.

A full discussion of Ableton Live is beyond the scope of this book, but you can get some amazing results pretty easily. If you have Ableton Live, simply drag an mp3 or wav into the Track view, set the tempo to your master tempo in ACID, and select File ⇨ Render. That's it. Now you can import the wav back into ACID as a one-shot, and the tempo will be in line with the ACID beat grid, although you may have to adjust the start point. This technique will work perfectly on about half of all variable tempo tracks. Of the remainder, an improperly detected beatmap may result in a measure here and there having an inappropriate length, so that the beats become offset. Fortunately, the offset is constant, so that if the beatmap strays from ACID's grid, you can perform a single cut-and-nudge, and the rhythm will again sync up with the grid for quite a long time.

Many people prefer the workflow of ACID over Ableton Live, so performing nothing but beatmapping in Ableton Live is not unheard of.

Breaking It Down

So that's the whole synchronization story. Now all your tracks are perfectly in time and in key. Soon, you'll learn how to fit them all together (in Chapter 11) and polish them up (in Chapter 12). You'll never be able to listen to one song at a time again. But first, it's time to sally forth into the mysterious world of unmixing. Good luck. You'll be a full-fledged "mashematician" soon.

Unmixing

When you're constructing mashups, you'll often want to isolate certain elements of the mix while eliminating others. Ideally, you'd always have a clean acapella to work with, but the sad truth is that there are only a limited number of acapellas actually made available to the public by the artists themselves, although there does seem to be an upswing in availability recently as artists and record companies discover the advantages of encouraging the remix, mashup culture.

Eventually you are sometimes faced with the ambitious prospect of *acapella extraction*, the process of separating the vocals from the instrumentation in a stereo mixed-down recording. This is an inexact science, and can produce widely varying results. Sometimes, you can create an astonishingly pristine vocal that sounds just as good as the original vocal recording. In most cases, however, some artifacts of the original mixdown remain. These may be quiet traces of guitars or subtle remnants of snare drums. Other times, so many elements of the mixdown remain that you can barely call the result an acapella at all, and you have to settle for a full mix with a background that's slightly quieter than before. Fortunately, you can often mix these imperfect acapellas with a new backing instrumental that drowns out many of its imperfections.

The following tools are available for vocal extraction:

- Stereo field manipulation
- EQ
- Noise reduction
- Transient elimination
- Gating

When venturing into the territory of vocal extraction, it's important to keep your expectations at a reasonably low level. There is no magic wand that lifts the lead vocals out of a mix, but even a slight reduction in the density of the vocal track can help you manage the overall density of the mashup. It's important to remember that you are not striving for perfection, but simply increased usability. Even messy acapellas can sound considerably cleaner when layered with other material.

in this chapter

- ☑ Center channel techniques
- ☑ Noise reduction
- ☑ EQ
- ☑ Transient elimination
- ☑ Gating
- ☑ Audio from surround sound

While vocal extraction is the most common motivation for unmixing, it's also useful for generally reducing the density of your mashup. If your mashup sounds like there's just too much going on, try creating a few unmixed wavs and see if they sound better instead of the full original audio file.

Always try to use the highest quality audio files you can get your hands on. A low-quality mp3 will perform poorly in unmixing. Wav-quality audio is preferable, typically ripped from a CD.

Vintage vs. Modern Stereo Recording

Although stereo sound recording dates all the way back to the 1930s, stereophonic recording wasn't commercialized until the 1950s and became quite popular throughout the 1950s and 1960s.

In the early days of stereo recording, when the novelty of stereo was still fresh, producers would pan isolated elements of the mix with more stereo isolation than they do today. For example, the drums might be only in the left speaker, the guitars might be entirely isolated in the right speaker, and the vocals might be dead center.

As time progressed, producers used panning with increasing subtlety. Also, the advent of stereo effects such as chorus and reverb smeared the tracks across the stereo spectrum, producing a fuller sound that was less pinpointed spatially. Today, although a vocal might still be panned dead center, the reverberations will often be spread between left and right. Although this might be pleasing to the ear, it is most unfortunate for the aspiring acapella and instrumental extractor because the recording's stereo spectrum is more complex and difficult to manipulate.

However, stereo field manipulation techniques can work really well for a number of recordings of the late 1960s. If you were to process many of the Beatles recordings, for example, you would notice a high amount of stereo separation and would find clean instrumental and acapella extraction quite easy to achieve in many cases.

Center Channel Techniques

Stereo audio has two channels: left and right. Often, it's useful to imagine that there are actually three channels: center, left, and right. If you were able to transform a two-channel stereo wave into a center channel wave and a remaining left/right stereo wave, you'd have more mixing flexibility. This is the goal of the center channel techniques and much of unmixing.

There is a long history of center channel manipulation. Phase cancellation techniques have been around since the early days of stereo, while more advanced computing has brought about new possibilities, best implemented by Adobe's Audition 2.0.

Note *Phase* refers to the position in the cycle of a sinusoidal component of a sound wave. Two sound waves can have identical amplitudes and frequencies, but different phase. If the waveforms are moving up and down at the same time, the waves are considered to be *in phase*. Phase is measured in degrees from 0∞ to 360∞ for an entire cycle, as shown in Figure 10-1. If two waveforms are not moving together — for example, if one waveform is at 0∞ every time another waveform is at 90 — the two waves are referred to as being 90∞ *out of phase* with each other.

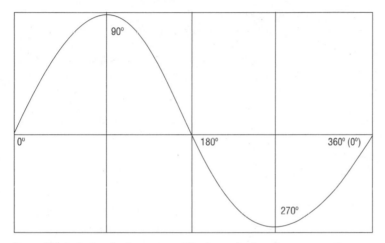

Figure 10-1: A simple sine wave with phase displayed

OOPS...

It's much more than a Britney Spears song. OOPS stands for Out Of Phase Stereo, also known as phase cancellation or the karaoke effect, and it's the oldest technique for manipulating the center channel, having been around for decades. It may seem counterintuitive, but sometimes when two sounds are added together, they aren't louder than just one of the sounds. If two perfectly identical sounds that are 180 degrees out of phase with each other, they will actually cancel each other out. This is the effect used in some home karaoke machines that eliminate the center channel, suppressing much of the vocals.

Some people have discovered this effect quite by accident after incorrectly wiring their speaker systems. If you simply switch the two wires in one of your speakers in a home stereo system, and you listen from a point precisely in between the two speakers, you can hear this phase cancellation to some extent, although it's imperfect. Alternatively, if you partially unplug headphones from your headphone jack just a little bit, often there is a "sweet spot" where the OOPS effect happens spontaneously. This works best using a 1/8-inch jack, and is simple and quite effective. There are other techniques that involve purposely miswiring your home stereo, but they may damage your equipment.

Luckily, you can perform this effect digitally as well. As previously discussed, a sound wave oscillates above and below a center equilibrium point. Figure 10-1 represented a simple sine wave. If the wave is inverted, turning it upside down, as in Figure 10-2, it is transformed into a vertically mirrored image of itself.

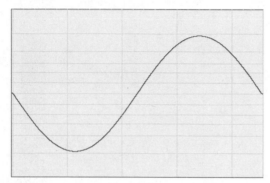

FIGURE 10-2: The same waveform as Figure 10-1, inverted (180 degrees out of phase)

Both sound waves will have the same frequencies at the same amplitudes. The magic comes when you add these waves together. Because the first wave is always equal and opposite from the second wave, their sum always adds up to exactly zero — a flat line. This has the effect of creating complete silence.

This experiment would not be so interesting by itself except for the fact that in a stereo recording, any track that is panned to the direct center has precisely the same component waveform in both the left and the right channel. If you were to invert either the left or right channel, turning it upside down, and then sum it with the other channel, you could totally eliminate the center frequencies.

Note
An OOPSed (left-minus-right) signal is called the *side* channel, and a left-plus-right signal is called the *mid* channel. A left/right waveform can be converted to a mid/side waveform and back again to left/right without any signal degradation.

Here is a simple example to demonstrate this phenomenon. Figures 10-3, 10-4, and 10-5 show three waves that have been added together in a mixdown (10-6 panned rhythmic pattern.wav on this book's CD-ROM). Panned hard left is a snare, designated as L (Figure 10-3). Panned hard right is a hi-hat, designated as R (Figure 10-4). Panned dead center is the kick drum, designated as C (Figure 10-5). Together they add up to a very simple drum pattern.

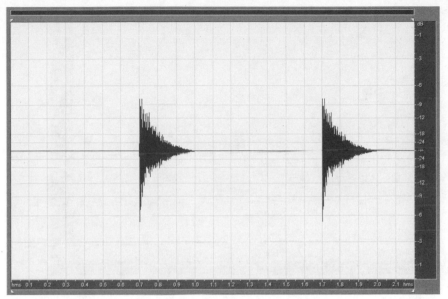

FIGURE 10-3: The snare drum, L, to be panned left

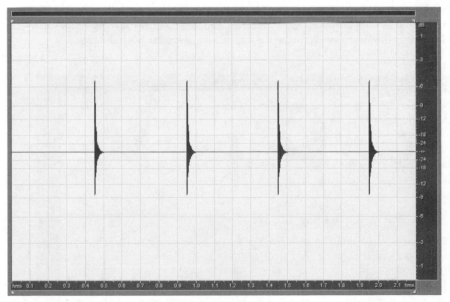

FIGURE 10-4: The hi-hat wave, R, to be panned right

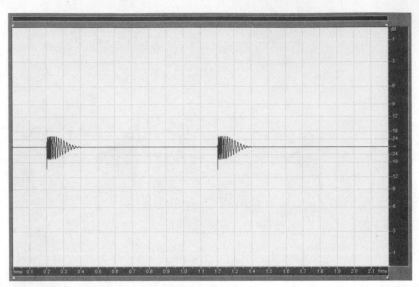

FIGURE **10-5: The kick, C, to be panned center**

Figure 10-6 shows the mixed-down stereo waveform, with the kick drum panned to the center, the snare drum panned hard left, and the hi-hat panned hard right. Notice that the kick drum can be seen in both channels, while in the left (upper) channel the snare drum can also be seen. In the right (lower) channel, the hi-hat can be seen, mixed in with the kick.

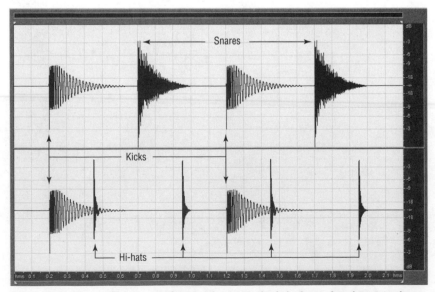

FIGURE **10-6: The mixdown waveform with L+C in the left channel and R+C in the right channel**

When presented with only the final mixdown, you would ideally like to be able to extract all three of these signals from a two-channel stereo recording. Figure 10-7 shows an attempt to do this, using only phase cancellation techniques. First, the right channel is inverted, turning the hi-hat and right-panned kick upside down. At first glance, this looks almost identical to the previous waveform, but if you look closely, you'll notice that the upward and downward spikes in the right (lower) channel are reversed.

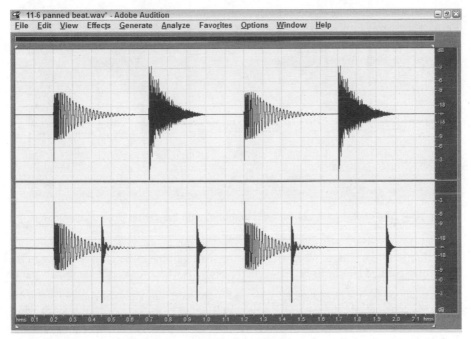

FIGURE 10-7: The same mixdown wave, with the right channel inverted — L+C in the left channel and R-C in the right channel

Then, you can simply sum up the two channels in a standard stereo-to-mono conversion, shown in Figure 10-8. You add L+C to -R-C, and the center channels cancel each other out, leaving you with just L-R. This is a mono waveform representing the left channel minus the right channel. Notice that the center channel has been entirely eliminated, leaving you with the snare from the left channel summed up with the inverted hi-hat from the right channel, but without the kick that was originally panned center.

Note A quick way to perform an OOPS phase inversion in Adobe Audition is to select Effects ⇨ Amplitude ⇨ Channel Mixer, choose the Vocal Cut preset, and click OK.

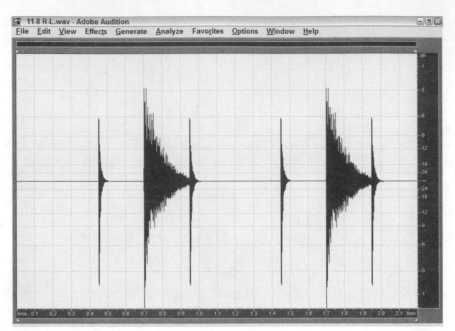

FIGURE 10-8: The stereo wave converted into mono, with the center channel eliminated

Now that you have a sound wave with both the snare and the hi-hat, it is tempting to try to get the center-panned kick by itself. After all, the center is where the vocals are usually panned.

If you were to take the resultant L-R wave and simply add it to the right channel of the original wave, R+C, you would end up with a wave representing L-R+R+C, or simply L+C, which is the left channel of the original wave. Alternatively, you could invert the L-R wave, creating an R-L wave, and add it to the left channel of the original wave, or L+C. You would end up with L+C+R-L, or C+R, the right channel of the original wave.

What if you converted the original signal to mono and then subtracted the snare/hi-hat wave from it? Converting the original wave to mono gives you L+C summed with R+C, or L+2C+R. Subtracting your snare/hi-hat wave would give you (L+2C+R) – (L-R), or 2C+2R, an amplified version of the right channel of the original wave.

So you are unable to isolate the center channel using this technique. You are also unable to create a stereo signal of the left channel and the right channel without the center channel, preserving the stereo panning of the L and R signals, although with some fairly straightforward manipulation you can eliminate the center channel, creating a single mono wave. The fact is, no matter how you manipulate these signals, you simply cannot isolate L, R, or C using this method. Many aspiring mashup artists have wasted many hours trying.

Note There's a list of Beatles tracks that respond well to OOPS effects at www.beatletracks .com/btoops.html. The tracks listed respond well to other techniques in this chapter as well.

The question remains: How can you eliminate the sounds from both the left and right channels from the center channel? Also, it would be great if you could get a signal containing L and R without C, maintaining the stereo separation. Luckily, a solution does exist, in the form of . . . (drum roll please) . . .

Adobe Audition's Center Channel Extractor

Adobe Audition has a remarkable tool for vocal and instrumental extraction. It can both remove the center channel from a stereo signal while maintaining the stereo imaging of the remaining signal as well as extract the center channel from the stereo wave, muting out the L and R signals. Using FFT (discussed in Chapter 8), Audition breaks apart a waveform into thousands of frequency bands. The levels of each frequency range can be analyzed and then processed. Breaking the signal apart in this way allows you to suppress or isolate similar frequencies in each channel without even necessarily requiring the signals to be exactly in phase with each other.

Now you can try to isolate each of the signals in the mixdown wav previously shown in Figure 10-6 using Adobe Audition.

After loading the "10-6 panned rhythmic pattern.wav" file, select Effects ⇨ Filters, and then choose the Center Channel Extractor (see Figure 10-9).

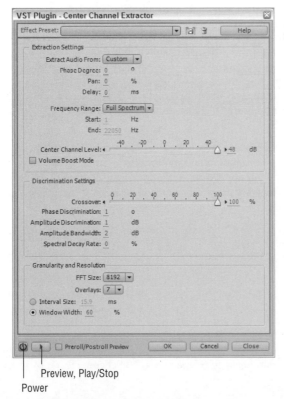

FIGURE 10-9: Center Channel Extractor

As you can see, there are many settings to choose from, and they will be discussed in detail shortly. But for now, do the following:

- Set the Frequency Range drop-down to Full Spectrum.
- Set the Center Channel Level slider to +48 dB.
- Set the Crossover slider to 100.
- Set the Phase Discrimination to 1.
- Set the Spectral Decay Rate to 0.
- Set the Amplitude Discrimination to 1.
- Set the Amplitude Bandwidth to 2.
- Set the FFT Size to 8192.
- Set the Overlays to 7.
- Set the Interval Size to 60%.

These are not typical settings for mixdowns of full songs, but they will work well for the simple wav file you're working with here.

Click OK, and you will find that the snare and hi-hats are completely removed. The center channel has been totally isolated. You will end up with a waveform very similar to the isolated kick previously shown in Figure 10-5, except that it will have two channels. Notice that after the center channel has been isolated, you still have two channels, but they are nearly identical, making them sound like a mono wave. Now, press Ctrl+Z to undo the isolation, and choose the Center Channel Extractor again. This time move the Center Channel slider all the way down to -48 dB, and the Crossover slider all the way down to 0 (zero). Click OK, and you will have a wave that contains only the snare from Figure 10-3 and the hi-hat from Figure 10-4, still properly panned, but without the kick.

It's important to realize that the Center Channel Extractor does not have quite the precision of the phase cancellation method. Phase cancellation will subtract each sample of the waveform exactly, and the Center Channel Extractor approximates the frequency content of the wave through FFT. Even with digital mixdowns with strong stereo separation, some artifacts are bound to remain.

Now that the general concept of the Center Channel Extractor has been demonstrated, it's time to discuss the parameters in more detail.

Material to Extract

These settings control the phase, pan, and frequency range of the material you want to extract or suppress.

Get Audio Phased At

This should be set at Center for almost all center channel extraction operations. You might change this to Custom for several situations. If for some reason one channel is out of phase with the other, you could change the Phase Degree setting to the number of degrees it is out of phase. This shouldn't occur with acapella extraction from prerecorded material. If the center channel isn't exactly dead center, but is slightly panned to the left or right of center, you can set the Pan from -100% to 100%. Usually you are interested in extracting the center, but in certain situations you may be interested in extracting something slightly off center — a background vocal, for instance. The Delay box is for entering any delay between the channels in milliseconds from -5 to +5. This will rarely be useful in extraction.

Frequency Range

Only the frequencies in between these two values will be included in the center channel extraction. Conversely, when you extract the side channels, any frequencies outside of this frequency range from the center channel will be included in the side channels.

When you're extracting the center channel where the vocals usually reside, you want the frequency range to be as narrow as possible, eliminating all frequencies outside the range. However, if you make the lower frequency too high, the vocals will start to become tinny. Also, if you make the higher frequency too low, the vocals will be muffled. The key is to find the balance that reduces the unwanted frequencies as much as possible, without reducing the quality of the vocals. In most cases, you want the upper frequency to be at or near the upper range. However, because the vocals usually share the same center pan as the bass and the kick drum, you often want to raise the lower frequency to a level where these tones are reduced. You can try several frequency range presets, but usually it's best to choose a custom frequency range, and then determine the ideal frequencies.

When you're extracting the side (instrumental) channels and muting the center (vocal) channel, only the frequencies within the range are muted. Any frequencies outside of these ranges from the center channel will be included in the filtered side channels, regardless of pan. Therefore, in most cases when muting the center channel, you want to suppress the full spectrum.

Center Channel Level

This setting basically sets the volume of the center channel in comparison to the side channels. Set this as high as possible to extract the center channel. Reduce this to the lowest possible value to mute the center channel, extracting the side channels. The only time you would want this to be somewhere in between would be if you wanted to generate a mixdown with a slightly raised or lowered center channel.

Caution Be aware that the uppermost value of the Center Channel Level is +48 dB, and the lowest value is -48 dB. It's easy to get confused when you're entering either of these values from the examples in this chapter, and the two settings have radically different results.

Volume Boost Mode

When this is checked, the center channel or side channel extraction is added to the original wave. This is typically not useful for acapella or instrumental extraction.

Discrimination Settings

These settings help the Extractor decide which material to manipulate based on the phase and amplitude of the frequency components. Each channel in the stereo signal is first broken down into small frequency bands using FFT. The Center Channel Extractor compares each pair of these frequency bands to each other, examining their amplitude and phase to see if they match and are considered a part of the center channel.

Crossover

This controls the stereo range width of material considered to be in the center channel. For acapella (center channel) extraction, you'll want to start with the Crossover at a fairly high value, which focuses the extraction on a very narrow portion of the stereo spectrum. If you want to include some of the material panned nearby the center channel, you might lower the crossover a bit. For example, you might want to include a bit of reverb. For instrumental (side channel) extraction, you'll often want to lower the Crossover almost all the way to maximize the width of the stereo spectrum to be eliminated.

Phase Discrimination

This setting determines how precisely each frequency band from the left and right channels need to be in phase with each other to be considered part of the center channel. With lower values, each frequency band in the two channels needs to have audio with more identical phase. Higher values relax this requirement.

Amplitude Discrimination and Amplitude Bandwidth

These values determine how precisely the amplitude of each frequency band from the left and right channels need to match each other to be considered part of the center channel. With lower values, each frequency band needs to have fairly similar amplitudes. Higher values relax this requirement, allowing more audio to be considered part of the center channel.

Spectral Decay Rate

This has a subtle (sometimes inaudible) impact on the center channel extraction. When a frequency band is considered to be a match, a high Spectral Decay Rate will influence decisions about the same frequency band in the immediate future, biasing the Extractor toward including the band in the center channel. This bias decays over time, more slowly for higher values, and immediately for a value of 0 (zero). High values of this parameter are CPU-intensive. In practice, this parameter doesn't receive a lot of focus, because it affects the sound less than the other discrimination settings.

Granularity and Resolution

You can set these values after setting all the values for the previous two sections. They will not have much effect on which material is extracted, but rather on the overall quality of the output. Higher quality sounds come at the expense of computing time. Depending on your computer's processing power, it is quite possible to set these values so high that you cannot listen to the results in real time. While determining the ideal values for the previous two sections, do not set the FFT Size and the Overlays to such high values that you cannot preview the results in real time. After you've determined all your settings from the first two sections, then you can set the FFT Size and the Overlays as high as you want for rendering.

FFT Size

This is the number of frequency bands the signal is split into. Higher values increase the sound quality of the frequencies and the processing time, but can smear the sound over time. Lower values increase the precision of the timing, but the precision of the frequencies suffers. Such is the dilemma of all things FFT.

Overlays

This setting determines the number of overlapping time windows for frequency analysis. Increasing this value increases the smoothness of the overall results, but it may smear the sound over time somewhat. The higher the value is, the longer the processing time will be.

Interval Size and Window Width

This is the size of the time window for each frequency analysis. You can set this either manually or as a percentage, usually 30% or higher.

Adobe Audition's Spectral Pan Display

With version 2.0, Audition has a powerful new feature that shows where your stereo wave-form's sound is panned in the stereo spectrum. Figure 10-10 shows the waveform from Figure 10-6 displayed in Audition's Spectral Pan Display, which you can access from the View menu or by pressing Shift+A. (Shift+W takes you back to Waveform Display.)

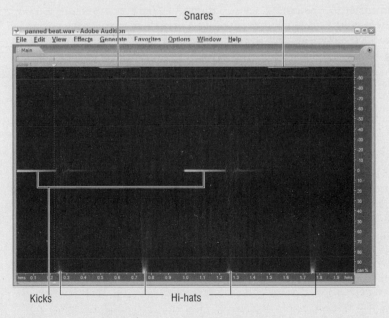

FIGURE 10-10: Adobe Audition's Spectral Pan Display

Continues

Adobe Audition's Spectral Pan Display *Continued*

The intensity of the color in the display represents the intensity of sound at each pan position for each moment. If you look at the pan % axis on the right side of the screen, you can determine where sounds are occurring in a mixed-down song. The display isn't perfect, and when there are sounds going on in multiple pan positions simultaneously, the graph can dart from one pan position to another, as if sound were actually traveling across. For example, in between 0.7 and 0.8 seconds in Figure 10-10 there is a thin blue line that starts off at the top with a snare sound and then swoops down to the bottom when the hi-hat starts. This doesn't represent actual movement. It's more important to notice where the energy seems to be concentrating over time. Actual full mixes can look quite complex in the Spectral Pan Display, but usually you can see general areas where instruments and vocals are panned. This can be a handy reference tool when you're manipulating the center channel.

General Center Channel Strategies

Start off by using a preset. At first you may find only one preset that's applicable, such as the acapella preset. Each time you render an extraction of a new wave, click the Add button and save the preset, giving it a new name. You may want to do this before raising the FFT Size and Overlays to values beyond what your computer can preview in real time. This way, the next time you perform an extraction, you can quickly step through all the previous settings you've saved, finding the one that works best and then adjusting it from there. Because the presets are listed alphabetically, you should name each of your acapella presets starting with *acapella* or simply *a-*, and name each instrumental preset starting with *instrumental* or simply *i-*. This way, the instrumental and acapella presets are grouped near each other, making it easier to step through them.

After you have picked the preset that most closely matches your goals, if you are extracting the acapella (center channel), adjust the lower frequency of the Frequency Range to as high a value as you can without the audio sounding tinny. Set the Center Channel Level to +48 dB. If you are extracting the instrumental (side channels), you'll usually want to set the Frequency Range to Full Spectrum and the Center Channel Level to -48 dB.

Set the Crossover to +48 dB for center channel extraction and -48 dB for center channel elimination. Next, experiment with different values for the three parameters of Phase Discrimination, Amplitude Discrimination, and Amplitude Bandwidth. It's important to realize that changing any of these three values may change the ideal value of all the other settings. Usually you need to adjust one setting, readjust another setting, and then go back and adjust the first setting. Repeat this process until your results sound good. Different songs may require radically different settings. You may even want to go back and adjust the lower frequency of the Frequency Range or the Crossover parameter. Because of the effort involved, you will want to save your settings as a preset. It may come in handy later.

The example for center channel extraction will use Harry Nilsson's song "One," from the album *Harry Nilsson: Greatest Hits*, which you can purchase from the iTunes Store and convert to a wav file using the burn-and-rip technique from Chapter 3. Make sure you are using the version from the album specified, because other versions have different panning and arrangement.

Even though compressed audio files are being used for the examples in this chapter, CD quality audio should be used if possible for all center channel operations.

Figure 10-11 shows "One" in Adobe Audition's Spectral Pan Display, revealing the strong panning in the song. In the left half of the displayed audio, there seem to be two events happening: in the upper half of the display is a sound with a defined start and end, panned strongly (around 90%) to the left, and a regularly occurring event on the right channel (the lower half of the display), panned around 40–50% to the right. About 8 seconds into the song, it looks like something is happening in the middle somewhere. A quick listen confirms this: There is a bass in the left channel, an organ in the right, and vocals in the center.

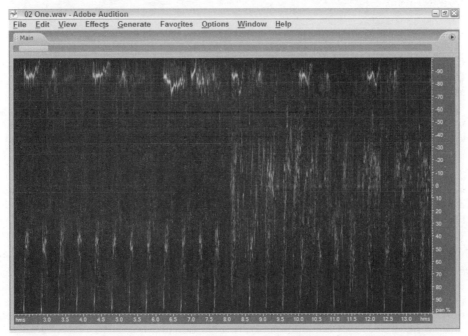

FIGURE 10-11: Harry Nilsson's "One" as seen in Adobe Audition's Spectral Pan Display

Zooming in to display just under 1 second of audio, a beautiful image emerges, showing the fluctuations in pan, as analyzed by Audition (see Figure 10-12). Again, the apparent instability of the pan shows up when there are multiple sounds at the same time, but there's still something of interest going on in the far left, and the energy seems most focused around the 50% pan on the right.

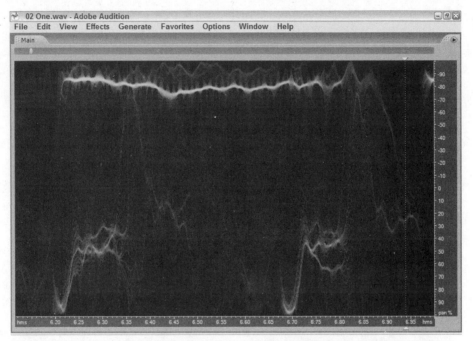

FIGURE 10-12: A closer view of "One" as seen in Adobe Audition's Spectral Pan Display

The main thing you can learn from this Spectral Pan Display is that there are very discretely panned events, making this waveform an excellent candidate for center channel extraction. The vocals seem to be panned dead center, as is usually the case.

Select Effects ⇨ Filters ⇨ Center Channel Extractor, choose the effect preset called Acapella, and click the Preview Play button near the lower-left corner of the Extractor. It's pretty effective as is. While the song is playing, move the crossover back and forth all the way down and then all the way up. Notice how the panned material is isolated more when the crossover is turned all the way up. Leave the crossover at 100%. You might notice the sound is fairly well isolated, but a bit tinny. Turn up the phase discrimination to its maximum value of 20. The vocals now sound full, but the organ sound has become a bit louder as well. Turning down the amplitude bandwidth to 0 dB can eliminate much of the organ while preserving the fullness of the vocals. There are still a few instrumental artifacts, but with this type of extraction, you usually accept that some unwanted remnants will remain.

Just for fun, move the center channel slider all the way down to -48 dB from +48 dB. The center channel is now suppressed, and the side channels are at normal levels. Much of the vocal that remains is from a reverb effect that was panned throughout a portion of the stereo spectrum. If you were using the extracted acapella for "One," you may choose to restore some reverb or other stereo ambiance, using techniques outlined in Chapter 12.

These settings are by no means universal, and each song requires that you adjust different parameters a bit, especially the Phase Discrimination, Amplitude Discrimination, and Amplitude Bandwidth. Eventually, you will find settings that strike a balance between the audio isolation and sound quality.

 Note   Center channel isolation can sometimes even be useful on commercially released acapellas. For example, suppose you have an acapella with the lead singer in the center and the background vocals, reverbs, and delays in the side channels. You may want to split the wave into two separate center and side waves so you can manipulate them independently.

Extracting the Acapella from the Instrumental and Full Song

The Center Channel Extractor works by either removing or isolating identical content between its two channels. Although it's designed for manipulating the levels of the audio panned to the center of a stereo waveform, if you paste different versions of the same song into the left and right channels of a stereo waveform, you could use this effect to eliminate identical content in any each waveform.

For example, you might have two separate sound files, one being a full mixdown of a song and the other being a full instrumental of the same song without the vocals. You might be interested in finding a third wave that would be the difference between the two. The resultant wave would be an acapella: the mixdown minus the instrumental. You can also use this technique to render the difference between two sections of the same song, which can yield pretty amazing results with modern electronically produced recordings. Older recordings may not work as well because the tempos and recording techniques generally aren't as precise, and the waveforms can have more subtle variation.

To begin with, you need a mono waveform of the full song and a mono waveform of the instrumental. Keep in mind that the two waveforms need to be in perfect sync with each other. If the instrumental is at a different tempo or has a different arrangement, this process will not work. You then paste one waveform into the right channel, paste the other waveform into the left channel, and line up the audio to the highest degree of accuracy possible. This creates a stereo wave with the instrumental in both channels and the vocal in only one channel. The instrumental then becomes panned to the center, and the vocal is panned hard to one side. After performing a side channel extraction, fully suppressing the center (instrumental) channel, you can end up with a stereo wave with near silence in one channel and the acapella in the other.

You can generate the mono waveforms using either of the following methods:

- Perform a stereo-to-mono conversion on both the instrumental and full mixdown waves.

- Simply copy only the left channel from both waves, or the right channel from both waves.

Using only one channel often has the advantage of having less sound in the instrumental, which you then need to suppress, so it is recommended in many cases. If you would like to preserve the stereo pan of the vocals, you can perform an extraction separately for each channel and then reassemble it into a stereo waveform.

The following example uses "Milkshake (Radio Edit)" and "Milkshake (Instrumental)," both from Kelis' *Milkshake – Single* album. Download it from the iTunes Store and convert it to a wav using the rip-and-burn technique from Chapter 3.

Open the radio edit in Audition and take a look at the Spectral Pan Display (Shift+A), shown in Figure 10-13.

The display is encouraging. There is a clearly defined center channel and other events panned far from center. Go to Effects ➪ Filters ➪ Center Channel Extractor, select the Acapella preset, and click Preview Play. The bass synthesizer is almost completely eliminated. Most of the percussion panned to the center, so it remains. But an acapella with percussion is certainly easier to combine with other material than a full song, and sometimes it's the best that you can do.

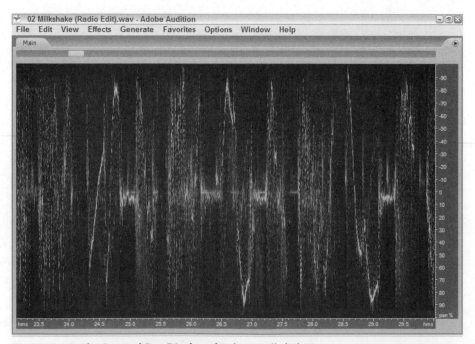

FIGURE 10-13: The Spectral Pan Display of Kelis' "Milkshake"

Because you happen to have an instrumental version of "Milkshake," it's possible to create a pure acapella with no percussion at all. Here's how:

1. Load up both versions of "Milkshake," dragging the wavs from iTunes into Audition.

2. Pull up the radio edit version of the song, select the entire left channel, and copy it by pressing Ctrl+A+L+C (A to select all, L to select left, and C to copy).

3. Create a new 16-bit 44100 Hz stereo waveform by pressing Ctrl+N and then click OK.

4. Press Ctrl+L+V to select the left channel of the new waveform and then paste in the copied content.

5. Pull up the instrumental version of the song, select the entire left channel, and copy it by pressing Ctrl+A+L+C. Make sure you take the same channel from each audio file.

6. Pull up the new waveform and press Ctrl+A+R+V to paste the instrumental into the right channel.

7. Press the Play button. The vocals are all the way to the left, but the instruments seem to have a lot of panning. Pull up the Spectral Pan Display (Shift+A), shown in Figure 10-14. Even in the instrumental sections, there seem to be heavy amounts of energy panned to the sides, which is confirmed by the strong stereo image you can hear. This is a sure sign that the two tracks are slightly misaligned — not so far that they sound like two separate sounds, but enough to cause problems. The tracks need to be realigned.

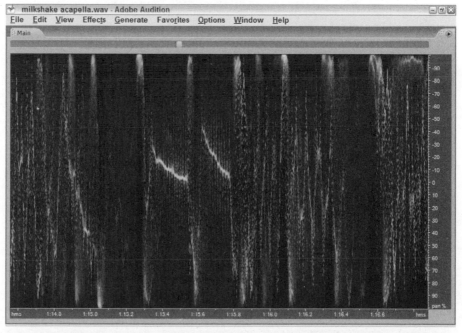

FIGURE 10-14: The Spectral Pan Display of a slightly misaligned instrumental and full song

8. Press Shift+W to return to the Waveform view. The goal now is to find a very distinctive feature in the waveform in one channel and then find the corresponding feature in the other channel. Any feature will do, as long as you can recognize it easily. Figure 10-15 shows the waveform zoomed in with almost identical features identified.

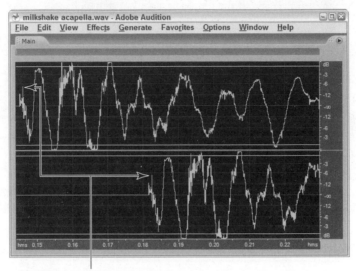

Identifiable corresponding features

FIGURE **10-15: A misaligned instrumental and full song in Waveform view**

9. Zoom in on each of the features you've picked and write down the corresponding times. You might find yourself zooming in farther than usual to find the exact time, usually to the tenth of a millisecond and maybe finer resolution (either four or five decimal places). Figure 10-16 shows the peak of the feature picked out in Figure 10-15 in very high magnification. You can see that the point lies .14604 seconds (146.04 ms) after the beginning of the song.

Zooming in just as close in the right channel will find the corresponding peak in the feature at .18248 seconds (182.48 ms) after the beginning of the song. Subtracting 146.04 from 182.48, you can calculate the difference between the two tracks to be 36.44 ms (0.03644 seconds).

Note

It may seem excessively precise to calculate the position of these features to the hundredth of a millisecond. But considering that a cycle of 22,050 Hz (the highest frequency renderable in 44.1 kHz digital audio) lasts 5/100 of a millisecond, it's wise to line it up with great precision. Sloppily aligned waves will cause the component frequencies to be out of phase, making eliminating them more difficult, especially the higher frequencies.

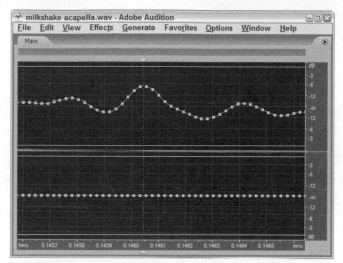

FIGURE 10-16: The cursor placed at the point chosen in left channel of Figure 10-15

10. Because the delay is very short, you can use Audition's Delay effect to correct it. Pull up the Delay effect by selecting Effects ⇨ Delay Effects ⇨ Delay. With the left channel, set the delay time to 36.44 and the mix to 100% (Wet). With the right channel, set the delay time to 0 and the mix to 100%. Make sure the Delay Time Units is set to ms and click OK.

11. Listen to the wave. The stereo image of the instruments now seems to come from one central location. Press Shift+A to view the Spectral Pan Display, pictured in Figure 10-17. (Compare this to Figure 10-14, which is the same stretch of audio before alignment.)

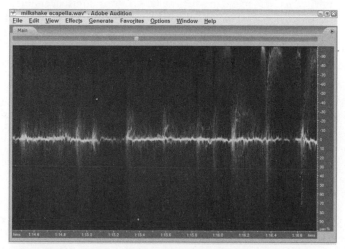

FIGURE 10-17: The Spectral Pan Display of the full song and instrumental properly lined up

At this point, the audio is so precisely aligned that you could perform a simple OOPS on it and get some pretty good results.

Note Although the volumes of the various elements are identical in the two versions of the "Milkshake" song, this isn't always the case. Different volumes would create bright areas panned off-center in the Spectral Pan Display. If this is the situation, you'll have to set the Extract Audio From setting to Custom and adjust the pan to match where the Spectral Pan Display shows the center audio to be.

12. To achieve the desired results for this exercise, you need to fiddle with a few more parameters in the Center Channel Extractor. Press Shift+W to return to Waveform view.

13. Select Effects ⇨ Filters ⇨ Center Channel Extractor and choose the acapella preset. Slide the Center Channel Level all the way down to -48 dB. Also slide the Crossover down to 0%. Change the Frequency Range to Full Spectrum and click OK.

14. Press Ctrl+A+R and then press Delete to get rid of the noise in the right channel. You now have a pretty decent mono acapella of "Milkshake" in the left channel. If you wanted a mono acapella, you could just paste this into a new mono wave. If you wanted to make a stereo version of the acapella, you'd repeat the entire extraction process for the right channels of the instrumental and full song and then again paste the left (acapella) channel of the resultant waveform into the empty (right) channel of the first extracted acapella, which should have the left channel of the acapella already in the left channel.

15. Save the wav file or keep it open. It will be used for later examples in this chapter.

Extracting the Acapella Through Shifting Time

The full song/instrumental technique is a pretty neat trick. But most often, an identical instrumental and full mixdown are not available. If only there were some other way to find a waveform that contained the sounds you want to remove without any of the sounds of the vocals you want to retain. Luckily, at least in the case of modern loop-based music production, there is a ready and elegant solution.

Most hip-hop, dance, and other electronic music forms repeat the same instrumental loops over and over. If you can line up the loop from one part of a song with the loop in another part of the same song, you can isolate the parts of the song that are different from each other. There are two variations on this technique: the loop technique and the time-shifting technique.

Loop Technique

Follow these steps to use this technique:

1. Delete the right channel of your full song.

2. In the left channel, find an instrumental loop of 1, 2, 4, 8, or 16 bars.

3. Copy the loop and paste it into the right channel, meticulously lining up the identifiable features of the loop with the identifiable features in the left channel.

You may have to paste each loop, one at a time in order to prevent drift. Or, if your full song is very regular, and consists entirely of sections that are multiples of your loop, you can first carefully paste two copies of your loop in the right channel, then copy the two loops from the right channel, and then paste the material afterward, lining it up with the left channel. You'll now have four loops perfectly aligned. Repeat this process to get 8 copies, and then 16, 32, and so on. (You can't simply paste 32 copies of your loop straightaway, because small errors will quickly build up, and you'll end up with your loop misaligned.)

4. Perform center channel elimination, removing the identical content in both channels.

5. Copy your left channel to a new mono wav, or save the results, repeat the entire process with the right channel, and construct a new stereo wav with the extractions from either channel.

Caution Resist the temptation to loop audio from the existing right channel and line it up with the full audio from the left channel. Both channels should contain audio from the same original channel. If you were to loop audio from the right channel along with the full song in the left channel, your center-panned instruments will be effectively removed, but the side-channel sounds will remain along with the isolated vocal.

Time-Shifting Technique

Follow these steps to use this technique:

1. Delete the right channel of your full song.

2. Copy the left channel into the right channel.

3. Delay the new right channel by exactly 1, 2, 4, 8, or 16 bars. You'll need to do this with sub-millisecond accuracy.

4. Perform center channel elimination, removing the identical content in both channels.

5. Copy your left channel to a new mono wav, or save the results, repeat the entire process with the right channel, and construct a new stereo wav with the extractions from either channel.

Do not simply shift the existing audio from the right channel, or you won't eliminate the side-panned audio. For example, suppose you have a song with a 16-bar verse followed by a 16-bar chorus, both sung over identical instrumental backing tracks. After deleting the right channel, you copy the entire left channel audio into the right channel and delay it by exactly 16 bars. Then you perform center channel suppression to isolate the material that is different in each channel. You'd end up with a stereo waveform with the verse acapella in the left channel and the chorus acapella in the right channel.

The only drawback to this method is that any material that is similar in both vocal perform-ances will also be eliminated. So if there are vocals in each channel at the same time, the extracted vocals can sound tinny. If you use this non-looped time shifting technique, you may want to create several acapellas, each with different delay times. Each acapella may become tinny at dif-ferent points, and you can assemble a decent-sounding acapella from the various extractions. For example, you may produce an acapella from time-shifting 16 bars, and another acapella from an eight-bar time shift. You can load each of them in ACID, and then alternate between them depending on which acapella sounds best at any given point.

Even with the danger of tinniness, time-shifting techniques can produce results that cannot be achieved any other way.

Here is a step-by-step example using "Milkshake (Radio Edit)" from the previous example. Usually you won't have access to the instrumental version of the song, and this example uses only the full song with the time-shifting technique instead, as follows:

1. Load the Radio Edit version of "Milkshake," dragging the wav from iTunes into Audition. Notice how regular the repeating bass synth line and percussion is.

   The bass line is panned, as you learned in the center channel extraction example earlier in this chapter. That example also revealed that the percussion is mostly panned to the center, sharing the pan position with the vocals. The challenge is to separate the vocals from both the percussion and bass synth without access to the instrumental.

2. Delete the right channel audio, copy the left channel audio, and paste it into the right channel. Alternatively, there is a shortcut to creating this two-channel mono wav:

   ▪ Select Effects ➪ Amplitude ➪ Channel Mixer.

   ▪ Choose the Both = Left preset and click OK.

3. Zoom in on the first downbeat of the first section, find an identifiable feature, and write down the time marker, as follows:

   ▪ Listening to the song from the beginning, there is a four-beat (one measure) intro before the first section begins. It's important to locate the fifth beat, which is the downbeat of the second measure and the first downbeat of the first section after the one-measure intro.

   ▪ Position the cursor close to the downbeat and zoom in a bit until you see some readily identifiable features, such as the quick upward spike towards the beginning of the downbeat's attack in Figure 10-18.

   ▪ Click the Zoom to Selection button one or more times, not allowing the selected feature in your downbeat to visually leave the screen. If you press it too many times, you can click the Zoom Out Horizontally button until the feature reappears.

   ▪ Repeat this process until you have zoomed in as far as you can, and then make note of the time marker. In this case, the value is 2.26992 seconds.

   This process is very similar to step 9 of the instrumental/full song extraction, pre-viously shown in Figure 10-16.

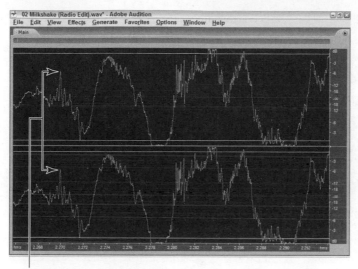

Identifiable feature at 2.26992

FIGURE **10-18:** The downbeat of the second measure in "Milkshake,"
zoomed in enough to find identifiable features

4. Zoom back out by clicking the Zoom Out Horizontally button repeatedly.

5. Listen to the sound file to determine the length of the repeating content. Ideally, this is where the material you want to isolate is not repeating, but the background instrumentation is. Usually the length will be 4, 8, or 16 beats, or some other multiple of 2, although other values may work. In this case, the main instrumental loop sounds like it is 4 beats (one measure), and the section length is 8 measures, or 32 beats. Probably 1, 2, 4, or 8 measures would work best here. Often delaying one channel by the length of an entire section works best.

6. Zoom in on the first downbeat of the second section, as you did in step 3. Listening to the song, the second section begins around 19 seconds into the song, right on the word "want," where Kelis is singing "I know you want it." Position your cursor close to the beginning of this beat and then zoom all the way in as you did in step 3, looking for an identifiable feature similar to the one you found earlier. Figure 10-19 shows the downbeat of the second section along with a very familiar waveform.

Zooming in even further (almost as far as possible), as in step 3, you can find that the peak of this waveform spike occurs at 19.26093 seconds.

Note If you are unable to find a recognizable feature similar to the one you found in step 3, you may need to go back and find another feature. It's not even essential that the feature be located on the downbeat. For example, if the snare on the second beat of the first section is more recognizable, you can compare it to the snare on the second beat of the second section. The exact points aren't important. What you're after is an extremely accurate value for the length of an entire section, the distance between the corresponding points.

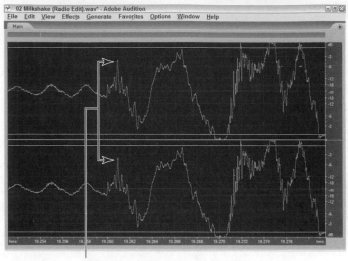

Similar identifiable features at 19.26093

FIGURE 10-19: The downbeat of the second measure in "Milkshake," zoomed in enough to find identifiable features

7. Subtract the value found in step 6 from the value found in step 3. In this case, subtracting 2.26992 from 19.26093 yields a section length of 16.99101 seconds, or 16991.01 milliseconds.

Note Because you have a section length defined with great precision, you can obtain a highly accurate tempo from this information. Multiply the number of beats (32) by 60 and then divide by the length of the section (16.99101). 32×60÷16.99101 = 113.0001 bpm, which is extremely close to the integer value expected in many modern recordings.

8. Delay the right channel of the wave by exactly 16.99101 seconds.

If this were a very short delay (under .5 seconds), you could use the delay effect like you did in step 10 of the full song/instrumental extraction. In this case, because the length of delay is so great, you have to perform the delay manually, as follows:

- Press Ctrl+A+R+X to select the entire right channel and cut it.

- Type **0:16.99101** in the Selection Begin (upper left) text box of Audition's Selection/View window, and press Ctrl+V to paste in the cut audio data. (You'll notice that the textbox only displays the value to the nearest millisecond — don't let that dissuade you from entering in the entire value, because the cursor is positioned with greater accuracy than is displayed in the text box.)

You have now created a single stereo signal, most of which has the looped material panned dead center. Any material that changes from section to section should be panned to the left or right. Listen to the waveform starting at around 20 seconds to hear this.

9. Perform center channel suppression by selecting Effects ➪ Filters ➪ Center Channel Extractor, and then doing the following:

- Choose the Vocal Remove preset.

- Because you are performing center channel elimination rather than isolation, set the frequency range to full spectrum.

- Set the Center Channel Level all the way down to -48 dB.

- Set the Crossover to Level all the way down to 0%.

- Turn the Amplitude Discrimination up to 9 dB.

- Click OK.

You now have two channels, each with a relatively isolated vocal. Press Ctrl+L and then play to listen to only the left channel, and then press Ctrl+R to listen to the right. You may notice fluctuations in the fullness of the vocal, as well as remnants of the signal from the other channel. This is a frequent occurrence with this type of acapella extraction.

Note Even though there are two acapellas in this stereo waveform, they are not components of a stereo wave. You may be tempted to delay the left channel another 16.99101 seconds to re-align it with the right channel. This is not recommended.

10. Select the left channel of this wave and copy it (Ctrl+L+C), create a new stereo waveform (Ctrl+N), select the left channel of the new stereo waveform, and paste (Ctrl+L+V).

11. Select the right channel of your extracted acapella waveform and copy it (Ctrl+R+C), create another new stereo waveform (Ctrl+N), select the left channel of the second new waveform, and paste again (Ctrl+L+V).

You are pasting both channels from your extracted wave into the left channels of two new waves because they are both derived entirely from the left channel of the original "Milkshake."

12. You are now finished with the extracted waveform, so you can close it. (Too many open waves are confusing.)

13. Repeat the entire process, from steps 1 through 9, except this time, extract the acapellas from the right channel, selecting the Both = Right preset in the Channel Mixer during step 2 instead of Both = Left.

When you're done, you'll have a second extracted acapella extremely similar to the original extracted acapella, only this time the vocals are from the right channel of the original "Milkshake."

14. Copy the entire left channel of the new extracted acapella (Ctrl+A+L+C), and select the *right* channel of the waveform you created in step 10, and paste in the data

(Ctrl+A+R+V). Now copy the entire right channel of the newly extracted acapella and paste it into the right channel of the waveform you created in step 11.

15. The second waveform (from step 11) contains the 16.99101-second delay. To remove this, make sure all of both channels are selected (Ctrl+A+B) and type **0:16.99101** in the Selection End (upper-middle) text box in the Selection/View window. Press the Delete key. Both acapellas now have identical timing.

Alternatively, you may choose a shortcut and simply create two separate mono acapellas. If you choose to do this, instead of performing steps 10-15, select the left channel of the extracted acapella wave and copy it (Ctrl+L+C), create a new *mono* waveform (press Ctrl+N and choose Mono), and paste (Ctrl+V). Repeat the process for the right channel, deleting 16.99101 seconds as outlined in step 15.

Whew!

You've just created two stereo acapellas. The first stereo acapella has all the sounds in the full song, eliminating all sounds that continue in the next section. The second stereo acapella has all the sounds in the full song with all sounds in the *previous* section eliminated. There is a good chance you may need to use both acapellas.

Suppose you have a simple song with four sections. The first section is just a drum loop, the second and third sections have vocals and the drum loop, and the last section is just a drum loop again. The goal is to isolate the vocals from sections two and three.

With the acapella that eliminates all sounds from the *following* section, the second section may sound tinny, because the frequencies from the third section's vocal will be eliminated from it. The third section will sound great, though, because only the loop from the fourth section will have been eliminated from it.

With the acapella that eliminates all sounds from the *previous* section, the second section will sound great, because the first section contains only the drum loop. The third section will sound tinny because you are subtracting vocal frequencies from the vocal.

The solution in this case is to use the second section from the second acapella, and the third section from the first acapella.

In practice, you can load up both acapellas as separate tracks in ACID and use whichever sounds better during each part. You may even want to go so far as creating more than one pair of acapellas using different delay times.

Note

Unmixing using the time-shifting technique can work wonders on modern extended dance remixes. Often, an intro will be very long and drawn out, while the instrumentation gradually gets denser and denser. Each new section introduces new sounds added on top of the sounds from the previous section. Shifting the time by exactly one section and performing side channel extraction will isolate the sounds that are introduced in each section. The extended outros offer similar extraction opportunities.

Combination Techniques

Sometimes you may want to use more than one method to get the acapella separated from the background. You can often isolate the vocal with standard center channel extraction, but some material still remains, like the snare drum and other center-panned sounds. Sometimes you can get rid of still more material by using the time-shifting technique afterwards. Just be aware that each time you perform center channel extraction, the sound quality is reduced a bit.

Noise Reduction

The Noise Reduction effect is designed to get rid of unwanted background frequencies, particularly those that are relatively constant throughout a recording. Some of its more common uses are for removing tape hiss, ground loop hum, or microphone noise. Noise reduction can also be helpful when used in conjunction with the Center Channel Extractor.

Noise reduction is a two-step process:

1. Select just a portion of the wave without the vocals. It should have similar content to the background noise behind the vocals. Capture a noise profile, which will contain information about the frequencies you would like to remove. You can do this by selecting Effects ⇨ Noise Reduction ⇨ Capture Noise Reduction Profile. Alternatively, you could simply press Alt+N.

2. Process the entire wave using the profile you have just captured, reducing the unwanted frequencies, by selecting Effects ⇨ Noise Reduction ⇨ Noise Reduction.

Center channel extraction often leaves undesirable artifacts along with the acapella. If after extraction, you end up with an unusually messy acapella, you can capture a profile of just the nasty artifacts and then reduce them somewhat with noise reduction. This type of processing needs to be used sparingly, or it might make your acapella sound even worse. Too much noise reduction will make your vocals sound like a pile of bubbly digital beeps.

The Noise Reduction Screen is shown in Figure 10-20.

The single most important parameter here is the Noise Reduction Level. The higher you set this level, the more noise is reduced.

If you are having a problem with bubbly sounding results, you can try a combination of raising the Reduce By parameter, the Smoothing Amount, and the Spectral Decay Rate. Be careful when raising the Smoothing Amount or Spectral Decay Rate, because this may also increase the noise level, so don't raise these too high.

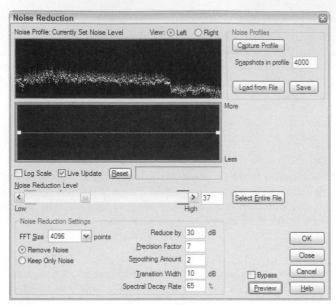

FIGURE 10-20: The Noise Reduction screen

Here's how to reduce some of the artifacts left over in the "Milkshake" acapella extracted from the full song and the instrumental. Load the wav file from that example now if it is not already loaded, and then follow these steps:

1. Select just under the first two seconds of the file. This is the *almost* silent part before the acapella starts. It contains the noise you want to eliminate without any vocals.

2. Press Alt+N to capture the noise reduction profile.

3. Select Effects ⇨ Restoration ⇨ Noise Reduction, enter the settings as shown in Figure 10-20, and click OK.

The noisy artifacts have been reduced without significant degradation to sound quality. Keep this wav file open or save it, because it will be further processed later in this chapter.

EQ

Because vocals occur in the middle range of frequencies, EQ is a valuable part of isolating them. A low-pass and a high-pass filter are built right into the Center Channel Extractor, to eliminate sounds that are outside of the range of the vocal.

If you use a phase cancellation technique to isolate your vocals instead, you will probably want to follow that up with some EQing to at least filter out the bass (see Figure 10-21).

Pro If you are making a mashup in ACID Pro, you can just EQ it there. The basic idea is to remove frequencies below 100–150 Hz. You can increase the rolloff for a more dramatic effect. (Chapter 12 provides a more complete explanation of ACID Pro's EQ.)

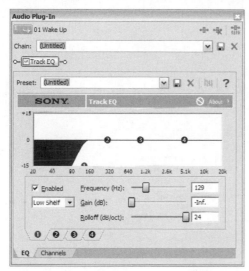

FIGURE 10-21: ACID Pro's EQ, removing the bass below the vocal range

Transient Elimination

Transient Elimination is one of the more overlooked methods of eliminating non-vocal sounds, especially drums. It can be labor-intensive, but remarkably effective. *Transients* are sounds that last only a very brief time, like hi-hats and the attack portion of snares. Often these sounds remain stubbornly noticeable after acapellas have been extracted using center channel extraction.

Adobe Audition has an effect called Click/Pop Eliminator, which is designed for getting rid of extremely short sounds, typically glitches in the recording process. These sounds usually have frequencies unrelated to the surrounding sounds, much like many percussive sounds you might be interested in removing.

You must painstakingly eliminate each one of these sounds individually. It would be great if you could just click a button and do this, but it requires many judgment calls to ensure that the intelligibility of the vocal isn't compromised.

 Note Don't confuse this with an effect called Auto Click/Pop Eliminator, which uses a much different algorithm and is of little use in transient elimination.

Adobe Audition's Spectral View

Although the Waveform view has the advantage of showing the wave data as it actually is stored, it can be hard to decode, especially when there are many different frequencies over-lapping each other.

The Spectral view addresses those problems by showing you a map of the intensity of all of the frequencies within the waveform over time.

In Audition's Spectral view, you can perform any operation on specific frequencies within a time window. To do this, follow these steps:

1. Switch to spectral view by selecting View ⇨ Spectral View.

2. Choose the Marquee selection tool, which looks like Figure 10-22.

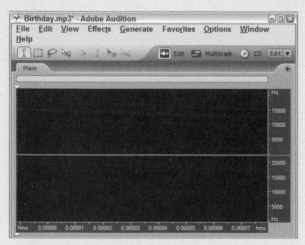

FIGURE 10-22: Marquee selection tool

3. Drag the mouse across the waveform, simultaneously selecting a time range and a frequency range.

4. Perform the operation. This can be any operation you would perform on the waveform in Waveform view.

Figure 10-23 shows you the Spectral view of the panned rhythmic pattern from Figure 10-6. The time scale is identical to that of the Waveform view, but now the vertical scale shows the frequencies within the wave rather than the position of the waveform itself. The color of the graph represents the intensity of the sound at that particular frequency, with blue being a low intensity, yellow being the highest intensity, and red being in between.

Adobe Audition's Spectral View *Continued*

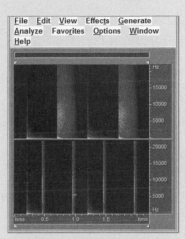

FIGURE **10-23: The Spectral view of the panned rhythmic pattern from Figure 10-6**

Notice the sharp attack on all three types of percussion sounds. This is typical for all kinds of percussion.

The leftmost event is the kick, which appears in both channels. You can see a sharp attack that has a broad spectrum of frequencies. The higher frequencies decay extremely rapidly while the lower frequencies linger, creating a shape like a capital *L*.

The other events in the right (lower) channel are hi-hats. You can see the short time span of this percussive event as well as its broad and relatively high frequency.

The snare is represented by the other event in the left (upper) channel. The snare differs from the hi-hat in that the decay is much longer and the frequency content, although still broad, is slightly lower.

To eliminate an offending drum sound, follow these steps:

1. Zoom in on the percussive sound.

2. Select the portion of the wave starting at a point just before the attack, and ending just beyond the last portion of the sound you want to eliminate. Do not select more than one percussive burst in your selection. In general, the less you select the better.

3. Choose Effects ➪ NoiseReduction ➪ Click/Pop Eliminator.

4. Click the Auto Find All Levels button.

5. Click the Fill Single Click Now button.

The percussive sound should be gone now. This unfortunately can sometimes also eliminate portions of the vocals as well, especially when explosive consonants (Ps, Bs, Ts, Ds, Ks, and Gs) coincide with the instrumental percussion. This is when the spectral view comes in handy. Often, when the Click/Pop Eliminator gets rid of intelligible vocal sounds, you can undo it: Highlight just some of the frequencies in the Spectral view and try again.

Gating

A *gate* is a form of dynamics processing that seeks to further attenuate the already quiet portions of a waveform. This can sometimes be used after center channel extraction to quiet down the remaining artifacts that occur in the gaps between the vocal phrases. When the sound drops below a certain level, the gate will shut it down entirely. Gating uses the same dynamics processing effect that you used in the last chapter in compression and limiting, but with much different settings. As you can see in Figure 10-24, the upper-right part of the dynamics curve is perfectly aligned with the dotted line, which represents the unprocessed sound. But below a certain threshold (-30dB in the figure), the sound attenuates sharply.

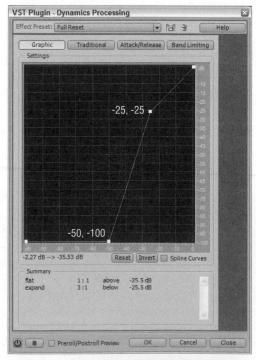

FIGURE 10-24: The Dynamics Processing screen, showing an example of noise gating

Here are the steps to finding the best gating curve for your signal:

1. Choose Effects ⇨ Amplitude ⇨ Dynamics Processing, and then choose one of the built-in Noise Gate presets.

2. Adjust the cutoff point (the second point from the top right). Click the Preview button and listen to the sound. If too much noise is coming through between the gaps in the desired sound, drag the cutoff point down and left along the dotted line. If too much sound is being cut out, drag the cutoff point up and right along the dotted line. Remember that for pure gating, the upper section of the curve remains on the dotted line, preserving the dynamics above the threshold. If you find that you need to lower the threshold below the floor point (the second point from the bottom left), you may need to first adjust the floor point, moving it to the left. (Leave the top-right and bottom-left points alone for this exercise.)

3. Adjust the floor point to achieve the most natural sounding cutoffs. If the on/off is too striking, then move the floor point to the left, and if the effect is not strong or sharp enough, move the floor point to the right. Vertically, leave the point at 0 (zero) or at a very low level.

Back in the noise reduction sample, you got rid of most of the noise in the "Milkshake" acapella extracted earlier in this chapter. But there are still remaining artifacts, particularly noticeable during the "silence" in the vocals. Here's how to reduce some of the artifacts left over in the "Milkshake" acapella extracted from the full song and the instrumental:

1. Load the wav from that example now if it is not already loaded.

2. Drag the existing point at -20,-20 so that it's located around -25,-25, as shown in Figure 10-24.

3. Create another point in the longer section of the blue line, clicking anywhere along its length. Drag this new point down to -50,-100, as shown in Figure 10-24.

4. Click OK and listen. The quiet portions of the wave are all cleaned up now. Not bad for a homemade acapella!

Audio from Surround Sound

Surround sound is simply a term used for recordings that use more than two channels. Although most music today is produced for stereo, increasing numbers of recordings are being released in multichannel surround sound formats. Additionally, record companies have figured out that if they remaster an old album in 5.1 surround sound, enthusiasts who already own the stereo recordings will go out and repurchase it.

Surround-sound techniques have been around in film since as far back as the 1940s, and most movies have been produced using multichannel sound for many decades. During the late 1960s, people began experimenting with quadraphonic recordings, which consisted of a left and right channel, like regular stereo, but added an additional left and right rear channel. A good number of recordings from the late 1960s and early 1970s were produced for four speakers.

Unfortunately, quadraphonic recordings didn't really catch on due to the expense of the stereo equipment and a lack of agreement on formats by manufacturers.

But with the advent of the VCR, and later the DVD, consumers began to demand stereo equipment that accurately reproduced the surround sound experience of the movie theater. Home movie viewing spurred the growth of multichannel consumer audio systems in the home.

The great thing about surround sound from the mashup producer's standpoint is that the unmixing has been given a big kick-start for you. Instead of spreading the sound across two channels, there are now six channels of sound. Many new possibilities for further unmixing will open up, possibly used in conjunction with the Center Channel Extractor.

Surround Sound Formats

Although there are many surround sound formats, the most common today is known as 5.1 Surround Sound. It consists of a left and right speaker, along with an additional center speaker, all set up in front of the listener. There are also two surround speakers, left and right, which sit to the left and right of the listener. There is also an additional subwoofer channel. Because lower frequencies are difficult for the human ear to pinpoint spatially, they can all be routed to a single speaker without a perceived loss of spatialization.

The term 5.1 refers to the five speakers plus one subwoofer. There are other less common configurations besides 5.1, such as 5.0, with no subwoofer; 6.1, with a center-back speaker; and 7.1, with a left-back and right-back speaker.

Surround sound can also be encoded in various formats:

- **Dolby Digital (also known as AC3):** The most common form of surround sound for DVD Video and cable, digital broadcast, and satellite TV. On your hard drive, this file will have an extension of .ac3, or it will be multiplexed with other DVD data and stored as a VOB file.

- **DTS:** Another method of encoding audio information on a DVD, although not all DVD players support it. DTS comes on both DVD and CD. DTS stores its information as encoded audio. On your hard drive, it may look like a wav file, and on a CD, it is stored as CD audio.

- **SACD:** A relatively new high fidelity proprietary format. It incorporates a copy-protection scheme and will work only on SACD-enabled CD players, which are becoming increasingly common. SACD will not work on a PC. Recent SACDs are hybridized, which means that they will work on a regular CD player, but will play back an audio signal from the disc identical to regular CDs.

- **DVD-Audio (also known as DVD-A):** A recent DVD format that stresses higher fidelity than either DVD Video or CD. DVD-Audio uses copy-protection schemes that make ripping the audio difficult, although tools do exist for DVD-Audio extraction.

Other formats are available as well, but because the majority of surround recordings available are either in AC3 or DTS, this section focuses on these two formats. Audio enthusiasts claim that DTS offers the higher fidelity of the two, using more data than AC3 to store the same duration of six-channel audio.

Ideally, a surround sound recording will be as unmixed as possible, with sounds recorded on some channels and not on others. Maybe the lead vocal will be soloed on the center channel. Maybe the drums are in both the front and surround channels, and the lead vocal is in the front channels.

To edit the surround sound data, you will need to rip and convert it into a six-channel wav file that Adobe Audition can understand. Following are techniques for ripping and converting both the AC3 and DTS formats.

AC3

Video DVDs have their sound encoded in AC3 (Dolby Digital) format. Many concert and music video DVDs are available in AC3 Surround. Look for "Dolby Digital 5.1 Surround" somewhere on the DVD.

Getting the VOB File

Inside a DVD are files with the extensions .IFO, .BUP, and .VOB. The VOB files contain the audio, usually in AC3 format, multiplexed together with video and subtitle data. To get into a .VOB file, you need to rip the DVD first.

Be aware that ripping a DVD may or may not be legal in your country. There are tools and information for copying the .VOB files onto your hard drive at www.doom9.org/software2 .htm#rippers. Doom9 also has guides that offer step-by-step instructions at www.doom9 .org/index.html?/descrambling-guides.htm.

Splitting the VOB

After you've loaded VOB files on your hard drive, you can pull out the AC3 and split it into six (mono) wavs, each representing one channel of the 5.1 Dolby Digital signal. The best tool to use for this is BeSweet, currently located at http://dspguru.doom9.net. Download the stable versions rather than the beta versions for best results. From this website you will need the following:

- BeSweet (from the stable page, dspguru.doom9.net/stable.htm)
- BeSweet GUI (also from the stable page)
- VOBInput.dll (from the Plug-ins&Source page, http://dspguru.doom9.net/ plug-ins.htm)

Unzip BeSweet, BeSweet GUI, and VOBInput.dll all into same directory. You may want to create a directory in your program files directory called BeSweet. Double-click BeSweetGUIxxxx.exe, where xxxx is the version number. You will see a window that looks like Figure 10-25.

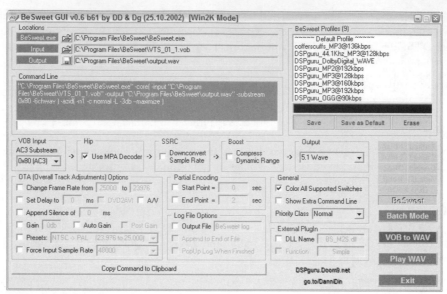

FIGURE 10-25: BeSweet GUI

You may need to alter the following four settings on the BeSweet GUI:

- **BeSweet location:** If the current path of your BeSweet.exe doesn't show up next to "BeSweet.exe" in the Locations section at the top-left of the BeSweet GUI, click the open folder icon, navigate to BeSweet.exe, and click OK.

- **Input file location:** Click the open-folder Input icon in the Locations section. When the Select Input window pops up, make sure the .vob suffix is selected in the Enter File Name drop-down, navigate to your VOB file, and click OK.

- **Output format:** This is located in the BeSweet Profiles section at the top-right of the BeSweet GUI. Set the Output to 5.1 Wave. Be aware that the output label may default to something other than the word "Output," depending on the initial settings.

- **Output file location:** Click the Output floppy disk icon in the Locations section of the BeSweet GUI. When the Select Output window pops up, enter the desired name of your output file, navigate to the folder you want to store it in, and click OK.

After you enter your settings, simply click the VOB To WAV button. You will end up with a six-channel wav file.

DTS

DTS is available on some DVDs and specially encoded CDs. Many classic quadraphonic-era recordings are available in this format, and other recordings have been remastered in surround sound and rereleased.

DTS CDs can be found in music stores online and retail outlets. DTS recordings can also be found on BitTorrent (as a search for "DTS torrent" will show you) and other P2P networks. There are also Usenet newsgroups devoted to files in the DTS format.

Ripping the DTS file

Because DTS data is not scrambled, but rather reencoded as a stereo wav file, you can obtain the data simply by ripping the CD to a wav. The simplest thing to do is rip it using iTunes. To make sure you have iTunes set to import as wav rather than mp3, choose Edit ⇨ Preferences and select the Importing tab. Make sure WAV Encoder is the Import Using selection. After inserting your DTS CD, click the Import button that appears in the upper-right of iTunes.

Do not play this wav or CD in iTunes, especially at full volume. It will sound like pure noise without a DTS decoder.

Converting the DTS-WAV into a Six-Channel WAV

Adobe Audition or Sony ACID will import a DTS-WAV file, but it will sound like pure static because it is encoded. You need to decode the DTS-WAV file first. A program to do just that is called DTSdec, and is located at `www.rarewares.org/others.html`. It is a very small and simple command-line utility. Create a new folder in your `C:\Program Files` folder, call it dtsdec, and unzip the downloaded files into the new directory.

The following process will convert a regular two-channel encoded DTS-WAV into a six-channel unencoded wav file:

1. Copy your DTS-WAV into the `C:\Program Files\dtsdec` folder, and rename it **dts.wav**.

2. Choose Start ⇨ Run and type **cmd** to open the command line.

3. Type **cd c:\program files\dtsdec** and press Enter to navigate to the appropriate folder.

4. Type **dtsdec.exe -o wavall > output.wav dts.wav** and press Enter.

The conversion should start up and soon you will have a file called output.wav, which is a six-channel wav file. Although some software can read this multichannel wav file, you'll need to do some further work before you can use any of the six channels in ACID.

Getting Mono and Stereo wavs from the Six-Channel wav

Open your six-channel wav in Adobe Audition. Audition immediately converts it into six mono waveforms. The first channel will bear the name of your initial wav, and the other five will have the numbers 2 through 6 appended to the end. For example, if your six-channel wav was called output.wav, after you've loaded it into Adobe Audition, your six mono waves will be titled as follows:

- **output.wav:** The left channel
- **output (2).wav:** The right channel

- **output (3).wav:** The center channel

- **output (4).wav:** The LFE channel (subwoofer)

- **output (5).wav:** The left surround channel

- **output (6).wav:** The right surround channel

In many surround recordings, the LFE channel will be empty. Additionally, if the recording has been converted from an old quadraphonic recording, the center channel may be silent as well. Each of the waves will be 32-bit if derived from DTS, and 16-bit if from AC3.

Using the Mono Files

Each of these channels represents a relatively unmixed version of the music compared with a stereo version. Often you'll find fantastic content in the center channel, such as raw vocals, or vocals mixed with minimal instrumentation. Often the front channels will provide a clean mixdown of the entire song without any reverberation or echo effects.

You can simply select the mono wavs you are interested in, choose File ⇨ Save As, and save the individual wav files, ready to be imported into ACID.

Note   Each of these wavs will have identical timing, and therefore should have identical offsets and bpm settings within ACID.

Creating Stereo wavs

On occasion, you might want to extract two of these mono waves and store them as a single stereo waveform. For example, you may want to combine the front-left and front-right channels into a stereo mixdown without the center channel or rear channel information. This can sometimes result in an instrumental mix with fewer effects than the original. Or you may want to generate a left-right mix of just the surround speakers.

The process of creating a new stereo wav is fairly straightforward. Using the extraction of the front left and right channels from a six-channel output.wav as an example, the steps are as follows:

1. Open the six-channel output.wav in Adobe Audition. The front left channel should be visible.

2. Press Ctrl+A+C to select the entire waveform and copy it.

3. Press Ctrl+N to create a new waveform, making sure you select Stereo.

4. Press Ctrl+L+V to select the new left channel and paste in the front-left channel data.

5. Select Window ⇨ Output (2).wav. Your wav name may be different, but the waveform with the (2) will be the front-right channel.

6. Press Ctrl+A+C to select the entire waveform and copy it.

7. Select Window ⇨ Untitled.

8. Press Ctrl+A+R+V to select the entire right channel of your new waveform and paste in the front-right channel data.

9. Select File ⇨ Save As and save your new stereo wav file.

Manipulating Stereo Waves

After you've created a stereo wav file from the surround sound, you can perform center channel extraction or suppression as discussed earlier in this chapter. In this case, you may not be interested in isolating or eliminating material actually panned to the center, but rather material shared between any two arbitrary channels from which you've just created your own stereo waveform. Of particular interest are situations where various elements of the mix have different distribution among the channels.

For example, suppose you happen upon a remastering of a vintage quadraphonic recording. There are drums, guitar, and bass in both the front and the rear speakers. Being a quadraphonic recording, there is no center channel or subwoofer channel. The vocals are centered between the front-left and the front-right channels, the guitar is panned left in both the front and the rear speakers, the drums are panned right in both the front and the rear speakers, and the bass is panned center in both the front and the rear. If you were to do a simple center channel extraction of the front-left and front-right channels, you would end up with the lead vocals along with the center-panned bass. However, if you create a stereo wave from the front-left and surround-left channels, your wave will have the formerly left-panned guitar at full volume in both channels, the formerly center-panned drums at a slightly lower volume in both channels, and the vocals in only one of the channels. Basically, you end up with a new stereo wave with the drums and bass panned somewhere near the center and the vocals panned hard left (or right, depending on the order in which you paste your channels).

Another example is when you have front-left and front-right channels with a full mixdown except for the vocals, and the vocals are in the center channel, except they are mixed with a bit of the left-front and right-front channels. In this situation, first create a stereo wave of the front-left and front-right channels. Then, select Effects ⇨ Amplitude ⇨ Channel Mixer. Choose the Average preset, which will sum the two channels into a mono mixdown (though there will still be two identical channels). Cut and paste one of these channels into the left side of a new stereo wave, and paste the center channel of the six-channel mix in the right side. You will now have an instrumental in both channels and the vocals in only the right channel.

In both of these examples, the stereo wave you've constructed may not have equal amounts of the material you want to eliminate in both channels. You may need to adjust the pan setting in your Center Channel Extractor. Check the Spectral Pan Display of any wavs you construct, especially if you are creating front or surround extractions. Then perform center channel suppression as detailed earlier in this chapter. Ideally, you will end up with a wave that is mostly silent, with the vocals in one channel. Copy just that channel (Ctrl+A+L+C or Ctrl+A+R+C) and then create a new mono wav and paste the copied material.

Breaking It Down

Hopefully, this chapter has inspired you to create your own acapellas and not solely rely on the commercially available vocals that everyone else is using. If you want to discuss ideas about acapella extraction, there's a section devoted to DIY acapellas in the forum at `http://acapellas4u.co.uk`. Unmixing can be hard work, but it's rewarding when you're able to create a remix with material that's never been remixed before.

Arrangement: Putting It All Together

By now you've learned how to pick songs to combine and how to make sure they are in time and in key. But given the exact same materials, different mashup artists will create wildly different sounding mashups. It turns out that there is a lot more to making mashups than just getting the tracks locked together. *Arrangement*, or the order and combination of the various elements in your component tracks, is where the real artistry comes in. Here is your chance to give your mashup a sense of drama and purpose. A great mashup shares many characteristics of a great song. In fact, many of the secrets to great songwriting and arranging very much apply to the mashup genre. After all, the ultimate purpose of creating a mashup is to generate music worth listening to. For this reason, it's good to look at what makes music worth listening to in the first place.

Mashup arrangement happens on multiple levels simultaneously. First, the pieces of each song need to be identified and broken up into sections and loops. The loops need to be smooth and steady, and the sections need to be complete, either beginning or ending on an important beat or perhaps some other logical point.

Second, these sections and loops are layered on top of one another, making sure that there are at least two tracks playing much of the time, and taking care not to create overlapping vocals, overly busy rhythms, or areas of key clash.

Third, these layered sections are arranged into a larger form of usually a few minutes. The mashup often has form borrowed from traditional or dance music, and will usually feature an intro, outro, and a verse/chorus/bridge structure.

Single-Song Techniques

Before delving into how to combine the various song elements, a discussion of how to find the parts of a song best suited for combining is in order. There are so many ways to cut up and rearrange a song. It's useful to create a bunch of sections and loops in order to play around with them, combine them in layers, and order them sequentially. These sections may be full song sections such as an entire verse or the entire intro, or they may be one- or two-bar loops that sound really smooth. It's useful to view your component songs as a collection of isolated sections at your disposal, rather than functioning as they are in the current context. Sometimes creating your own sections and listening to them individually can be useful, because it takes you a step away from the original, which may allow you to make your own arrangement without preconception.

Usually by the time you've decided on a particular song combination, you've already laid the songs down in ACID and listened to them play at the same time. Often this is the only way to really tell if two songs have chemistry together. Although it's tempting to simply tweak this haphazard duet, it's often wise to take a step back and really take inventory before you start structuring your mashup. Sure, the intro to Song A sounds great against Song B. But just because you've painted them each at the beginning of the track doesn't mean that this is the best option.

Having a variety of usable sections and loops at your disposal will not only give you a big picture of what's going on in each of your songs, it will also allow you flexibility and control. Because so much of what happens in a mashup is out of your control, every little bit of control helps!

A mashup artist's worst enemy is inaction. Always remember, just because an original song has a certain flow doesn't mean your mashup has to have the same flow. Play with your tracks. Cut them up. Rearrange them. Have fun.

The Instrumental Loop

The instrumental loop is a fundamental building block of a mashup. Along with an acapella, a single instrumental loop as a background can make a complete (albeit a bit boring) mashup. However, if you simply vary a few different instrumental loops behind a minimally edited acapella, you may very well be able to produce a mashup that sounds pretty good.

Referring back to Chapter 4, in the section on the basics of form, you'll find a few sections that are typically instrumental in nature: the intro, outro, instrumental break, and breakdown. These are usually the first places to look for your instrumental loops.

Intros are great sources for instrumental loops in many cases. Often a song will introduce a groove and chord progression before the vocals kick in. If you're lucky, you'll get a long intro with several sections, each introducing a new theme or each building in intensity. In dance music and remixes particularly, you'll find long intros that build. This extra instrumental material is put there to allow a beatmatching DJ time to bring in the new song, but it's perfect for mashup artists too.

Outros can be a decent source in some cases. Often the end of a song can have a repeating instrumental that is perfect for looping, although in many pop songs the chorus is simply repeated over and over at the end. However, in dance music, you'll usually find great long instrumental bits after the vocals end and the rhythm goes on.

Instrumental breaks offer good opportunities to nick instrumental bits. Although they are usually short, slipped in between two verses, they can often produce gems. Classic rock "jam" style bands will often have long instrumental sections, although if there's too much instrumental soloing going on, it might make for an overly dense pairing.

If your song has a breakdown, that's very good news. Not only are breakdowns typically entirely instrumental, but the density is pared way down, which makes it combinable with other songs. If the breakdown goes on for long enough, you may find yourself with enough material for several instrumental loops.

Making the Loop

So now you've found an instrumental section that you like, and you want to make a loop out of it. Generally, you'd like it to be as long as possible — the shorter the loop, the quicker the ear tires of it. Ideally, you'd be able to make a loop that's as long as the entire musical section. Successful loops can be short, such as a one- or two-bar pattern, but shorter loops are often made to sound less monotonous by layering them with loops of longer duration. Additionally, the loop's length is usually in a musically repeatable duration such as 1, 2, 4, 8, 16, or 32 bars. Shorter, longer, and unusual durations are possible but not common. Because other elements in your mashup will probably share these same durations, the sections should align and layer nicely.

Most importantly, an instrumental loop *sounds* repeatable. This means that the end of the loop flows into the beginning of the loop without sounding jarring. So if there's a singer whose last note ends on the first beat of your instrumental loop, it's probably not going to sound so smooth when the loop starts again and the vocal bit starts again mid-phrase. Likewise, if the instrumental section ends with a few guitar notes leading into the next section, it might sound funny cut off without resolution.

Often instrumental sections will have fills, drop-outs, or other elements toward the last measures to punctuate the section or give the listener an idea that a new section is coming. This sometimes sounds okay repeating, but other times it results in an anticlimax when the expected change doesn't happen. Ultimately, whether a section sounds repeatable is up to you.

Hacking the Loop

Sometimes, you have the choicest piece of music but the looping transition is just a little bit off, or there's a bit of vocals you'd like to eliminate somewhere in the loop. There are a few ways to go about this.

For example, suppose you have a great eight-bar instrumental section with just the vibe you are looking for, as represented in Figure 11-1.

Bar 1 Wind Up Chord W	Bar 2 Chord X	Bar 3 Chord Y	Bar 4 Chord Z	Bar 5 Chord W	Bar 6 Chord X	Bar 7 Chord X	Bar 8 Wind Down Chord Z

FIGURE 11-1: An instrumental section that a loop could be made from

You split the event at the beginning and end of the section and then paste a few copies of it, but the transition doesn't sound right, because the section seems to spend the first bar winding down from the previous section and the last bar winding up for the next section. The simplest thing to do would be to simply create a shorter loop, avoiding these wind-ups and wind-downs.

If there is a four-chord repeating pattern, with two complete progressions in the eight bars, even those who don't know what a chord is will intuitively feel an anomaly if the chord progression is scrambled. So ideally you'd like to preserve it. Simply taking bars 1 through 4, or 5 through 8, will preserve the chord progression, but this will not alleviate the looping problem because each four-bar loop contains a problem bar you are trying to eliminate. And a simple two-bar loop consisting of bars 3 and 4, or bars 5 and 6, would work well, but replacing an eight-bar loop with a two-bar loop seems a bit extreme, and the chord pattern is altered.

A simple and elegant solution would be to simply take bars 3 through 6 as a four-bar instrumental loop. Although this solution does indeed work, it needs to be used with caution. Remember that you ideally will preserve the chord progression, and that while bars 3 through 6 have the same chords, the order is displaced by two bars. If you were to place this new loop directly after another section of the same song, the chords wouldn't sound right. The solution to the problem is to place bars 5 and 6 at the beginning of the loop and bars 3 and 4 next. The loop progresses in the same order, but it just starts at bar 5, so that the chord progression remains intact, as shown Figure 11-2.

Bar 5 Chord W	Bar 6 Chord X	Bar 3 Chord Y	Bar 4 Chord Z	Bar 5 Chord W	Bar 6 Chord X	Bar 3 Chord Y	Bar 4 Chord Z

FIGURE 11-2: The instrumental section made into a smooth four-bar loop

Suppose there is a great little lick in bar 2 that you just need to have, and you miss it terribly in this 5-6-3-4 concoction. Well, there's nothing wrong with creating a 5-2-3-4 loop or even a 5-6-7-4 loop — as long as the loop length remains a nice power of two and you can vary the loop's start and end points. You can even place them in the middle of a bar or beat, as long as both ends of the loop are at exactly the same point within the bar or beat.

Now suppose you really like both bar 2 and bar 7. In fact, you're pretty fond of all the instrumental section except for those pesky bars 1 and 8. This is when you really need to hack a loop together. Remember: Preserve the placement as much as possible to avoid nasty chord-progression-altering experiences. In this case, you have bar 1 with the same chord as bar 5, and bar 4 with the same chord as bar 8. If you simply split bar 5 at its beginning and end, you can copy it and then paste a copy directly over bar 1. Similarly, you can place a copy of bar 4 on top of bar 8. The result is a great eight-bar instrumental loop with even more musical variety than the four-bar solution, as shown in Figure 11-3.

Bar 5 Chord W	Bar 2 Chord X	Bar 3 Chord Y	Bar 4 Chord Z	Bar 5 Chord W	Bar 6 Chord X	Bar 7 Chord Y	Bar 4 Chord Z

FIGURE 11-3: An eight-bar instrumental loop with more variety than the previous loop

Even if you don't know or don't want to know how long the chord progression is, you can still use this technique. Just remember to follow the principals of placement preservation and get the replacement material from 16, 8, 4, or 2 bars away within the same section. Experiment and let your ears be your guide. Be aware that different sections often have different chord progressions.

Placement Preservation

Sections of audio material are routinely moved about when you're arranging your mashups within ACID. It's important to keep in mind that when you're moving a bit of music from its original spot to a new spot, there are preferred places for that piece of music to go, where it will fit in best. Remember that in music, there are many levels of repetition going on simultaneously, whether it is a hi-hat pattern repeating every quarter note, a drum rhythm repeating every bar, a chord progression repeating every four bars, or a verse/chorus repeating in 32-bar increments.

A bit of music will sound best if it's placed in a position similar to its original position within the repeating pattern. For example, if you take a snippet from the third bar of a repeating four-bar pattern, it most likely will sound best in the third bar of another four-bar pattern elsewhere. If the original was from the second repetition of that four-bar pattern and can be dropped in the middle of another second repetition, so much the better.

As long as your displacement coincides with the natural beat, measure, and section lengths of your material, multiples of larger displacements typically work best. So for example, a four-, eight- or twelve-bar displacement will usually sound better than a two- or six-bar displacement, both of which in turn usually sound better than a one- or three-bar displacement. Displacements that add half measures to the whole-measure displacements fall next in order of preference, followed by displacements involving quarter notes, eighth notes, and so on. Generally, music that is displaced by higher multiples of two sounds best. This makes it probable that the snippet's new home is very similar to the place it left. Of course, if your section length is unusual, or if you are operating in triple or some other meter, you may need to make appropriate adjustments.

Sections Containing Vocals

After you get some good instrumental loops together, you probably want to combine them with some vocals sections. Although acapellas offer the easiest way to layer without clash, you can often achieve good results with full-mixed songs, and you can often create partially isolated vocals using the techniques from Chapter 10. The important thing to remember with vocals (or any other sections of music) is that you don't need to leave things as they are. You can drop out portions of the vocal to make room for other elements, and you can rearrange the words and phrasing.

Looping a vocal section would turn it into a refrain, but most of the time a vocal section will simply be played once before moving on to another section. It's a good idea to just create vocal sections to see what is possible before deciding on the ultimate form of the mashup. These sections are just building blocks to be used later.

Hybrid Vocal/Instrumental Sections

If you are creating vocal sections from full songs, quite often you will find that an instrumental loop from the same song shares the same chord progression as a part with vocals. This presents a great opportunity for vocal manipulation by switching between the vocal portion and the instrumental portion to create sections with just the phrases you want while eliminating the ones you don't. The result is a hybrid vocal/instrumental section. This can come in handy when you're layering two sections containing vocals while trying to avoid unnecessary vocal overlap between the two songs.

If you can't find a decent instrumental loop in your song to manipulate, you can always try to create your own instrumental loop through center channel suppression, outlined in Chapter 10, and combine a section from that with the section from the full mix.

The general process to create a hybrid vocal/instrumental section is as follows:

1. Create an instrumental loop, using the techniques from the previous section. Make sure that your instrumental loop has a bass line if the vocal section has one too, or the bass will drop in and out. Ideally, the loop will have instrumentation, density, and chord progressions similar to those of the vocal section.

2. Duplicate the original track, and then copy and paste your instrumental loop for several minutes (the duration of the song).

3. Draw the complete song on the original track or create another duplicate track and draw the complete song.

4. If the complete song has irregular section lengths, you may need to shuffle the instrumental loops around a bit to keep the "1"s from happening simultaneously.

5. Identify the sections where the song sounds good with the instrumental loop. (These sections probably have identical chord progressions as the loop.) Line up two compatible sections, one with vocals and one without, making sure that the vocal sections have bass lines as well. (Because different simultaneous bass lines result in muddy, ugly key clash, you will be able to recognize the compatible parts by the fact that they don't sound like doo-doo.)

6. Using either the erase tool or by splitting the event and dragging the edges, eliminate the vocals you don't want to hear in the vocal track.

7. Again using either the erase tool or by splitting the event and dragging the edges, eliminate from the instrumental track the portions of the event that occur while the vocal track is playing. What is left is an instrumental track that is playing while the vocal track is silent, and is silent while the vocal track is playing.

You now have a vocal section with only the vocals you want. You can use this trick with two vocal sections or two instrumental sections if you want to experiment. The main thing to remember is that when you are ending an event on a particular measure and beat in a section, the event you want to try placing after it will probably start on the same measure and beat in another section.

Here's an example using "Sweet Dreams" by the Eurythmics. If you beatmapped this song already in Chapter 7, you will not have to re-beatmap it when you drop it into ACID again. The first four bars of this song sound great as an instrumental loop. Just follow these steps:

1. Drop the song into ACID, and Ctrl+click with the paint tool, creating an event that contains the entire song.

2. Duplicate the track, zoom in if necessary, put your cursor at beat marker 5.1 on the second track, and type **S** to split it.

3. Click the four-bar section you've just cut off at the beginning of track two and press Ctrl+C to copy it.

4. Place your cursor at beat marker 5.1 again and press Ctrl+B to multiple-paste it.

5. Enter **25** and click OK.

You now have two tracks, one with an instrumental loop and the other with the full song. Click the Play button. The tracks sound doubled, but they sound pretty compatible for at least the first 20 bars.

The goal of this exercise is to isolate "Who am I" from the first four-bar vocal section of the "Sweet Dreams" vocals, where Annie Lennox sings, "Sweet dreams are made of this. Who am I to disagree?" By playing measures 5 through 8 with the beginning instrumental section looped underneath, you've determined that the two layers are perfectly compatible, though doubled. The key is to get rid of the doubling, deleting material from each track until just the vocals you want remain. Here's how:

1. The phrase "Who am I" occurs just after bar 7 and ends by bar 8. Place your cursor on the first track on bar 7 and type **S** to split it. Repeat this on bar 7 of the second track.

2. Type **S** two more times, once on bar 8 in track 1 and again on bar 8 in track 2.

3. Split the first track at beat marker 5.1. Measures 5 through 8 of your ACID project should look something like Figure 11-4.

4. It's time to get rid of what you don't need. A single song with similar sounds should rarely be doubled as it is currently. Click the event in the first track between 5.1 and 7.1 and press Delete.

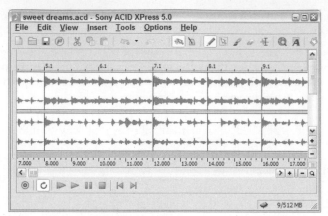

FIGURE 11-4: "Sweet Dreams" after layering an instrumental loop and splitting

5. Repeat the process for the event in the first track between 8.1 and 9.1, and then the event in the second track between 7.1 and 8.1.

6. Place the cursor at 5.1 and click Play. This sounds *almost* like the intended results, with the vocal saying only "Who am I to." This kind of rough approximation is a common first step, and you only need to move the edges of the events a little bit to get rid of the word "to."

7. Drag both edges that are on beat 8.1 one-quarter note to the left (that's one quarter of the distance from 7.1 to 8.1). Your project should now look something like Figure 11-5.

8. Place the cursor at 5.1 and click Play.

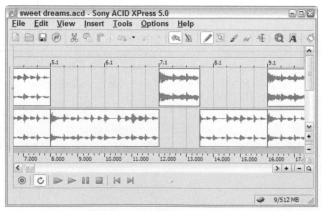

FIGURE 11-5: "Sweet Dreams" with a hybrid vocal/instrumental section

The goal has been achieved! You have a hybrid vocal/instrumental section where the chord progression is smooth, the instrumentation is constant, and the vocals have been eliminated except for the one desired phrase.

You can use this technique to isolate a few words of a song to alter their context, or you might want to insert a brief vocal line from one song during a pause of the vocals in the other song.

Acapellas

Acapellas are a bit easier to mangle and chop up than full songs, but because of the lack of strong rhythmic cues, they can be easily misaligned. Acapellas are usually best placed in the same position in any new section as their original placement. But because of the simplicity of the musical material, usually a single melody, they can often be placed more flexibly, two bars displaced, one bar displaced, or even ½ or ¼ bars displaced.

If you somehow get an acapella and you've never heard the full song, it's a good idea find it and listen to it. Because there aren't as many rhythmic cues in an acapella as there are in a full song, it's easy to mishear the rhythm. This could result in placing the vocals in a position offset from where they are in the original song without even being aware of it. Although this placement may sound normal to your ears, it will sound different to those familiar with the song. Not that offset placement is wrong, but it ought to be intentional.

Cross-Reference Beatmapping acapellas is discussed in Chapter 7.

It's best to beatmap the entire acapella before starting to cut it up and move it. This way, all your timing is solved from the beginning, and as long as you place the acapella in similar spots, you'll retain the timing. For this reason, it's sometimes easier to shift the start of vocal tracks to important beats before you move them.

For example, suppose you have a vocal track that starts one sixteenth note before the downbeat, you have Snap turned on, and your current grid is one beat. As you drag this vocal to its new location, the beginning of the event will snap to the beginning of the beat, even though it ought to start one sixteenth note early. If, however, you shortened the vocal event so it started on the downbeat, removing the very beginning of the vocal, you could drag this vocal and it would snap right in place, making precise placement easy. After finding the vocal's proper placement, you'd zoom in and extend the track to the left, once again allowing the vocal intro.

Transitions

Now that you've covered some ground on how to make the sections, you might be curious about putting the sections in sequence, one after another. Typically, a good transition will be invisible, and the listener will have no idea that they are suddenly listening to a different section of the song. Other successful transitions will draw attention to themselves, but in a pleasant and artistic way. What you generally want to avoid are transitions that are unintentionally obvious or jarring. Because each audio file is cut up into many sections and pieced back together, there are almost as many transitions as there are sections.

Often a sloppy transition can be partially masked by layering it with other tracks. Although it's still audible upon careful listening, it may not jump out at you when you're listening to all tracks play at once. For this reason, it's a good idea to solo each track in your final mashup and listen to each play all the way through. This will expose your transitions and let you more easily spot any that need additional work.

On the One

This is the simplest and most common transition. Your previous event ends right on a downbeat, and your next event starts on a downbeat, so you paste in the event right at the downbeat where the previous event ended, as shown in Figure 11-6. You play back the two events in ACID, and everything sounds great. Mission accomplished.

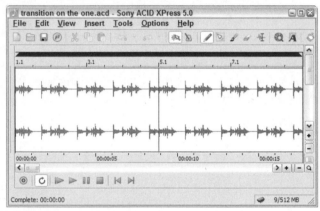

FIGURE 11-6: Transition on the one

Displaced

Suppose your previous transition's event ends right on a downbeat, and your next event starts on a downbeat but is missing a few words from before the downbeat, so when you play the events, the timing is right but a few words are missing. What you'll need to do is displace the transition so it occurs earlier. To restore the missing words in ACID, use the select or draw tool to drag the right edge of the first event to the left, and then drag the left edge of the second event to the left by the same amount. Alternatively, you could paint from within the second event to the left until the proper amount of material is replaced (in ACID Pro 6, the second event must be beatmapped for this method). If the material in both events is similar, your transition point can be placed almost anywhere. If the material is quite different, the transition will be noticeable. In this case, instead of trying to mask the transition, place it square on a beat and let it make a statement when it comes in. Early transitions work only as long as nothing terribly important is happening in the tail end of the first event.

Similarly, if your first event gets prematurely cut off when you place your second event on the downbeat where you want it to start, and there is not important material in the beginning of the second event, you can drag the right side of the first event to the right, and the left side of the second event as well, as shown in Figure 11-7. In the case of a late transition, it's best if the two events' material sounds pretty similar. Often, an obvious early transition can sound okay, but an obvious late transition can sound awkward. This is due to a tendency of music to change up and increase activity right before major downbeats, especially leading up to the first beat of a new section.

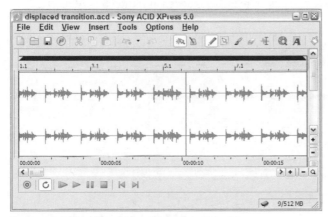

FIGURE 11-7: Displaced transition, occurring late

Crossfade

Sometimes your transition on the one sounds sudden and jarring, and you can't find a displacement point that sounds good. Consider a crossfade. This will create a brief period of transition between the two tracks where your first event gradually fades out while the next event fades in, keeping a constant total volume throughout.

To create a crossfade leading up to the one in ACID Pro 6, first make a simple transition on the one. Then, drag the left edge of the right event to the left. ACID automatically creates the crossfaded transition, and you're done, as shown in Figure 11-8.

FIGURE 11-8: Single track crossfade in ACID Pro 6

If you're using ACID XPress, first make a simple transition on the one, and then duplicate the track. Delete the second event on the first track, and then delete everything but the second event on the second track. Now drag the left edge of the second event (on the second track) to the left for the duration of the desired crossfade. Select both events and type **F**. A fade-out and a fade-in are created in each event, producing a crossfade, as shown in Figure 11-9. Of course, you are stuck with a transition straddling two tracks, which is a bit more unwieldy to manipulate, but the one-track crossfade is a great feature that was added in version 6 of ACID Pro.

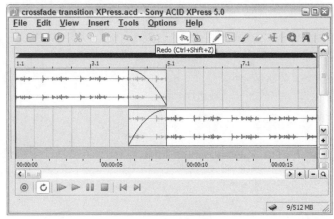

FIGURE 11-9: Crossfade transition with ACID XPress

You could also create a crossfade starting on the one, or even starting before the one and ending after the one, straddling the downbeat. As with the displaced transition, the ear generally prefers to hear the second section early rather than the first section late, but there are exceptions.

Drop-Out

Another transition alternative is the drop-out. Place the second event squarely on the major downbeat where the first event ends, and then simply delete the very end of the first event, either by dragging the right edge of it to the left with the select or draw tool or by erasing it with the erase or paint tool. This creates a brief silence before the next section starts. Although this transition can possibly sound good if the events are on the only track playing, it has even greater potential when layered with other sections on other tracks. It creates a brief drop in density before the transition, which can sometimes sound very good, especially if there is rhythmic material in it. Try erasing an entire measure or perhaps half a measure, as shown in Figure 11-10. Although drop-outs at the beginning of a section are not unheard of, they are not nearly as common.

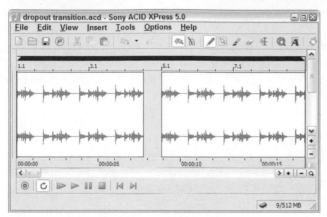

FIGURE **11-10: Half-bar drop-out transition**

Drop-In

Instead of erasing the end of your first event, you might want to simply replace it with material from a different section. Perhaps you could replace the final measure of event one with the final measure of some other section that has a really cool drum fill or other transitional snippet that you like. This type of drop-in is shown in Figure 11-11.

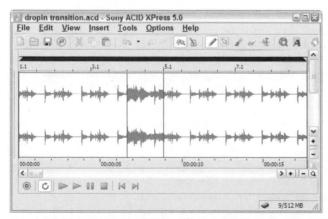

FIGURE **11-11: Drop-in transition with material from elsewhere in the track**

One interesting variation of drop-in is to split off the last bit of the first event (a measure, half a measure, or some other length), and then reverse it by selecting it and typing **U**. This trick should be used sparingly, but it can be a bit of fun sometimes.

Layered

You could layer a chunk of music on a new track, leaving the first event intact. This is like a drop-in without dropping out the original material. Try this only if the dropped-in segment doesn't duplicate sounds in the material it's being layered with, because doubling identical sounds can produce undesirable effects. Like a drop-in, often a half measure or measure of material works, but let your ears be your guide.

Beginnings and Endings

When material from a component song starts or stops, it is essentially a special type of transition, from silence into a section, or from a section into silence. Many of the techniques for handling beginnings and endings are similar to those of transitions.

On the One

As with transitions, the simplest thing to do is to start your musical material at the downbeat at the beginning of your section, and to end it on the downbeat at the end of your section. This works great much of the time, especially for beginnings, but endings can sometimes sound abrupt and awkward when music stops immediately before an important downbeat. If at the same time, the density suddenly picks up in another track or a new song is introduced, it might help to soften the discomfort of the transition.

Displaced

As with transitions, sometimes dragging the edges a bit to the left or right can make an entry or exit more natural. For example, suppose you have a song ending with an instrumental section that lasts four measures followed by a big power chord. It's almost obvious that you wouldn't simply cut the instrumental track off right before the one. In this case, you'd let the music finish. Similarly, if there are a few notes of melody before the downbeat, or a really cool drum fill or musical transition, by all means extend the left edge of the event to include relevant material.

Fade-Ins and Fade-Outs

Other times, the smoothest way to bring a track in or out is to ease it gradually. Fade-ins and fade-outs are essentially crossfade transitions with silence, but there are different means to achieve them in ACID. To create a fade-in, drag the uppermost portion of the left edge to the right for the duration of the desired fade-in. For the fade-out, grab the uppermost portion of the right edge of the event and drag to the left. Fade-ins can be less than a sixteenth note in duration, or they may last the duration of several sections.

Echoes

Using echoes is a pretty neat trick that is not only a great way to rescue an awkward fade-out, but it can also sound pretty cool when done in the right places. It's not something you want to overuse, but it's a great tool to have in your arsenal.

The idea behind an echo fade-out is that by the time the potentially awkward ending takes place, a delayed version of the same sound is already playing, masking out the sudden drop-out of the original sound. You can use this with a drop-out that happens suddenly or in combination with a rapid fade-out that sounds awkward. Additionally, because you are repeating only the very last part of the audio, you may want to fade it in on the delayed portion in order to prevent smoothing out the sound. You can do this using either "flavor" of ACID.

You need to decide on a delay time for your echo. The usual suspects work well, like one bar or half a bar. But with echoes, other values work nicely too, like three quarter notes or three eighth notes. This echo creates a polyrhythm, which can sound really cool in some places.

The next example uses "Sweet Dreams" by Eurythmics again. Drop the file into ACID and draw a four-bar loop. It will cut off suddenly, and this is the cutoff you will mask with the echoes.

Echoes with ACID XPress

 Although echoes can most easily be done in ACID Pro using effects, they can be faked pretty well with ACID XPress.

1. Zoom in until the grid markers show eighth note values, so there are eight tick marks per measure.

2. Place your cursor at the gridline one eighth note past 4.3 and type **S** to split the event. (It's 4.3.384, although you may not be zoomed in enough to see the tick values.)

3. Create an eighth note fade-out by dragging the upper portion of the left edge of the audio to the left by one grid line (an eighth note).

4. Set the volume to 0.0 dB.

5. Duplicate the track by right-clicking it in the track list and selecting Duplicate Track from the context menu.

6. In the new track, select the first event and delete it. You will be left with only the end portion of the loop, which lasts three eighth notes with a fade on the last eighth note.

7. To smooth the overlap, extend the event on the second track back (to the left) one eighth note.

8. Create an eighth note fade-in on this event by dragging the upper portion of the right edge of the event to the right by one grid line (an eighth note).

9. Lower the volume by 4 dB. (For the second track, that means the volume will be 4 dB.)

10. Drag the event on the newest track three eighth notes to the right.

11. Duplicate this track.

12. Repeat steps 9 through 11 as many times as you like, or until ACID XPress' track limit is reached. The final results should look something like Figure 11-12. Notice that each track has a lower volume than the previous one, eventually approaching silence.

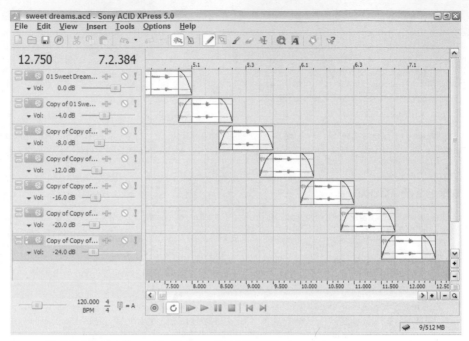

FIGURE 11-12: A manually created echo using ACID XPress

If you run out of tracks, render your echoed track and reimport the output as a one-shot. Remember that you want to perform time-warping only once, so if you change the tempo after you render, you may want to rerender at the new tempo rather than rewarping the rendered output.

Echoes with ACID Pro

 ACID Pro has a slightly more elegant way to achieve similar results using ACID Pro's built-in effects.

1. Zoom in until the grid markers show eighth note values, so there are eight tick marks per measure.

2. Create an eighth note fade-out by dragging the upper portion of the left edge of the audio to the left by one grid line (an eighth note).

3. Choose Insert ⇨ Assignable FX and select Simple Delay from the pop-up window.

4. Set the Dry Out level to -Inf dB with the slider all the way to the bottom, leaving the Delay Out level at -6.0 dB (as shown in the bottom-left of Figure 11-13).

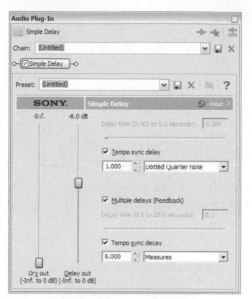

FIGURE 11-13: ACID Pro's simple delay

5. Check the Tempo Sync Delay check box, and set the value of the delay to Dotted Quarter Note.

Note "Dotted" means the length of a note is multiplied by 1.5. So a dotted half note is equal to three quarter notes, while a dotted quarter note is equal to three eighth notes.

6. Check the Multiple Delays check box.

7. Check the Tempo Sync Decay check box and set the decay to 6.000 Measures. Your audio plug-in settings should look like Figure 11-13.

8. Right-click your track, and select Insert/Remove Envelope ⇨ FX 1.

9. Double-click this envelope at both beat 4.3 and at an eighth note after 4.3 (4.3.384).

10. Drag the envelope point at both 1.1 and 4.3 downward to the value of –Inf at the bottom of the track, leaving the envelope point at 4.3.384 as is.

Your ACID Pro screen should look like Figure 11-14. The envelope controls the input to the assignable FX.

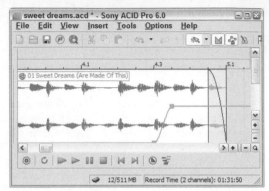

FIGURE 11-14: ACID Pro 6 with the envelope for the simple delay's assignable FX

Note If you were to perform the more usual method of placing the effect directly on the track, you would be able to control only the effect's input, but not its output. This means that as your envelope's value increased, the echoes, which would have been generated but at no volume, start to become audible. This means that there may be echoes of material from before the envelope rose. Using an assignable FX means that only the material after the envelope's value rises are echoed. In traditional mixing parlance, this is similar to using a send/return instead of an insert.

Layering

Now that you've gotten a bunch of sections together, you probably want to know more about combining them. After all, that's what mashups are all about. You've probably already tried out different combinations of your loops, and brute-force trial and error is a great technique — experimenting and seeing what works, using ACID as a sketchpad, playing around, and not worrying about structure and flow. You can structure elements in your sketch later, after you've gotten inspiration from playing around. When the sections don't layer well, usually it's either because the total sound is just too dense, or specific elements within the two tracks are incompatible. The harmonies could clash, the rhythms could clash, or the lyrical material could clash.

Controlling Density and Complexity

Most recorded music consists of many layers of sound already. The vocalist, the guitar, the bass, and each one of the drummer's different drums could potentially be playing simultaneously. People expect a variety of simultaneous sounds for pleasing music. Having multiple things happening at once is stimulating, and if they all relate to each other, the listener can recognize the tonal and rhythmic patterns. However, if the rhythm or the tonality becomes too complex, with many independent harmonies and rhythms that do not relate to each other in some kind of pattern, the listener can get confused. If there are too many patterns, it can cause a bit of sensory overload.

The problem is that most music is recorded with a fairly reasonable amount of density. When you layer just two tracks, you can double the density and create a sound that is just too much. In fact, many, many mashups fall prey to this problem.

This is a major reason why mashup producers love working with acapellas, which are usually not meant to be listened to by themselves, because the low density is not enough for many to enjoy. Of course, there are other ways of managing density. The most obvious is to find the parts of the song where there's less happening. The intro, outro, and breakdowns are great places to find low-density material. Sparseness is your friend, and all low-density portions of your component songs should be considered.

Another approach is to use some form of center channel extraction or isolation. Because this will usually entirely mute at least some of the tracks in the original song, it's a great tool for lowering the density. If you've got a guitar part you like in the left channel, why include the center and right channels? Unmixing can be a great part of lowering your mix density. It's almost always worth trying to process each of your songs with both center channel isolation and center channel elimination and seeing what happens. If the results are at all interesting, and they often are, save one or both of the extracted and isolated wav files. You may also consider copying just the left or right channel in an audio file whose center channel has been eliminated into a new mono file and saving these, if the results are interesting. Load each of them into ACID, and copy the Beatmapper tempo and offset information from the original full track to the new processed tracks. If a particular passage is too dense with the full mix, you could try to substitute a section of your extracted wav instead.

Transient elimination, gating, and noise reduction are all potentially useful for reducing complexity. Review Chapter 10 for more on how to use these processes. Additionally, EQ, covered in Chapter 12, can be helpful in eliminating portions of the signal.

One important aspect of density to remember is the need to vary it. If there is similar instrumentation throughout your mashup, it might be a bit boring. Most produced songs will vary the density, and your mashup should too. (More on this later in this chapter.)

Clash

Things don't have to get dense to get uncomfortable. Two singers out of key from each other can make some pretty sour harmonies. And a drummer with a bad sense of timing can even make his kick drum clash with his snare drums.

So the art of layering doesn't just address the idea of *how much*. It's also interested in the issue of *how independent*. If pitches or rhythms do not relate to each other at all, they will be perceived as clashing. In fact, very dense tracks can sound great if they relate to each other. Think about a symphony orchestra. You are listening to a hundred different musicians, each playing his or her own "track." But somehow, because they are all using related rhythms and harmonies, it sounds like one piece of music.

The Groove Is in the…

What we call *groove* is a recurring pattern of timing and dynamics. Usually the period of repetition is one or more measures. Different melodies, bass lines, and riffs can be placed over the groove, but each part usually responds to the groove in some way. In a live band, musicians naturally feel a groove and will play along with each other with a shared pattern, even when they're not playing the same notes or rhythms.

Sometimes musicians will purposely rush or delay certain notes within a groove. This can alter the mood of the rhythm by making it seem more laid-back or more aggressive. In the case of *swing* grooves, every other sixteenth note (or sometimes eighth note) has some delay. All musicians in a group will share the same rhythmic offsets each time they play a note at a certain point in the groove.

Some musicians will emphasize different time intervals in the groove more than others. For example, a groove may emphasize the sixteenth note before the fourth beat while deemphasizing the fourth beat. Increased emphasis means louder sounds, increased probability that a sound will occur, and changes of tone and pitch.

In typical Western music, there is a general set of expectations built on each type of meter. For example, if you have a 4/4 meter, it's generally expected that the downbeat will have a large amount of emphasis. The midpoint between the downbeats (the third beat) is typically expected to have slightly less emphasis than the downbeat. The midpoints between the downbeats and third beats (the second and fourth beats) will have slightly less emphasis still. The eighth notes in between the beats will receive even less emphasis, followed by the sixteenth notes in between these eighth notes.

This hierarchy of emphasis is abstract, and rarely does an actual groove follow this generic groove. Indeed, a groove would seem boring if it followed this pattern exactly. A groove that closely adheres to the generally expected patterns of emphasis dictated by the meter is called *straight*, and a groove that significantly deviates from the generic set of expectations is called *funky*.

Additionally, a groove that has timing close to the expected evenly spaced timing suggested by the meter is called *tight*, and a groove with more subtle timing variations is called *loose*. By this definition, a song with swing will necessarily be loose. Variation of emphasis and timing can be independent, so a groove can be straight but loose, or tight and funky. More often, straight grooves tend to be tight, and funky grooves might be a little looser.

The important thing to remember is that if you layer two rhythms, their grooves ought to be compatible, both in the patterns of emphasis and the patterns of timing.

Rhythmic Clash

The rhythmic events in two layers of a mashup do not have to have identical or even similar patterns to sound good in combination, but they are required to share identical underlying rhythmic grids.

Usually, if both layers' beatmaps are aligned with ACID's internal grid, you will encounter little rhythmic clash. However, if there are significant differences in the groove offsets, the parts may be incompatible. For example, a track that has plenty of swing will probably clash with a track that is straight. Luckily, although there could theoretically be an infinite combination of offsets that go into a groove, a swing-type groove is the most common pattern of looseness within a groove. As long as the two songs have similar amounts of swing (that is, similar amounts of delay on the alternating sixteenth or eighth notes), they should be compatible.

If you have clashing grooves or your beatmaps are sloppy, your percussive sounds will not form a coherent groove, and your mashup will sound rhythmically messy. When the layers' rhythms are only a little bit off, the groove can sound coherent and well-defined. However, there are very subtle cues that the timing is a little bit off. If you have two percussive sounds happening at nearly the same time, they sound doubled. You can actually hear both sounds. Often when two percussive sounds happen exactly simultaneously, they seem to blend into a single sound, and you couldn't really tell which part of what you're hearing came from which percussive sound. For example, if you are blending two songs, each having kick drums, there is a point where the two kick drums may seem to actually become a single super-kick drum. It's this sweet spot of rhythmic precision that helps to make a mashup really tight. It's useful to put your cursor at the point of a shared attack and zoom way in. Look at the attacks of both sounds. Do they line up to a high degree of precision? If not, why not? Perhaps the grooves are different, or even more likely, perhaps the beatmapping is slightly off.

The rhythmic movement can clash at a higher level as well. The sections of each track need to line up with each other. If you have an irregular six-bar vocal section followed by a regular eight-bar section, it won't sound good accompanied by an eight-bar instrumental loop. For the most part, the sections should change at the same time. This means you have to either figure out how to hack up an eight-bar instrumental section into a smooth-sounding six-bar section, or you'll have to repeat parts of the six-bar vocal section to stretch it out to eight bars. This type of rhythmic clash is subtle and may not jump out at you, but it's common and almost inevitable if you do not bother to first split up your songs into sections before arranging them.

Tonal Clash

As you learned in Chapter 4, the various pitches present in a piece need to have a certain kind of mathematical relationship with each other or the music will sound dissonant. Getting the music to harmonize and the pitches to gel is one of the hardest parts of creating a good mashup. Musicians have plenty of flexibility to match their instrument to a chord or key that's in a piece, but mashup artists only have the bits and pieces of already existing songs that need to be coaxed into a harmonic relationship with the other material. For this reason, maintaining harmony throughout a piece is one of the greatest challenges mashup artists face.

Microkey Clash

Some pretty bad dissonance can result when two layers are only slightly out of key by less than a semitone. If the chromatic scale is shifted in increments of less than a semitone in one layer, then none of the pitches in either layer are shared, and every single pitch pairing will be dissonant, because the mathematically compatible values are no longer available. (To refresh your memory, the chromatic scale is the set of 12 semitones from which all chords and scales are selected, as discussed in Chapter 4.)

If the two scales are only ever-so-slightly different (perhaps up to five or ten cents different), the ear may perceive the scales to be compatible. Beyond that, the ear will hear the combination as unpleasant. The first sign that your layers may be suffering from microkey clash is that no combinations seem to sound good, even when you transpose the sections up and down one or several semitones. If you suspect this kind of clash, you may want to review Chapters 6 and 8, which discuss microtuning in detail. A quick check with tONaRT can usually tell you with precision if your mashup has this problem. No amount of arranging or layering will fix it.

Note   It may not be a bad idea to run all your component songs through tONaRT at some point, just to make sure that there isn't a subtle microkey clash that you're unaware of. If tONaRT detects a Standard Pitch more than 2 Hz away from 440, you may want to consider a fractional pitch shift.

Key Clash

Like microkey clash, you should be able to avoid key clash if you follow the guidelines in Chapter 6 and select songs with compatible keys. However, some individual songs actually go through several key changes. If this happens, you may need to transpose sections of one of the two tracks into identical or compatible keys, using the techniques discussed in Chapter 8.

Bass Clash

The human ear has a very difficult time recognizing multiple simultaneous pitches in the lower register. For hundreds of years, composers have recognized that when music is being orchestrated, there needs to be more space between the lower voices than the upper voices. In an orchestra, the distance between the pitches played by bass violin and the cello are greater than the distance between the violin and the viola. In many rock bands, there may be two or even three guitarists, but you will never find a band with two bass players. In a similar vein, a bass player will rarely play more than one simultaneous note, but guitarists strum chords of multiple notes all of the time. Chords played on the bass are not unheard of, but they have a deserved reputation of making the bass sound muddy.

Long story short: bass needs room! Two different simultaneous notes in the bass register almost never sound good together. If your two bass lines happen to be playing the same note, it might sound okay, but chances are that the two lines will diverge at some point.

Bass clash is one of the most common sources of muddiness in a mashup mix and should be avoided at all costs. If you are plopping an acapella down on top of an instrumental, you will have no problem, because the acapella is bass-free. But if you are layering two full songs, you'll need to take care to avoid bass clash. Here are some ways to do this:

■ Simply use the parts of the song without bass. This can be difficult, because most parts of most songs contain bass.

- Perform EQ to suppress the bass frequencies in one of the tracks. You may still be able to hear remnants of the altered bass line, but it will be dominated by the unaltered bass. As long as you do not have chord clash, the thinned-out bass may sound fine in combination with the other track.

- Perform center channel suppression on one of the tracks. Basses are almost always panned center in modern recordings. Of course, you will be eliminating other sounds that are also panned center, but this can also help in managing density. Early stereo recordings may have the bass panned in locations other than center, but it will almost always be panned in one defined spot and not spread across the stereo spectrum.

Chord Clash

Chord clash was discussed in Chapter 8, and this kind of clash can actually be cured by proper arrangement. As previously mentioned, the level of chord clash is primarily determined by the number of shared pitches between the two chords. Two songs may sound great together for the most part, but all of a sudden there seems to be a sour note or dissonance. It doesn't last long, but it is noticeable. In Chapter 8, the possibility of raising or lowering the pitch of one of the dissonant parts was brought up as one possible solution. But now that you are rearranging the parts of the song, there are new possibilities. When you're rearranging individual measures of a song, probably instrumental sections work best, but don't be afraid to shuffle your vocals about either, as long as the lyrics still make some sort of sense.

Note   When you're rearranging your chords, remember to consider the principles of placement preservation discussed earlier in this chapter. Although the need to find a compatible chord dominates the decision-making, if you can move a segment four or eight bars, it may be preferable to moving it three or five bars.

Figuring out chords and chord progressions can be tough, and if you can find a solution by trial and error, it may actually be quicker. But if you are willing to spend a little time and energy on the problem, you may find some elegant solutions you didn't expect.

Here's an example of chord clash. Suppose you have two tracks, both in the key of C. Track one has a four-bar repeating chord progression of C major, F major, G major, C major. The other track has a four-bar repeating chord progression of C Major, A minor, F major, G major. The two chord progressions are illustrated in Figure 11-15.

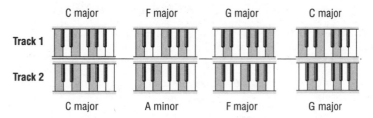

FIGURE **11-15: Example of chord clash, with the third pair clashing the most**

In Search of the Lost Chord

If you want to resolve chord clash, it might be useful to figure out what chord is playing. Figuring out the chord is a lot like figuring out the key, which was covered in Chapter 6, in the "Key Detection Techniques" section. A chord progression is a lot like a rapid series of key changes. Each chord has a new root and at least two other pitches, usually each falling on one of the seven pitches in the current key. The difference is that when the chord changes, the entire scale does not change. A key consists of an entire scale of seven pitches, and a chord usually consists of three or four pitches.

Probably the easiest way to determine a chord is to isolate just the section with the chord. In ACID, solo the track with the chord in question. In the Transport bar, click the Loop Playback button. Drag the cursor across the beat ruler above the timeline, and select just the portion of the track that contains the mystery chord.

The simplest thing to do is to use the chord MIDI files on this book's CD-ROM as described in Chapter 6. Because there is only one chord in your looped selection, when you layer a correctly transposed MIDI loop with the mystery chord in your track, the correct chord should be even more obvious than when you were figuring out the overall key.

As discussed in Chapter 6, you can also use ACID's built-in piano, and follow a similar technique to figure out which pitches sound most "at home" with the current chord. Usually, but not always, the bass note is the root of the chord. If you can play a pitch on the piano that sounds the same as the main bass note for the section of audio, you may have figured out the root of the chord. Play each of the pitches three and four semitones higher. If the pitch three semitones higher sounds good, your chord is probably minor, and if the pitch four semitones higher sounds good, your chord is probably major.

In the worst case scenario, where you can't figure out what a certain chord is, write down which pitches sound best with it. Even a partially recognized chord may be useful.

For the sake of thoroughness, inspect each chord pairing and resolve chord clash one bar at a time. For example, using the chord clash shown in Figure 11-15, here's what you'll find:

1. The first pairing, C major versus C major, has three of three pitches identical and needs no adjustment.

2. The second pairing, F major versus A minor, has two out of three identical pitches. This is often an adequate level of compatibility and may not need any adjustment.

3. The third pairing, G major versus F major, has no identical pitches, and is the most severe chord clash of the two progressions. The incompatibility will need to be fixed.

   One solution is to simply transpose either the F major up two semitones or the G major down two semitones. That would make the chords identical and completely eliminate the key clash.

Suppose, however, that you don't like how the tracks sound transposed by that amount. After all, two semitones of transposition can be on the edge of sonic acceptability. Another solution is to locate a G chord (or compatible chord) somewhere in the second progression or to find an F chord (or compatible chord) somewhere in the first progression.

Luckily, there is an F chord in the second measure of the first progression, so if you copy the second measure of the first progression and paste it on top of the third measure, the chord clash will be completely eliminated without any transposition. This works best when the track being rearranged (in this case the first track) is not the dominant track. If there are vocals or a very recognizable instrumental hook, the rearranged track might not sound so good, although some mangling can be surprisingly interesting and pleasant sounding.

An alternate solution would be to alter the second progression instead, copying the fourth chord, G major, and pasting it on top of the third chord, F major.

4. The fourth pairing, C major versus G major has one of three identical pitches, and will probably sound clashy. There are two solutions. Altering the first progression, you can copy the third chord (G major) and paste it on top of the fourth chord (C major), matching the G major in the second progression. Alternatively, you can alter the second progression, copying the first chord (C major) and pasting it on top of the fourth chord, matching the C major in the first progression.

Take another look at the second chord pairing. When there are two of three identical pitches, this creates a special situation that may or may not result in chord clash. Just how clashy it sounds depends largely on the bass. Of course, only one of the tracks should contain bass. A common variation of the three-note triad chord is the four-note seventh chord. Whereas a triad has a note at its root, a note two steps above the root, and another note another two steps above that, a seventh chord takes this even further, adding another note two steps above the third note of the triad.

The example in Figure 11-15 is in the key of C major. In the second chord pairing, if you were to add a seventh to the F chord, it would be an E, which is contained in the A-minor chord. If you were to add a seventh to the A-minor chord, it would be a G, which is not contained in the F chord. Suppose that the first progression has the bass line, and during the second pairing, both the A-minor and F-major chords are played with an F in the bass, as shown in the left chord in Figure 11-16. This is essentially an F-major seventh chord, and can sound pretty good. However, if the second progression has the bass line, the compatibility picture changes a bit. Even though there are the same notes playing, the fact that the bass is playing an A can make you hear the combination as a variation of A minor instead of F major. The additional note not in A minor is the F, which occurs one step above E, the highest note in A minor. Although this is in actuality the same chord, it may sound less resolved and more out of place than the seventh chord with the root in the bass. This kind of clash doesn't sound dissonant, but it may sound a bit unresolved. Both of these chords are pictured in Figure 11-16.

Figure 11-16: F major seventh chord with F in the bass (left) and with A in the bass (right)

This effect is even more apparent with melody. If a melody from the first progression hits F (the root of the second chord in the first progression), this will sound pretty unresolved over an A-minor chord, like the melody was supposed to land somewhere but never made it. However, if a melody from the second progression hits an A (the root of the second chord in the second progression), that is a note actually contained within the F-major chord of the first progression and will sound quite good. This kind of compatibility is similar to the relative minor/major key relationships discussed in Chapter 6.

One other kind of chord compatibility that echoes key relationships is that of the fourth/fifth relationships (also discussed in Chapter 6). If two chords that are a fifth apart are played simultaneously, it results in a ninth chord, which can sound good, although it has a certain jazzy kind of dissonance. The thing to remember is that the bass needs to be in the chord that is a fifth below the other. So a C-major chord might sound good with a G-major chord as long as the C is in the bass. If the G is in the bass, it will likely sound more unresolved.

Acapellas create a special set of circumstances because they are not so strongly associated with chords. The general rule is that some notes from the acapella ought to be in the accompanying chord, but even this needn't be the case 100 percent of the time. It is more important that notes given special emphasis by the singer or notes at the end of phrases be contained in the accompanying chord.

Vocal Clash

There is one simple guideline when it comes to layering two sections that have vocals: don't.

This Is Your Brain on Music

Words seem to occupy a different part of the brain than music. Perhaps you've heard of the concept of left and right hemispheres of the brain, where the left half of the brain is more logical and analytical, and the right half of the brain is more intuitive and creative. Interestingly, it has been found that the area that recognizes melodies and notes in the right brain closely mirrors the area that processes words and letters in the left brain. No wonder they sound so good together!

But although the right brain takes great pleasure in hearing multiple notes simultaneously, the left brain hurts when given too much information. If you've ever had two people talking to you at the same time, you know the feeling.

Few things are more annoying than competing vocal lines in a mashup. Usually it's due to underproduction and too much "leaving things as they are." If different lyrics happen simultaneously, the left brain is almost certain to overload, and the mashup will seem like it's a bit much. So the first thing to ask yourself if your mashup has overlapping vocals is: "Did I intend to do this, or did this just happen?"

There are some exceptions however. As you're probably aware, many songs actually have overlapping vocals, usually with a foreground vocal interacting somehow with a background vocal. If you can mimic this interaction, perhaps your vocal overlapping will not hurt so much. Two forms of acceptable vocal overlap are background vocals and lead-in/tail-out overlaps.

Background Vocals

Background vocals are usually sung at the same time as the main vocals, but they are less dominant. They usually don't add much meaning to the lyrics, so your left brain can handle them even though it's processing meaning from the foreground vocals.

The simplest kind of background vocals are harmonies or doubling of the foreground vocals. This means that the background vocals are saying the same thing at the same time as the foreground vocals. Although this may seem next to impossible with two different songs with different lyrics, it's not unheard of. Maybe the vocal has a one or two words that have special emphasis, and these same words exist in another full song or acapella. If you can snip out just those few words and line them up with the foreground vocals, the results can be pretty cool. You can even Google the few words of the foreground lyrics just to find another song with a complementary doubling background vocal.

A more common kind of background vocals is where the singers are not singing words or anything that will stimulate the left brain too much: "Aaaahhhh," "Doo doo doo," "sha la la la la" — that kind of thing. Because these vocals were probably originally meant to be background vocals, they may work well as the background to a different vocal.

One other kind of background vocal worth mentioning is the refrain. A *refrain* is a short, usually one-phrase, repeated vocal line. If a vocal line is repeated often enough, the left brain stops gathering meaning from it. It's kind of like if you say the word "chair," you may think of a chair. But if you say the word "chair" a hundred times, you will start hearing it as a collection of sounds rather than the word it represents semantically. For this reason, if a vocal refrain is repeated enough, you probably can put a foreground vocal over it. The important thing to remember is that the refrain probably ought to be repeated by itself a few times first, so that when the layering occurs, the refrain is no longer imparting any meaning.

Lead-In/Tail-Out Overlaps

If you have one vocal line start a little before the downbeat, while the previous vocal line ends right on the downbeat, it may sound okay. Although the left brain cannot process two different simultaneous vocal lines well, it can store a few words while the other line is finishing up, and then process them later, after the second vocal line takes over. In general, this overlap shouldn't be more than a few words.

Two conditions will allow you more overlap than this, however. If your second vocal is repeating the same words as the first vocal, the left brain has no new words to process and will not be confused. Also, if the second vocal is repeating itself, it may become like a refrain and not create any new words for the brain to process.

Form

Form, or structure, is one of the most important elements in a mashup, and definitely one of the more overlooked. Without structure, your mashup may sound good at any given moment, but it will not have a satisfying sense of pacing. By paying attention to structure, you will impart a sense of drama to your mashup and introduce musical elements to the listener at a digestible pace, with a comfortable balance between repetition and novelty.

Here's a brief review of the basics of form that were first discussed in Chapter 4. Classic song structure is a great way to give form to your mashups, and there are many variations so the limitations are not too stifling. Classic song structure will typically repeat two or three types of sections several times: a verse, possibly a pre-chorus, and a chorus. Some of these sections are more similar than others. Switching between different section types gives the listener variety, and repeating the similar sections gives the listener familiarity. After two or maybe three cycles of this, the song will often go to some sort of variation, such as a bridge, an instrumental break, a total breakdown, a rap, or something to break up the song and give it novelty now that the listener has heard the verse/chorus sections a few times. After the break, the song usually goes back to another verse/chorus cycle or possibly just the chorus. Additionally, there are intros and outros to begin and end the song.

You may find the concept of fitting your mashup into a rigid structure stifling. You may want to be free from constraints and make music as you please. This is fine. But song structure has evolved for good reasons. If you do not repeat sections, the listener may experience too much variety and become disinterested. A nonrepeating piece requires a lot of concentration and does not offer the pleasure of a hook that allows you to listen to music and know what to expect. On the flip side, if your mashup has too much repetition, it becomes dull. Not enough variety leaves the mind craving more.

Even if you reject standard song structure, at least consider why it exists. There are only two or three sections that cycle, because the brain cannot digest much more than that. After a couple of cycles, the brain has probably digested the information and can handle more. Indeed, the brain may even hunger for more variety at this point. After having some time away from the cycles, it feels good to hear them again, like seeing an old friend. So if your form deviates significantly from traditional song structure, make sure to take into account how much repetition and novelty listeners can handle, and try to strike an appropriate balance.

In addition to providing a healthy balance of repetition and variety, a good structure can provide a sense of drama. You can start small, building gradually into a big crescendo. You can introduce little hints of material to create a sense of mystery, and then resolve the mystery later. You can build up expectations and then satisfy them. You can build up expectations and the violate them. It's up to you. But do have a big picture. Music is more than a moment-by-moment experience, a series of loops that sound good together. A great piece of music is like a fantastic journey, each step taking you further until you reach your destination.

Strategies

If you've been playing around with ACID for a bit and have been experimenting with layers, you probably already have some pretty cool combinations in mind. You may even have layered sections in a sequence that sounds great. There is a danger, however, of letting your sketchpad determine your structure. Remember, a sketchpad is for determining which sections work together, not for creating the structure. In fact, it's very hard to build the structure until you know which sections work together. So if you're playing around with the sections, don't let that determine your structure. At some point during your mashup construction, take a step back to look at the big picture.

After playing around in your sketch area, your component songs are hopefully pretty chopped up, segmented, and mangled. In fact, after playing around for a while with your sections, you may forget what the original songs sound like. This may actually be a good thing because it will allow you to recontextualize the elements more freely. However, when you're thinking about structure, it's a good idea to listen again to each of the component songs in its entirety. You might actually hear some great parts that you missed as you chopped and moved the chunks around. When you listen to each song, note the song's structure. Does it have an intro? A verse/chorus structure? A bridge or break? Many times, a mashup's structure will closely mirror one of the component song's structures. This is especially true in a song with only one dominant vocal. Often the lead vocal forces the background instrumentation into the vocalist's structure, especially if the acapella is relatively unaltered.

In addition to reexamining each song, you may want to listen to any remixes, instrumentals, or acapella versions you can get your hands on. You may end up using a version of the song that you didn't start off needing or considering.

If your background instrumentation is not instantly recognizable, it's a good idea to somehow make the song identifiable at some point during the mashup. This might be achieved by inserting a few words from the backing track somewhere during a break in the lead vocals. Alternatively, you could use vocals from the backing track as a bridge. One of the pleasures of listening to mashups is the recognition of multiple songs at once. If your backing track remains unidentifiable, this pleasure may be missing for your listeners.

As you listen to your sketch, make a note of your favorite combinations. If a layered section is really catchy, and the lyrics are repeatable, maybe it's a good candidate for the chorus. If a layered section contains lyrics from a component song's verse, maybe the combination can serve as the mashup's verse. If a layered section just sounds really cool, but maybe is so unusual that it needn't be repeated, maybe it's a good candidate for the bridge section. Each element of song structure as it relates to mashup arrangement will be discussed over the next several pages.

Sections

A great new feature of ACID Pro 6 is the introduction of a Sections feature. This feature helps you rearrange the entire content of your mashup, including all audio, envelopes, and markers, with a simple drag-and-drop operation.

One approach to arranging your mashup is to create sections that sound good, and then arrange them into an order that works on a larger scale. If you do decide to use ACID's sections, it's a good idea to define them for every portion of your mashup.

To define an ACID section:

1. Above the beat ruler, select a portion of the timeline that corresponds to your section.

2. From the menu, choose Insert ⇨ Section, or press Shift+S. The colored section will appear above the beat ruler in the timeline.

3. Type in the name of your section.

Note

To undefine an ACID section, right-click on the section above the beat ruler and select Remove Label. Your audio data will remain unaffected.

To move an ACID Section:

1. Click on the section (above the beat ruler in the timeline) and drag it to the left or right, dropping it in the location you want. You can select multiple sections with Ctrl and Shift, just like events.

2. If the edges of your section are in the middle of any events, they will be automatically split before you move the section.

3. If you drop your section in the middle of existing events, the events will be split to make room for the new section.

4. No material is lost or created when you move sections; if you move a section backward, the material in between the old section location and the new section location will be moved forward to compensate, and vice versa. The total length of your arrangement will not change.

5. You cannot move one ACID section to the middle of another ACID section, splitting it. You are only allowed to move an ACID section in between two existing sections or in space not yet defined as an ACID section. This keeps all defined sections intact. If you are using ACID sections, it's a good idea to define all of your sections to more easily control where you drag and drop them.

To change the length of an ACID section, simply drag either edge of it, just like you would do with an event using the Draw tool.

To copy an ACID section, drag it while holding down the Ctrl key. A copy will be placed in the timeline where you drop it, and all material afterward will be shifted by the duration of your section, lengthening your overall arrangement.

To delete an ACID section, click on it above the beat ruler, and press the Delete key. All material after your section will be shifted earlier by the duration of your ACID section, shortening your overall arrangement.

To delete all events from your ACID section without shifting subsequent audio, right-click the section above the beat ruler and select Clear Events. The events will be removed (and split if necessary), but all other audio remains unaffected.

To change the color of your ACID section, right-click it above the beat ruler, and select a new color from the Color menu.

ACID sections are a great way to experiment with different forms in your mashup, and they also encourage you to pay attention to your overall form, allowing you to view it quickly. It's a good idea to color all your choruses one color and all your verses another color. Color your bridge, intro, outro, and other sections yet another color. This way you can get a sense of your overall form just by looking at the colors above the beat ruler.

Intro

Intros are typically simple and relatively sparse. Often they are instrumental, although a smattering of vocals might be okay. Intros are usually conceived of and created after the main verse/chorus structure is in place, and then tacked on to the beginning. Quite often, the intro to a mashup consists simply of the intro of one of the component songs. It's usually worth a try.

One trick is to drop in a little snippet of material that will be more fully explored later in the chorus or the bridge. When the full material finally comes in, the ear is primed for it and there is already some familiarity.

A great intro should grab your interest immediately. Some mashups will introduce several elements right away to let listeners know that this is a mashup, and others will simply use a single recognizable instrumental intro, startling the listener when the unexpected vocals come in from an altogether different song.

Verse

The main characteristic of verses is that they usually have similar melodies but different words. Usually, all the verses within a mashup are from various verses of one of the component songs. Some mashup producers combine verses from different songs, which can sound good, but should be done with caution. Make sure that your chorus is very well-defined in this case, because the chorus becomes the only clue to the mashup's structure. Resist the urge to follow up a verse from one song with the verse from another song, unless there's a really good reason. Remember that you are making a single song from several, so it's necessary to leave some parts out of the mashup, even if you really like all of both songs. This can't be emphasized enough, especially when combining two full songs. If one song has a verse, a chorus, and a bridge, and the other song has these as well, you are dealing with six sections, which is most likely too much variety for the listener to concentrate on. Choose your favorite layered combinations, drop the rest, and don't look back!

Typically, your mashup verse will contain vocals from a verse of a component song, and it will be complemented by an instrumental loop. If there are several instrumental loops with similar chord progressions, by all means use different loops for each of the verses. Often, a sparser, low-energy loop works best for a verse near the beginning, and a denser, higher-energy loop might work for a later verse.

Also, don't forget to use parallel structure. If you cut up the first verse in some way, cut up the second verse in a similar way. If you silence the lead vocal and drop in a vocal from another song at a certain point in the verse, do something similar in another verse. With verses, the name of the game is to repeat yourself, but with some variations.

Chorus

The chorus is the most important part of a song, and therefore will be the most important part of your mashup. Choruses tend to be the catchiest part of the song. If you have a strong instrumental hook in the background layer that works with the chorus vocals, it could sound great. This is the place to pull out all the stops.

Choruses tend to have higher energy and more density than the verses. You may reserve an instrumental accompaniment section to bring in just during the chorus and drop it out otherwise. You may allow another song's vocals to sing a few words during the space between the main vocal's phrases. You may even eliminate a phrase or two of the main vocals in order to put another catchy few words from another song in its place. Be adventurous, but make it good! The chorus is the part of the song people should remember.

Often, but not always, a chorus will have a different chord structure than the verse to help add variety. If your instrumental accompaniment has sections with different chord progressions, use them. At the very least, make sure that the chorus has different instrumentation behind it than the verse. Your mashup will become tedious if you do not offer this level of variety.

Many times a song will end with several repetitions of the chorus, often with some variations. Because the ear is getting pretty used to the words and music by this point, it can often handle added complexity or density. An ending chorus-repeat is often the densest part of a song, and can be the most layered part of your mashup as well. Again, you are balancing repetition versus variety.

Whatever your choices of structure are, it's usually pretty important for your mashup to have a chorus or at least some chorus-like section. Make sure it returns frequently, but not too frequently.

Bridges and Breakdowns

After a few verse/chorus repetitions, the ear is ready for some novelty. The bridge is a big opportunity to really let loose and have fun. Some of the craziest and most unusual sections can be placed in the bridge, because the listener's ears need a little break and welcome something out of the ordinary at this point. Usually the bridge takes place between halfway and three-quarters of the way through a song.

Often songs will have a breakdown before, after, or instead of a bridge. In mashup terms, a breakdown would be a stripped-down version of some material that may or may not have already occurred. The main characteristic is low density and fewer layers. Breakdowns usually precede or immediately follow the moment of highest intensity in a song.

If the verses and choruses are dominated by the vocals from one or two songs, but you are dying to put in the vocals of an additional song, now is the time to do it. Surprise your audience! They are ready now.

Outro

Endings, like beginnings, are often lifted directly from one of the component songs. If one of your songs has a big splashy ending, use it. Usually, listening to the endings of each of your songs will guide you. In the worst case scenario, you can do a gradual fade-out of some looped content. Sometimes a sudden song ending can be covered up with the echo effect discussed earlier in this chapter.

Even though your mashup may not mirror the traditional song structure, there is much to be learned from how it balances the need for variety with the need for repetition. This balance is something most every composer (mashup or otherwise) strives for.

Lyrics

The words of your mashup have been discussed in various sections in this book. Choosing compatible lyrics is one of the factors involved in song selection. If your lyrics relate to each other naturally, that's great. But you may be surprised at how you can make seemingly unrelated lyrics relate to each other when the context is changed.

It's a good idea to read the lyrics to all your component tracks at some point. A Google search for the title of your song along with the word *lyrics* usually takes you to a website that will display the lyrics. Reading the lyrics divorced from the song may give you ideas on how the lyrics of different songs might relate to each other. You might even read the lines of the song out of order, just to further remove them from the original context.

Call and Response

Call and response is a vocal tradition where a vocalist will sing a short phrase and a backup chorus will respond with another phrase or sometimes an echo of the lead singer's phrase. Examples include Ray Charles' "What'd I Say," The Who's "My Generation," and the B-A-N-A-N-A-S section of Gwen Stefani's "Hollaback Girl."

Using the techniques for hybrid vocal/instrumental sections detailed earlier in this chapter, you can create some great examples of call and response, and can really mess with the meanings of the lyrics, especially when combined with other lyrics from different sources.

For example, I once made a mashup containing, among other songs, Scissor Sisters' "Filthy/Gorgeous" and Fischerspooner's "We Need a War." "Filthy/Gorgeous" is essentially a light-hearted song about prostitution, featuring the lyrics "Cuz you're filthy, ooooh, and I'm gorgeous. You're disgusting, ooooh, and you're nasty." "We Need a War," on the other hand, is a serious antiwar statement, featuring the title of the song as its main lyric. Although these two songs are seemingly unrelated, I snipped out bits of "Filthy/Gorgeous" and replaced them with portions borrowed from an instrumental section using the hybrid vocal/instrumental technique, so only "Cuz you're filthy" and "You're disgusting" remained. Inserted into the gaps already existing in the "We Need a War" track, the resultant lyrics said, "Cuz you're filthy, we need a war. You're disgusting. We need a war." With the context changed, the lyrics' meanings changed.

In general, the more the lyrical content's placement is preserved, the better. If you have a section where one vocal dominates, examine the lyrics of the other songs in your mashup. Look at each song phrase by phrase and see if any of the phrases may relate to your main vocal section when removed from their original context. If the placement of a phrase you find corresponds with gaps in the main vocal, try placing the phrase in the gap. If there are competing vocals in the corresponding spot in the main vocal, consider eliminating them by replacing them with an instrumental part (or silence if the main vocals are from an acapella). Of course, you can shift the placement of any found phrases, keeping in mind the principles of placement preservation outlined earlier in this chapter.

Cut-Ups

The difference between a cut-up and a call-response mashup is essentially that of scale. A call-response may rearrange phrases and alternate between phrases from different sources, but cut-ups will rearrange the words of a vocal and sometimes even the syllables and phonemes (the individual sounds that make up language).

One of my favorite mashups by Soulwax is a remix of Kylie Minogue's "Can't Get You Out of My Head," featuring a cut-up vocal where at one point they transform the lyrics "I just can't get you out of my head, boy your loving is all I think about, I just can't get you out of my head, boy it's more than I dare to think about" into "I can't get my head to think about boys." They went as far as to find an "s" and tack it on to the end of "boy" to create a believable-sounding "boys."

If you have one or more acapellas to play around with, you can really have fun. I was playing around with the acapellas for Jennifer Lopez' "Jenny from the Block" and TLC's "No Scrubs," and I noticed how similar the two vocal tracks sounded, harmonies and all. I took "I'm still Jenny from the block" from J-Lo and cut it up with "Hanging out the passenger side of his best friend's ride" from TLC to create "I'm still hanging out the passenger side of Jenny from the block, his best friend's ride." Pretty absurd lyrics, but both originals are pretty absurd anyway.

Giving Up

It's the same old story. You think you've found a perfectly compatible match. There's real chemistry right off the bat, and an air of excitement. All is full of promise, and your day brightens with the expectation that something beautiful could come of this.

But after a little while, things get difficult. Conflicts start to arise, and you grow more aware of certain possibly insurmountable differences. You try different ways to smooth things over, changing, compromising. You even leave for a few days, hoping that when you return, things will be better. At some point, you reluctantly realize that maybe this pairing just isn't meant to be. It just doesn't feel right anymore.

Most mashups are not meant to be. Seriously. If you try and try to get a mashup to work, and it just doesn't seem to gel, it's probably because the songs just weren't meant to be together. You may have spent a lot of time and poured lots of energy into the project, but if it doesn't look like it's going to come together, there's no shame in simply trashing it. I expect that most of the greatest mashup artists' hard drives are littered with unfinished projects that just seemed to dead-end. But even a discarded project has value. While working on it, you probably learned some valuable lessons about song selection that you can use in your next mashup, and possibly picked up some production techniques along the way. Each component song may be compatible with a song you find in the future, so if you've logged your tempo and key information, they may pop up again. Any unmixed parts may be useful in future mashups as well. Who knows, maybe the entire mashup is just waiting for that one last ingredient to make it all come together. Some mashups are shelved only to be reopened when a new song comes along with a compatible key and tempo.

Breaking It Down

On the other hand, perhaps your mashup is really working out, and you need to just give it a little bit of polish to get it to the next level. You've created your instrumental loops and some hybrid vocal/instrumental sections. You've ironed out your transitions, fade-ins, and fade-outs, and layered your sections without any rhythmic, tonal, or vocal clash. You've arranged your sections into a compelling structure that balances variety and repetition. You've explored the lyrical content and created some interesting interactions between the vocal lines. And you haven't given up. It's time to get this thing to shine! The next chapter talks about fine-tuning your mashup with mastering and effects. This will give your mashup slick production values, and make it sound better in subtle but important ways.

Finishing Touches

B y now, all your tracks are in sync and in key and arranged into a sensible structure. All that is left is some sound processing and tweaking of both the individual tracks and the overall mix to make sure that the elements you want to hear are heard, and the elements you want to hide are hidden.

Traditionally, mixing and mastering have been two separate processes, although with current audio production software, the lines between the two activities are getting fairly blurry. For most of the history of recorded music, a song would be mixed in the recording studio, where the levels, pan, and effects would be adjusted. The recording engineer would create the best-sounding mix he could. The mixed-down recording would then be shipped to the mastering plant, where additional processing would take place on the entire mix to make sure that the recording would sound good on a record, tape, or CD. Each medium had different characteristics and needed to be treated differently. Having a mastering engineer finalize the mix added the advantage of new ears tweaking the mix with a fresh perspective and objectivity (which a mixing engineer can sometimes lose after too many hours working on the same project).

Another traditional goal is to create as loud a signal as possible to increase the signal-to-noise ratio when transferred onto a playback medium. This is usually done with dynamics processors such as compressors, and also has the side effect of making the overall song seem louder in comparison to other songs, and so it would stand out on the radio.

Recently, recording studios have begun to deliver the final mix to the mastering engineer on several tracks, called *separations* or *stems*. The vocals will be on one track (possibly with the background vocals), the drums on another track, the keyboards and guitars on another track, and the bass on yet another. This separation gives the mastering engineer greater control over the final output.

Mixing a mashup is a lot like the mastering process in a modern recording. The components are mostly premixed, and it is up to the mashup producer to balance out the elements. Of course, it's a bit more challenging, because the components were not meant to be mixed together. Each component has already been mixed and mastered on its own, and now they all need to be mixed and remastered at the same time. From the world of mixing and mastering, mashup producers borrow the following processing techniques to achieve balance and a pleasing sound:

- **Mixing:** Adjusting the levels of the components
- **Panning:** Adjusting the stereo placement of the components
- **EQ:** Altering the presence of various frequencies
- **Dynamics:** Altering levels based on the audio's loudness
- **Effects:** Various other tricks to enhance the sound

Because the entire process often takes place within ACID, a producer may perform all of these processes simultaneously, starting the mixing and mastering even as the arrangement is taking form.

 ACID Pro has effects built in, but ACID XPress cannot use effects internally. Throughout this chapter, if you are using ACID Pro, you'll be placing effects and processors both on individual tracks as well as the entire mix using the master bus. If you cannot see the master bus track, choose View ⇨ Show Bus Tracks. The Master FX button looks just like the Track FX button, and behaves in the same way, except the effects process the entire mix.

VST Plug-Ins

Before diving into this chapter in detail, it's important to understand some general concepts of Virtual Studio Technology (VST) plug-ins. VST is a standard developed by Steinberg. It has become the most common platform for both audio processors and software-based sound modules, and most audio-production software can handle the standard.

 VST plug-ins are types of effects, and can function only in the Pro version of ACID.

Usually, all the VST plug-ins in your computer are located in a single folder. Sometimes they are in C:\Program Files\Vstplugins, or perhaps C:\Program Files\Steinberg\Vstplugins\. ACID Pro allows you to specify up to three folders to search for VST plug-ins. Choose Options ⇨ Preferences ⇨ VST Effects. Here you can type or browse to the location where your plug-ins are stored. These are the effects and processes not provided by Sony, but are created by any number of third-party developers.

There is a dizzying array of plug-ins available, many of them free to download. Probably the most comprehensive source of up-to-date information on VST effects (and instruments) is www.kvraudio.com. It offers news, reviews, and a complete catalog of plug-ins in VST and other formats.

 A VST plug-in designates an audio effect, and a VSTi plug-in is an instrument. VSTis are great for original music production, but they are not as useful for mashup production.

Follow these steps to search for free VST plug-in effects:

1. Go to www.kvraudio.com/get.php and scroll down to Advanced Search.

2. In section 1(a), select Effects as the general plug-in/host type.

3. In section 1(b), in the Effects subsection, select the type of effect you are interested in, or don't select any specific effect if you want to see them all.

4. In section 2(a), select VST as the format.

5. In section 3, uncheck the operating systems you're not using.

6. In section 4, uncheck Unreleased and also uncheck Commercial, unless you want to view commercial plug-ins.

7. Click the search button at the bottom of the page.

You will be rewarded with a rich selection of free plug-ins to play with. Download them, and dump them into the folder you've specified in ACID Pro. If ACID is open, you won't be able to access your new plug-ins until you restart. Keep in mind that some of the plug-ins are made by hobbyists, and some are extremely sophisticated.

Mixing

The goal of mixing is to achieve a proper balance between all the various elements in your mashup. In the arrangement phase, you've ensured that certain elements didn't overlap, while others did. Now, in the mixing phase, you'll make sure that the elements that do overlap have pleasant relationships to each other. Proper mixing can ensure that the various sounds are audible even though they are occurring at the same time. Proper mixing can also make certain sounds inaudible if you want to diminish their presence.

Chances are that you've already done some volume adjustment on the various tracks. The mixing of some mashups is so simple that adjusting the volume is the only thing required to make it sound good.

Achieving Balance

In the case of a simple A-plus-B mashup, the only real decision to make is how loud the vocal should be compared to the instrumental background. The vocal should be loud enough to be intelligible, but not so loud as to overpower the instruments. Vocals that are too soft are often obvious, because you can't really make out the lyrics, and they seem buried. A more common mistake is to make the vocals too loud. If you can lower the vocal levels by a decibel, and they still sound intelligible, chances are they were too loud. Try lowering the vocals until they are obviously too quiet and then gradually raising them from there until they sound loud enough.

Avoiding Clipping

If you've ever turned up a stereo too loud, you have already experienced the unpleasant effects of clipping. A sound that is amplified beyond the capacity of the software or hardware to handle it can make a distorted sound, adding frequencies that weren't in the original signal and reducing clarity. Most of the time, this clipping is unwanted; however, this distortion is what gives electric guitars their distinctive tone. Figure 12-1 shows three identical sounds. The top signal peaks at just under 0.0 dB, while the middle signal shows slight distortion. The bottom signal exhibits extreme distortion. Notice that even though the signal was amplified tremendously, the overall output never goes above 0.0 dB. The waveform is simply cut off at 0, and the shape of the wave is flattened out.

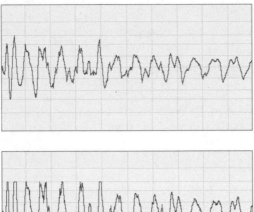

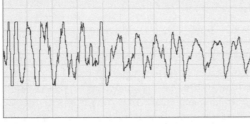

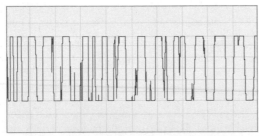

FIGURE 12-1: A waveform with varying degrees of clipping

As a general rule, you never want to add distortion to your signal through the simple act of overloading your software. If you want distortion for artistic purposes, it should be done through a distortion effect instead, where you can exercise much greater control over the output.

If your signal ever gets above 0.0 dB, on the master bus or any other bus, you will get clipping. You can easily hear heavy distortion, but light distortion can be subtle. Luckily, ACID has a few ways of letting you know if you are distorting or even getting close. In Figure 12-2, you can see two images of the master bus in the mixer. The first is a healthy level for a signal. The numbers above the colored level meters represent the peak level of the signal since the project started playing. These numbers should always be below 0, as in the left pair of meters. When the signal goes above 0.0 dB, the numbers turn red and display a positive number, as in the right pair of meters. Additionally, the level meters are colored. If your signal is at a reasonable level, the meters are green, but if you get close to 0.0 dB, the faders start to turn yellow, and then orange, and if they get all the way to red, then you've gone too far. There is no distortion until they actually hit red.

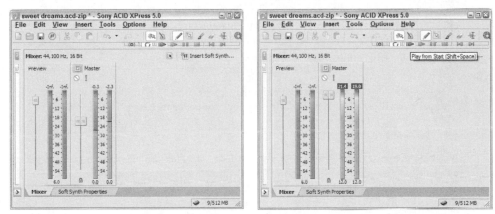

FIGURE 12-2: A signal with a reasonable level, compared to an overloaded and distorted signal

If your signal is overloaded, simply turn down the volume. The level of amplification for the signal is adjusted by sliding the faders up and down, and is numerically displayed by the pair of numbers underneath the meters. In the case of the example on the right of Figure 12-2, the peak level of the left channel is +21.4 dB, and the amplification level is +12.0 dB. To bring it down so the level doesn't go past 0.0 dB, you'd have to move the faders down at least 21.4 dB to -9.4 dB (+12.0 dB – 21.4 dB). You might want to go to -9.5 dB just to be safe. Alternatively, you can adjust the levels of your component tracks, although if you want to maintain your mix, you'll have to adjust the levels of each component equally. In this case, each individual track would need to be decreased by at least 21.4 dB instead of lowering the master fader. You could also perform a combination of lowering the master fader and each of the component tracks.

If you are fretting because you want a louder output, don't worry. There are methods for achieving loudness that do not involve the risk of clipping, which are discussed in the "Dynamics" section later in this chapter.

Masking

If you have multiple instrumental songs or an extracted acapella with instrumental remnants remaining, you may not be able to hear all the individual elements of each song. Indeed, you may not want to hear each element. The ear can only take in so much information at once. There is a phenomenon known as *masking*, where the ear perceives certain information and discards the rest.

Frequency masking occurs when two events occur simultaneously with very similar frequencies. Typically, the louder sound in that frequency range is heard, but the quieter sound is not. You can use this to your advantage when layering multiple instrumental tracks. For example, you may have an acapella you extracted yourself with some bass and drum remnants remaining. Even though you've eliminated the bass frequencies in your extraction, the instrumental artifacts are unpalatable when your acapella is listened to by itself. However, when layered with another rhythmic track, the rhythmic elements in your acapella may be drowned out by the rhythmic elements in the backing track, but the vocal is still clear because the background contains no competing sounds in the vocal frequency range. You may be surprised at how clean a messy acapella can sound when layered properly.

Temporal masking occurs when two percussive events occur very close to each other in time. The ear perceives only one event, with the louder one dominating. Two drum tracks synced up pretty well will blend into a single drum track with stacked snares and stacked kicks being perceived as single events.

Masking is used extremely frequently in mashup construction. If you can't seem to isolate the elements you want, camouflaging them with competing material is often the way to go. Masking can also be your enemy, however, and can make the mix unintelligible. For example, if you have distorted guitars playing from two separate tracks, chances are that they will have competing frequencies, mask each other, and become one big garbled mess.

Bass clash is also an example of masking. If you can't seem to find decent levels where you can hear each sound, you may also try solving the problem using pan and EQ to separate the sounds. Of course, going back to fix the arrangement is always a possibility.

Envelopes

If you have ACID Pro, judicious use of volume envelopes can sometimes help in maintaining appropriate mix levels. If a certain track sounds good for the majority of your mashup, but is buried for only a passage, you can use volume envelopes to raise only that portion. Traditionally, engineers would sit at the mixing console and nudge the faders while the mix went to tape. Eventually mixing consoles were fitted with automated faders that would change the levels at predetermined times. ACID Pro's envelopes fulfill the same role, nudging up the volume of a track for just the portion of the song where it needs to be fixed.

Panning

Since the advent of stereophonic sound, music producers have used panning to separate and clarify different elements of a mix. In Chapter 10, the chapter devoted to unmixing, you used this fact to your advantage to isolate elements according to their location in the stereo field. When mixing, you can use panning to separate elements that otherwise might mask each other. If two elements share similar frequencies, they can blend together and be indistinct if panned to the same location. Panning them to different locations can allow each sound to be heard more plainly.

The conventional goal of panning is to simulate the stereo field of a live performance. However, in mashup production the dominating goal is to create as distinct and crisp a mix as is feasible with possibly more elements than were meant to be mixed together.

Separating Elements

Extreme panning should be used sparingly, because the ear prefers balance overall. If you pan some elements to the left, usually other elements should be panned to the right so your mix doesn't end up lopsided. In general, most of the time you won't pan mono tracks all the way to either side, because extreme panning can be jarring. Also, it's not a good idea to pan multiple mono tracks to the same location other than dead center, unless you want to blend the sounds together.

As it is, most instrumentals, full songs, and even many acapellas are already in full stereo to separate the individual elements in the recording. If you pan a stereo track, you will compress the stereo field of that track. Although your panning may help to separate the stereo track from other elements in your mashup, the compression of the stereo field will bring the elements within the track closer together. In practice, when you're mixing several stereo tracks together, most occasions call for simply leaving the panning as is and using other tools to separate the tracks. Many stereo tracks have a decent amount of stereo separation already built in, which you may not want to reduce.

Traditionally, lead vocals are always panned dead center. Bass, kick, and snare are also typically in the very middle. Background vocals are often panned, with equal amounts of voice panned to the left and right, often with different notes in the harmony panned to different positions. Usually, there is an overall balance between the left and right levels. Cymbals, toms, hi-hats, and other percussion can often be panned somewhat to the left and right, maintaining an overall balance. Guitars can be panned, sometimes with two distorted guitars panned one to each side.

As the frequency of a sound increases, the ear's sensitivity to spatial placement increases as well. You can place the subwoofer of a stereo system off-center, and it will still sound good, but if you misplaced a tweeter, it would sound lopsided. Due to the ear's increased sensitivity, take extra care to balance the high frequencies between the left and right channels.

Front/Back

To create convincing front/back spatial relationships, you'll need to use a combination of techniques outside of the realm of panning. To make a track sound farther back:

- Lower the volume.
- Increase the amount of reverb and delay.
- Use a high shelf filter to roll off the higher frequencies.

The use of filters and reverb is discussed later in this chapter.

Mono-to-Stereo Imaging

Certain types of sounds, such as some guitars, ambient synths, and background vocals, can be spread across the stereo spectrum, creating a stereo effect while maintaining left/right balance. Sometimes you don't want the imbalance that panning a sound to the left or right of center can create, but you want to create stereo imagery either to help separate an element from others in the mix or create a fuller sound. There are a few techniques that will either first break a mono sound apart into components or create multiple copies of the sound, each processed slightly differently. These elements are then spread across the stereo spectrum.

Stereo Delay

A simple way to create a stereo image from a mono image is to first create two identical copies of the audio and pan them left and right in equal amounts. Then delay one of the sounds a very slight amount, perhaps 30 or 40 milliseconds. This amount is small enough that the audio is still perceived as a single sound, but large enough that the stereo placement can be perceived. The overall sound is still balanced around the center, but because each part of it is off-center, it seems separated from whatever audio in the mix is still panned center.

This can also be performed with a stereo delay effect, discussed later in this chapter, or by just duplicating the track in question, panning each track equally to the left and right, and then selecting all the events in one of the tracks and shifting them ever so slightly back in time. You may want to include an additional duplicate of the track that remains panned center, and adjust the volume of the center-panned track in relation to the side-panned tracks to your taste.

Left/Right EQ

Another way to add stereo imaging to a mono signal is to EQ the left and right channels slightly differently.

Pro EQ is discussed in detail in the next section, and is available only in ACID Pro.

Pan the mono sound to the center, and add two track EQs to a single track. In the Channels tab of the first Track EQ, uncheck the Enable Left check box, and then uncheck the Enable Right check box in the other Track EQ. This puts a different EQ effect on each channel of the mono signal. Now, make very small adjustments in the upper range of the EQ on each channel. Make sure that you are not raising or lowering similar frequencies in each effect, so each channel has a distinct character. Don't go crazy with this effect, however. You are not trying to create an EQ-type effect, but just enough to make the sound have a fuller stereo image.

Plug-Ins

Here are two free VST plug-ins that are dedicated to creating stereo sounds from mono sources:

- **Voxengo Stereo Touch**: Available at www.voxengo.com/product/stereotouch. It basically performs a stereo delay, with the addition of a low-pass filter on the delayed and panned signals (see Figure 12-3).

FIGURE 12-3: Voxengo Stereo Touch

- **Klanglabs StereoFaker:** Downloadable at http://klanglabs.siliconemusic .com/freebies/sfaker/sfaker.htm. It provides up to six separate signals, each with its own pan, delay with feedback, and filtering (see Figure 12-4).

FIGURE 12-4: Klanglabs StereoFaker

Enhancing Stereo Imaging

Most of the audio you will deal with is likely already in stereo. However, you may want to alter the existing stereo spectrum of this signal beyond the simple panning of the track to the left or right. Plug-ins are available that can compress or expand a stereo signal, moving the panned elements within the audio further from or closer to center. This effect uses the OOPS technique outlined in Chapter 10 to separate the signal into mid and side components, and then manipulates the levels independently before changing them back into left and right signals. The net effect is that the side channels are raised or lowered compared to the center channel, and therefore, the stereo image is widened or narrowed. If elements in the two tracks are panned and seem to be competing with one another, you can use this effect to separate them.

One example of a free VST plug-in that implements this effect is Spatty (pictured in Figure 12-5), which is available from MB Plugins at `http://mitglied.lycos.de/mbplugins/`. To widen the stereo image, raise the side level higher than the mid level, and to narrow it, raise the mid level higher than the side level.

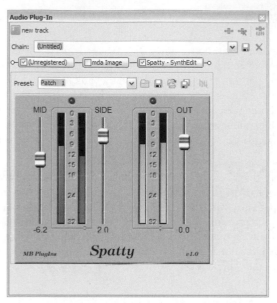

FIGURE 12-5: Spatty stereo-width-adjusting plug-in

Life in Mono

Some people will inevitably end up listening to your mix with reduced stereo separation, either in true mono or with the stereo speakers close enough to each other that the stereo channels are mixed together pretty well. It's important that your mix sounds good in mono. With all the stereo field manipulation that mashup producers engage in, some very strange things can sometimes happen when the mashup is heard in mono. Sounds can disappear due to phase cancellation, or at least have drastically different levels than they do in the stereo signal. Selecting all of your tracks and then panning them all the way to the left or right can simulate this phenomenon, allowing you to listen to your entire mashup in mono. Just press Ctrl+Z to undo this action afterwards.

EQ

EQ refers to the raising or lowering of only a certain range of frequencies in a signal. In a music studio, EQ is used so extensively in mixing that it is almost as important as adjusting the overall levels of the individual tracks. With mashups, EQ is also used quite frequently, although perhaps not quite as often, because the component tracks have presumably already been EQ'd in their mastering process.

Only ACID Pro supports EQ and other effects.

If you've ever adjusted the treble or bass on your home stereo, you've already performed a rudimentary form of EQ. A slightly more advanced form of EQ for the home user is the *graphic EQ*, a frequently-seen hardware component in hi-fi systems that has a bank of around 5 to 15 sliders, each controlling the volume of a different frequency band. Both of these types of EQ may enhance the experience for the home user, but they lack the precision of a professional EQ. The frequencies that each knob or slider affects are fixed, and although you can precisely affect the levels, you cannot affect the exact frequency or how other nearby frequencies are affected.

An overall goal of EQ is to spread out the tone of the final mix through the frequency spectrum. EQ not only irons out any irregularities in the sound, but it also purposely creates irregularities that increase the track's compatibility with the rest of the mix. The levels of the various frequency components are reduced, each track making room for the other, with the net result being a very full sound. But paradoxically, in order to create the full sound, sometimes the individual components need to be thinned. It's not as important how each track sounds on its own as how it sounds in combination with the other tracks.

Filters

A *parametric EQ*, as opposed to a graphic EQ, allows you precise control over the level, frequency, and width of frequency response. This is the type of EQ most commonly used in music studios and is the EQ included in ACID Pro. ACID's EQ is comprised of a series of processors called *filters*. These filters come in two basic varieties: band filters and shelf filters.

Band Filters

A *band filter* raises or lowers the levels of the signal at and around a chosen frequency. The following three parameters define the filter:

- The *frequency* (in Hz) at which the signal is most amplified or attenuated

- The *gain*, or the amount (in dB) of amplification or attenuation of the signal

- *Bandwidth* (in octaves), also known as Q, which defines how much the frequencies near the center frequency are affected

Shelf Filters

Shelf filters are similar to band filters except that rather than affecting a range of frequencies, they affect the level of all frequencies above or below a given frequency. A low shelf will reduce or increase all of the frequencies below the frequency of the filter, and a high shelf will affect the frequencies above it. The frequency and gain parameters of a shelf filter are identical to those of the band filters, but the bandwidth parameter is replaced by a rolloff parameter, measured in dBs per octave. This represents how many decibels will be reduced or increased for each octave beyond the frequency of the filter.

A high shelf filter that attenuates is commonly known as a *low-pass filter*, and an attenuating low shelf filter is also known as a *high-pass filter*. A filter that attenuates both low and high frequencies is called a *band-pass filter*. The word "pass" refers to the fact that those frequencies are allowed to pass through the filter.

ACID's Track EQ

Several shelf and band filters are typically used at the same time, and they bundle together into a single effect in ACID Pro known as Track EQ, shown in Figure 12-6. The curve depicted in the figure is a graph of the amount of volume adjustment in dB for each frequency in the track in Hz. By default, Track EQ consists of a low shelf filter, a high shelf filter, and two band filters. In Figure 12-6, there is a low shelf filter with a very low rolloff, compared to a high shelf filter with a high rolloff. The relatively gentle slope of the low shelf filter on the left side of the curve contrasts with the steep slope of the high shelf filter on the right side. The two band filters, represented by the numbers 2 and 3, have a very narrow bandwidth and a very wide bandwidth, respectively. As you can see, the narrow bandwidth only affects a small number of frequencies, and the wide bandwidth affects a greater portion of the signal.

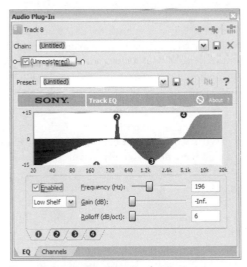

FIGURE 12-6: ACID Pro's Track EQ

In ACID's Track EQ, you can alter the frequency and gain parameters by clicking the number associated with the filter, and dragging it up and down for gain, and left and right for frequency. Move the slider below the graphic window to define the bandwidth for band filters and the rolloff for shelf filters.

Overcoming Masking

One great use of EQ is minimizing frequency masking. Suppose you have a vocal track mixed with an instrumental track that occasionally has loud guitars that interfere with the clarity of the vocals. When the guitar is not playing, the vocals are fine, but when the guitar plays, the voice seems buried. You might try panning, but the mix seems lopsided. You might try turning up the vocals, but they seem too loud when the guitar isn't playing. You might try adding a volume envelope to the vocals, but the change in volume is too obvious.

Because the vocals and guitar are competing in the same frequency range, there is another trick you can use. With a band filter, you can lower the frequencies in the guitar that compete with the vocals. You can possibly combine this with raising the volume of the frequencies in the same band on the vocal track. Although doing this may affect the overall volume of each track very little, if the band of frequencies is appropriate, it can have a profound effect on the clarity. This sort of EQ adjustment should be very subtle, with relatively small amounts of gain. Be aware that your ear quickly adjusts to the sound of EQ, so it's easy to go too far. It's a good idea to occasionally bypass the EQ and then reactivate it, just to remind yourself how the track sounds unaltered and how much you've altered it.

It's easy for a mashup with multiple instrumentals to have certain competitions of sound in the low and mid ranges. If you are hearing muddiness in the mix, try using an EQ's band filter to lower a band of frequencies significantly, with the gain at first lowered all the way down to -Inf, and the bandwidth set to one octave. While the clashing parts are playing, sweep the frequency of the filter up and down across the entire frequency spectrum, and notice when there is an increase in clarity. That's the frequency you're looking for. Now raise the gain back upward toward a less extreme level, until you've given the track back some of its body, but not enough to create conflict with the other track.

Ironically, although the end goal is to create a full-sounding mix, the way to go about it is to thin out the individual elements. This is true in traditional music mixing and mastering, and even more so when you're combining elements that were not originally meant to be combined.

Raising vs. Lowering

In the real world, very few natural processes raise a range of frequencies in a sound, although there are various situations where a group of frequencies is absorbed and therefore lowered. If you've ever heard loud music in the next room with your door closed, you may have noticed that the bass frequencies are clearly audible, but the higher frequencies are totally eliminated. This is because the door absorbs and reduces the high frequencies. Due to this sound absorption in nature, the ear generally expects a reduction rather than an amplification in a frequency band. Therefore, it is usually preferable to use EQ with a negative gain. If you think frequencies in your two tracks are competing with each other, try eliminating the frequencies in one track before you try raising them in the other. If you do find you need to raise the frequencies, it's possible that the amount of gain is less than the amount you would need if you were lowering the other track.

Bass Elimination

Most of the adjustments you'll make with EQ are fairly subtle, but there is a notable exception in the case of avoiding bass clash. If you have two tracks with bass lines playing at the same time, you will almost certainly need to eliminate the bass on one of the tracks. Although you may be able to do this with center channel elimination, EQ is more commonly used. Try a low shelf filter with very steep rolloff, the gain set to a large negative value, and the frequency set between 100 and 150 Hz. You may still hear the bass notes, but they will sound thin, and will quite possibly disappear when masked with the accompanying tracks. The key here is to balance the need to eliminate the bass with the need for fullness in the rest of the track. If your track begins to sound tinny, you may need to lower the frequency of the shelf filter or set the gain so the bass isn't reduced so drastically.

Spectral Analysis

Even people experienced with EQ may have difficulty determining exactly what frequencies are present in the audio. If you are trying to eliminate masking for example, it would be useful to know what frequencies are present in each component, and at what levels. Fortunately, there are tools called *spectral analyzers* that can graphically depict the level of all frequencies within a given signal. You can use this information to help guide you through the equalization process.

ACID Pro doesn't have a built-in spectral analyzer, but a great free plug-in called SPAN is available from Voxengo at www.voxengo.com/product/SPAN/. Figure 12-7 shows a spectral analysis of an acapella. Notice the peak near 2,000 Hz and the steep rolloff between 200 and 100 Hz, typical of acapellas. Most of the default settings are appropriate for the purposes of mashup construction; however, you may want to change the monitor from RealT to Avg, as highlighted in Figure 12-7.

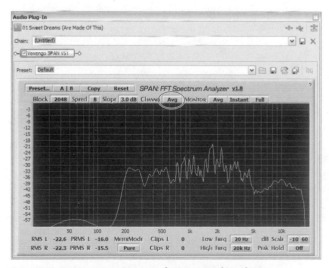

FIGURE 12-7: Voxengo SPAN, a free spectral analyzer

Comparing the spectral analysis of two tracks in your mashup may be able to help you determine if competing frequencies are the cause of a lack of clarity in your mix.

An alternative to SPAN is to use Adobe Audition's built-in frequency analysis. In Adobe Audition, press Alt+Z to bring up the window. You may want to uncheck the Linear View check box, so the high frequencies do not take up the majority of the window, and each octave is given equal visual prominence.

Equalizing the Master Bus

EQ can also come in handy when you're processing the entire mixdown. Although each of the component tracks in all probability have been EQ'd well, there is a possibility that the processing of individual tracks, including EQ and center channel manipulation, may have created an imbalance in the overall sound, which needs to be corrected by equalizing the mixdown. You may want to perform a spectral analysis of your entire mixdown, and then compare the output to the spectral analysis of a reference audio file, which could be any song you think is well mixed and mastered and is in a similar style to your mashup.

Another piece of information spectral analysis of your mixdown will provide is an accurate assessment of the sonic energy in the bass register below what your sound system can reproduce. Ideally, there shouldn't be a lot of bass energy your ears aren't aware of, and if your speakers aren't capable of producing the low frequencies, that doesn't mean they're not in the audio file. If you notice a large spike in the very low end that your speakers aren't reproducing, you might consider applying a low pass filter on your entire mix, and then reanalyzing the spectrum. Alternatively, find a friend with a boomin' subwoofer and subject your victim to your latest mashup experiment.

There are software packages that will automatically analyze the spectrum of a reference audio file, and then apply the necessary EQ on your final mix to raise and lower the appropriate frequencies until your frequency spectrum exactly matches the spectrum of the reference audio file. Commercial products include the following:

- **Voxengo CurveEQ:** www.voxengo.com/product/curveeq/
- **Elevayta Clone Boy:** www.paulrharvey.co.uk/elevayta/product2.htm

Resonant Filters

A *resonant filter* is a special type of filter that doesn't simply remove sound beyond a certain frequency, but creates an additional spike in volume in frequencies adjacent to the cutoff point. The most commonly used type is a resonant low pass filter, which is like ACID Pro's low shelf filter with an extra boost in the frequencies just below the cutoff. Figure 12-8 shows the frequency response of a typical low shelf filter (the dotted line), contrasted with the frequency response of a resonant filter (the solid line). The higher the resonance, the taller and sharper the peak will be.

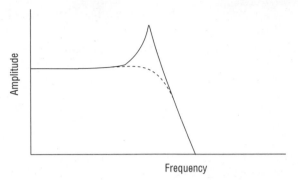

FIGURE 12-8: The frequency of a low shelf filter and a resonant low shelf filter

Resonant filters are used extensively in modern dance music, where they can add tension and release, and they can be a lot of fun in mashups as well. Typically, the frequency will be swept from low to high or from high to low, with all other parameters kept constant.

ACID Pro has a built-in resonant filter effect, with settings for resonance, frequency, wet/dry (which determines the amount of processed versus unprocessed signal), filter type (low pass, band pass, or high pass), and filter order, which determines the rolloff. Although ACID's resonant filter is decent, I prefer the free VST plug-in from Ohm Force called Frohmage (shown in Figure 12-9), which is available at `www.ohmforce.com/ViewProduct.do?p=Frohmage`. It has a beautiful analog sound, and includes built-in distortion and other neat features that just sound great! Ohm Force is one company that knows how to make cool effects. The only drawback is the somewhat cryptic interface. The knob in the lower-left corner is the resonance, and the big knob in the middle is the frequency. Turn up the resonance to a level you like, and then add an envelope on your track that controls the frequency. Play around with the other knobs. It's a (formerly) secret weapon in my arsenal that I can't seem to tire of.

FIGURE 12-9: Ohm Force Frohmage

Dynamics

EQ alters the level of audio components based on their frequency, but *dynamics* alters the level of the audio components based on their original level. Although mixing can alter the relative loudness of the various tracks, dynamics can alter the relative loudness of various points within a single track or the entire mix. Compression is the most common kind of operation on dynamics, but gating, expansion, and limiting also can come into play. There may not be a single commercially mixed track that doesn't use dynamics to some extent, and many modern electronic music producers depend on it heavily as an artistic effect.

Like EQ, the goal of dynamics is to create a fuller-sounding mix, and often the elements are shrunk in order for the full mix to have a larger sound.

 Dynamic processing requires ACID Pro.

Compression

Compression seeks to lessen the difference between the quieter portions of a sound compared to the louder portions by decreasing the amplitude of the sound when the sound has surpassed a certain volume, called the *threshold*. If the signal has a lower volume than the threshold, the audio is unaltered. But after the audio passes the threshold, the amount of gain beyond the threshold is reduced by a constant ratio. The ratio represents the number of decibels in the input signal above the threshold compared to the number of decibels in the output signal above the threshold.

For example, if you have a ratio of 2:1 and the threshold is -10 dB, the output signals would be affected as follows:

- A -15 dB signal would remain unchanged at -15 dB because it's under the threshold.

- A -10 dB signal would remain unchanged at the threshold of -10 dB.

- A -5 dB signal would retain only half the gain beyond the threshold, reducing the output to -7.5 dB.

- A 0 dB signal would similarly be reduced to -5 dB.

This relationship of input to output is graphically displayed in Figure 12-10. The solid thin line represents the pure unadulterated signal with the input equal to the output. The solid bold line represents the compressed signal, and the dotted bold line represents the same compressed signal after the gain is adjusted so that it again peaks at 0.0 dB.

As you can see, the act of compression reduces the amplitude of the louder portions of the signal. Assuming that your original signal peaked at 0.0 dB, after being processed by a compressor with a 2:1 ratio and a -10 dB threshold, your signal would now peak at -5 dB, allowing you to raise the entire signal by 5 dB afterwards and still not go over 0.0 dB. Every portion of the audio below the peak of 0 dB has been given some amount of gain without clipping. The quieter

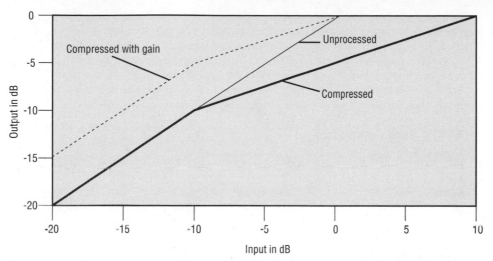

FIGURE 12-10: The response curve of a compressor with a 2:1 ratio and a -10 dB threshold

sounds (below the threshold) are most affected and are easier to hear, and the increase in gain gradually disappears for the loudest signals. The net effect of a compressor is to smooth out the audio, making the sound more constant. Although a compressor itself makes an audio signal quieter, the newly allowed gain added afterwards can make the overall signal louder than it was before without the clipping that would occur with straightforward amplification.

Suppose you have an acapella that seems to have a great level when the singer is belting out the big notes in the chorus, but your accompanying instrumental seems to bury the vocalist when she's whispering the verses. One solution would be to place a volume envelope on the acapella track and raise the volume during the verses. A simpler solution would be to place a compressor on the whole track, and experiment with the threshold, gain, and ratio to find settings that balance the vocalist with the instruments throughout the mashup.

Compressors are often used on the entire mix to help iron out volume fluctuations and to help bring the whole mix together and make it sound like one cohesive piece. Almost all commercial music has some compression on the entire mix, giving the music maximum loudness and punch. Although there is always the danger of overdoing it, mashup producers need every tool available to blend different elements together. If you are compressing your entire mixdown, unless you are doing an extreme artistic effect, it's probably a good idea to add the compressor late in the mixing-and-mastering process. Because compression smoothes out the mix so much, mixing with a compressor on the master bus can make you lazy, and you'll make fewer decisions than you would otherwise. When the mix sounds good without a compressor, consider putting compression on the master bus. It can make a good mix a bit better, but can make it hard to fine-tune the mix while peering through its glossy sheen. Most mashups will not need any compression at all on the master bus. If you're unsure, render a few different versions with various levels of compression or none at all. Listen to each on various systems later, and decide after a day or so.

Like so many other aspects of mashup production, the best way of learning how to use compressors is to experiment with them. After a while, you'll gain an intuitive feel for what they do. Like EQ, compressors are easy to overuse, and your ears can get too comfortable with the sound. You may want to periodically turn off the compression just to remind yourself how the unprocessed track sounds and to verify that the compression is actually necessary. Also, remember that most of the tracks you are manipulating have most likely already been compressed, so most often, additional compression on the individual tracks will be unnecessary.

ACID's Track Compressor

Figure 12-11 shows ACID Pro's Track Compressor.

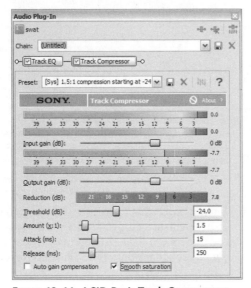

FIGURE 12-11: ACID Pro's Track Compressor

Here's a description of the Track Compressor features, from top to bottom:

- **First stereo meter:** Shows the level of the input signal in real time.

- **Input Gain:** This slider adjusts the level of the signal before compression.

- **Second stereo meter:** Shows the level of the signal after processing.

- **Output Gain:** This slider can be used to amplify (or attenuate) the signal after it's compressed. Remember that after you have a compressor on a track, you'll need to resist the impulse to adjust the level with the volume slider as you usually do. This will affect the portion of the signal that is above the threshold and change the sound in unexpected ways. If you want to change the overall level of the track, you'll need to do it after compression using the Output Gain.

- **Reduction:** Basically, this meter lets you know, in real time, how much attenuation is being applied to the signal. In Figure 12-11, the track is currently being lowered 7.8 dB. If you play your entire track and you never see any orange on the reduction meter, it means that either your signal is never reaching the threshold or your ratio is 1:1. In either case, no actual compression is happening. You'll need to raise the input gain or the volume on your track, decrease the threshold, or increase the ratio (amount) if it is indeed 1:1 (which it never should be).

- **Threshold**

- **Amount:** This is the ratio of compression. 1.0 means there is no compression. Bringing it all the way up to Inf. (infinite) turns the compressor into a serious limiter, which is discussed in a little bit.

- **Attack:** This parameter (measured in milliseconds) adjusts the amount of time that it takes for the compressor to go from a 1:1 ratio while the signal is below the threshold, to the designated ratio when the signal surpasses the threshold. Typically the compression is not instantaneous but takes a very brief time to reach the desired ratio. This slight lag in reaching maximum compression helps to preserve the transient attacks that would otherwise be so ironed out that the percussive elements in the track could be lost and become muddy. The faster the attack time, the more the transient attacks are muted.

- **Release:** This parameter (measured in milliseconds) controls the amount of time that the compressor returns to the 1:1 ratio after the signal again descends below the threshold. This amount of time is typically much slower than the attack time. This is because sounds generally start quickly and decay more gradually. As a result, you can take your time in returning to normal levels, and make the transition smoother and less noticeable.

- **Auto Gain Compensation:** When this box is checked, the output gain is automatically adjusted to make up for the threshold and amount (ratio) settings. This feature exists because people will usually turn up the gain to balance out the gain reduction brought about by the compression. This is automatic, so you'll still need to adjust the output gain, but you'll find you need to do less fine-tuning to the gain as you change the threshold and amount settings.

- **Smooth Saturation:** When this box is checked, the compressor distorts the sounds less harshly, mimicking analog circuitry and giving the compressor a bit of warmth. This is similar to the analog-style distortion as opposed to the harsh digital clipping.

Knees

ACID Pro's track compressor is what is known as a *hard knee* compressor. Go back to Figure 12-10 and look at the transition from 1:1 compression to 2:1 compression. As soon as the attack and release period are over, any signal below the threshold receives one treatment, and anything above the threshold receives an entirely different treatment. The bend in the graph is reminiscent of a knee, hence the name.

A *soft knee* compressor would have a smooth curvature at the bend instead of a sharp angle. This has the effect of further smoothing out the compression and making it sound more natural and less sudden. You may encounter this feature in more advanced compressors.

Pump It

Although the traditional use of compressors has the attack at a fairly quick duration, many dance producers have been seriously playing around with compressors lately. Using a compressor on the entire mix, and giving the attack a longer duration than usual makes the entire mix seem to swell rhythmically. This fluctuation is traditionally frowned upon, but it is being increasingly used for artistic effect in some circles. Pumping can give the entire mix a rhythmic feel, even if the background is a pad or some constant sound.

Note

Often dance music pump is implemented with *side-chain compressors*, which compress a signal according to the input amplitude of an altogether separate signal (often the kick drum track).

Know Your Limit

A *limiter* is a specialized kind of compressor with a very high ratio approaching infinite, usually with an extremely quick attack. Adjusting the ratio and attack time with ACID Pro's track compressor can create an effective limiter. The main purpose of a limiter is to make absolutely sure that the signal doesn't clip and distort in an ugly way. Unless you are getting really creative with your compressor, you probably wouldn't want a limiter to be reducing your signal for any significant duration of time. Limiters are used mostly for very brief transient attacks, which are brought under control. Because the period is so brief, it should be barely noticeable in most cases. If every drum sound is being limited, you probably are overusing this process.

A limiter with an infinite ratio is called a *brick wall* limiter, and if used, is usually placed as the very last process on an entire mix. Brick wall and other limiters are frequently used in live situations where you cannot know beforehand what the peak amplitude of a signal will be. However, in ACID you have the opportunity to listen to the same signal repeatedly, so most of the time limiters shouldn't be necessary. There may be exceptions, however, such as if you are using an effect with a random or periodic component that changes each time you play it.

Big Bands

One type of compression used frequently during mastering the entire mixdown is a processor called the *multiband compressor*, or Multi-Band Dynamics in ACID Pro. This type of compressor breaks down the audio signal into discrete frequency ranges and operates a separate compressor on each. This is handy during mastering when you are trying to optimize the levels for all frequencies. Sometimes multiband compression works better than EQ on the entire mix, because it can smooth out the levels in a problem frequency range.

Multiband compression can be used to flatten out the bass and make it constant. It is also used to reduce sibilance in vocals (high frequency sounds like "s" and "t").

Hammer Time

If you want to get your signal *really* loud, you may want to use the Wave Hammer effect included with ACID Pro. It consists of a compressor followed by a limiter, and features a look-ahead function, which means that the signal can be attenuated *before* the attack. While the track compressor is modeled after traditional analog compressors, the look-ahead functionality of the Wave Hammer reads the audio ahead of time and pre-compresses the audio. This plug-in might give you the extra decibels you are looking for, but the look-ahead might give you an annoying pre-pump.

Expansion

Expansion, although similar in concept to compression, has the opposite effect. Instead of attenuating the sounds above the threshold, expansion attenuates the sounds below the threshold, as shown in Figure 12-12. The thin solid line is the unprocessed signal, the thick solid line is the signal processed with a 2:1 ratio and a -10 dB threshold, and the thick dotted line represents the processed signal with an infinite:1 ratio.

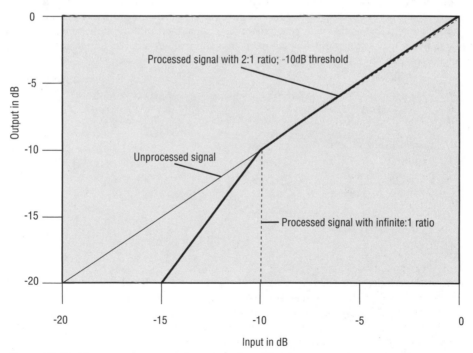

FIGURE 12-12: The response curve of an expander with a 2:1 ratio and a -10 dB threshold

This should look familiar from Chapter 10, when the gate was used to remove artifacts from extracted acapellas. A gate is just an extreme form of an expander with an infinite:1 ratio. In traditional music production, expanders and gates are typically used to remove noisy parts from a recorded signal. In mashup production, this type of dynamic processing is more likely to be used to remove ugly parts from a signal that hasn't been elegantly unmixed.

Note   Often simply deleting the noise manually in ACID is a better solution and gives you greater control. You can choose whether to fade in or out each segment, simulating expanders with various ratios.

Graphic Dynamics

The Graphic Dynamics plug-in, shown in Figure 12-13, can function as multiple simultaneous dynamics processors. It can act as two different compressors with different ratios and thresholds, or it can act as a combination compressor/limiter and gate, as in Figure 12-13. It's great if you want that extra bit of control over dynamics beyond the typical two-stage compressors and expanders. You can even get fancy and create an inverse dynamic processor, making the output actually get louder as the input gets quieter. You can also create soft-knee compression with it by drawing multiple straight-line segments that approximate a curve. Check out some of the presets for examples.

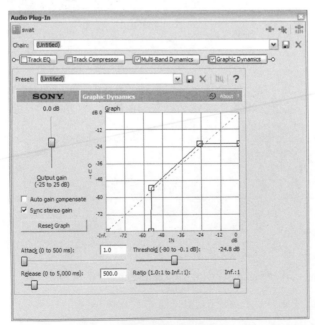

FIGURE 12-13: The Graphic Dynamics plug-in, with simultaneous limiting and gating

Santa Barbara Public Library System

www.sbplibrary.org
Renewal Line: 1-800-354-9660
Customer Service Line: (805) 962-7653

Borrowed Items 3/10/2015 10:49
XXXXXXXXX3972

Title	Due Date
...ashup construction kit	4/1/2015

...ou for using self-check!

Chapter 12 — Finishing Touches   **259**

Effects

Effects are the spice that gives your tracks a little something extra, but as with spice, you don't want to use too much — just a tasty amount. There are hundreds of effects available, as you may have realized if you've visited www.kvraudio.com, but only a few of them are commonly used with regularity.

 Effects are available only in the Pro version of ACID.

Delay

Delay effects are very simple but useful for a variety of purposes. A delay simply creates a copy of the audio signal and replays it slightly later than the original signal. Usually the original signal is played as well, and typically, the delayed signal has a lower amplitude than the original. Sometimes the delayed signal is panned to the left or right, and sometimes the delayed signal itself is fed back into the delay. If there is feedback and the delayed signal is set to a lower level than the original, the delay will produce an echo effect. Sometimes the echo will be panned back and forth between the left and right channels and is called a *ping-pong delay*.

ACID Pro comes with two types of delay: simple delay and multi-tap delay.

Multi-Tap Delay

ACID Pro's Multi-Tap Delay window, pictured in Figure 12-14, gives you precise control over up to eight independent delays.

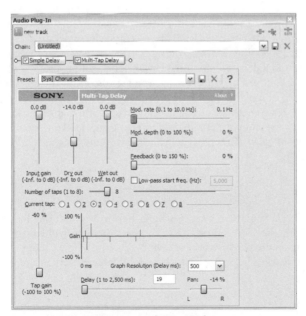

FIGURE 12-14: ACID Pro's Multi-Tap Delay

The upper portion of the window lets you control the input gain, allowing you to attenuate the signal before processing. It also has Dry Out and Wet Out controls to balance the delayed effect with the unprocessed signal. The modulation (Mod.) parameters allow you to vary the delay times. This can create a chorus-like effect (discussed shortly). The Feedback parameter can transform the delay into an echo, although to achieve rhythmic echoes would take a bit of math and may be easier to achieve by other means. The Number Of Taps defines how many independently delayed signals there are.

The Low-Pass check box and frequency slider can filter the delays, cutting out some of the high frequencies. Often, a multi-tap delay is used to create the illusion of space, with the delayed signals simulating reflections or echoes of the sound from walls or other surfaces. Low frequencies travel farther than high frequencies, so by the time a sound wave has traveled to a distant surface and back to the listener, chances are that the high frequencies will be attenuated more than the low frequencies. Including a low-pass filter in the delay allows you to simulate this effect.

The bottom half of the Multi-Tap Delay window allows you to set the parameters for each of the independent delays. You can control the gain, pan, and delay amount of each delay here. To edit each delay signal, click the corresponding number next to Current Tap. The amplitude and pan of each delay, including any feedback, is depicted in the graph. You can change the time window of the graph with the Graph Resolution drop-down menu.

You can use the multi-tap delay to create stereo width from a mono signal, and to create chorus-like and reverb-like effects, although dedicated choruses and reverbs may do the job more elegantly. Use this effect with caution in mashup production, as it can muddy a signal quickly.

Simple Delay

The name of this effect makes it seem less useful than the multi-tap delay, but the simple delay (shown previously in Chapter 11, Figure 11-13) has some attractive features that make it an extremely useful tool. The ability to easily create delays that are tempo-dependent makes the simple delay rhythmic and musical. Creating delays on only a portion of the signal was covered in Chapter 11, but if you want to add a delay effect on the entire signal, simply use it as an insert effect instead of a bus effect and turn up the dry level. You can also enter the delay and decay times in seconds rather than in musical durations if you want to. But the simple delay really shines with the tempo sync delay checkbox checked. You can soften the abrupt ending of a track, as you learned in Chapter 11, and you can create interesting rhythms on percussive material. Using musically significant delay times prevents your mix from getting as muddy as it would with imprecisely timed delays.

Reverb

Reverb is actually a form of delay. If you are in a space where there are so many reflected sounds that they seem to smear together and you no longer can hear them individually, you've left the realm of the delay/echo and entered the world of reverb. An echo is like yelling into the Grand Canyon, and hearing a clear voice hollering back at you a bit later. Reverb is like yelling in a cathedral (frowned upon — author accepts no responsibility) and hearing a blurred response that contains the same frequencies, but none of the intelligibility. Because reverb smears a sound over time, pitch irregularities can seem to be ironed out as well.

It is probably unnecessary to use reverb on an instrumental or full mix. You may, however want to add a bit of reverb to an acapella to give it a bit of depth. Also, if you are extracting your own acapellas using center channel isolation, most of the reverb in the original recording will be lost, because reverb typically will be spread across the stereo spectrum. Adding reverb to this dried-out signal may help to restore life and ambience to it.

Here are a few guidelines:

- Never use reverb on a bass. It will just muddy it up.

- Reverb, along with volume and filtering, can impart a sense of distance to audio. Signals that are farther away have a greater wet-to-dry ratio.

- Add reverb late in the mixing process. Get the levels, compression, and EQ right first.

- Don't overdo it. It's easy to use too much.

- If you are using reverb on vocals, make sure you are not losing intelligibility. Reverb can make some consonants disappear.

History

Well before the advent of recording technology, musicians were keenly aware of the pleasant effect of reverb. Churches and auditoriums were designed to create reverbs that would maximally accentuate musical performances. In the early days of recorded sound, the effect was created by using actual reverberant spaces, either with the sound being recorded in the room, or played back and rerecorded in the space.

In the 1950s, a new piece of technology called *plate reverb* was introduced to music studios. A large thin sheet of metal resonated with recorded sound, and created a simulated space. Plate reverbs may seem huge today, but they are much smaller than the reverberant rooms they replaced.

By the late 1970s, digital reverbs started appearing, which used various algorithms to simulate the smeared multiple reflections of a reverberant space.

ACID Pro's Reverb

The effect that is simply called *reverb* in ACID Pro is an example of a simple digital reverb (shown in Figure 12-15). This reverb (and most reverbs, both real and virtual) contains two elements: the reverberation, which is the smeared portion of the signal, and the early reflections, which hit the ear first and are more discrete and defined (similar to a multitap delay).

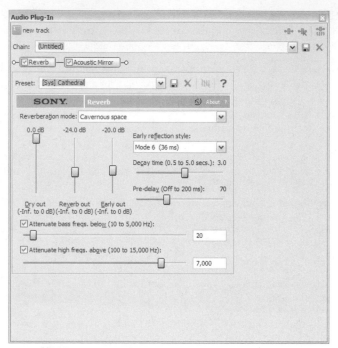

FIGURE 12-15: ACID Pro's reverb

The Dry Out slider controls the level of unaffected signal. The Reverb Out and Early Out sliders control the levels of each component of the reflected sound. The Reverberation Mode drop-down menu selects from a set of predetermined modeled spaces. The Early Reflection Style lets you choose the timing and panning of the early reflections, which help your ear perceive the size of the room. The Decay Time affects the reverberant portion of the signal, which also helps the ear perceive both the size of the room and the reflectivity of the surfaces. Pre-delay is the amount of time before the reverberant portion starts — the longer the pre-delay, the bigger the room. ACID Pro's reverb also allows you to roll off the high and low frequencies of the reverb over time if the Attenuate check boxes are checked, which helps to model different reflective surfaces. Some surfaces reflect higher frequencies better than others.

You Say You Want a Convolution?

More recently, *convolution reverbs* started making their mark. Convolution is *really* cool, and is implemented in ACID Pro with the Acoustic Mirror plug-in.

To implement a realistic convolution reverb, an engineer goes to a reverberant space and plays a special sound called an *impulse*, which has a very short duration and equal strength in all frequencies. The reverberations are recorded, and then compared with the original sound. In a reverberant space, each frequency has different patterns of absorption and reflection, and this is all recorded in stereo by the engineer. This recording is further processed to generate an *impulse response*, which is essentially an idealized stereo recording of the reverb. This information is stored in a simple audio wav file. This wav file is a map of the frequency response over time of the reverberant space. So if the level of sound at 1,000 Hz has decayed to half of its original volume at two seconds into the impulse response, it means that frequency components at 1,000 Hz in the original reverberant space also decayed to half their original volume by two seconds after the original sound. This map of frequency levels over time can be basically multiplied by any new waveform, and produce a pristine and stunning recreation of the original reverb. The sound quality of convolution reverbs is unmatched, but convolution is extremely processor-intensive, because every point in the waveform needs to be multiplied by every point in the impulse response. For this reason, you may need to render the results of a convolution reverb and reimport it into ACID Pro.

An interesting aspect of convolution is that because it measures the entire frequency response over time, not only can every delay and reverb effect be cloned by convolution, but EQ and other nonreflective effects can as well. Microphones and speakers can be modeled and stored as impulse responses. Also, because the impulse response is actually a wav file, you can use *any* sound wave as an impulse response. Try a convolution reverb with a snare drum as your impulse response. Or a gong. Or a drum loop. The results can be overly exotic sometimes, but it sure is fun to play around with, and you never know when you'll come up with something useful.

Acoustic Mirror

Acoustic Mirror, shown in Figure 12-16, is a most excellent convolution reverb included with ACID Pro.

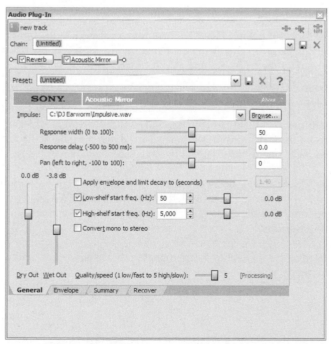

FIGURE 12-16: ACID Pro's Acoustic Mirror convolution reverb

Here's a quick rundown of the Acoustic Mirror settings:

- **Impulse:** This is the most important setting. It is the wav file that contains the impulse response. You can select your impulse and, without changing any other setting, achieve amazing results.

- **Response Width:** Applies a compression or expansion of the stereo field of the impulse response. This is the same effect as Spatty, discussed in "Enhanced Stereo Imaging" earlier in this chapter, except it is applied only to the reverb. A width of 50 leaves the width untouched.

- **Response Delay:** Creates a delay before the wet signal begins. You can actually set this to a negative value, which makes the wet signal precede the dry signal. You could potentially use negative values to create interesting backward-type reverb effects.

- **Pan:** A pan other than 0 will simply skew the stereo image of the reverb to the left or right.

- **Dry Out and Wet Out:** Behave much like the previously discussed reverbs and delays.

- **Apply Envelope:** If this is checked, the impulse response will have a volume envelope possibly prematurely fading it out. This is similar to the volume envelopes on ACID Pro's tracks. The envelope is not shown in Figure 12-16, but is available when you click on the Envelope tab. You can control the duration of the envelope on both the General and Envelope tabs. The envelope can be as complex as you like, with multiple stages of decay.

- **Low- and High-Shelf Start Frequency (Freq.):** These filters behave like the filters discussed in the "EQ" section earlier in this chapter, attenuating the high and low frequencies of the reverb. You can set the frequency and gain for each.

- **Convert Mono To Stereo:** Checking this box will artificially create a stereo reverb if your impulse is in mono.

- **Quality/Speed:** Determines the fidelity of the effect. Ideally, this would be at 5 at all times, but it really eats up the CPU of your computer. Turn down the quality if your audio is stuttering, but make sure to turn it up all the way before you render!

The Recover tab of Acoustic Mirror provides a set of tools for you to create your own impulses. This topic is beyond the scope of this book, but is covered in the online help. You can create impulses either with microphones and speakers in a real acoustic space or by processing the impulse with a variety of processors.

Note   In many scenarios, simply changing the impulse to an appropriate wav file will suffice, and you may not need to adjust any other parameter.

Impulses

When you have a convolution reverb, you'll probably want to get your hands on some impulse response (IR) files, unless you're extremely motivated and want to create your own. Here's a short list of freely available IRs:

- `www.prosoniq.net/html/ir.html`

  You will need StuffIt Expander (available from www.stuffit.com/) to decompress the .hqx files meant for a Mac. You will also need to convert the aif files to wav files using Adobe Audition, Audacity, or some other editing software capable of reading aif files. It's a bit of work, but worth it for a great collection.

- `www.cksde.com/p_6_250.htm`

- `www.voxengo.com/impulses/`

If you're still not satisfied, go to `http://staff.cofa.unsw.edu.au/~simonhunt/2005SoundList.html#ir`, where you'll find a list of more than a dozen websites that offer free impulse responses.

Other Effects

A variety of other effects can be used to give certain tracks a bit of exotic flair. This section is by no means comprehensive, but it contains some of the more commonly used special effects.

Flanger/Phaser/Wah-Wah

Both flangers and phasers layer multiple phase-shifted copies of the input signal on top of the original signal. The net result is a sweeping, psychedelic, 1960s-ish sound, with the flanger periodically highlighting certain harmonics within the audio, and the phaser more smoothly sweeping through the audio. Both of these effects are subsets of ACID Pro's Flange/Wah-Wah effect.

The third member of Flange/Wah-Wah, wah-wah is the classic sound of the guitar funk of the early 1970s. It is essentially a low-pass resonant filter that periodically sweeps up and down through the frequency spectrum.

Try checking the Tempo Sync check box to synchronize the frequency sweeps of this effect with the rhythms in your project.

Chorus

The chorus effect creates multiple copies of your audio, detunes them slightly, and stacks them on top of each other. The net result is a thicker, more layered sound. Chorus can sound good on vocals, especially background vocals, where you might expect more than one singer. Try using the chorus effect if you are using a snippet of a lead vocal acapella as a background vocal.

Distortion

Although accidental distortion by clipping is a big no-no, distortion can be used purposefully for artistic effect. As opposed to a compressor, which has a (barely) perceptible attack and release time, distortion operates in absolute real time, squishing each cycle of the wave as it crosses the threshold. The sonic effect is completely different than compression, because distortion alters the spectrum of the signal, introducing discordant nonharmonic elements. ACID Pro's distortion provides all the flexibility of the graphics dynamics effect, giving you total control over the relationship between the input and output of the signal.

Hear, Hear

Finalizing and mastering your mix should take place after your ears have had a rest from mixing and arranging. Often, if you wait a day after you've finished the basic construction of the mashup to polish it off, you'll catch issues you wouldn't have caught otherwise.

When you think you're done with mixing and mastering your mashup, you'll need to listen to it in a variety of situations to make sure it's perfect. Different sound systems will highlight different aspects of your mix. Listen to it on as many different systems as you can. Close your eyes, or at least look away from the computer screen. Listen to it first thing in the morning. Listen to it from the next room. Anything you can do to alter your perspective can be handy.

Remember, music should make you happy. If listening to your mashup doesn't inspire you or make you feel something, well, something's wrong. If you are listening to your creation and you feel a sense of joy, you probably have done something right.

Sound Systems

Many people listening to your work will do it on their home stereos. If possible, check out your mix on friends' stereo systems as well as your own. If your mashup doesn't sound so hot on your friend's system, make sure that the stereo sounds good on other songs. It's possible that the stereo just sounds bad.

It's valuable to listen with headphones on, especially when you're examining the stereo separation of your mix, because headphones offer the purest reproduction of the stereo field. However, do not try to adjust your bass levels with headphones, because they are notoriously bad at bass reproduction.

In fact, if you have access to a sound system with kickin' bass, it's great to listen to your mix with it. Often the bass in some home stereos will not be deep enough to reproduce all the frequencies in your mix. You may be surprised to hear what's happening in the lowest registers. If you do not have access to a sound system with good bass, you can perform a spectral analysis on your mix. Comparing the output to the analysis of a reference song can alert you to problems with the bass in the registers lower than your sound system is capable of reproducing.

If have access to a good car stereo, it's a great way to check out the mix. Some engineers at major music studios will take their masters outside to the car to check them out. Also, changing the location has a subtle psychological effect that can change your perspective slightly.

Time

One of the greatest ways to alter your perspective is simply to wait. After several hours of listening to your mix over and over, your ears become used to the way the music sounds, and you can easily lose objectivity. You may be surprised at what you'll hear the next day after you thought you had totally finished your mix. In general, a mix is never truly finished on the day you're done working on it. If you come back a day or two later and it still sounds good, that's a good sign! Be patient. Although it's tempting to render and distribute your mashup the moment it's done, quality control may require a bit of time.

Friends

One of the best ways to achieve a fresh perspective is to use a different set of ears. If you have friends with good taste and judgment, they can be very useful. Listen to what they say with an open mind, and don't get too defensive. It's easy to discard what they have to say, especially if they question choices you made that you're very happy with. Give their opinions a bit of time to settle in, and then decide what parts of their feedback to act on. Don't forget that different people have different ways of expressing what they hear. Often, non-musicians may use imprecise words to express what they are hearing. For example, a busy part of a song may be described as "fast," or a jarring frequency may be described as "loud." They may hear a problem that actually exists, but not be able to identify it with precision.

Breaking It Down

So now you've learned how to make a mashup from the ground up, from basics of music and music software, to keeping the tracks in time and in key, to arrangement, unmixing, and remixing. All that's left to do is get your mashup in distributable form, consider the legalities, and put it out there.

Rendering

By now you've gotten your mashup stretched, pitch-shifted, arranged and mastered. It sounds great coming out of your computer, and you're probably itching to share your masterpiece. To do this, you will need to render your mashup to an audio file, probably in CD or mp3 format.

CDs have the advantage of great sound quality, but because they are tied to a physical medium, they depend on physical distribution. mp3s, on the other hand, are easily beamed through the magical Internet, but the smaller and more transportable they are, the more the sound quality suffers. Often, mashup producers will render both formats and use each one for different circumstances.

Audio Files

Rendering to an audio file from ACID is simple. Choose Render from the File menu, and a window will pop up asking you what filename and type you want to save as. The filename is up to you, and you can choose from the following file types in ACID XPress:

- **mp3:** The most popular and supported audio compression format. ACID XPress allows only 20 mp3 encodes, and ACID Pro offers unlimited encodes.

- **rm:** RealMedia; a proprietary audio compression format developed by RealNetworks.

- **wma:** Windows Media Audio; a proprietary audio compression format developed by Microsoft.

★ **Pro** | Additionally, see the following list for formats that are available in ACID Pro.

- **pca:** Perfect Clarity Audio; a proprietary audio lossless compression format.

- **wav:** Waveform Audio; uncompressed audio format developed by Microsoft and IBM.

- **aa3:** ATRAC; a proprietary audio compression format developed by Sony.

- **ac3:** Dolby Digital, an audio format popular on DVDs.

- **aif (also known as AIFF):** Audio Interchange File Format; uncompressed format developed by Apple, but not proprietary.

- **ogg:** Patent-free audio compression format.

- **w64:** Wave64; a proprietary uncompressed audio format designed by Sony to create very large sound files.

- **video formats:** ACID Pro supports a variety of video formats to export to. These do not pertain to audio projects, but include **mov**, **avi**, **wmv**, and **mpg**.

Although there are many competing compression algorithms, mp3 is by far the most popular. The most common format for uncompressed audio on Windows is wav. Although many people argue that ogg is superior to mp3 in terms of sound quality, its lack of popularity makes it a poor choice for sharing with others. If you render to an mp3, you can guarantee that almost anybody will be able to listen to the file, and if you render to wav, you can guarantee that any CD-burning software will be able to burn it to a CD.

After you've chosen a file type, you may select a template, which is a set of parameters for your file type, or you may click Custom to set the parameters manually. The particulars of these parameters are covered in the following sections.

CDs

Burning a CD is the best way to ensure top quality in your output. To create a CD, do one of the following:

- **ACID Pro:** Render the ACID Pro project to a wav file (or aiff) and then burn the audio files to CD with an external program such as iTunes, or burn a CD directly within ACID Pro.

- **ACID Express:** Render the ACID XPress project to an mp3, and then burn the audio files to CD with an external program such as iTunes.

Rendering to a wav file first gives you the flexibility to create a CD using a combination of previously rendered wav files, but burning within ACID Pro is the quickest way to get your material to CD.

Remember, these CDs are for promotional purposes only. You may want to label them as such, and selling them may be asking for trouble.

Rendering to WAV

When you're rendering to a wav file, there are three settings: the sample rate, the bit depth, and the number of channels.

 Only ACID Pro is capable of rendering to a wav file. Rendering to mp3 with ACID XPress is covered in the next section.

Sample rate refers to the number of samples per second per channel in the output. This sample rate is twice the frequency of the highest pitch the wav can render. So if you are rendering a wav at 44.1 kHz, the default, the wav can render frequencies of up to 22,050 Hz, which is above the human threshold of hearing. This is the standard frequency of an audio CD, and if you render at any other sample rate, you will have to resample it later, so it's best to simply render it at the default.

Bit depth refers to the amount of information contained in each sample. The sample rate measures how many sample points are created per second, and the bit depth counts how many bits are contained in each one of these samples. A *bit* is just a zero or a one, the smallest amount of data a computer can hold. The greater the bit depth, the greater the amount of *dynamic range*, or the difference between the quietest and loudest possible sounds, in the wav file. Although it may seem like a good idea to have a sample rate as large as possible, this will be downgraded to 16 bits before rendering to a CD, so it's probably best to leave this setting at 16, the standard bit depth for audio CDs.

The *number of channels* simply determines whether your rendered wav file will be in mono or stereo. Again, a CD defaults to stereo, and hopefully your project has stereo audio files and effects (if you're using ACID Pro). So it's best to render to stereo.

ACID's default template should be 44.1 kHz, 16 bit, Stereo. You can simply render the wav, and then open it up in iTunes. After you have all the wavs for a CD together, create a new playlist in iTunes (press Ctrl+N). Then drag over all the wav files you want on the CD, select your playlist, and click the burn icon in the upper-right corner.

Rendering to WAV with ACID XPress

Chapter 3 mentioned the audio recording software Audacity, which allows you to record the audio output of any other software on the same computer. Audacity could allow you to record ACID XPress' audio to Audacity and then store it as a wav file.

Burning within ACID

A more direct approach is to burn CDs within ACID. The disadvantage is that you either have to have the entire CD laid out in one project, or you need to load the projects in the same order that they will appear on the final CD.

 CD burning is supported by ACID Pro, but not ACID XPress.

Burning Your CD Track-At-Once

You can load each project in order into ACID, burn each project as a track, and then close your CD, making it listenable on any CD player. To do this, select Burn Track-At-Once Audio CD from the Tools menu when your project is open and ready to render. Keep Burn Audio selected as your action and click the Start button.

Repeat this process for each ACID project you want to add as a track on the CD. When you are done burning the last track of your CD, make sure to check the Close Disc box. This will finalize your CD and make it playable on other CD players.

Keep in mind that each project will render as a single track *including any currently muted tracks*, which will render as silence of a corresponding length. If you want to render only a portion of a project, first select that time window using the time selection tool, and then make sure to check the Burn Selection Only box in the Burn Track-At-Once Audio CD pop-up window.

Burning Your CD Disc-At-Once

You can also burn your project into a single CD with ACID Pro 6. The advantage to burning your entire CD at once is that you can create a CD with tracks that are continuous. Also, if you were to make a CD for mass duplication, the Disc-At-Once option creates an industry-standard master disc.

First, line up all your audio in a single project. If your musical sources are your mashups, you will need to first render them as wav files and then load them in a master project. They should probably all be one-shots unless you really have a good reason to be doing time-stretching at this stage of the game.

 Remember — time-stretch and/or pitch-shift any audio material once and once only. If you find yourself restretching material that has been previously stretched, perhaps it should have been differently stretched in the previous render.

Setting the CD track markers is easy. Put the cursor where you want it and type **N**. Do that at the beginning of each track, and you're ready. Select Burn Disc-At-Once Audio CD from the Tools menu, insert a blank CD, and click OK.

MP3s

Although CDs offer premium sound quality, they are tied to the quaint tradition of physical objects. Pure audio files are more transportable and easily duplicated. The drawback is that the larger the files are, the longer it takes to download them. Most audio is compressed for this reason, and the sound quality suffers somewhat, although a high-quality mp3 is pretty tough to differentiate from the uncompressed wav file of the same material. The most important question is how much you compress the material, closely followed by the question of how you compress it.

 ACID XPress is limited to only 20 mp3 encodes. ACID Pro has unlimited mp3 encodes.

How MP3s Work

The mp3 compression algorithm relies on psycho-acoustics to eliminate portions of the sound that the human ear might not notice. The algorithm converts the time-varying waveform into a spectrum of frequencies that changes over time. Using knowledge of human perception, certain frequencies are then eliminated. Frequencies underneath the threshold of hearing are thrown out, as are frequencies that are much quieter than other simultaneously occurring frequencies, due to the human ear's inability to hear the quieter frequency. Often mp3 compression sounds worst for crash cymbals and other similarly noisy sounds. Generally, the cleaner the sound, the easier it is to compress.

Bit Rate

The more the signal is compressed, the more the sound quality of the mp3 decreases, along with the file size. *Bit rate* measures the amount of computer data needed to store a given duration of audio, and is usually measured in kilobits per second (kbps). A CD at 44,100 Hz with two channels of 16-bit audio has a bit rate of $44,100 \times 2 \times 16$ bps, or 1411 kbps. The very highest quality mp3 available is 320 kbps, less than ¼ as large. In general, a 128 kbps mp3 is considered not very good, and the compression will be noticeable in most environments. 192 kbps seems to be the standard that most people use nowadays, which produces reasonably clean compression for many tracks. 160 kbps lies in the grey area in between. Some mashup producers render at greater than 192 kbps for improved fidelity. A rule of thumb should be: If it sounds better bigger, make it bigger (Internet bandwidth permitting).

One misconception of rendering mashups is that if you are mashing up tracks of questionable sound quality, then it's worthless to render your mashup at high quality. For example, if you're combining two 128 kbps tracks into a lo-fi mashup, is it really worth rendering the final project at greater than 128 kbps? The answer is yes. Even though the end product will sound very much like a 128 kbps mp3, a further rendering at 128 kbps would degrade the sound quality even further. Much like time and pitch manipulation operations, the fewer compression operations the better. The deterioration is cumulative.

Constant vs. Variable Bit Rate

Additional sound quality per bit can be achieved by using a *variable bit rate* (*VBR*). While a *constant bit rate* (*CBR*) of 192 will always use 192,000 bits of data every second, a variable bit rate will use more bits when there is more sound activity. So when there is a silent portion, the bit rate drops, and when there is a big commotion and lots of frequencies are heard, the bit rate goes up. Because the bits are used more efficiently, the quality goes up, or the file size goes down, or some combination of the two. Some older mp3 decoding software and hardware cannot handle VBR mp3s, although support is rapidly becoming widespread.

Joint Stereo

The term *joint stereo* has been much maligned and misunderstood. In standard stereo, the audio file is treated as two separate streams, each one encoded separately. This creates a stereo file that is exactly double the size of a similar mono file. Joint stereo tries to take advantage of similarities between the two channels to compress the signal further. Much of the confusion surrounding joint stereo lies with the fact that there are two completely different techniques used to compress a stereo signal: mid/side stereo and intensity stereo.

Mid/Side Stereo

The *mid/side stereo* technique uses the out-of-phase stereo effect discussed in Chapter 10. First, this compression algorithm starts with two signals, L and R. Then it calculates the sum and difference signals, L+R and L-R, each of which becomes a channel in a new stereo wave. Here are a couple of interesting things about this new two-channel wave:

- It can be recombined to form L and R *exactly*. [Don't believe me? (L+R) + (L-R) = 2L. (L+R) - (L-R) = 2R. Divide each of these by two and you have L and R again.]

- The L-R difference signal is usually much quieter than the L+R signal. Remember, the L-R signal only contains sound that is panned off-center. A quieter signal means that it can be encoded with fewer bits, which is the whole goal of compression in the first place.

So the main thing to remember is that mid/side stereo conversion is *lossless*, meaning that there is no signal degradation. However, the compression that might follow is *lossy*, meaning that there is some signal degradation, as there is with all mp3 compression.

Intensity Stereo

Intensity stereo is the source of most audiophiles' rants over joint stereo. This is because the intensity stereo algorithm detects similar frequencies in each channel, and then replaces them with a single signal along with intensity and pan of that frequency. If the phase of these frequencies is different in each channel, that difference is lost. It is claimed that for mid-range and low frequencies, the ear cannot detect this phase discrepancy, so the information is discarded. Generally, unless you are encoding at low bit rates, intensity stereo should be avoided.

To sum up, render your mp3s at a reasonably high bit rate, VBR is preferable to CBR, and joint stereo is good if it's Mid/Side, perhaps not if it's intensity stereo.

Rendering Your MP3

Choosing mp3 as your file type after choosing Render As from ACID's File menu will bring up a set of templates you can choose from. Most likely, you'll want to take the extra step of clicking the Custom button and setting all of these settings yourself. You may want to perform a few renders to compare the sound quality at different bit rates as well. Generally, selecting Joint Stereo with the Mid/Side Stereo option checked works well, as shown in Figure 13-1. The Quality should be set to the highest quality. You can choose a constant bit rate from the drop-down, or you can click the VBR check box and use the slider next to it.

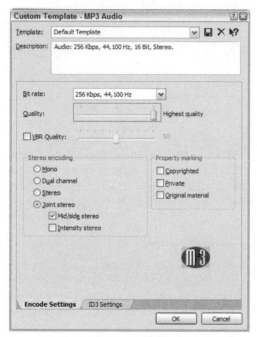

FIGURE 13-1: The custom template encode settings

The Custom Template — MP3 Audio window also has an ID3 Settings tab, shown in Figure 13-2, which allows you to enter additional information. mp3s have embedded information about artist, title, album, and other items typically associated with music files. In the ID3 Settings tab, you can put in information that might help the recipient identify the mp3. Sometimes mp3s are renamed in transit, so you can't count on the mp3 having the same filename as it passes from person to person. ID3 tags are altered far less frequently than filenames, so it's a good idea to use them for any mp3 you intend to distribute. Information can contain your name or pseudonym, the name of the track, any tracks or artists used, your e-mail address or website, and any other information or smart-aleck remarks you want to include.

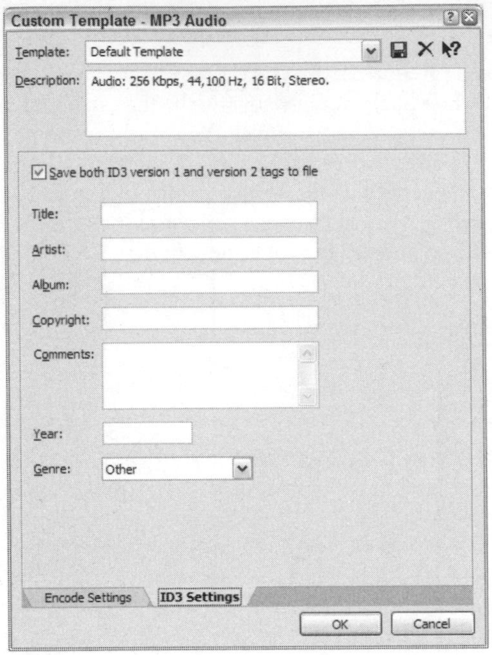

FIGURE 13-2: The custom template ID3 settings

LAME

LAME, an open-source mp3 encoding algorithm, is considered by many to be the highest quality encoder available. Although it may not be as simple to use as ACID Pro's built-in encoding, it may be worth the extra effort to render your project to a wav file and then encode it with one of the many software packages that use the LAME algorithm. One easy-to-use piece of software is winLAME, which is downloadable at `http://winlame.sourceforge.net/download.php`, and sounds great.

Breaking It Down

A high-quality mp3 if your best bet if you're distributing your material through the Internet, but a CD is probably best for face-to-face distribution. The next two chapters discuss both distribution as well as the legal aspects of mashup creation and distribution.

I Fought the Law and...

One of the first questions people ask in regard to mashups is, "Is this legal?" I have bad news for y'all. Mashups have never been definitively declared legal. But there is good news too. Mashups have never been declared illegal either. In fact, there has never been a U.S. court case definitively declaring unauthorized sampling to be illegal. How can this be? It turns out that every single case has been settled out of court, and the cases that have been brought to court have been decided on issues other than the legality of the appropriation itself.

So the legal status of mashups is arguably still in question, and although there's not a red light to stop mashup production altogether, there isn't a green light that gives you unfettered freedom either. In fact, the light is decidedly a bright yellow blinking caution signal.

For the purposes of this chapter, the discussion will be strictly limited to U.S. law. Other countries have different copyright laws. Additionally, this area is rapidly changing, so it's important to keep updated on the latest decisions and laws.

Copyright Basics

A *copyright* refers to the exclusive rights given to the creator of a work by the government of the nation where the work is created. This right governs the reuse of that work by others. The concept of modern copyright dates back to 1709 in Britain, where a law was created stating that the author of a book had the exclusive rights to publish his work for 14 years, with an option to renew it for another 14 years at expiration. Even back then, authors routinely sold their rights to publishers, so the concept of larger companies owning artists' intellectual properties is not new.

Modern U.S. Law

In 1790, the United States created its first copyright law that also allowed a 14-year copyright with an optional 14-year extension. Although some adjustments to the law were made in the following centuries, the copyright law of 1976 was a significant overhauling, addressing many of the technological advances of the twentieth century. Before this law, works that didn't specifically have a copyright notice were considered to be in the public domain. After this law was enacted, basically any work that was created was considered to be copyrighted by default. Sections 106 and 107 of this law probably have the most relevance to mashup producers.

Section 106 basically gives the following six rights to the copyright holder:

1. The right to reproduce the work.

2. The right to prepare derivative works.

3. The right to distribute copies of the work.

4. The right to perform the work.

5. The right to display the work.

6. The right to perform through digital audio transmission. (This right was amended in 1995.)

Because mashups are derivative works, and because they are most likely distributed, section 106 arguably may not favor mashup artists.

Fair Use

Fortunately, section 107 outlines some exceptions that seem to be in the mashup producer's favor. This section outlines something called *fair use*, which helps to define and defend certain forms of what might otherwise be considered copyright infringement. Fair use modifies the draconian prohibitions of section 106 and softens them up a bit. Instead of a blanket denial of rights to create derivative works and distribute them, section 107 basically seems to say that you need a good excuse. Although this provision may have been written primarily for libraries, schools, and corporations, it could benefit mashup producers as well.

Interestingly, there has never been a fair use case involving borrowed sound material that has ever gone to court! Although there have been many lawsuits, they have all been settled out of court. A judge granted an injunction against the distribution of sound recordings while a case was pending, as in the 1991 case of *Grand Upright Music, Ltd. v. Warner Brothers Records, Inc.*, involving a Biz Markie song. This case had a chilling effect on hip-hop music, creating in its wake a general policy by record companies of obtaining preapproval from the original copyright owners. Notably, a final decision was never reached in this trial, although the preliminary injunction had a huge effect on commercially available sample-based music.

Another significant case was made by Bridgeport Records against Terminator X of Public Enemy, who used an unauthorized George Clinton sample. George Clinton was named as a plaintiff, much to his surprise and befuddlement. The defense was that the sampled recording was so short in duration that it wasn't significant. The court ruled that this was not an adequate defense in and of itself, but never made a decision on fair use. Clinton was basically okay with the sampling, and his disagreement with the record company over ownership ultimately derailed the lawsuit.

At this point in time, the issue arguably seems to be undecided. But fair use might be the most reasonable defense if the issue were to be decided. So it may behoove you to know what constitutes fair use and what factors a court would consider, if it were to ever consider the issue. Four factors are legally relevant to fair use: the nature and character of use, the nature of the original work, the quantity and quality of the appropriated work, and the effect the use has on the original work. There is no magic formula that weighs or compares these four factors; rather it would be up to a judge or jury to weigh all of them and reach a decision.

Nature and Character of Use

In general, this factor would probably seem to work in favor of the mashup artist. There are two subfactors to be addressed: the commercial nature of the use and the transformative nature of the use.

Commercial vs. Noncommercial

This is fairly simple. Did you make money on your appropriation? If you are selling your mashups, the answer may seem to be clear. It's probably not a good idea to sell CDs or records without obtaining clearance, or this factor may work against you. Selling ads or related merchandise may not be a great idea, although these endeavors may be less directly profiting from the appropriated work. If you make no profit, this subfactor of nature and character may work in your favor.

Transformative Nature

This question addresses how much the derivative work has altered the original. In general, the more that your work transforms the original, the more this subfactor of nature and character may weigh in your favor. Did you really change the work, or did you simply duplicate it? If you only altered a few seconds of the source material, your work might be considered to function as a substitute. If you broke the original sound recording into hundreds of pieces and then rearranged them, altering the pitch and rhythm into something almost unrecognizable, you probably have significantly transformed the work.

One notable court decision involving transformation was the case of *Roy Orbison vs. 2 Live Crew*. 2 Live Crew was sued after they did a parody of a Roy Orbison track. The court ruled that 2 Live Crew's interpretation was a commentary on the original and that it was sufficiently transformative enough to be considered fair use. Although this case involved the appropriation of another song, it did not involve the appropriation of the sound material itself.

Nature of the Original Work

This factor addresses the concept of whether the original work was creative or factual in nature. If the work you are mashing up is an original song, it would probably be considered to be creative rather than factual. If you were mashing up a famous historical political speech, however, perhaps this factor would work in your favor. Remember, all four factors are weighed, so even if this factor seems to work against you, others may work for you.

Quantity and Quality of the Appropriated Work

This factor consists of two subfactors: how much and how important.

Quantity

This is simply the question of how much appropriated material you used. Did you use the entire work, or just a millisecond? In general, the more material you use, the more this factor may work against you.

Quality

This subfactor addresses the issue of which part of the work you appropriated. Could it be considered to be the heart of the work? Was it the main hook of the song, or was it a forgettable intro that no one remembers? The issue of quality is subjective. Also, if you really wanted to create a transformative work, it may turn out to be necessary to use the heart of the song to get your point across.

"Ice Ice Baby" by Vanilla Ice lifted only six notes from "Under Pressure" by Queen without permission. Although this seems like a very insignificant quantity, it was argued that it was of significant *quality*, because it was the main instrumental hook of the song. The case was settled out of court.

The Effect the Use Has on the Original Work

This factor also consists of two issues: substitution and licensing.

Substitution

This issue addresses the question of whether or not the appropriated work functions as an effective substitute for the original work. This is also related to the transformative nature of the work. If your mashup seems to replace the need for the original work, this may not work in your favor. However, if your mashup is significantly different, it may not be considered to substitute for the original. In practice, good mashups seem to actually spur interest in and sales of the original works rather than depleting interest in them.

Licensing

This issue addresses the question of whether the appropriated work competes with any existing or potential licensing agreements. If your appropriation is not licensed, but *could have been licensed,* this factor may not work in your favor. This may be the case even if the work is not currently available for license.

Remember, in determining fair use, all these issues are weighed together. Some seem to work in a mashup artist's favor and others may not. If this were to go to trial (which has never happened) the decision would be subjectively based on all these factors.

Real World

Although it is important to be aware of the legal implications, in practice the most trouble any mashup artists seem to have gotten in is a *cease and desist letter*, or *C&D*. This is a letter written by a representative of a copyright holder asking for an immediate stop of the distribution of disputed material. Usually a mashup producer's web host will receive the C&D, and either remove the material themselves or send a warning to the producer to remove the material. Some great mashups have been removed from the web in this manner. Danger Mouse's *The Grey Album* was a famous victim of a C&D, as was the innovative *American Edit* Green Day mashup album.

Letters have been sent out to operators of the servers that host questionable files, and also to operators of servers simply linking to files. Artist's reactions have been varied. Some simply retire and quit making mashups. Others switch web servers and move their site elsewhere, because the Internet Service Provider (ISP) is usually the recipient of the C&D rather than the artist himself. Some people go so far as to change their identities, and then start up again on a new server with a new alias.

Although it's tempting to think that an anonymous alias could protect you from identification, in reality, if you were to be sued, your identity would most likely be revealed quite quickly. If you ever use your home computer or a traceable e-mail address, your identity could be pinpointed. Even anonymous e-mail addresses are not as anonymous as you may think. There are people who go to great lengths to protect their online identity, but it is quite difficult, and unless you have a high level of specialized knowledge, you probably would be unable to effectively shield yourself in this manner.

The most reasonable thing to do upon receipt of a C&D is simply to comply. The only other alternative is to send a counter-notice to your ISP. If you truly believe that your activity is non-infringing, and you are willing to face a costly and time-consuming lawsuit, a counter-notice should result in your ISP allowing your files to remain online. However, you'd basically be asking for a real full-fledged lawsuit. Sure, the law seems to be murky in this area, but would you really want to be the hero who clears it up? If you were sued, the courts would possibly ask for all of your computers, CDs, DVDs, and hard drives, and you'd have to swear under penalty of perjury that you'd supplied the court with all the data it had asked for. If you had any illegal mp3s or software, you could be charged with the piracy of those files in addition to the mashups that started the mess in the first place.

Although criminal charges seem to be unlikely, the threat of civil action is real, and potentially costly. If a court were to find you to be infringing, the copyright holder could ask for both actual and statutory damages. The actual damages relate to how much money you made on the mashups and how much money the copyright holder lost. It would seem that the actual damages would be very little if you were not selling your mashups. Additionally, it may be difficult for a copyright holder to prove that a mashup was causing them to lose profits. However, the statutory damages are somewhat more frightening. Even if you did no harm to the copyright holder, if the court found you to be infringing, you could be asked for $750 to $30,000 per infringement, at the jury's discretion. Each song use could contain two infringements: one for the song writing and the other for the actual sound recording. So there are two potential infringements for each track used, and a mashup has at least two tracks in it. So a single quadruply infringing A+B mashup could cost you $120,000! As stated, no mashup has ever gone to court, and in practice, a lawsuit would probably be preceded by a C&D letter, giving the mashup artist an opportunity to comply. Even Danger Mouse was never sued. He complied with the C&D letter, and was later hired by Sony and went on to co-produce the Gorillaz's sophomore album.

People have been sued for unauthorized mix CDs. Usually, the organizations who press the discs are the recipients of the lawsuit. Because they are actually selling copyrighted music that may be relatively untransformed, the concept of fair use seems to apply less to these recordings than they might to mashups. If you sell copyrighted material, it may not matter whether you are aware of it or not. Intent and knowledge are probably irrelevant.

Duplicators have been shut down, as have underground hip-hop record stores. Although they haven't been shut down for selling or pressing commercial mashups, the potential may remain. It seems that the commercial nature of the duplicators and record stores has been a factor in getting sued. Individuals who work at these businesses can get sued or charged with criminal offences. Duplicators are required to send tracks they intend to press to a system that the Recording Industry Association of America (RIAA) has set up, called Repli-Check, which is an automated system intended to recognize copyrighted material. If a duplicator doesn't use Repli-Check, the RIAA will probably sue them simply for not using it. Even after passing Repli-Check, a duplicator doesn't have immunity.

Even the live performance or transmission of mashups may not be clear-cut, even when a venue has the rights to perform the individual mashup components. Because mashups may be classified as derivative works, organizations that protect and license copyrighted music — American Society of Composers, Authors, and Publishers (ASCAP), Broadcast Music, Incorporated (BMI), or SESAC — could consider their performance not licensed, and a radio station or club that plays mashups could potentially find itself slapped with a C&D or lawsuit. A venue could comply with the C&D or attempt to argue fair use in a court of law. It's possible that any kind of layered style of deejaying, or even using the loop function on a CD player may create a derivative work and may not be covered under the license agreement of a venue. Although no one's ever been sued for looping a CD at a bar, there seems to be no legal precedent that explicitly allows it.

For some examples of real C&D letters, as well as a discussion of related copyright issues, check out www.chillingeffects.org.

Public Domain

If this chapter has put you into panic mode, there is a way around the question of whether your use of copyrighted material is or is not fair use. The simplest solution is not to use copyrighted material in the first place. Several types of music recordings are free to use without legal risk.

Vintage Recordings

All recordings from before 1923 are considered to be in the public domain. This means that there is no existing copyright holder, and you can copy them, manipulate them, and distribute them both in the original form and any derivative form that you create. Unfortunately, there are not a lot of recordings from before 1923, and the sound quality is not great for the recordings that have survived. Also, unless you are creating mashups for your great-grandmother, the songs may not be terribly recognizable, which might adversely affect the impression your mashup creates on the listener.

Creative Commons

Creative Commons is a nonprofit organization that seeks to find more flexible alternatives to existing copyright licenses. It breaks down ownership rights into several categories. Each work under the Creative Commons license has at least one, but not all of these rights:

- **Attribution:** Any copies, distributions, or performances of the original music must be accompanied by crediting the original author in a manner specified. All Creative Commons licenses include the obligation of attribution.

- **Noncommercial:** Some Creative Commons licenses may include a ban on selling the work or any derivative work made from it.

- **No Derivative Works:** Some Creative Commons licenses may allow you to perform, copy, and distribute the work, as long as it remains intact in its original form. This would seem to ban the creation of mashups with the work.

- **Share Alike:** This allows derivative works (including mashups) as long as they are distributed under a Creative Commons license identical to the license of the original work. The No Derivative Works option and the Share Alike option will not exist on the same work.

For more on Creative Commons licenses, as well as a collection of works licensed under Creative Commons, check out http://creativecommongs.org. As with vintage recordings, you may find that works licensed under Creative Commons may not be as recognizable as works licensed under more traditional copyright. Creative Commons also runs a community-oriented website especially devoted to remixes and mashups at http://ccmixter.org.

For a thorough examination of works in the public domain, a great resource is a book entitled *The Public Domain: How to Find and Use Copyright-Free Writings, Music, Art & More*, published by Nolo Press.

Ethical Considerations

Apart from the legal question of "can I do this" is the ethical question of "should I do this." Although every person is free to create their own moral code, here are some issues you may want to consider:

- **Consideration of the interests of others.** Are you hurting people? Would the artists you are mashing up be offended? Are you hurting artists financially? Are you hurting others who have a legitimate interest? Are you being fair?

- **Honesty.** Are you claiming credit for the component tracks? Are you claiming credit for someone else's mashup?

- **Lawfulness.** Are you following the law? If not, are you practicing a reasonable form of civil disobedience in defiance of an unjust law?

- **Goodwill.** Are your actions having a positive effect on the world? Are you giving more than you are taking?

This book will not attempt to answer these personal ethical questions, which all mashup producers need to settle for themselves. If you don't feel that what you are doing is right, don't do it.

Breaking It Down

Mashup creation and distribution exists in a legal grey area. Be aware of the implications of creating and distributing unauthorized derivative works. If you still want to distribute your mashups into the world, read on: The subject of the next chapter is distribution.

Distribution

After you've created your mashup masterpiece, you're probably itching for others to hear it. There are a few ways of getting your work heard. First, you need to post the mashups somewhere, usually on the web, although peer-to-peer (P2P) networks can also be useful.

 Note   Make sure you have a handle on the legal status of your creation and the terms of service of any ISP or software you are using.

Setting Up a Website

To put their creations online, most people create websites. There are a few different kinds of websites that mashup producers make. Although most known producers eventually make their own traditional websites, there are other options available to those just getting their feet wet.

Traditional Website

If you opt for a regular website, that means you are creating your page from the ground up, HTML and all. This requires a bit of effort, but it means you can control exactly how your site will look. It also may help to give the impression that you are serious about your creations. Some people already have blogs, which are transformed into a platform for their mashups.

Many people who host mashups on their own websites choose to put disclaimers somewhere on the page. Basically, this states that you are not the copyright owner of the component songs and expresses a willingness to cooperate with the copyright holders or their representatives. This may or may not have any legal effect, but it might help to let the artists know that you will respect their wishes.

If you choose to use advertising on your website, this could be construed as directly profiting from your mashups, and could hurt any potential fair use argument outlined in Chapter 14. For the same reason, you should *never* sell your mashups from your website. This is just asking for trouble.

Building and maintaining websites is a gargantuan topic, much too broad to cover in a measly 300-page mashup book. Here are some websites to check out if you are just getting started:

- www.w3schools.com/
- www.learnthenet.com/english/section/webpubl.html
- www.davesite.com/webstation/html/

Most web designers use software to help them such as the following:

- **Macromedia Dreamweaver:** www.adobe.com/products/dreamweaver/
- **Microsoft Frontpage:** www.microsoft.com/Frontpage/

When designing your website, don't forget the main reasons people have come to your mashup website: *mashups*. Other information, rants, ramblings, upcoming gigs, press, beauty shots, or cute flash animations may all be of interest, but make sure that the music is accessible and obvious within seconds of viewing the page. Most people have very little patience when surfing the net, and if their struggle to find the music lasts for more than a few seconds, many will give up. After they're hooked, they may become curious and read the other material you offer up.

Bandwidth Considerations

If you opt for a traditional website, make sure you have enough *bandwidth*, which is amount of allowed data transmission in a given time period. A single link in a popular blog can make your traffic skyrocket overnight. Bandwidth is getting cheaper all the time, so you can get several hundred gigabytes of data transfer per month from many web hosts. If you purchase less bandwidth, you may find yourself suddenly scrambling if people start linking to you. On the other hand, if you're only getting a few hits a day, you don't want to waste your money. Many web hosts offer an array of services with varying costs and bandwidths. Some may choose to purchase a small amount of bandwidth and deal with spikes as they come in by setting up BitTorrents or getting other people to temporarily mirror their file.

Nontraditional Websites

Some people opt to simply place their mashups on a music-sharing website, such as http://multiply.com or social networking sites such as www.myspace.com. Make sure you understand the terms of service. Although enforcement seems to be sporadic, you may be banned from these sites if you're found to be sharing copyrighted material.

The great thing about having a website is that people always know where to find your latest project and can easily keep track of what you've been up to. The major drawback is that you have to pay for all that bandwidth. One solution to the bandwidth problem is to use P2P networks.

P2P

P2P networks were briefly touched on back in Chapter 3 as a potential source for mp3s. They are also a cheap way to distribute your own mp3s. The basic premise behind P2P networks is that the same people who download content act as servers to the network, allowing users to download content other users have already downloaded. In a web server situation, each content consumer downloads from a central content provider. In P2P situations, each content consumer is a content provider as well, the distribution is decentralized, and the bandwidth is distributed among the users or consumers, rather than the content provider.

This may seem like a free ride, and in some ways it is. However, there are significant drawbacks to this approach as well. First of all, depending on the P2P client, your material can be hard to locate. Needless to say, if you can't locate the material, it's impossible to download it. Also, the bandwidth on P2P networks can be frustratingly slow. Generally, the more popular the content, the more people will be offering it for download on the network, and the faster the download speed. This popularity can be short-lived, however. A popular file on the network can quickly fade into obscurity as users delete, move, or otherwise make the content unavailable. Another drawback is that not everyone has the client software, and many are resistant to installing new software, no matter what its demonstrated trustworthiness. Offering up your mp3s *only* via BitTorrent is guaranteed to reduce your total number of downloads and exposure.

There are two major approaches to P2P distribution. The Gnutella network and other similar networks allow you to search other users' shared collections in order to find the content you seek. There are many users on these networks, so if the content you're looking for is popular, it's often easy to find. Drawbacks are that you often can't find the exact content, and also there are many Trojans, viruses, fake files, and other inconveniences. BitTorrent allows you to identify the source of the shared download to some extent, so the content can be trusted as long as the source is trusted. You cannot search within BitTorrent, however, and you'll need to locate the content on the web or elsewhere.

Another added advantage to P2P networks is that since the mashup producer is no longer hosting the music, it cannot be shut down by the RIAA or similar organizations. For example, DJ BC's Beatles/Beastie Boys albums, *The Beastles* and *Let it Beast*, are no longer available on his website, but are downloadable via BitTorrent, as is Dean Gray's infamous *American Edit* Green Day mashup album.

Gnutella, FastTrack, and eDonkey2000

The early days of P2P technology saw the rapid development of various networks of users sharing their files.

Gnutella is one of the more widely known networks, accessible through various free client applications such as LimeWire and BearShare. It has many users and works fairly well, although it is littered with fake files and Trojans.

FastTrack was the more popular network for some time, with Kazaa being its primary client. Kazaa is no longer legal in some parts of the world, and the official version of Kazaa is packaged with so much malware and potential spyware that its installation is not recommended. In fact, many P2P clients can be dangerous, so it's a generally good idea to research any P2P software before downloading and installing it.

eDonkey2000 is another large network of users, with sharing files of typically larger sizes. Although development of eDonkey2000 has ceased due to legal action by the RIAA, the network continues to operate.

Shareaza is a P2P client that operates using multiple networks, including Gnutella and eDonkey2000. It has no adware or malware, and combines many features of competing applications. It can be found at www.shareaza.com.

There are problems with using any of these networks to distribute content. First of all, it can be difficult for mashup fans to find your content. The user needs to search for your content via the P2P application. Hopefully, someone on the network will be sharing your content. Even if you are sharing the content yourself from your own computer, it isn't guaranteed that a search on the network will find your files. Also, there are so many false files and nasty software that many users no longer trust these networks. For these reasons, BitTorrent has gained dominance in the world of P2P recently.

If you are using Gnutella or similar P2P networks to distribute your content, it might be a good idea to put terms in your filenames and ID3 tags that people might search for, like *mashup* or *vs*.

BitTorrent

Before you can understand BitTorrent fully, you need to first understand the concept of a torrent, as well as a few other terms. A *torrent* file is a small metadata file that contains the name and size of the files to be downloaded as well as information about the tracker. The *tracker* is a server that acts as a hub for communication between all of the peers. Neither the tracker nor the torrent file contains any actual data from the actual download. A *seeder* is a peer on the network with full copies of the files being downloaded. Every torrent needs a seeder to get started, and torrents can potentially go dead if no seeders remain online.

One of the most full-featured BitTorrent clients is Azureus, available at http://sourceforge.net/projects/azureus/. It has many great features, and it's great for downloading content from BitTorrent as well as for creating torrents yourself. Here are the key elements to serving up content via BitTorrent:

- **Torrents:** If you have Azureus, creating the actual torrent is easy. From the File menu of Azureus, choose New Torrent. A wizard guides you through the process. First, you are asked for the tracker URL. This will be discussed shortly. You can then drag and drop a file or directory onto the Make A Torrent window. Clicking Next twice and then Finish will complete your torrent. It's that simple. The big question is what tracker to use.

- **Tracker:** Because the tracker is a server pointed to in the actual torrent file, its address needs to be fixed. If you are going to use your own computer as a server, it should have a static IP. Unfortunately, most computers have dynamic IPs, making your torrent invalid as soon as your IP changes. Many people opt to use public trackers, and a quick Google search for *torrent tracker* will guide you to the latest sites. These trackers often face legal challenges, so a popular tracker today may be shut down months later. Azureus also has the option to create a decentralized, or tracker-less torrent. This type of file is not as universally compatible, however, and is not recommended.

One other alternative to using a third-party tracker or using your own computer as a tracker is to set up a tracker on your website if you have one. Blogtorrent (www .blogtorrent.com) has a great system for setting up a BitTorrent tracker on your website. Users can even download a rudimentary BitTorrent client along with your torrent all in one step. If you have a website and are simply using BitTorrent to save on bandwidth, this is a great route to go.

Running trackers such as Blogtorrent may be against your web host's terms of service. Because neither the tracker nor the torrent contain any data from the eventual download, if there are any issues with infringement, the trackers and the torrent hosts may not bear responsibility. The peers, however, may be considered responsible.

- **Seeder:** If you've made a torrent with Azureus, you are already are hosting a full copy of the data shared. This makes you a *seeder*. Azureus will give you feedback letting you know how many other seeders and leechers are on your network. A *leecher* may be a bit of a misnomer, because it refers to downloaders with incomplete copies of the content. However, there is still a pretty good chance that they are sharing the data chunks they've downloaded. When there are other seeders with complete copies, you could turn off your BitTorrent client, allowing other seeders to take over. This is not recommended for any but the most popular torrents, because you will be relying on strangers to stay online and distribute your content. Unless you know the seeders personally, and they've promised not to go offline, it's in your best interest to keep your BitTorrent client up and running for the lifespan of your torrent. This means leaving your computer on and online.

A major advantage BitTorrent has over other P2P networks is trust. Because the user downloads a very small torrent file from a website, e-mail, or other known source, the content of the download is as trusted as the source of the torrent. So if you trust a website enough to download content from it, you probably would trust it enough to download a torrent from it as well. Although creating and distributing content via BitTorrent requires a few steps beyond placing it in a shared directory as in other P2P clients, the user knows that the content delivered is the content asked for. There is a considerably lower chance of fake names, Trojans, viruses. or malware.

One cool feature of BitTorrent is that partial files can be shared immediately. BitTorrent breaks content into smaller chunks, and these chunks are available for upload as soon as they are downloaded. So the moment a peer starts downloading content from a seeder, the portion of the content is immediately shared, reducing the burden on the seeder right away. A BitTorrent client requests the chunks that are most rare on the network, so all parts of the file tend to distribute themselves across the network equally, and the upload demands spread out as well.

Promoting Your Mashups

The great thing about being part of this modern networked culture is that you really have to do very little promotion at all. If you have good content, those who appreciate your mashups will direct others to download them as well. E-mails, blogs, instant messages (IMs), websites and message boards all allow popular buzz to build and can generate huge amounts of traffic effortlessly. If you have a great mashup, all you need to do is plant a seed in a few places, and it will grow naturally. If a natural buzz doesn't build, it may be that you need to try extra hard on your next mashup.

Get Your Bootleg On, or GYBO (www.gybo.org) is the premiere mashup-oriented message board, and has acted as an incubator for some of the finest talents in "mashupdom." Many of the greatest mashup artists around the world are members of this community. GYBO doesn't host files or even allow posting direct links to downloadable files, so you will still need to figure out how to host your material. If you create a great mashup and post it here, it will get recognized and probably start popping up on various locations throughout the net, because mashup fans regularly check GYBO. On the other hand, if your mashup is lacking, people may comment with helpful tips that can help you in your next production. You'll need to sign up before you can access the portion of the message board where people post links to their mashup websites and discuss each creation. Another active message board is http://acapellas4u .co.uk, which also has some great forums on acapella extraction. As an added bonus, this site has been known to offer limited downloads of acapellas.

You may also try posting links on message boards devoted to the artists contained in the mashup. Although this may generate attention, many avid fans do not like the "pure" works bastardized. If you choose this route, make sure you have thick skin!

Various free mp3 sites on the web allow you to submit mp3s that include mashups. When people search for one of the artists contained in your mashup, your mashup may pop up. Just type **free mp3** in Google, and about half of the results will be from these types of sites.

Which brings up another point: It's important to tag your mp3s correctly. You can do this while rendering (see Chapter 13) or in iTunes. If your artist, title, and album fields are filled out, even if the mp3 gets copied, renamed, and linked to from some obscure website, when people download it, they will know where it came from and where to get more. If you have a website, put it in your ID3 tag. Often people download mp3s and don't listen to them until much later, completely forgetting where the mp3 came from. I can't tell you how many times I've listened to a great mashup and had no idea who created it, because the filename had changed and there were no ID3 tags.

If you have a website, make sure it's been optimized so people can find it on search engines. Search engine optimization is a large topic, and it's summarized rather well at http://en .wikipedia.org/wiki/Search_engine_optimization.

You may also consider burning a bunch of CDs and giving them away. People love free stuff! Don't forget to label them "For Promotional Use Only."

In general, be careful not to be overly aggressive or assertive in your self-promotion. What may seem to you like an earnest attempt to direct people's attention to your work may come across to others as annoying spam. Generally, people you don't know probably don't want unsolicited messages from you. Although there may be some radio DJs or podcasters who appreciate mashups, usually they will check out blogs, message boards, and websites where the buzz is naturally building and download the mashups from there. Likewise, if you do not get the response you want on a message board, it won't help you to repost, bump, or whine.

If you're generating a fair amount of traffic on your mashups and want to retain the viewers, consider creating a mailing list, so people can sign up for notifications. Another idea is to put your mashups in podcast format, so people can automatically download each mashup as it comes out.

Breaking It Down

So that's it! Grab some tunes, slap 'em together, and put 'em out there! The world awaits your creation. Making mashups is a lot of fun, as you've probably figured out by now. It's also maddeningly addictive, as thousands of mashup producers can attest. The mashup is arguably the most unoriginal genre ever, yet somehow it has seemed to produce some of the freshest sounds of this new century. Your new creations will add to this burgeoning movement, and perhaps the next masterpiece that's got the web buzzing will be yours.

Good luck, and enjoy!

What's on the CD-ROM?

Included on the CD-ROM are several software packages used throughout this book, including:

- Sony's ACID, music production software excellent for use in creating your own mashups. Provided are two distinct flavors:
    - ACID XPress 5.0, Sony's free version of ACID with some limitations.
    - A 30-day trial version of ACID Pro 6.0, fully functional with the exception of exporting to mp3 and other proprietary formats.
- A 30-day fully functional version of Adobe Audition 2.0, a powerful sound editing application.
- A fully functional demo of zplane's tONaRT, an amazing little piece of software that detects the key of a piece of music.
- A limited-feature demo of zplane's élastique Pro, software that can perform high-quality independent manipulations of the time and pitch of an audio file while maintaining important aspects of the sound's quality.

Also included is a song database spreadsheet that will help you manage your music collection and pick out compatible songs for your mashups.

Additionally, many audio examples and ACID (.acd) files are provided to illustrate many of the concepts discussed throughout the book.

Hardware Requirements

Make sure that your computer meets the minimum system requirements listed in this section. If your computer doesn't match up to most of these requirements, you may have a problem using the contents of the CD.

For Windows 9x, Windows 2000, Windows NT4 (with SP 4 or later), Windows Me, or Windows XP:

- Intel® Pentium® III or 4 or Intel Centrino™ (or other SSE-enabled) processor
- Microsoft® Windows® XP Professional or Home Edition with Service Pack 2
- 512MB of RAM (1GB recommended)
- 700MB of available hard-disk space
- 1024×768 display
- Sound card with DirectSound or ASIO drivers

Installing the Software

Installation of both Adobe Audition and Sony Acid are covered in Chapter 5.

ZPlane's products need no installation and can be run directly from the CD-ROM or copied onto your hard drive in a location of your choice. Simply double-click on either tONaRT.exe or elastiquePro.exe on the CD-ROM.

To use the spreadsheet, you'll need to have either Microsoft Excel or OpenOffice, freely downloadable at `http://download.openoffice.org/index.html` installed. Simply double-click on "mashup song database.xls" in the Chapter 6 section on the CD-ROM.

Using the Software

Usage of both Adobe Audition and Sony Acid are covered in depth in Chapter 5. Usage of tONaRT is covered in Chapter 6, and élastique Pro is discussed in Chapter 8.

The Mashup Song Database Spreadsheet

Included on the CD-ROM is a spreadsheet that you can use to store and analyze tempo and key data for your song collection. For an introduction to this spreadsheet, see Chapter 6.

How the Spreadsheet Works

The spreadsheet performs the following calculations for each song in your collection to arrive at a score for each song:

1. The tempo ratio is calculated, from the song's tempo and the target tempo.

   - The slower tempo divided by the faster tempo. This gives you the unaltered tempo ratio.

- The song's tempo is halved, and then again compared to the target tempo. The slower of these two tempos is divided by the faster tempo. This gives you the half-tempo ratio.

- The song's tempo is doubled, and then again compared to the target tempo. The slower of these two tempos is divided by the faster tempo. This gives you the double-tempo ratio.

- The highest of these three ratios represents the closest tempo relationship, and is considered to be the tempo score, and will range from 0 to 1.

2. The transposition amount is calculated between each song's key and the target key. This calculation represents the difference in semitones between the song's root pitch and the root pitch of the target key. The calculation is repeated for each of the following root notes of the keys related to the target key.

- The transposition amount is found between the song's key and the target key.

- The transposition amount is found between the song's key and the relative minor or major to the target key.

- The transposition amount is found between the song's key and 5th above the target key.

- The transposition amount is found between the song's key and 4th above the target key.

- The transposition amount is found between the song's key and the relative minor or major to the 5th above the target key.

- The transposition amount is found between the song's key and the relative minor or major to the 4th above the target key.

3. For each of these six relationships, a key score is calculated. First, each key difference is multiplied by the pitch transposition penalty, and subtracted from 1, giving you a base key score. The default value of the pitch transposition penalty is 1/12, but can be changed to any value the user wants. At a penalty of 1/12, songs that are 6 semitones apart would receive a base key score of .5, while songs in the same key would receive a base key score of 1. These six base key scores are then adjusted as follows:

- For the relative, relative/5th, and relative/4th relationships to each song's key, the key score is penalized by an amount set by the relative key penalty. This value has a default of 5%, but can be changed to any value the user wants.

- For the 5th and relative/5th relationships to each song's key, the key score is penalized by an amount set by the 5th penalty. This value has a default of 10%, but again can be changed to any value the user wants.

- For the 4th and relative/4th relationships to each song's key, the key score is penalized by an amount set by the 4th penalty. This value has a default of 10% as well.

- If the modes are different, (or if they are the same for the relative, relative/5th, and relative/4th relationships), the key score is given an additional parallel penalty. This value has a default of 20%.

Note that there can be multiple penalties for each of these six key relationships. For instance, suppose the target key is C minor, and you are calculating the score for A minor. When calculating the relative/5th relationship key score, you would first calculate the key difference. In this case, the relative major to A minor is C Major, 3 semitones above A. A fifth above C Major is G Major. G is five semitones away from your target of C, so you start with a penalty of 5 * 1/12, or .4167. Subtracting this from 1 gives you a base key score of .5833. Since you are calculating a relative relationship, this score is penalized 5%, to give you a key score of .5542. Since this is a 5th relationship, the score is now penalized 10%, to give you a score of .4988. Finally, since this is supposed to be a relative relationship, but the modes are both in the same key, you penalize the score a final 20%, to arrive at the final key score of .399.

This example is just the key score for the relative/5th relationship. Each song has six key scores calculated for each of the six key relationships. The highest of these six scores is considered to be that song's final key score, which balances the strength of the key relationship with the need to transpose.

4. The final key score is multiplied by the tempo score and then multiplied by 100, to give a final score for each song.

The spreadsheet then sorts the songs by score, putting the highest score first, and then describes the tempo and key relationship in plain English.

You may wish to adjust the penalties on this spreadsheet which are located on the "penalties" worksheet. If you want to highlight songs in your collection that would need less pitch shifting, raise the pitch transposition penalty. If you don't mind shifting the pitch of your songs, then you may lower the pitch transposition penalty. You may even want to adjust this each time you are matching a target song, depending on how good that song sounds pitch-shifted.

If you want to allow more songs with relative minor/major relationships, then lower the relative penalty. To suppress these relationships, raise the relative penalty. For example, your target song may be in major, but the verse may be in the relative minor. In this case, the key may even be ambiguous, and so you may wish to lower the relative penalty to zero.

If you want to allow more songs with 4th or 5th relationships, then lower those respective penalties, or raise the penalties to suppress these relationships. Again, if there is key ambiguity, or the key shifts into the 4th or 5th above the root for sections of the song, you may wish to lower the penalties.

If you want to allow more songs with parallel relationships, then lower the parallel penalty. For instance, if you have dance track with very little melody, you may wish to lower this value. If you have an acoustic guitar singer/songwriter track with lots of melodies and chords, you may wish to raise this value.

In practice, you may wish to just leave all these penalties alone. The default values work pretty well for most situations.

How to Add More than 1,000 Songs

The spreadsheet can handle up to 1,000 songs as is. This is to conserve on computing power. However, if you want to expand it to handle more, it is possible. In Excel:

1. Go to Format ⇨ Sheet ⇨ Unhide, select "calculations," and hit OK.

2. Select cell A1000.

3. Select the entire bottom row by pressing Ctrl+Shift+Right Arrow.

4. Select the number of rows you want to add by pressing Shift+Down Arrow or Shift+Page Down a number of times.

5. Press Ctrl+D to copy the last row into the newly selected rows.

6. If you wish, choose Format ⇨ Sheet ⇨ Hide to once again hide the calculations worksheet.

Troubleshooting

If you have difficulty installing or using any of the materials on the companion CD, try the following solutions:

- **Turn off any anti-virus software that you may have running.** Installers sometimes mimic virus activity and can make your computer incorrectly believe that it is being infected by a virus. (Be sure to turn the anti-virus software back on later.)

- **Close all running programs.** The more programs you're running, the less memory is available to other programs. Installers also typically update files and programs; if you keep other programs running, installation may not work properly.

- **Reference the ReadMe.** Please refer to the ReadMe file located at the root of the CD-ROM for the latest product information at the time of publication.

Customer Care

If you have trouble with the CD-ROM, please call the Wiley Product Technical Support phone number at (800) 762-2974. Outside the United States, call 1(317) 572-3994. You can also contact Wiley Product Technical Support at `http://support.wiley.com`. John Wiley & Sons will provide technical support only for installation and other general quality control items. For technical support on the applications themselves, consult the program's vendor or author.

To place additional orders or to request information about other Wiley products, please call (877) 762-2974.

Online Resources

I f the Internet didn't give birth to the mashup phenomenon, it certainly hastened its development. Logically, the place to find mashups and information on mashups is online. Not only can you find an endless number of mashups, some of them even listenable, but there are also forums, blogs, podcasts, and tutorials devoted to mashups. Listed here are a number of useful links for your exploration, including all the links to software mentioned in this book.

For your convenience, a clickable HTML copy of this appendix is located on the CD-ROM.

Software

Following is a list of websites where you can find the software mentioned in this book.

Music Software

There are many types of music software helpful in mashup construction. These are all mentioned in this book, and most of them are free.

Music Production

- ACID: www.sonymediasoftware.com/products/acidfamily.asp
- Audition: www.adobe.com/products/audition
- Ableton Live: www.ableton.com
- élastiquePro (formant-preserving pitch shifting demo): www.zplane.de/Downloads/elastiquePro.zip

Tempo and Key Analysis

- TapTempo: www.analogx.com/CONTENTS/download/audio/taptempo.htm
- MixShare (tempo/key detecting music database): www.mixshare.com/software.html
- tONaRT (key detection software): www.zplane.de/Downloads/tONaRT.zip
- aufTAKT (tempo detection software): www.zplane.de/Downloads/aufTAKT.zip

---

in this appendix

- ☑ Software
- ☑ Mashup artists
- ☑ Forums
- ☑ Blogs
- ☑ Podcasts
- ☑ Other Useful Information and Tutorials
- ☑ iTunes Downloads

Pitch Shifting

- Prosoniq's TimeFactory: `http://products.prosoniq.com/cgi-bin/register?service=prodbycategory&category=Application%20PC&num_items=10`
- Celemony's Melodyne: `www.celemony.com/cms/index.php?id=358`

Surround Sound Audio Manipulation

- BeSweet (converts 5.1 AC3 audio to wav): `http://dspguru.doom9.net`
- DTSdec (converts 5.1 DTS audio to wav): `www.rarewares.org/others.html`

VST Plug-ins

- KVR Audio (a complete guide to VST plug-ins): `www.kvraudio.com`
- Frohmage (Resonant Filter): `www.ohmforce.com/ViewProduct.do?p=Frohmage`
- Voxengo's SPAN (spectral analyzer): `www.voxengo.com/product/SPAN/`
- Voxengo's CurveEQ (spectral cloner): `www.voxengo.com/product/curveeq/`
- Elevayta's Cloneboy (spectral cloner): `www.paulrharvey.co.uk/elevayta/product2.htm`
- Voxengo's StereoTouch (mono to stereo): `www.voxengo.com/product/stereotouch`
- Klanglabs' StereoFaker (mono to stereo): `http://klanglabs.siliconemusic.com/freebies/sfaker/sfaker.htm`
- MB-Plugins' Spatty (stereo width manipulation): `http://mitglied.lycos.de/mbplugins/.`

Impulse Responses

- Prosoniq's impulses (requires Stuffit Expander): `www.prosoniq.net/html/ir.html`
- Impulses from Cyber Kitchen Sound Design Enterprise: `www.cksde.com/p_6_250.htm`
- Voxengo's impulses: `www.voxengo.com/impulses/`
- Large list of IRs: `http://staff.cofa.unsw.edu.au/~simonhunt/2005SoundList.html#ir`

Other Music Software

- iTunes: `www.apple.com/itunes`
- Audacity: `http://audacity.sourceforge.net`
- winLAME (high quality mp3 encoder): `http://winlame.sourceforge.net/download.php`

P2P Software

- BitTorrent: http://azureus.sourceforge.net/download.php
- LimeWire: www.limewire.com
- Shareaza: www.shareaza.com
- Blog Torrent: www.blogtorrent.com

Usenet Software

- Forte Agent: http://forteinc.com
- Xnews: http://xnews.newsguy.com

Website Building Software

- Dreamweaver: www.adobe.com/products/dreamweaver/
- Frontpage: www.microsoft.com/Frontpage/

Other Software

- Open Office (Free Microsoft Office substitute): http://download.openoffice.org
- DVD Rippers: www.doom9.org/software2.htm#rippers

Mashup Artists

So many mashup producers are out there it would be impossible to list them all. Be aware that some web sites are short lived or may change location. If the artist is no longer at the site listed, they may have closed up shop, moved to another site, or even changed their online identity. Following are artists who have developed their skills and created interesting or beautiful mashups, downloadable from their websites. This list is by no means exhaustive, and new artists are popping up all the time.

- A Plus D (aka DJs Adrian & the Mysterious D): www.rebeldjs.com
- Agent Lovelette: http://agentlovelette.intenseactionkrew.com
- Aggro1: www.Aggro1.com
- Andrew Herring: www.andrewherring.co.uk/
- Audiodile: www.audiodile.com
- Axel: www.djaxel.com
- Carrasco: www.carrascomusic.com

- ccc: www.mashups.blogspot.com
- Churchill: www.andychurchill.co.uk
- CRFTP: www.crftp.com
- Cropstar: www.cropstar.co.uk
- Cry on my Console: http://josh-console.co.uk
- Divide and Kreate: www.divideandkreate.com/
- DJ BC: www.djbc.net
- DJ Cal: www.robootlegs.com
- DJ Earworm (yours truly): www.djearworm.com
- DJ Freddy, King of Pants: www.djkingofpants.com
- DJ Jay R (aka C.H.A.O.S. Productions): www.djjayr.com
- DJ John: www.djjohn.net
- DJ Lumpy: www.scottcairo.co.uk/Lumpy/
- DJ Matt Hite (your faithful technical reviewer): www.beatmixed.com/music
- DJ Mei-Lwun: www.mei-lwun.com
- DJ Moule: www.djmoule.com
- DJ Payroll: www.bootleg.dj
- DJ Prince: www.djprince.no
- DJ Reset: www.resetmusic.com
- DJ Riko: www.djriko.com/html/tunes.html
- DJ Schmolli: www.thomasschmoll.net/dj_schmolli.html
- DJ Tripp: www.bass211.com
- DJ Zax: www.djzax.com/download.html
- DJ Zebra: http://djzebra.free.fr
- Dopplebanger: http://shocker.club.fr/music.html
- Dsico, that No-Talent Hack: www.lukecollison.com/dsico/download.html
- Dunproofin': www.dunproofin.co.uk
- Elektric Cowboy: www.elektriccowboy.net
- Essexboy: http://ebrotunes.blogspot.com
- Eve Massacre: www.evemassacre.de/bootie_mp3.htm
- Evolution Control Committee: http://evolution-control.com
- Erol Alkan: www.erolalkan.co.uk
- FettDog: www.fettdog.com
- Freelance Hellraiser: www.thefreelancehellraiser.com
- GameOver: www.gameoveronline.tk

- Go Home Production: www.gohomeproductions.co.uk
- Grafyte: www.earsoup.co.nr
- Instamatic: www.mutantpop.net/artists
- Jimmi Jammes: www.djjj.tk
- JoolsMF: www.joolsmf.co.uk
- Juxtaposeur: www.thejuxtaposition.co.uk/mitunes.html
- Kitty Glitter: www.solcofn.com/kittyglitter
- Kleptones: www.kleptones.com/
- Lance Lockarm: www.lancelockarm.com
- Lenlow: http://luke.enlow.net/music.html
- Loo & Placido: www.looandplacido.com
- McSleazy: www.mcsleazy.net
- Miss Frenchie: www.missfrenchie.co.uk
- Mr. Fab/RIAA: www.m-1.us
- Mr. White Label: www.mrwhitelabel.f2s.com
- Osymyso: www.osymyso.com
- Party Ben: www.partyben.com
- Pheugoo: www.pheugoo.com
- Phil 'n' Dog: www.radio-earwax.tk
- Pilchard: www.scottcairo.co.uk/pilchard
- Prosac: http://prosac.sitesled.com
- Poj Masta: www.pojmasta.co.uk
- Rolo: www.mixstreet.net/artist.aspx?artistid=22880
- Roy Batty: www.mashamerica.com/roybatty
- Sam Flanagan: www.samflanagan.co.uk
- The Silence Xperiment: www.thesilencexperiment.com
- Solcofn: www.solcofn.com
- Soulwax (aka 2 Many DJs): www.2manydjs.com
- Soundhog: www.atew86.dsl.pipex.com/soundhog/
- SoundWasta: www.soundwasta.com
- Team 9: www.team9.net/home.htm
- Thriftshop XL: www.thriftshopxl.com
- Tim G.: www.timgmusic.co.uk
- Tristan Shout: www.tristanshout.net

Forums

Online Forums provide opportunities to get feedback on your productions, listen to other people's work, learn new techniques and interact with other mashup artists. Some mashup artists have their own forums as well, as do most major recording artists.

- Acapellas 4 U: www.acapellas4u.co.uk
- ACIDplanet: www.acidplanet.com/forum/
- Get Your Bootleg On (GYBO): www.gybo.org

Blogs

There are a variety of blogs out there covering the mashup scene. Here are some of the better ones.

- Beatmixed: www.beatmixed.com/
- Bootie Blog: www.bootie.fm
- Bootlegs Fr: www.bootlegsfr.com
- Mash Culture: www.mashculture.nl/english
- Mashup Town: http://mashuptown.com

Podcasts

If you're too busy to search for and download mashups, you can have a podcast deliver them directly to you. You can subscribe using iTunes (Click on Advanced ⇨ Subscribe to Podcast and paste in the podcast URL) or any of a variety of podcast receivers.

 Note   Even though the word *Podcast* comes from a combination of the words *iPod* and *broadcast*, you do not need an iPod or even a portable mp3 player to enjoy or create podcasts.

Some podcasts will have two different URLs for the website describing the podcast and the podcast itself. Where applicable, both addresses are listed.

If your favorite mashup artist doesn't have a podcast, don't fret! You can quickly generate your own podcast from any web page. Go to http://mfeeds.com, enter the URL in the lower textbox and hit Enter. MFeeds will generate a podcast for you consisting of all the mp3s on the web page.

- Dancecast (DJ JayR)

    Web Site: www.dancecast.net

    Podcast: http://djjayr.com/wp-dancecast/nfblog/?feed=rss2

- Delicious mashups (aggregated from all del.icio.us users): http://del.icio.us/tag/system:media:audio+mashup

- MashMix (Loo & Placido): `http://www.looandplacido.com/pages/downloads.php?lang=en`
- Mashup.Podcast
    - Web Site: `www.tbr.pwp.blueyonder.co.uk/mashup`
    - Podcast: `http://feeds.feedburner.com/Mashuppodcast`
- Mashuptown.Podcast: `http://www.mashuptown.com`
- Radio Clash (Instamatic):
    - Web Site: `www.mutantpop.net/radioclash`
    - Podcast: `www.mutantpop.net/radioclash/rssfeed.php`
- Smash Mix (DJ Paul V):
    - Web Site: `www.thesmashmix.com`
    - Podcast: `www.thesmashmix.com/?feed=rss2`
- Twisted Radio:
    - Web Site: `www.podcast.net/show/86063`
    - Podcast: `www.twisted.co.nz/radio/podcast/The_Mashup_Show.rss`
- WoBcast (West of Bastard):
    - Web Site: `www.thejuxtaposition.co.uk/wobcasts.html`
    - Podcast: `www.thejuxtaposition.co.uk/feed.xml`
- ZebraMix (DJ Zebra):
    - Web Site: `www.ouifm.fr/media.php?action=podcast&id=4`
    - Podcast: `www.ouifm.fr/podcast/zebramix.rss`

Other Useful Information and Tutorials

- Guide to unprotecting audio files: `http://wiki.ehow.com/Convert-Protected-Audio-Into-a-Plain-MP3`
- DJ Prince Mixing Tips (includes a database of tempo and keys for popular music.): `http://www.djprince.no/`
- Camelot Sound Services (sells bpm and key data): `www.harmonic-mixing.com/services.mv`
- A list of "oops-able" Beatles songs plus tutorial: `www.beatletracks.com/btoops.html`
- DVD ripping tutorial: `www.doom9.org/index.html?/descrambling-guides.htm`
- Guide to EQ: `www.modcam.com/emusic/Frequency_ranges.pdf`
- Search Engine Optimization: `http://en.wikipedia.org/wiki/Search_engine_optimization`.

HTML Tutorials

- W3 Schools: www.w3schools.com
- Learn the Net: www.learnthenet.com/english/section/webpubl.html
- Dave's HTML Code Guide: www.davesite.com/webstation/html

Sites that Host Music

- Multiply: http://multiply.com
- MySpace: http://myspace.com

Search Engines

- Isohunt (BitTorrent search engine): www.isohunt.com
- Audiofind (Usenet music search engine): http://audiofind.com

iTunes Downloads

Here's a complete list of iTunes Store audio files used in the examples throughout this book. Since the easiest way to convert the files involves burning a CD, you may wish to buy and burn several songs at once in order not to waste blank CDs.

Table B-1

Title	Artist	Album	Chapters Used
Whoomp! (There It Is) [Acappella Mix]	Tag Team	Whoomp! (There It Is) - EP	1, 5, 7
Stand Up Tall (Instrumental Version)	Dizzee Rascal	Stand Up Tall - EP (CD 1)	1, 5
Policy of Truth	Depeche Mode	Violator	7
Sweet Dreams (Are Made of This)	Eurythmics	Sweet Dreams (Are Made of This)	7
Whoomp! (There It Is) [Radio Edit]	Tag Team	Whoomp! (There It Is) - EP	7
I Know There's Something Going On	Frida	Something's Going On (Remastered)	9
Milkshake (Instrumental)	Kelis	Milkshake - Single	10
Milshake (Radio Edit)	Kelis	Milkshake - Single	10
One	Harry Nilsson	Harry Nilsson: Greatest Hits	10

Glossary

♭ —See *flat*.

♯ — See *sharp*.

3/4—A triple meter representing three quarter notes per measure; a waltz meter.

4/4—The most common meter in popular music representing four quarter notes per measure.

33 ⅓—Standard number of revolutions per minute (rpm) for a standard long-playing vinyl album.

45—The number of revolutions per minute (rpm) for a 7-inch vinyl single; a popular format for delivery of singles, especially in the 1950s and 1960s.

78—The number of revolutions per minute (rpm) of early vinyl recordings.

AAC—Advanced Audio Coding, the preferred audio codec format for songs sold in Apple's iTunes Store. Although its compression is superior to that of mp3s, AAC's popularity hasn't approached that of the mp3 codec, and many software packages still do not offer AAC decoding/encoding.

Ableton Live—Music production software that offers a great array of tools for mashup production, including variable tempo beatmapping and real-time manipulation.

AC3—Also known as *Dolby Digital*, the most common form of surround sound for DVD video and cable, digital broadcast, and satellite TV

acapella—A version of a song with all the instrumentation removed and only the vocal parts remaining. (See the "Searching for Accappellazz" sidebar in Chapter 3 for a discussion of the various spellings and misspellings of acapella.)

acapella extraction—The process of separating the vocals from the instrumentation in a stereo mixed-down recording.

accent—A rhythmic event having greater emphasis than other surrounding rhythmic events

.acd—The windows extension given to Acid project files.

.acd-zip—The windows extension given to Acid project files that contain all of the sound files used in the project.

ACID—Multitrack music production software from Sony that is capable of manipulating pitch and tempo in real time; a favorite production tool of mashup artists.

ACID Music Studio—An intermediate level version of ACID that offers more features than ACID XPress or XMC, but is not as full-featured as ACID Pro.

ACID Pro—The top-of-the-line version of ACID, used by serious mashup producers. It is available as a demo on the CD-ROM in this book.

ACID XPress—A free version of ACID, with a reduced feature set, that is only available in version 5.0. It is included on the CD-ROM in this book.

ACID XMC—Introductory version of ACID, with more features than XPress, but fewer than ACID Music Studio or Pro.

AcidPlanet—A website operated by Sony that is dedicated to ACID, where users can upload their tracks, enter contests, and download remix kits.

acoustic mirror—An effect provided with ACID Pro that performs convolution reverb.

acoustics—(1) The science of sound. (2) The sonic characteristics of a space, including reflections and absorptions.

Agent—Newsreader software from Forté.

.aif—Windows extension for the AIFF format.

AIFF—Audio Interchange File Format, the primary format for storing uncompressed audio on Mac computers.

algorithm—A procedure, especially used in computers, to accomplish a particular task.

amplify—To increase the volume of a sound.

amplitude—The size of a sound wave's vibration, perceived by the ear as loudness.

amplitude bandwidth—Along with amplitude discrimination, a parameter in Adobe Audition's center channel extractor that shifts the balance of center channel detection between the phase and amplitude of the component frequencies.

amplitude discrimination—See *amplitude bandwidth*

analog—In audio, an electrical representation of a sound wave in which the electrical signal directly corresponds with the waveform and which is continuous in nature.

arrangement—The aspect of music creation concerned with the order and layering of elements.

artifact—An undesirable component of a sound wave that is created as a result of processing.

ASCAP—American Society of Composers, Authors and Publishers. Along with BMI and SESAC, this organization protects and licenses copyrighted music.

assignable effect—A routing component in ACID Pro that allows for processing of single or multiple tracks before being sent to the master bus; similar to a bus with the addition of an input level control.

atonal—Not tonal; refers to music that largely ignores the concepts of key and scale.

attack—(1) The onset portion of a sound; usually the time from the beginning of the sound until the sound has reached peak volume. (2) In a compressor, the amount of time that it takes for the compressor to go from a 1:1 ratio to the designated ratio after the signal surpasses the threshold.

attenuate—The opposite of amplify; to decrease the volume of a sound.

Audacity—Open-source sound editing and recording software that allows you to record any audio your computer is producing, regardless of the software platform used to produce the sound.

audio effect—See *effect*.

audio file—A computer file that holds sound wave data in digital format, either uncompressed or compressed.

audio signal—An electronic representation of a sound wave.

Audiofind—A website that catalogs audio files available on the Usenet.

Audition—Sound editing and multitrack production software by Adobe; particularly useful in mashup production for its acapella extraction capabilities.

automation—In ACID Pro, the capability to record changes in volume, pan, and effects parameters throughout the playback of your project.

A vs. B—A type of mashup composed of only two songs, usually featuring the acapella of one song overlaid on top of the instrumental from the other.

Azureus—A full-featured, multiplatform, open-source BitTorrent client.

background—Elements in a musical composition that do not attract the listener's attention.

background vocals—Singing that accompanies the lead singer, sometimes harmonizing with the lead, sometimes repeating a refrain, and sometimes participating in a call and response; vocals that do not attract attention.

balance—(1) The proper and aesthetically pleasing amplitudes of each element of a mix in proportion to the others. (2) Having similar amounts of sound energy in the left and right sides of the stereo spectrum.

band filter—A filter that raises or lowers the levels of the signal at and around a chosen frequency.

band pass filter—A filter that lowers the levels of a signal outside of an area around a chosen frequency.

band stop filter—A band filter that lowers the levels of the signal at and around a chosen frequency.

bandwidth—(1) In a band filter, the range of frequencies around the center frequency affected. (2) On the Internet, the quantity of data that can be delivered in a certain period of time.

bar—See *measure*.

bass—(1) The lower range of audible frequencies. (2) A stringed instrument that plays notes in the bass register.

bass clash—Clash that occurs when two bass lines are simultaneously present; to be avoided in mashup production.

bastard pop—See *mashup*.

BearShare—A Gnutella client for Windows.

beat—(1) A relatively steady series of events that defines a rhythmic grid for a piece of music. (2) A single event in this series; (3) Colloquially, a rhythmic pattern or groove of a piece of music.

beatmap—To locate all of the beats in a an audio file. In ACID, this information consists of a single offset and tempo.

Beatmapper Wizard—The component of ACID Pro that helps to automate the process of beatmapping an audio file.

beatmatching—The practice of playing two or more different audio recordings simultaneously, lining up the rhythms with each other so they are perceived as a single rhythm.

beat ruler—In ACID, the element above the timeline that marks the number of measures and beats.

bel—A measure of the intensity of a sound wave, each unit representing a ten-fold increase in amplitude; 10 decibels.

BeSweet—An audio file converter for Windows that can convert a surround sound AC3 to a Windows wav file.

binaural—See *stereophonic*.

bit—Consisting of either a 0 or a 1, the smallest possible amount of digital information.

bit depth—In an audio file, the number of bits stored in each sample.

bit rate—In a compressed audio file, the amount of data used to store a particular duration of sound, usually measured in bits per second (bps).

BitTorrent—A P2P protocol that allows for the decentralized distribution of files.

bleed-through—A portion of an unwanted audio signal that is found mixed into a wanted audio signal.

blend—See *mashup;* a term favored by turntablists more than computer-based mashup artists.

bootie—See *mashup*.

bootleg—See *mashup*.

borrowing—The copying of preexisting music; typically used in the context of copying a musical composition, not copying actual recorded material.

BMI—Broadcast Music, Incorporated; see *ASCAP*.

bpm—Beats per minute, a measure of tempo.

bps—Bits per second, a measure of bit rate.

break—A section of a song with only percussive instruments playing.

breakdown—A section of a song with similar parts but much lower density than the surrounding sections.

break-in—A predecessor to the mashup that intersperses comedic dialog with snippets of popular music.

breaks—An early name for hip-hop.

brick wall limiter—A limiter with an infinite ratio, usually placed as the very last process on an entire mix.

bridge—A section of a song structure that contains new musical and lyrical material apart from the verse and chorus, usually occurring after some repetition of the verse/chorus pattern.

bright—A term used to describe a sound that has significant levels of high-frequency harmonics.

burn—To create a CD-R or CD-RW, either putting music or audio on it.

bus—A routing component in ACID Pro that allows for processing of single or multiple tracks before they are sent to the master bus.

call and response—A vocal tradition where a vocalist will sing a short phrase and a backup chorus will respond with another phrase or sometimes an echo of the lead singer's phrase.

C&D—See *cease and desist*.

CBR—See *constant bit rate*.

ccMixter—A website dedicated to sharing, mixing, and mashing up Creative Commons licensed material.

CD-R—A recordable CD that can be burnt once.

CD-RW—A recordable CD that can be burnt multiple times.

cease and desist—Also referred to as a C&D; a letter written by a representative of a copyright holder asking for an immediate stop of the distribution of disputed material.

cent—One hundredth of a semitone.

center channel—(1) The channel in a surround sound audio file meant to be played from a speaker located directly in front of the listener. (2) The audio located in the center of stereo audio after processing with center channel extraction.

center channel extraction—An algorithm included in Adobe Audition 1.5 and higher that mashup artists and remixers use to isolate or suppress material in a stereo wave depending on the material's pan position; designed as a component for stereo-to-surround conversion.

Chamberlin—An early predecessor to the sampler; a music keyboard that played back a strip of magnetic tape for each key on the keyboard pressed.

channel—A discrete waveform that, along with other channels, comprises stereo or surround sound audio, with each channel meant to be heard from a discrete location, creating the illusion of space.

Chipmunk—Named after the popular novelty group The Chipmunks, the usually unwanted effect of formant-shifting during pitch-shifting up, creating the illusion of the sound being generated by a source smaller than the actual source.

chopper—A tool in ACID Pro that allows you to quickly select portions of an audio file and create new events on tracks.

chord—A collection of harmonically related pitches, usually played simultaneously.

chord clash—The phenomenon that occurs when two unrelated chords are played simultaneously, creating an unpleasant sounding result; to be avoided in mashup production.

chord progression—A repeating sequence of chords, either sounded or implied, underlying a piece of music; also called *harmonic progression*.

chorus—(1) The most recognizable, repetitive, and catchy part of a song, with mostly identical lyrics each time it's repeated. (2) An audio effect that thickens a sound wave by multiplying a signal, and then processing each copy with a variable delay, usually coupled with pitch-shifting and sometimes panning.

chromatic scale—A scale consisting of all 12 pitches in standard Western music.

clash—The disorienting simultaneous presence of elements not normally found together. It can be pleasant or interesting, in the case of genre clash or era clash, or unpleasant and jarring, as with bass clash, chord clash, key clash, or vocal clash.

click track—A recording that consists of an automatically timed pulse, designating the intended tempo and timing or a recording; often listened to by live musicians in order to keep their playing at a constant and predetermined tempo.

Click/Pop Eliminator—An effect included in Adobe Audition used to remove sudden unwanted spikes in a waveform; helpful in removing transients and other sounds with sharp attacks, as well as artifacts left over after center channel extraction.

clip—(1) Any of possibly several different media files on a track in Acid Pro 6.0, along with information on type of playback and beatmap information if applicable; a new feature in ACID Pro 6.0. (2) The often unwanted effect that occurs when a wave is amplified beyond the maximum allowable signal level of the device handling it, warping the waveform and creating inharmonic overtones.

clip pool—In ACID Pro 6.0, the collection of clips available for a track.

clip properties—In ACID Pro 6.0, the window that defines the type of playback and beatmap information of a clip.

Clipboard—The area in Windows memory where data is held after a cut or copy operation and made available to subsequent paste operations.

cochlea—The snail-shell-shaped inner ear component; contains frequency-responsive hair cells.

collage—A style of mashup and related forms that is composed from multiple sources of prerecorded music.

color—See *timbre*.

compatible—Having frequency relationships with simple and familiar ratios to each other, producing a pleasant, tonal effect; also known as *related*; pertains to pitches, melodies, keys, scales, and chords.

compression—(1) When referring the propagation of a sound wave, the area of air that has greater density due to the pressure of a sound wave. (2) When referring to loudness or dynamics, sound processing that limits the dynamic range of a piece of audio. (3) When referring to stereo image, sound processing that narrows the perceived stereo field. (4) When referring data or audio, the reduction of the size of a file. (5) When referring to time, see *time compression*.

compressor—A hardware or software component that performs dynamics compression.

concert A—440 Hz, a standardized pitch of the note A that allows different musicians to be in the same key.

constant bit rate—A feature of an mp3 file that uses a pre-determined amount of data to store a given length of audio, regardless of the complexity of the waveform; usually abbreviated as *CBR*.

convolution—An algorithm that performs a type of multiplication of two waveforms; a process used to create realistic reproduction of reverberant spaces.

copy protection—A method of stopping users from duplicating media files.

copyright—The exclusive rights given to the creator of a work by the government of the nation where the work is created.

Creative Commons—A nonprofit organization that seeks to find more flexible alternatives to existing copyright licenses.

crescendo—In music, a gradual increase in volume.

crossfade—In music production or deejaying, the fading in of one audio signal while fading out another audio file; a method of smoothly transitioning from one sound to another.

crossover—A parameter in Adobe Audition's Center Channel Extractor that helps adjust the amount of bleed-through and separation for the effect.

cutoff—(1) In a filter, the frequency beyond which the levels are attenuated. (2) In dynamics processors, the amplitude beyond which the levels are attenuated.

cut-up—A form of music or spoken word related to the mashup that largely relies on a single audio source, which is then cut apart and heavily rearranged.

cylinder—A very early form of phonographic sound recording, predating the 78 and having a cylindrical shape rather than the disc shape of modern records.

dark—A term used to describe a sound with harmonics of low amplitude.

dB—See *decibel*.

decay—(1) The final portion of a sound; usually the time from the peak or sustained amplitude until the sound is completely gone. (2) In reverb, the amount of time it takes for the reverberant signal to dissipate. (3) In delay, the amount of time it takes for the feedback portion of the signal to dissipate.

decibel—A measure of the intensity of a sound wave; $\frac{1}{10}$ of a *bel*; considered to be the smallest change in amplitude the ear can readily discern.

decompression—The area of air that has less density due to the pressure of a sound wave.

degree—In phase shifting, the amount that a sinusoidal component has been shifted from its original position; measures $\frac{1}{360}$ of a wavelength of the frequency component.

delay—Hardware or software processor that plays back one or more copies of an audio signal at various time periods, amplitudes, and pan positions.

density—The amount of independent sound activity in a composition or recording.

derivative—At least partially composed of or copied from preexisting work.

digital—In audio, an electrical representation of a sound wave in which a waveform is represented as a discrete series of amplitudes.

dissonance—The simultaneous occurrence of unrelated pitches.

distortion—The warping of a waveform, often caused by clipping, that alters the harmonic characteristics of an audio signal, creating inharmonic partials.

DLS Soft Synth—Short for Downloadable Soundfont Software Synthesizer, the built-in sample-based instrument that ships with ACID.

Dolby Digital—See *AC3*.

dotted—A modifier that multiplies the duration of a note by 1½.

doubled—Having two nearly identical versions of a sound playing simultaneously; can be purposeful, such as to thicken or alter the pan characteristics of a sound, or accidental, such as when layering similar tracks.

downbeat—The first beat in a measure; a strong beat, sometimes referring to both beats one and three in a 4/4 meter.

downbeat offset—In ACID, the number of samples between the beginning of the waveform and the first downbeat specified.

draw tool—In ACID, the tool that both creates and selects events.

drop—See *drop-out*.

drop-in—A brief introduction of a new sound, particularly in the final measures of a phrase, leading up to a downbeat.

drop-out—A brief reduction in density of an arrangement, particularly in the final measures of a phrase, leading up to a downbeat.

dry—The portion of an audio signal that is left unprocessed after signal processing.

DTS—Digital Theatre System, a method of encoding surround audio information on a DVD.

dub—A version of a song with most of the vocals stripped out.

duplicator—A company that presses CDs.

DVD-A—See *DVD-Audio*.

DVD-Audio—A recent copy-protected DVD format capable of higher fidelity than either DVD Video or CD; also referred to as *DVD-A*.

dynamic range—The difference in dB of the quietest and loudest possible sound reproducible by audio hardware or software or an audio storage mechanism.

dynamics—The area of sound and music related to loudness.

dynamics curve—In a dynamics processor, the mapping of the relationship between input volume and output volume.

dynamics processor—A signal processor that can alter the level of the output audio signal based on the level of the input audio signal.

eardrum—The part of the ear that vibrates with a sound wave and passes the sound into the inner ear.

early reflection—The portion of a reverb processor that hits the ear first, and is more discrete and defined than the reverberant portion.

earworm—(1) A song that gets stuck in your head that you can't get rid of. (2) Yours truly. (3) A voracious moth larva that insatiably eats crops like corn and cotton.

echo—A delay with feedback; a reflected sound wave.

effect—A signal processor that acts on audio signals, altering the audio characteristics in various ways.

effects chain—A series of effects, one after another, stored together as a package.

eighth note—A note with the duration of half a beat and an eighth of a 4/4 measure.

envelope—A series of values over time that controls volume, pan, or an effects parameter in ACID's automation; in general, any non-repeating variable control of a parameter

envelope tool—The tool in ACID used to draw and manipulate envelopes.

EQ—Equalization, the raising or lowering of only certain ranges of frequencies in a signal.

equalization—See *EQ*.

era clash—Common in mashups, the usually pleasant and disorienting practice of mixing elements lifted from songs in different time periods.

erase tool—In ACID, the tool that can remove portions of events from the timeline.

event—In ACID, a segment of an audio file, along with playback speed and pitch-shift information.

expander—A hardware or software component that performs dynamics expansion.

expansion—(1) When referring to loudness or dynamics, sound processing that increases the dynamic range of a piece of audio. (2) When referring to stereo image, sound processing the widens the perceived stereo field.

extraction—Isolating parts from stereo or multichannel audio using techniques such as phase cancellation or center channel extraction.

fader—A slider that controls volume.

fade-in—Starting with silence, the gradual increase in volume of an audio signal.

fade-out—The gradual decrease in volume of an audio signal until it is silent.

Fairlight—An early digital sampler.

fair use—An exception in copyright laws that allows for the creation of derivative works in certain cases.

Fast Fourier Transform—See *FFT*.

feedback—In signal processing, the looping back of a portion of the processor output back into the processor's input.

FFT—Fast Fourier Transform, a mathematical process that breaks down a waveform into its sinusoidal components and represents each small frequency band as a discrete time-varying signal; used in many time-warping and pitch-shifting algorithms, center channel extraction, and noise reduction.

fidelity—The capability of a software or hardware device to accurately reproduce a signal.

fifth—An interval consisting of seven semitones; a frequency ratio equal or close to 2:3; also called *perfect fifth*.

fill—A short percussive break, usually with a syncopated and dense rhythmic pattern.

filter—A component of EQ, capable of affecting the amplitudes of a single range of frequency components or a single audio signal within them.

flange—(1) The usually unpleasant effect of doubling very similar sounds when their phases aren't perfectly aligned, usually occurring when layering very similar portions of a track or slightly misaligning identical portions of the track. (2) See *flanger*.

flanger—An effects processor that creates multiple copies of the input signal on top of the original signal with an oscillating phase shift, resulting in a sweeping sound similar to a jet airplane taking off, with certain harmonics within the audio periodically highlighted.

flat—(1) A note that has been lowered a semitone from the notes normally present in the key; when outside of the context of key, used to designate pitches other than the seven letter-named pitches; represented by the symbol ♭. (2) Pertaining to frequency response, having no effect on the levels of any frequency components.

foreground—Elements in a musical composition that attract the listener's attention.

form—The structure of a piece of music, usually referring to the larger, more general structure.

formant—Natural frequency peaks of the frequency spectrum that occur in the resonance of a tone.

fourth—An interval consisting of five semitones; identical to a fifth with the lower pitch transposed up an octave or the upper tone transposed down an octave; also called *perfect fourth*.

frequency—The number of oscillations occurring in a fixed amount of time in a sound wave.

frequency band—A narrow range of frequencies to be independently analyzed or manipulated.

frequency masking—Masking that occurs when two events occur simultaneously with very similar frequencies, usually making the quieter sound imperceptible.

frequency response—A curve that represents the relationship between input and output amplitude for every audible frequency.

front channel—The channel in a surround sound audio file meant to be played from a speaker located in front and left or right of the listener.

fundamental—The lowest and usually loudest sinusoidal component of a timbre.

funky—Pertaining to groove, having accents on beats displaced from the underlying regularly spaced rhythmic grid; syncopated.

Fx—Effects in ACID Pro.

gain—Amplification given by a signal processor.

gate—A dynamics processor that mutes the quiet portions of an audio signal based upon a defined threshold.

genre clash—Common in mashups, the usually pleasant practice of mixing songs of completely different musical styles.

glitch—A form related to the mashup that usually manipulates a single track at a time, chopping it up into very small fragments and rearranging them, and using sounds that are reminiscent of various malfunctioning pieces of digital technology.

Gnutella—A P2P network with many clients, such as LimeWire, BearShare, and Shareaza.

gramophone—The name for a *phonograph* outside of the United States.

Graphic Dynamics—In ACID Pro, a flexible dynamics processor that has a response curve that can be drawn in the by user.

Graphic EQ—In ACID Pro, a flexible EQ that has a frequency response curve that can be drawn in by the user.

grid—In ACID, the underlying pattern of divisions and subdivisions that mark the hierarchy of rhythmically significant points in time.

grid line—A visible manifestation of the grid, appearing as a vertical grey line in the background of the timeline.

groove—A recurring pattern of timing and dynamics.

GYBO—Get Your Bootleg On, the Internet's premiere forum for mashup-related discussion.

hair cells—The cells in the inner ear, each of which is tuned to pick up a particular frequency.

half note—A note with the duration of two beats and half the length of a 4/4 measure.

half step—See *semitone*.

harmonic—An overtone with an integer multiple of the fundamental.

harmonic progression—See *chord progression*.

harmonic spectrum—The collection of harmonics or a timbre.

harmonious—Consisting of compatible pitches; also known as *tonal*.

harmonize—To create a melody with pitches compatible with another melody.

harmony—The aspect of music that deals with chord relationships and progressions.

hertz—A measurement of frequency, signifying of cycles per second, abbreviated as *Hz*.

high-pass—A filter that allows high frequencies through, attenuating the low frequencies.

high-shelf—A filter that attenuates the high frequencies.

hook—A very catchy part of a song, instrumental or sung.

Hz—See *hertz*.

ID3—The tag in an mp3 file that contains the title, artist, album, and other information about the mp3.

impulse response—In convolution, the file that records the reverberation of a space.

inf.—Abbreviation for *infinity* or *infinite*.

infringement—An instance of copyright violation.

inharmonic—In overtones, having a frequency of a non-integer, dissonant relationship to the fundamental.

insert—An effect that operates on the entire signal in a track or bus; compare to *send*.

instrumental break—A section in the middle of a song where there are no vocals; useful for looping underneath acapellas in mashups.

intellectual property—An idea that is owned and has restrictions placed on its use.

intensity stereo—A form of joint stereo, typically used for mp3s with low bit rates, that assigns a single pan to each frequency in the spectrum; not recommended for high-quality mp3s.

interval—The relationship between two different pitches, either played simultaneously or in sequence.

in the pocket—In sync with the current groove.

intro—In song structure, the first part of a song, usually without any vocals.

invert—With a waveform, to turn it upside down, shifting its phase 180 degrees.

ISP—Internet Service Provider; the fine people who you pay to access the Internet.

iTunes—mp3 playback and management software from Apple.

join—In ACID, turning two separate events into one.

joint stereo—A method of stereo mp3 compression that takes advantage of similarities between the two channels to compress the audio beyond the amount that could be achieved by compressing each channel independently.

kbps—Kilobits per second, a measure of bit rate.

key—A set of related pitches that influence the pitches chosen for chords and melodies in a musical piece.

key clash—Clash that occurs when incompatible keys are mixed together.

key compatibility—The ability of two different keys to sound good together; strongly dependent on the number of shared pitches between the two keys.

kHz—See *kilohertz*.

kilobit—1,000 bits; abbreviated *kb*.

kilohertz—1,000 hertz; abbreviated *kHz*.

knee—The bend in the response curve of a dynamics processor near the threshold.

lead-in—The portion of a phrase or piece of music that occurs before a major downbeat.

lead vocals—Vocals that draw the listener's focus.

leecher—In BitTorrent, a downloader with incomplete copies of the content.

LFE—Low Frequency Effects; in a surround sound file, the channel routed to the subwoofer.

LimeWire—A P2P software platform that relies on the Gnutella network.

limiter—A specialized kind of compressor with a very high ratio approaching infinite, usually with an extremely quick attack.

loop—(1) A repeating waveform. (2) In ACID, a mode of playback that stores the audio file in RAM and repeats the playback in its entirety.

loopback—In audio software, the capability to have as an input the audio output of another piece of software on the same computer; helpful to record audio in which no rendering or saving capability is present.

loose—In a groove, having offsets so that the rhythmic events do not occur at rigid intervals.

lossless—In audio compression, having identical fidelity to the original audio file.

lossy—In audio compression, having lower fidelity to the original audio file, but a smaller size than would be possible with lossless compression.

Low Frequency Effects—See *LFE*.

low-pass—A filter that allows low frequencies through, attenuating the high frequencies.

low-shelf—A filter that attenuates the low frequencies.

m4a—A type of AAC created by Apple's iTunes.

m4p—A protected type of AAC downloadable from Apple's iTunes Store.

major—When referring to scales or keys, one of two modes most common in Western music; usually considered the more cheery of the two.

major second—See *whole step*.

mashup—A piece of recorded music composed entirely of several pieces of pre-recorded music; also known as *bastard pop, bootie, bootleg, blend;* sometimes spelled *mash-up*

Masking—A phenomenon in which the ear perceives certain information and discards the rest.

master bus—In ACID, the bus that all tracks, busses, and assignable effects get routed to before being mixed together into the final output.

mastering—The process by which a mixed-down piece of music is refined for playback on different media and sound systems.

mastering engineer—The sound engineer who performs mastering in commercial music production; usually a different person than the *recording engineer*.

master FX—In ACID, effects placed on the master bus.

measure—In music, the smallest grouping of rhythmic beats, usually consisting of two to four beats; also called a *bar*.

medley—A series of musical pieces, woven together in a musical piece; distinguished from a mashup in that the pieces are not layered and have minimal editing

megamix—A long remix of a medley of several songs, usually by a single artist.

Mellotron—A tape-based successor to the Chamberlin and predecessor of the sampler.

melody—A series of pitches, one after the other.

meter—A hierarchy of potential rhythmic events, with repetitious patterns of emphasis on various levels simultaneously.

metronome—A device that emits a constant pulse; in ACID, a click track that corresponds with the beats of ACID's beat grid.

microtuning—The practice of pitch-shifting in increments of less than a semitone, usually in order to get the pitches in line with the standard Western set of frequencies built on the concert A of 440 Hz.

mid/side—(1) A lossless transformation of a stereo signal that converts the left and right channels into sum (mid) and difference (side) channels. (2) A type of joint stereo mp3 encoding that uses mid/side transformation in hopes of further compressing the side channel, which typically has lower amplitude than the mid channel.

millisecond—A thousandth of a second.

minor—When referring to scales or keys, one of two modes most common in Western music; usually considered the more sad and serious of the two.

minor second—See *semitone*.

mix—To combine multiple audio signals into a single signal using volume, pan, EQ, dynamics processors, and other effects; see *mixdown* and *version*.

mixdown—A recording of a piece of music after the mixing process.

mixer—(1) In ACID, a dockable window that controls the levels of all the busses. (2) A hardware device that allows the DJ or recording or mastering engineer to blend sounds from various sources, controlling the levels, pans, and other parameters.

mode—In music, the type of scale or key, defined by a particular sequence of half steps and whole steps.

mono—Having only a single channel of music, designed for playback from a single speaker.

monophonic—(1) Having only a single melody line. (2) See *mono*.

mp3—A popular compressed, lossy audio file format.

muddy—A term describing a mix with competing frequency components, often affecting clarity and intelligibility.

multiband compressor—A dynamics processor that breaks down the audio signal into discrete frequency ranges and operates a separate compressor on each.

multipurpose slider—In ACID, a slider that can adjust any of several parameters, depending on the setting of other controls.

multitrack—Having many (usually more than two) tracks; a term used to describe tape recorders and digital music production software.

music concrete—Music consisting of recorded sounds and noises from the environment, pioneered in the early days of magnetic tape.

mute—In ACID, to temporarily silence a track, bus, or assignable effect.

natural—A note that is neither raised nor lowered a semitone from the notes normally present in a key.

needle drop—The difficult DJ practice of dropping the needle into the groove of a record in time with the music already playing.

newsgroup—A discussion group on Usenet.

newsreader—Software capable of reading and posting on Usenet.

news server—A computer that archives Usenet messages.

noise—Sound activity that contains frequencies with no clear relationship to one another.

noise gate—A gate dynamics processor specifically for the purpose of removing noise from an audio signal.

noise reduction—A signal process that analyzes the frequency spectrum of the noise in an audio signal and attempts to remove the noise while leaving the rest of the audio intact.

note—An instance of a musical event that has a specific pitch and rhythmic duration.

Nyquist frequency—In digital sampling, the highest frequency that can be represented by a particular sample rate; a frequency half that of the sample rate.

octave—An interval where the frequencies have a 2:1 ratio.

octave equivalence—A phenomenon in which pitches an octave apart are perceived as identical.

offset—(1) An amount of displacement in time. (2) In groove, the amount that the timing of rhythmic events deviate from a strict, regularly subdivided grid. (3) As used in ACID, see *downbeat offset*.

one—See *downbeat*.

one-shot—In ACID, a mode of playback that does not use pitch-preserving time-warping, but rather shifts the pitch with the playback speed, maintaining the tempo-to-pitch relationship.

on the one—Occurring on the first beat of the measure.

OOPS—Out Of Phase Stereo, a technique to eliminate the center channel from a stereo signal, creating a mono signal of the side channels summed together.

open source—Free software with the code available for any programmer to customize; contrast with *intellectual property*.

optical recording—The transcription of a sound wave onto a piece of film, to be played back by shining a light through it and converting the light back to an electric signal.

original tempo—In ACID, the tempo at which a clip (Pro 6.0) or a track (XPress) originally played; to be sped up or slowed down to match the project tempo.

oscillation—One of a series of regular back-and-forth movements of an object, a signal, or any quantitative measure.

out of phase—Having the same frequency but different phase from another signal, often resulting in variable frequency attenuation when summed with the other signal.

outro—In song structure, the ending part of a song.

overload—To amplify a signal beyond what the hardware or software can handle, usually resulting in clipping.

overtone—Sinusoidal components of a timbre with higher frequency than the fundamental.

P2P—Peer-to-peer; technology that allows users to download files from a distributed network of other users sharing them.

paint tool—In ACID, a tool that can create new events and extend existing events on one or multiple tracks.

pan—The position of a sound in the stereo spectrum.

parallel major—A major key with the same root as a minor key.

parallel minor—A minor key with the same root as a major key.

parameter—A usually numeric measure that controls some aspect of the behavior of a signal processor or other algorithm.

parametric EQ—An EQ in which you can control the bandwidth or rolloff of the filter components.

PCM—Pulse code modulation, a method of storing uncompressed audio in a file.

peer-to-peer—See *P2P*.

percussive—In sound, having a sharp attack immediately followed by a decay, without a sustained portion of the sound.

perfect fifth—See *fifth*.

perfect fourth—See *fourth*.

phase—The position in the cycle of a sinusoidal component of a sound wave.

phase cancellation—The phenomenon that occurs when summing out-of-phase audio signals, resulting in some frequency components being attenuated or entirely muted.

phase discrimination—A parameter in Adobe Audition's Center Channel Extractor that adjusts the amount of bleed-through and separation for the effect.

phase inversion—Flipping a waveform upside down, often in preparation for phase cancellation; phase shifting by 180 degrees.

phaser—An effect processor that creates multiple copies of the input signal on top of the original signal with an oscillating phase shift; similar to *flanger*, but resulting in inharmonically spaced filtering.

phase shifting—Altering the phase of each frequency component of a waveform.

phonoautograph—An early predecessor of the phonograph that recorded audio but did not play it back.

phonograph—A device that plays sound from a disc or cylinder; also known as record player or turntable.

phrase—A short section of a melody.

pitch—The musical term for frequency.

pitch-shifting—Sound processing that alters the pitch of an audio file, possibly without changing the length.

plate reverb—An early reverb processor that used a large thin sheet of metal, which resonated with recorded sound and created a simulated space.

plug-in—An effect (or instrument) developed by any number of organizations that can act as a signal processor within a different piece of software, often written by a different set of developers.

podcast—A method of automatic content delivery that helps users automatically download mp3 files to their PC or portable mp3 player.

polyphonic—Having more than one pitch occurring at once.

polytonality—A piece that has multiple keys playing simultaneously. Usually frowned upon in mashups, because it usually isn't intentional, but it's present in many classical pieces that contain aspects of borrowing from multiple sources.

power chord—A chord that occurs when a guitar player plays only notes from a perfect fifth (or fourth), with the distortion adding strong harmonics; can sound minor or major depending on other elements in the accompaniment.

pre-chorus—In song structure, a short section after the verse and before the chorus.

preset—A set of stored parameters that defines the behavior of an algorithm.

preview fader—The fader that controls the volume of the metronome, chopper, and Beatmapper Wizard; also controls the volume of new audio files added to the project.

project—In ACID, a complete set of instructions for a musical composition.

project key—The overall key of an ACID project; used to automatically transpose any clips that have their root note set.

project tempo—The overall tempo of an ACID project; used to automatically warp any beatmapped or looped clips.

project time signature—The overall meter of an ACID project; defines the pattern of subdivisions in the ACID grid.

psychoacoustics—The branch of acoustics concerned with how the mind perceives sound.

public domain—Refers to material that cannot be considered intellectual property, due to unknown authorship, expired copyright, the creator's intention to make the material public, or a variety of other reasons.

pulse—A series of regularly repeating events.

pulse code modulation—See *PCM*.

pump—The usually undesirable, noticeable variation in volume when using a compressor with a slow attack; sometimes done on purpose for artistic effect.

Q—In a band filter, the range of frequencies around the center frequency affected; also called *bandwidth*; abbreviation for quality

quadraphonic—A type of surround sound that uses four speakers, two in the front and two in the back.

quarter note—A note with the duration of one beat and a quarter of a 4/4 measure.

ratio—In a compressor, the number of decibels in the input signal beyond the threshold compared to the number of decibels in the output signal beyond the threshold.

recording engineer—The sound engineer who performs recording and mixing in commercial music production; usually a different person than the *mastering engineer*.

reflection—An instance of a sound wave bouncing off a surface, creating a delayed copy of the original wave.

refrain—A section of a song consisting of a short, usually one-phrase, repeated vocal line.

register—A broad range of frequencies.

related—See *compatible*.

relative major—A major key with the same notes as a minor scale with a root three semitones lower than the major root.

relative minor—A minor key with the same notes as a major scale with a root three semitones higher than the minor root.

release—In a compressor, the parameter that controls the amount of time for the compressor to return back to the 1:1 ratio after the signal descends below the threshold.

remaster—The act of mastering an old recording after it has been released.

remix—A different version of the song from the original released version.

render—To convert your entire mixdown to an audio file.

Repli-Check—RIAA's automated system intended to recognize copyrighted material.

resonance—Selective frequency amplification, usually produced by an object that unevenly amplifies a sound source.

resonant filter—A special type of filter that doesn't simply remove sound beyond a certain frequency, but creates an additional spike in volume in frequencies adjacent to the cutoff point.

response curve—(1) In dynamics processing, the set of relationships between each possible input level and corresponding output levels. (2) As used in EQ, see *frequency response*.

reverb—(1) The phenomenon that occurs in a space where there are so many reflected sounds that they seem to smear together, and you no longer can hear them individually. (2) An effects processor that mimics this phenomenon.

rhythm—A pattern of sound events over time.

RIAA—Recording Industry Association of America, an organization that represents the copyright holders of sound recordings.

rip—To convert CD audio to a wav or mp3.

ripple edit—A mode in ACID where pasted audio pushes everything after it back a duration equal to the length of the pasted material.

rolloff—In a shelf filter, a parameter that represents how many decibels will be reduced or increased for each octave beyond the cutoff frequency.

root—(1) In music, the note in a chord on top of which other notes are built. (2) The tonic of a key. (3) In the track properties of ACID XPress and the clip properties of ACID Pro 6.0 (when a track is beatmapped), the note signifying the tonic of the audio file, used as the basis for transposition when the project key is set.

routing—In ACID, the path a signal takes through busses and assignable effects.

rpm—Revolutions per minute; a measure of phonograph playback speed.

SACD—A relatively new high fidelity proprietary CD format that incorporates a copy-protection scheme.

sample—(1) A single discrete numeric value that represents the amplitude of a waveform at a single point in time. (2) A snippet of a digital audio signal. (3) To create a snippet of a digital audio signal from an analog source.

sampler—A hardware or software musical instrument that records and plays back snippets of digital audio.

sample rate—The number of samples per second of a digital waveform.

saturation—A condition usually associated with magnetic tape recording, in which the hardware cannot handle any further increase in volume; produces distortion that is generally considered more pleasant than the clipping of a digital signal.

scale—A sequence of related notes, usually in ascending or descending order of frequency and consisting of each note in a key.

scratching—A version of slip-cueing with the audio turned on so the audience can hear the back-and-forth motion of the record for artistic effect.

scroll—In Windows, to move the visible portion of the window in order to see information currently off-screen.

scroll bar—In Windows, the control that allows the user to perform scroll operations.

seeder—In BitTorrent, a peer on the network with a full copy of the files being downloaded.

selection—The event or events currently being operated on.

selection tool—In ACID, a tool that allows you to make or alter a selection.

Selection/View window—In Adobe Audition, a numerical way of looking at the portion of your waveform that is selected and currently in view.

semitone—A twelfth of an octave; the smallest interval in standard Western music; also known as a *half step* or *minor second*.

send—The routing of a duplicated signal from a track or bus, to be processed via a bus; the processor on the bus operates on only the portion of the signal sent to the bus; compare to *insert*.

separation—In music mastering, a track that consists of a portion of the final mix; also called a *stem*.

SESAC—Society of European Stage Authors & Composers; see *ASCAP*.

sharp—(1) A note that has been raised a semitone from the notes normally present in the key; when outside of the context of key, used to designate pitches other than the seven letter-named pitches; represented by the symbol ♯. (2) When referring to an attack or a transient, this means very quick and well-defined.

shelf filter—See *low shelf* and *high shelf*.

side channel—Terminology used when distinguishing panned components from center components in center channel extraction; see *front channel*.

signal—See *audio signal*.

signal processor—A hardware or software device that performs operations on an audio signal.

simple delay—In ACID, a delay effect that allows for synchronization of the decay and delay times to the project tempo.

sine wave—The purest tone possible; the basic building block of all sound.

sinusoidal—Having the form of a sine wave.

sixteenth note—A note with the duration of a quarter of a beat and a sixteenth of a 4/4 measure.

slider—In ACID, a component that allows you to change a parameter through horizontal or vertical movement.

slip-cueing—The practice of putting a felt mat on a turntable, allowing the turntable to spin at full speed underneath the stationary felt mat with a record on top, and releasing the record at a rhythmically significant moment, with the record rapidly accelerating to full speed.

smearing—The phenomenon in which frequency components have imprecise placement in time; usually a desired effect of reverb, but an undesirable effect in time-stretching and pitch-shifting.

snap—In ACID, the mode where placement of events is restricted so their beginning or ending edges are perfectly aligned with ACID's beat grid.

solo—In ACID, allowing only a single track or bus to play, temporarily muting out the others.

Sonic Foundry—The company that originally developed ACID, before Sony bought them out.

song structure—The typical form of a modern pop song, almost always consisting of verses and choruses, and usually including bridges and other sections.

Sony—The company that owns and currently develops ACID.

sound editor—A piece of software that performs operations on digital audio files.

sound wave—The physical manifestation of sound, usually propagated through the air.

spatialization—The aspect of performed or recorded music that deals with the location of the audio.

spectral analysis—A method that can graphically depict the level of all frequencies within a given signal.

spectral decay rate—In Adobe Audition's Center Channel Extractor and noise reduction, a parameter that seeks to minimize background distortions.

Spectral view—In Adobe Audition, a method to view a waveform as a map of frequency components over time.

spectrum—(1) When referring to stereo field, a mapping of the amplitudes for each position in real or perceived space. (2) When referring to frequency, a mapping of the amplitudes of each frequency component in an audio signal.

split—In ACID, turning a single event into two events.

stem—See *separation*.

step—In music, the interval between adjacent notes in a scale, usually consisting of one or two semitones.

stereo—Sound recorded with two separate channels, transmitting the perception of space to the listener; also known as *stereophonic* or *binaural*.

stereo delay—A delay that pans the delayed signal.

stereo field—The range of real or perceived space that a stereo signal occupies.

stereo imaging—The presence of stereo elements in an audio signal; often referring to the introduction of stereo elements into a mono signal.

stereophonic—See *stereo*

straight—In a groove, having accents on beats occurring on the underlying regularly spaced rhythmic grid; not syncopated.

stretch—Time-warping that increases the duration of an audio signal.

stripping—Removing the copy protection from a media file.

structure—The ordering of elements in a musical composition.

subwoofer—A loudspeaker dedicated solely to reproducing very low frequency components of an audio signal.

surround channel—In surround sound, a channel placed to the side or rear of the listener.

surround sound—An audio format that includes front/back as well as stereo information, usually with at least four discrete channels.

swing—In groove, the regular offset delay of alternating eight or sixteenth notes.

sync—See *synchronize*.

synchronize—To align two separate events, rhythms, or rhythmic grids.

tail-out—The portion of a phrase or piece of music that occurs after the final downbeat of the section.

tap—A single reflection in a delay effect.

tape—Technology that allows transcription of a sound wave onto a thin flexible strip, which can be wound around a reel and played back.

tape delay—An early delay effect using magnetic tape.

tempo—The pace at which beats are occurring.

tempo marker—In ACID, an instruction to change the project tempo to a specified value at a specified time.

temporal masking—Masking that occurs when two percussive events occur very close to each other in time, with the louder one dominating.

tempo sync decay—In ACID's simple delay, a tempo-dependent decay time.

tempo sync delay—In ACID's simple delay, a tempo-dependent delay time.

threshold—In dynamics processing, the point beyond which the amplitude of the sound is manipulated.

through-composing—A practice in early Western music in which each new section of text would have entirely new music written for it, as opposed to the mostly derivative composing that preceded the practice.

tick—The smallest time subdivision in ACID, representing $1/768$ of a beat.

tight—In a groove, having little rhythmic offset so the rhythmic events occur at fairly rigid intervals.

timbre—A characteristic set of harmonics for a given sound; also known as *tone* or *color*.

time compression—Time-warping that shortens an audio file.

timeline—In ACID, the area where events are created and manipulated.

time marker—In ACID Pro, a visible indicator in the time ruler that stays at the same point in time regardless of the project tempo.

time ruler—In ACID, the optionally visible element below the timeline that marks the time in minutes and seconds.

time selection tool—In ACID, a tool that creates a selection of a duration of time, as opposed to selecting events.

time-stretching—Time-warping that lengthens an audio file.

time-warping—Sound processing that alters the length of an audio file, possibly with pitch preservation.

tonal—See *harmonious*.

tonal clash—See *key clash*.

tONaRT—Software from zplane that performs automatic key detection in a wav file.

tone—(1) The mood of a piece of music. (2) See *timbre*. (3) See *pitch*.

tonic—The initial pitch of a scale.

torrent—In the BitTorrent protocol, a small metadata file that contains the name and size of the files to be downloaded as well as information about the tracker.

track—(1) In ACID, a place in the timeline where you arrange events. In XPress, tracks are associated with a single audio file, and in Pro 6.0, the tracks can hold clips from several audio files. (2) Colloquially, a complete mixed audio recording of a song.

track compressor—ACID's built-in compressor.

Track EQ—ACID's built-in parametric EQ.

tracker—In BitTorrent, a server that acts as a hub for communication among all of the peers.

Track FX—In ACID, an effect that operates on a single track.

track list—In ACID, the area where each track's volume and pan are set, as well as the overall tempo of the project.

Track Properties—In ACID, the window that displays more detailed information about the currently selected track than is shown in the track list area.

transient—A brief sound component, often consisting of overtones, usually heard during the attack portion of a sound.

transient elimination—An effect that seeks to minimize the presence of transients in an audio signal.

transient smearing—The degradation in sharpness of the transients in an audio signal, where their durations are lengthened, decreasing their sharpness; usually an unfortunate side effect of FFT-based processes.

transition—The changeover from one ACID event or audio signal to another.

transport bar—The area in ACID for controlling project playback.

Transport window—The area in Adobe Audition for controlling project playback.

transposition—The shifting in key of a musical composition

triad—A three-note chord.

turntable—A modern version of the phonograph; a term often used by DJs.

turntablism—The art of manipulating sound with a DJ mixer and turntables.

unmixing—A process that attempts to isolate instruments or vocals from a mix to the highest degree possible.

unpitched—Not having a recognizable frequency.

upbeat—The beat before the downbeat; often refers to beats two and four in 4/4 meter, where the snare will typically play in popular music.

URL—Uniform Resource Locator, a location on the Internet

Usenet—An Internet-based system for hosting discussion groups on various topics, including a large amount of binaries.

variable bit rate—A feature of an mp3 file that uses a changing amount of data to store a given length of audio, depending of the complexity of the waveform; usually abbreviated as *VBR*.

VBR—See *variable bit rate*.

verse—Along with the chorus, the most prevalent section in song structure, with identical melodies but different lyrics in each repetition.

version—A mixdown with a variation of the elements found in the original; a remix.

vinyl—What modern records are made of.

VOB—Video object, a file containing video and sound information on a standard DVD.

vocal clash—Clash that occurs when two vocalists are singing at the same time, usually from two separate songs in a mashup.

volume—A musical term for amplitude.

VST plug-in—An instrumental or effects plug-in that conforms to a commonly used standard, usable in many software platforms such as ACID or Audition; VST stands for Virtual Studio Technology.

wah-wah—An effect consisting of a low-pass resonant filter that periodically sweeps up and down through the frequency spectrum.

warbly—Having unsteady frequency components; a usually undesirable effect of noise reduction or Center Channel Extraction and other processes.

wav—An uncompressed PCM audio file on the Windows platform.

wave—(1) See *sound wave*. (2) See *oscillation*. (3) See *wav*.

waveform—The shape of a sound wave, often referring to the visual representation of the shape.

wave hammer—Provided with ACID Pro, an effect consisting of a compressor followed by a limiter that features a look-ahead function, attenuating the signal before the attack.

wavelength—The distance from one peak of a wave to the next peak; inversely related to frequency.

web host—A company that operates a server offering websites on the Internet.

Western music—A term for a collection of genres of music originating in Europe.

wet—The portion of an audio signal that is processed in signal processing, usually used with a dry signal that is left unprocessed.

white label—A vinyl record, usually pressed in limited quantities and often containing unauthorized remixes of commercially available music.

whole note—A note usually with the duration of four beats and the length of a 4/4 measure.

whole step—An interval consisting of two semitones; also known as a *major second* or *whole tone*.

whole tone—See *whole step*.

zoom—In Windows, to view more or less data in the current window.

zoom tool—In ACID, a tool that can control how much audio to show in the timeline.

zoom window—The area in Adobe Audition for controlling the amount of the waveform to be displayed.

zplane—A software company that creates powerful tools for time-warping, pitch-shifting, and key, pitch, and tempo analysis.

Index

Note to the Reader: Throughout this index **boldfaced** page numbers indicate primary discussions of a topic. *Italicized* page numbers indicate illustrations.

BUILD IT
TWEAK IT
KNOW IT

The best place on the Web to learn about new technologies, find new gear, discover new ways to build and modify your systems, and meet fascinating techheads...just like you.

EXTREMETECH™

▶ Visit www.extremetech.com.

How to take it to the Extreme.

If you enjoyed this book, there are many others like it for you. From *Podcasting* to *Hacking Firefox*, ExtremeTech books can fulfill your urge to hack, tweak and modify, ...ch tips and ...ed to get ...their

EXTREMETECH™ Availa... ...ILEY

Now you know.

Wiley and the Wiley logo are trademarks of John Wiley & Sons, Inc. and/or its affiliates. The ExtremeTech logo is a trademark of Ziff Davis Publishing Holdings, Inc. Used under license. All other trademarks are the property of their respective owners.